WESTERN FILMING LOCATIONS

MASTER INDEX

The Sons of Katie Elder, Durango, Mexico
(l to r) Dean Martin, John Wayne

WESTERN FILMING LOCATIONS

MASTER INDEX

compiled and written by
Jerry L. Schneider

A CP Book
First Edition
March 2025

Published by
CP Books

For a list of our books, please visit our web site at
www.CPEntBooks.com

Copyright © 2025 CP Entertainment Books

isbn 979-8-990058118

All rights reserved. No part of this book may be reproduced or transmitted in any form by any means, electronic, mechanical, photocopying, recording, or by any information source and retrieval system now known or to be invented, without prior written permission of the publisher, except for the quoting of brief passages in connection with a review of this book.

CP Entertainment Books
www.CPEntBooks.com

This Master Index contains those locations and films which are identified in the currently published books in the Western Film Locations series of books, as well as many other films which have not been written up in the series. This book contains over 4,500 listings. This published Master Index will contain as close to 100% of western films from 1929 to 2023 as humanly possible, but will most likely be missing some.

Special thanks are given to the following individuals who have helped and/or supported my efforts in publishing this series of books: Carlo Gaberscek, Kenny Stier, Tinsley Yarbrough, and Marc Wanamaker (for photographic help).

The research for this book began in the late 1950s. Over the years as I watched old westerns on television, I would take note of where they were filmed. As time went by, the obsession grew and the viewing of the films became one of watching the background no matter what the foreground actors were doing or saying. Over the years, I have come into contact with fellow researchers on the same subject. Their work is interspersed with my work for this comprehensive location guide to western locations. I have not been able to check all of the films to make sure that what has been gathered is accurate (I would be extremely old by the time I saw all of them—totally out of the question). However, the work is being presented NOW and not a hundred years from now!

LOCATIONS INDEX

This locations index contains both the book designation (CA1, AZ, UT) and page number for each location in the format XXX-999 where the XXX to the left of the hyphen designates the book designation and the number after the hyphen designates the page number on which the location begins.

1504 N. Commonwealth Ave, CA5-39
20th Century Fox Ghost Town Street, CA7-5
20th Century-Fox Ranch, CA2-6
20th Century-Fox Studio, CA3-6, CA5-31
4363 Sunset Dr, CA5-40
A L Gatzman Ranch, CA7-135
Acton Train Depot, CA6-11
Acton, CA4-151
Adams Port, CA2-168
Alvin Judd Ranch, UT-1
Amado Ranch, AZ-1
Anchor Ranch/Anchorville, CA6-114
Andreas Canyon Club, CA7-19
Andy Jauregui Ranch, CA4-62
Apacheland, AZ-3
Arboretum, CA3-94
Arches National Park, UT-3
Arizona Biltmore Hotel, AZ-13
Arizona State Fairground, AZ-14
Aspen Mirror Lake, UT-9
Ava Ranch, AZ-15
Avra Valley, AZ-16
Babacomari Ranch, AZ-17
Balboa Park, CA7-25
Baldwin Hills Oil Field, CA5-47
Banning House, CA3-17
Barkely Cattle Ranch/Quarter Circle U Ranch, AZ-18
Barney Oldfield Country Club, CA7-8
Barrett Ranch/Crummer Ranch, CA2-30
Beale's Cut/Fremont Pass, CA4-60
Beaumont, CA6-33
Berry/Bell Location Ranch, CA1-58
Bidwell Park, CA7-41
Big Bear, CA3-112
Big Bend, UT-11
Big Sky Movie Ranch, CA1-99
Big Water, UT-12
Bisbee, AZ-22
Bishop Creek Intake II, CA6-153
Bishop, CA6-149

Black Butte, AZ-23
Blacks Beach, CA7-27
Bloomquist Ranch, AZ-24
Blue Canyon, AZ-25
Blue Cloud Ranch, CA4-125
Bodie, CA6-171
Boulder Creek, CA7-121
Bradshaw Ranch/Bitter Creek, AZ-27
Brandeis Ranch, CA1-42
Brant Ranch, CA2-27
Bridgeport, CA6-173
Bronson Canyon, CA2-180
Bryce Canyon, UT-14
Buffalo Flats, CA1-163
Bull Farms, AZ-30
Burro Flats, CA1-70
Busch Gardens, CA3-92
Buttermilks, CA6-155
C. E. Toberman Estate, CA3-84
Calaveras Big Trees, CA7-51
Calico Ghost Town, CA 5-159
Camulos Rancho, CA1-166
Canoa Ranch, AZ-32
Canyon de Chelly, AZ-33
Caravan West, CA4-139
Carefree Studio, AZ-35
Carlotta Hotel, CA7-65
Carlotta Lumber Company, CA7-66
Carmel Mission, CA7-109
Carson & Colorado Railroad, CA6-121
Castle Valley, UT-15
Catalina Island, CA3-16
Cave Creek Canyon, AZ-38
Cave Lake Dude Ranch, UT-19
Cave of Munit, CA5-20
Cedar Breaks, UT-21
Cedar Lake, CA3-125
Cerro Gordo, CA6-118
Chaplin Studio, CA3-52
Chatsworth Lake and Manor, CA2-35
Chatsworth's Trains, CA2-40
Chavez Ravine/Elysian Park, CA3-85
Chico Meadows, CA7-42
China Flats, CA1-139
Circle J Ranch, CA4-130
Circle Z Ranch/Sonoita Creek, AZ-40
CJS Film Studio, AZ-43
Clarence Brown Ranch, CA2-11

Coconino National Forest, AZ-46
Columbia Ranch, CA2-123
Columbia, CA7-145
Conejo Valley Airport, CA1-116
Consumers Rock and Gravel Company, CA2-173
Convict Lake, CA6-161
Coral Pink Sand Dune, UT-25
Corrections to Previous Books, CA5-197, CA7-1
Cougar Buttes, CA5-145
Cowtown, AZ-48
Crannell, CA7-68
Crestline/Lake Gregory/Camp Seeley, CA3-136
Crystal Lake, CA5-46
Cuddeback Lake, CA5-192
Cudia City, AZ-50
D. W. Griffith Ranch, CA2-175
Dead Horse Point, UT-27
Deadman Hill (Granite Mountain) CA5-124
Deadman Point, CA5-127
Death Valley, CA6-132
Deerwood Stock Farm, CA1-132
Devonshire Farms, CA2-53
Diamond Bar Ranch, AZ-55
Disney's Golden Oak Ranch, CA4-76
Dolomite, CA6-82
Donnell Vista, CA7-149
Douglas Station, CA7-150
Dragoon Mountains, AZ-57
Drais Ranch, CA7-117
Dry Canyon Reservoir, CA4-121
Duck Creek/Meadow View Movie Ranch, UT-29
Dugout Ranch, UT-32
Eagle Gate Arch, UT-34
El Mirage Dry Lake, CA5-63
El Monte, CA3-96
El Paso and Southwestern Railroad Depot, Tucson, AZ-62
El Rey Hotel, CA5-27
Elgin, AZ-59
Eureka, CA7-69
Fairbank, AZ-63
Fairfax, CA7-93
Fairplex Park, CA3-97
Fairview Mountain/Sycamore Rocks, CA5-101
Fairview Valley/Reeves Dry Lake, CA5-117
"Fat" Jones Ranch, CA4-72
FBO Studio, CA7-7
Fillmore to Valencia Railroad, CA1-168
Fillmore's State Fish Hatchery, CA1-167

Fine Arts Studio, CA3-68
Five Lakes, CA7-113
Four Mile Beach, CA7-122
Foxboro Ranch, AZ-65
Frank LaSalle Ranch, CA4-104
Frank Staubinger Ranch, CA2-12
Franklin Canyon Lake, CA2-187
French Ranch, CA1-136
Fryman Ranch, CA5-25
Gadsden Hotel, AZ-67
Gammons Gulch, AZ-68
Gap, The, UT-36
Garden Court Apartment, CA3-83
Garner Ranch, CA3-152
Gaviota Train Bridge, CA6-11
George Lewis Mansion, CA3-3
Gila Bend, AZ-70
Glendale Grand Central Air Terminal, CA3-86
Glendale Train Depot, CA5-43
Goblin Valley State Park, UT-38
Goldfield Ranch, AZ-74
Goldfield, AZ-71
Goldwyn/United Artists Studio, CA3-47
Goulding's Trading Post, UT-39
Grafton, UT-42
Grand Canyon, AZ-75
Grand National Studio, CA6-21
Green Valley, AZ-77
Greenfield Ranch, CA1-135
Griffith Park Observatory, CA2-178
Hackberry, AZ-78
Hal Roach Ranch, CA3-43
Harold Lloyd Estate, CA2-189
Harry Carey Ranch, CA7-12
Harry Quinn Ranch, CA5-190
Hart Ranch Western Street, AZ-80
Hayden Movie Ranch, CA5-171
Heber Valley Railroad/Heber Creeper Village, UT-47
Helvetia Mine & Ghost Town, AZ-82
Highland Springs Guest Resort, CA6-31
Highway 18/Joshua Road Area, CA5-98
Hitchcock Ranch, CA3-134
Holcomb Valley, CA3-133
Hollywood Legion Stadium, CA6-25
Honey Run Covered Bridge, CA7-44
Hoot Gibson Ranch, CA4-126
Hornitos, CA7-99
Hot Creek Geological Site, CA6-162

Hot Creek, CA6-168
House Rock Valley, AZ-85
House, CA17085 Rancho St., CAEncino, CA5-24
Hoyt Chamberlain Property, UT-49
Humboldt Redwoods State Park/Williams Grove, CA7-71
Hurrah Pass, UT-52
I. S. Ranch, CA3-124
Ida Gulch, UT-53
Idyllwild, CA3-149
Imperial County Sand Dunes/Buttercup Valley, CA3-108
Inceville, CA3-12
Intersection Country Club Dr, N Sunset Canyon, & E Olive Ave, CA2-164
Intersection N. Figueroa St. and N. Avenue 57, CA6-26
Iron Springs, UT-55
Iverson Movie Ranch, CA1-1
Jack Ingram Motion Picture Ranch, CA2-88
James L. C. Sherwin Ranch, Round Valley, CA6-154
Janet Gaynor Ranch, CA6-18
Janns Janss Conejo Ranch, CA1-110
Jawbone Canyon, CA7-83
Joel McCrea Ranch, CA6-37
John Huston Ranch, CA2-57
Johnson Canyon, UT-56
Joshua Tree, CA5-173
Jungleland, CA1-115
Kanab Canyon/Slot Canyon/Robinson Ranch, UT-62
Kanab Race Track, UT-79
Kanab, UT-60
Keen Camp, CA3-160
Kennedy Meadows, CA7-151
Kernville Movie Street, CA6-63
Kernville, CA6-54
Kings Bottom, UT-82
KTLA Studio (Warner Brothers Sunset), CA3-71
La Grange Mine, CA7-141
La Mesa, CA6-3
La Sal, UT-83
Laguna Dam, CA7-31
Lake Alpine Area, CA7-94
Lake Arrowhead, CA3-140
Lake Elsinore, CA3-105
Lake Havasu City, AZ-86
Lake Hemet, CA3-158
Lake Mary, AZ-88
Lake Sherwood/Sherwood Forest, CA1-123
Lakeside, CA6-1
Lancaster's Lake, CA2-177
Lang Train Depot, CA4-135

Lazy K Bar Ranch, AZ-89
Lebec/Tejon Ranch, CA2-5
Leo Carrillo State Beach, CA3-15
Leupp/Grand Falls, AZ-92
Little Hole on Green River, UT-84
Little Rock Dam, CA4-154
Lone Pine Canyon, CA5-69
Lone Pine Train Depot, CA6-120
Lone Pine/Alabama Hills, CA6-84
Long Valley, UT-86
Los Angeles Riding Academy, CA3-4
Los Angeles Stock Yard, CA5-41
Los Encinos Ranch, CA2-58
Lovejoy Butte/Lake Los Angeles, CA5-48
Lucerne Dry Lake, CA5-141
Lucerne Valley, CA5-140
Lucky Baldwin Mine, CA3-132
Lyon Canyon/Valencia Oaks, CA4-102
M & T Ranch, CA7-45
Mad River, CA7-72
Magma Arizona Railroad, AZ-93
Malibou Lake, CA1-164
Malibu Beach, CA6-19
Mammoth Lakes, CA6-165
Marble Canyon, AZ-95
Marwyck Ranch/Northridge Farms, CA2-50
McDonald Ranch, UT-87
Mckinley School for Boys, CA5-26
Mecca, CA5-178
Mesa Grande Indian Reservation, CA6-5
Mesa, AZ-96
Mescal, AZ-98
Metro-Goldwyn-Mayer Ranch, CA1-109
Metro-Goldwyn-Mayer, CA3-21
Metropolitan Airport, CA2-71
Mexican Hat, UT-88
Midwick Country Club, CA3-89
Mill Creek Canyon, UT-91
Mirror Lake, UT-92
Miscellaneous Antelope Valley Areas, CA5-60
Miscellaneous Victor Valley Areas, CA5-154
Mixville, CA3-19
Moenave, AZ-102
Mojave, CA5-181
Mono Lake, CA6-169
Montezuma Castle, AZ-103
Monument Valley, AZ-105
Mormon Rocks, CA5-71

Morrison Ranch, CA1-140
Mount Gaines Mine, CA7-101
Mount Wilson, CA5-44
Mountain Brook Ranch, CA4-158
Movieland Frontier Town, CA3-165
Mt. Kalmia, CA3-45
Mulholland Dam, CA5-29
Muroc Dry Lake, CA5-185
Murphys, CA7-52
N. B. Murray "Overall Wearing" Dude Ranch, CA5-94
Navajo Lake, UT-93
Neil McCarthy Estate, CA6-38
Newhall Oil Field, CA7-11
Newhall Ranch & Newhall, CA4-119
Newhall Train Depot, CA4-132
Niles, CA7-35
North Ranch, CA1-118; 5-3
North Verde Ranch/Kemper Campell Ranch, CA5-78
Northridge Train Depot, CA6-17
Oak Park, CA5-4
Oatman, AZ-109
Olancha Sand Dunes, CA6-78
Old Town Victorville and Railroad Depot, CA5-73
Old Tucson, AZ-110
Oliver Drake Ranch, CA4-161
Orick, CA7-73
Oroville Area, CA7-46
Orville Robinson Ranch Fort, UT-94
Orvis Cattle Company/Snow Ranch, CA7-118
Oscar Robinson Ranch, UT-101
Owens Dry Lake, CA6-80
Pacific Lumber Company, CA7-74
Pacoima Dam, CA2-174
Painted Desert, AZ-125
Palm Springs/Palm Canyon, CA5-177
Palmdale & Lake Palmdale, CA4-169
Palms Depot, CA3-20
Paloma Ranch, AZ-126
Panguitch Lake, UT-104
Pantano Creek, AZ-127
Paradise Springs, CA4-164
Paramount Ranch, CA1-149
Paramount Studio, CA3-53
Paria Canyon, UT-106
Paria Ghost Town, UT-111
Paria Movie Set, UT-119
Parowan Gap, UT-126
Pasadena City Hall, CA3-88

Patterson Grade, CA7-154
Paulden, AZ-128
Paulson Packing Company, CA2-172
Peña Blanca Canyon, AZ-129
Perkinsville, AZ-130
Pico Canyon/Mentryville, CA4-98
Pierre Domec's First Adobe, CA5-22
Pine Valley Reservoir, UT-128
Pioneer Church, CA2-39
Pioneer Living History Village, AZ-131
Pioneer Trail State Park, UT-129
Pioneertown, CA5-160
Pipe Springs, AZ-133
Piru Creek, CA1-165
Piute Butte/Antelope Valley Indian Museum, CA5-55
Placerita Canyon Road and Aqueduct, CA4-59
Point Dume State Beach, CA3-14
Polsa Rosa Ranch, CA4-137
Porter Ranch, CA2-169
Prescott/Granite Dells/Watson Lake, AZ-134
Preston Swapp Ranch, Sink Valley, UT-148
Professor Valley, UT-132
Providencia Ranch, CA2-149
Quartzite Mountain Area, CA5-72
Rabbit Dry Lake, CA5-138
Rain Valley, AZ-136
Rainbow Bridge National Monument, UT-137
Ralph M. Like/Monogram Studio, CA3-73
Rancho El Escorpion, CA2-29
Rancho Maria, CA4-96
Rancho Placeritos/Rancho Placeritos/Melody Ranch, CA4-28; 5-9
Rancho Seco, AZ-137
Ratto Ranch, CA7-155
Ravenna Train Depot, CA4-136
Ray Corrigan Movie Ranch/Corriganville, CA1-76
Reading Island, CA7-125
Red Hills Ranch, CA7-156
Red Rock Canyon, CA6-41
Relief Reservoir, CA7-159
Republic Studios, CA2-72
Ridgecrest, CA5-193
Rio Rico, AZ-139
Riviera Country Club, CA3-11
RKO Culver City 40 Acres, CA3-33
RKO ENCINO RANCH PHOTO GALLERY, **CA**3-167
RKO Encino Ranch, CA2-61
Rosamond, CA5-183
Rowland V. Lee Ranch, CA2-44

Roy Rogers Double R Bar Ranch, CA1-69
Rush Valley, UT-139
Russell Ranch/Albertson Ranch/Glenmoore Cattle Ranch, CA1-119
Russian Gulch State Beach, CA7-105
Russian River near Monte Rio, CA7-131
Sabino Canyon, AZ-141
Sable Ranch, CA4-92
Sacramento River, CA7-47, CA7-127
Saguaro Lake Guest Ranch, AZ-143
Saguaro National Park, AZ-144
Salt River Canyon, AZ-145
Salt Spring Valley Reservoir, CA7-55
Saltdale, CA5-195
San Andreas, CA7-57
San Fernando Mission, CA2-166
San Fernando Train Depot, CA5-28
San Gabriel Canyon and Morris Dam, CA3-98
San Gabriel Mission, CA3-91
San Juan Capistrano, CA3-106
San Luis Rey Mission, CA3-107
San Manuel Arizona Railroad, AZ-147
San Rafael Valley, AZ-149
San Rafael, CA7-95
San Xavier del Bac Mission, AZ-152
Sand Flats Recreation Area, UT-140
Santa Ana River/Canyon, CA3-103
Santa Barbara Mission, CA7-15
Santa Fe Depot, CA7-28
Santa Susana Pass Area, CA1-67
Santa Susana Pass Road, CA1-65
Santa Susana Pass State Historic Park, CA1-66
Santiago Canyon/S & M Ranch, CA3-104
Saugus Train Depot, CA4-133
Scotia, CA7-76
Sedona/Oak Creek, AZ-154
Seven Mile Canyon, UT-141
Shadow Hills, CA2-176
Shay Ranch, CA3-122
Sherwin Summit, CA6-159
Sidney Valley, UT-142
Sierra Madre, CA6-28
Sierra Railway, CA7-160
Silver City Ghost Town, CA6-69
Simi Valley Ranches, CA1-106
Sky Castle, CA4-166
Slaughter Ranch, AZ-164
Smith River, CA7-61
Snegoff Ranch, CA2-96

Snow Canyon, UT-149
Sonoita Valley, AZ-165
South Haiwee Reservoir, CA6-77
Southern Pacific Railroad/San Fernando Pass, CA2-171
Spahn Ranch, CA1-55
Spanish Valley, UT-155
Spin & Marty Ranch/Sunshine Ranch, CA2-49
Springdale/Virgin River, UT-144
St. Peter Indian Mission School, AZ-168
Stanislaus River, CA7-167
Stillwell's Resort, CA5-172
Strawberry Point, UT-156
Strawberry Valley, UT_158
Sunshine Ranch/Spin & Marty Ranch, CA5-197
Taft, CA5-189
Tarzana Ranch, CA2-55
Tec-Art/California Studio, CA3-62
Telegraph Pass, AZ-169
Texas Canyon, AZ-170
The Prospect Studios, CA3-82
The Traveling Western Towns, CA4-5
Three Lakes, UT-160
Thunderbird Ranch, CA7-21
Tinemaha Reservoir, CA6-148
Titus Ranch, UT-162
Tom's Place, CA6-160
Tombstone, AZ-171
Tooby Ranch, CA7-77
Toulumne City, CA7-168
Towsley Canyon, CA4-111
Trem Carr Ranch, CA4-10
Triangle T Ranch, AZ-172
Tropico Mine, CA5-187
Tsegi Canyon, AZ-174
Tumacacori Mission, AZ-176
Tuolumne County, CA7-169
Turkey Crossing, UT-164
Universal Studios, CA2-97
University of Southern California, CA3-67
Unknown Ranch, CA1-131
Uplifters Club, CA3-13
Upper Desert Knolls Area, CA5-91
Upper Narrows, CA5-88
Valyermo Ranch, CA4-156
Valyermo-Big Rock Springs Store, CA4-159
Van Duzen River, CA7-79
Vanderlip Stables, CA3-18
Vasquez Rocks, CA4-140

Veluzat Movie Ranch, CA4-123
Verde River, AZ-177
Victory Pictures Studio, CA6-23
Villa Leon, CA6-20
Vincent Train Depot, CA4-153
Virgin Oil Field Area, UT-165
Walker Ranch, CA4-83
Walt Disney Studio, CA2-159
Warner Brothers Studio, CA2-137
Warner Hot Springs, CA6-6
Warner Ranch, CA2-13
Warnerville, CA7-136
Weldon Adobe Town, CA6-73
Weldon, CA6-70
Westlake Blvd, CA5-6
White Ranch, UT-167
White Stallion Ranch, AZ-178
White Wash Sand Dunes Recreation Area, UT-170
Whitehorse Ranch, CA5-156
"Wild Bill" Elliott Ranch, CA2-60
Willcox Dry Lake, AZ-180
William Mackelprange Ranch, UT-171
Willow Gate Stable, CA2-47
Winkelman, AZ-181
Winnedumah Hotel, Independence, CA6-147
Wrightwood/Grimy Gulch, CA3-145
Yosemite National Park, CA7-179
Yrigoyen Ranch, CA1-148
Yuma, AZ-183
Zion National Park, UT-179

The **WESTERN FILMING LOCATIONS** series of books which are referenced in the above index are for sale at online book stores, such as amazon.com and others, as well as at the CP Entertainment Books website located at www.CPEntBooks.com.

MASTER FILM INDEX

$50,000 Reward (1924 Clifford S. Elfelt) Ken Maynard. LOC: California: Mulholland Dam

... And Now Miguel (1966 Universal) Michael Ansara. LOC: New Mexico: Abiquiu Ghost Ranch; San Ildefonso Pueblo.

'Neath Canadian Skies (1946 Screen Guild) Russell Hayden. LOC: California: Corriganville.

'Neath the Arizona Skies (1934 Monogram) John Wayne. LOC: California: Trem Carr Ranch; Kernville.

13 Fighting Men (1960 20th Century Fox) Brad Dexter. LOC: California: Century Ranch.

1313: Billy the Kid (2012 Rapid Heart Pictures) Brandon Thornton. LOC: California: Malibu; Sylmar.

3 Godfathers (1949 MGM) John Wayne. LOC: California: Lone Pine; Death Valley; Keeler; RKO Encino Ranch.

3:10 to Yuma (2007 Columbia Pictures) Russell Crowe. LOC: New Mexico: Abiquiú Ghost Ranch; Abiquiú Reservoir; Bonanza Creek Ranch; Cook Ranch/Cerro Pelon Ranch; Galisteo; Diablo Canyon North of Santa Fe; Gilman; Santa Fe National Forest.

6 Guns (2010 The Global Asylum) Sage Mears. LOC: California: Paramount Ranch; Snegoff Ranch; Whitehorse Ranch.

Abe Lincoln in Illinois (1940 RKO) Raymond Massey. LOC: California: RKO Encino Ranch; Oregon: McKenzie River, Eugene.

Abilene Town (1946 United Artists) Randolph Scott. LOC: California: Agoura Ranch; Columbia Ranch.

Abilene Trail (1951 Monogram) Whip Wilson. LOC: California: Iverson Ranch.

Aces and Eights (1936 Puritan) Tim McCoy. LOC: California: Trem Carr Ranch; Walker Ranch; Universal Studio.

Ace High (1918 Fox) Tom Mix. LOC: California: Big Bear.

Aces 'N' Eights (2007 RHI Entertainment) Casper Van Dien. LOC: California: Corriganville; Paramount Ranch; Veluzat Ranch; Rancho Placeritos.

Aces Wild (1936 Commodore) Harry Carey. LOC: California: Kernville; Kernville Movie Street.

Across the Badlands (1950 Columbia) Charles Starrett. LOC: California: Iverson Ranch; Corriganville.

Across the Great Divide (1976 Pacific International) Robert Logan. LOC: Utah: CANADA: Alberta; British Columbia.

Across the Plains (1938 Robert J Hoerner) Ted Wells. LOC: California: Fat Jones Ranch; Vasquez Rocks.

Across the Plains (1939 Monogram) Charles Starrett. LOC: California: Lone Pine.

Across the Rio Grande (1949 Monogram) Jimmy Wakely. LOC: California: Walker

Ranch.

Across the Sierras (1941 Columbia) William Elliott. LOC: California: Iverson Ranch; Columbia Ranch; Brandeis Ranch.

Across the Wide Missouri (1951 MGM) Clark Gable. LOC: Colorado: Durango; La Plata Canyon; Ouray County; Molas Lake; Haviland Dam; Little Boyce Lake.

Adios Amigo (1975 Atlas Prod) Fred Williamson. LOC: New Mexico: J. W. Eaves Movie Ranch, Santa Fe.

Advance to the Rear (1964 MGM) Glenn Ford. LOC: California: Janss Janss Conejo Rancho; MGM backlot.

Adventure of the Texas Kid, An: Border Ambush (1954 Franklin) Hugh Hooker. LOC: California: Corriganville.

Adventures in Silverado (1948 Columbia) William Bishop. LOC: California: Iverson Ranch; Columbia Ranch.

Adventures of Bullwhip Griffin, The (1967 Disney) Roddy McDowall. LOC: California: Walt Disney Studio backlot.

Adventures of Don Coyote, The (1947 Comet) Frances Rafferty. LOC: California: Corriganville; Bronson Canyon.

Adventures of Frank and Jesse James (1948 Republic) Clayton Moore. LOC: California: Iverson Ranch; Republic Studio backlot.

Adventures of Frontier Fremont, The (1977 Sun Classics) Dan Haggerty. LOC: Utah: Heber City; Kamas; Park City.

Adventures of Gallant Bess (1948 Eagle Lion) Cameron Mitchell. LOC: California: Iverson Ranch.

Adventures of Mark Twain, The (1944 Warner Bros) Fredric March. LOC: California: Bronson Caves; Sacramento River; Warner Ranch; Warner Bros Studio backlot.

Adventures of Red Ryder (1940 Republic) Don Barry. LOC: California: Iverson Ranch; Lake Sherwood; Burro Flats; Republic Studio backlot.

Adventures of Texas Jack (1934 Security) Wally Wales. LOC: California: Trem Carr Ranch; Newhall.

Adventures of the Masked Phantom, The (1939 Equity) Monte Rawlins. LOC: California: Iverson Ranch; Brandeis Ranch.

Adventures of the Texas Kid: Border Ambush (1954 Franklin Productions) Hugh Hooker. LOC: California: Corriganville.

Adventures of the Tucson Kid, The (1953 Tucson Kid Prod) Tom Keene. LOC: California: Ingram Ranch.

Adventures of the Wilderness Family (1975 Pacific International) Robert Logan. LOC: Utah: Heber City, Kamas, Uinta Mountains; CANADA: British Columbia.

Adventures of Tom Sawyer, The (1938 Paramount) Tommy Kelly. LOC: California: Malibou Lake; Paramount Ranch.

Adventurer of Tortuga, The (1965 Eichberg-Film) Guy Madison. LOC: SPAIN: ITALY: Incir De Paolis, Rome.

Against a Crooked Sky (1975 Doty Dayton) Richard Boone. LOC: Utah: Park Avenue, Arches National Park; The Windows, Arches National Park; castle Valley; Professor Valley; Dead Horse Point State Park.

Al Jennings of Oklahoma (1951 Columbia) Dan Duryea. LOC: California: Iverson Ranch; Agoura Ranch; Lone Pine; Burro Flats.

Alamo (2004 Buena Vista) Billy Bob Thornton. LOC: Texas: Austin/Driscoll Hotel and Paramount TheatreBastropJim Small's Big Thicket, BastropPedernales Falls State Park, Johnson CityDripping Springs/Reimer's RanchSteiner Ranch, Bastrop.

Alamo, The (1960 United Artists) John Wayne. LOC: Texas: Brackettville.

Alamo: the Price of Freedom (1988 Imax) Enrique Sandino. LOC: Texas: Alamo Village Brackettville.

Alamo: Thirteen Days to Glory, The (1987 NBC) James Arness. LOC: Texas: Alamo Village BrackettvilleRancho Rio Grande/Moody's Ranch Del Rio.

Alaska (1944 Monogram) Kent Taylor. LOC: California: Rancho Placeritos.

Alaska Highway (1943 Paramount) Richard Arlen. LOC: California: Azusa.

Albuquerque (1948 Paramount) Randolph Scott. LOC: California: Iverson Ranch; Rancho Placeritos; Arizona: Sedona.

Alias Billy the Kid (1946 Republic) Sunset Carson. LOC: California: Iverson Ranch; Republic Studio backlot.

Alias Jesse James (1959 United Artists) Bob Hope. LOC: California: Iverson Ranch.

Alias John Law (1935 Superior) Bob Steele. LOC: California: Kernville; Ralph M. Like Studio.

Alias Smith and Jones (1971 Universal-TV) Peter Deuel. LOC: Utah: Professor Valley.

Alias the Bad Man (1931 Tiffany) Ken Maynard. LOC: California: Jauregui Ranch; Vasquez Rocks; Warner Bros Studio backlot.

Aliens in the Wild, Wild West (1999 Full Moon Entertainment) Taylor Locke. LOC: ROMANIA: Izvorani; Castel Film Studios backlot.

All Hat (2007 New Real Films) Keith Carradine. LOC: CANADA: Ontario: Alliston; Fort Erie Racetrack; Hamilton.

All Hell Broke Loose (2009 Barnholtz Entertainment) David Carradine. LOC: California: Pollock Pines.

All the Pretty Horses (1999 Columbia Pictures) Matt Damon. LOC: New Mexico: Abiquiú Dam; Abiquiú Ghost Ranch; Bonanza Creek Ranch Santa Fe; Charles R Ranch Las Vegas; El Rancho de las Golondrinas Santa Fe; Las Vegas; Río Chama; San José; The White Place/Plaza Blanca Abiquiú; Zia Pueblo; Texas: Helotes; Hill Ranch.

Allegheny Uprising (1939 RKO) John Wayne. LOC: California: Lake Sherwood.

Almost Heroes (1998 Turner Pictures) Chris Farley. LOC: California: Big Bear; Holcomb Valley; Black's Beach, La Jolla; Humboldt Lagoons State Park, Trinidad; Montana.

Along Came Jones (1945 RKO) Gary Cooper. LOC: California: Iverson Ranch; Arizona: Nogales; Sasabe; Tucson.

Along the Great Divide (1951 Warner Bros) Kirk Douglas. LOC: California: Lone Pine.

Along the Navajo Trail (1945 Republic) Roy Rogers. LOC: California: Corriganville; Republic Studio backlot.

Along the Oregon Trail (1947 Republic) Monte Hale. LOC: California: Iverson Ranch; Vasquez Rocks.

Along the Rio Grande (1941 RKO) Tim Holt. LOC: California: Jauregui Ranch; Walker Ranch; Cougar Buttes, Luzerne Valley; Rancho Placeritos.

Along the Sundown Trail (1942 PRC) Frontier Marshal. LOC: California: Iverson Ranch; Corriganville.

Alvarez Kelly (1966 Columbia) William Holden. LOC: Louisiana: Baton Rouge.

Ambush (1950 MGM) Robert Taylor. LOC: California: Corriganville; Arizona: Lupton; New Mexico: Gallup; Navajo.

Ambush at Cimarron Pass (1958 20th Century Fox) Scott Brady. LOC: California: Iverson Ranch.

Ambush at Tomahawk Gap (1953 Columbia) John Hodiak. LOC: California: Corriganville.

Ambush Trail (1946 PRC) Bob Steele. LOC: California: Corriganville.

Ambush Valley (1936 Reliable) Bob Custer. LOC: California: Kernville; Kernville Movie Street.

American Bandits: Frank and Jesse James (2010 Barnholtz Entertainment/ARO Entertainment) Peter Fonda. LOC: California: Canyon County.

American Empire (1942 United Artists) Richard Dix. LOC: California: Kernville.

American Outlaws (2001 Morgan Creek Productions) Colin Farrell. LOC: Florida: Fort De Soto Park, Tierra Verde; Texas: Texas State Railroad, Rusk-Palestine; U.S. Western Town Austin; Wimberley.

Americano, The (1955 RKO) Glenn Ford. LOC: California: Riverside; Brazil.

And Starring Pancho Villa as Himself (2003 HBO) Antonio Banderas. LOC: MEXICO: Guanajuato: Dolores Hidalgo, Hacienda San Diego de Jaral de Berrio; San Felipe Torres Mochas; San Luis Paz, Mineral de Pozos; Queretaro: San Luis Potosi.

Andersonville (1996 TNT) Jarrod Emick. LOC: North Carolina: Wilmington; GEORGIA: Turin.

Angel and the Badman (1947 Republic) John Wayne. LOC: Arizona: Sedona; Arizona/Utah: Monument Valley.

Angel and the Badman (2009 The Hallmark Channel) Lou Diamond Phillips. LOC: CANADA: British Columbia: Bordertown, Maple Ridge, Vancouver.

Angel in Exile (1948 Republic) John Carroll. LOC: California: Corriganville.

Angels' Wild Women (1972 Ind-Intl Pictures) Ross Hagen. LOC: California: Spahn

Ranch.

Animals, The (1971 MGM) Henry Silva. LOC: Arizona: Old Tucson.

Annie Get Your Gun (1950 MGM) Betty Hutton. LOC: California: MGM backlot.

Annie Oakley (1935 RKO) Barbara Stanwyck. LOC: California: RKO Encino Ranch.

Another Man, Another Chance (1977 Majestic Films) James Caan. LOC: California: Lake Sherwood; Arizona: Old Tucson; Rancho Romero, Tucson.

Another Pair of Aces: Three of a Kind (1991 Pedernales Films) Willie Nelson. LOC: Texas: Austin; Manor.

Apache (1954 United Artists) Burt Lancaster. LOC: California: Corriganville; Agoura Ranch; Vasquez Rocks; Burro Flats; Warner Ranch; Solemint Canyon; Dardanelle; Russell Ranch.

Apache Ambush (1955 Columbia) Bill Williams. LOC: California: Iverson Ranch; Sierra Railroad, Tuolumne County; Columbia Ranch.

Apache Blood (1975 Key Int'l) Ray Danton. LOC: Arizona: Carefree; Tucson.

Apache Chief (1949 Lippert) Tom Neal. LOC: California: Corriganville; Walker Ranch.

Apache Country (1952 Columbia) Gene Autry. LOC: California: Rancho Placeritos.

Apache Drums (1951 Universal) Stephen McNally. LOC: California: North Verde Ranch/Kemper Campbell Ranch, Victorville; Fairview Valley/Reeves Dry Lake, Apple Valley; Red Rock Canyon.

Apache Kid, The (1941 Republic) Donald Barry. LOC: California: Iverson Ranch.

Apache Kid's Escape, The (1930 R J Horner) Jack Perrin. LOC: California: Jauregui Ranch; Lake Sherwood.

Apache Rifles (1964 20th Century Fox) Audie Murphy. LOC: California: Red Rock Canyon; Bronson Canyon.

Apache Rose (1947 Republic) Roy Rogers. LOC: California: Iverson Ranch; Vasquez Rocks; Leo Carrillo State Beach; Republic Studio backlot.

Apache Territory (1958 Columbia) Rory Calhoun. LOC: California: Red Rock Canyon.

Apache Trail (1943 MGM) Lloyd Nolan. LOC: California: MGM backlot; Arizona: Starr Pass.

Apache Uprising (1966 Paramount) Rory Calhoun. LOC: California: Vasquez Rocks; Paramount Studio backlot.

Apache War Smoke (1952 MGM) Gilbert Roland. LOC: California: Iverson Ranch; Arizona: Starr Pass.

Apache Warrior (1957 20th Century Fox) Keith Larsen. LOC: California: Corriganville; Vasquez Rocks.

Apache Woman (1955 American Releasing Corp) Lloyd Bridges. LOC: California: Iverson Ranch; Corriganville.

Appaloosa (2008 New Line Cinema) Ed Harris. LOC: New Mexico: Abiquiú Dam;

Bonanza Creek Ranch Santa Fe; Cook Ranch/Cerro Pelon Ranch Galisteo; Diablo Canyon North of Santa Fe; La Madera/Palovista Ranch Rio Arriba County; Lamy; Río Chama; Río Pecos Algodones; San Cristobal Ranch Galisteo; Texas: Dripple Springs/Mexican set Austin.

Appaloosa, The (1966 Universal) Marlon Brando. LOC: California: Lake Los Angeles; Lone Pine Canyon; Utah: St. George; Virgin; Silver Reef area; Ivins Bench; Sand Mountain area.

Apple Dumpling Gang Rides Again, The (1979 Buena Vista) Tim Conway. LOC: California: Disney's Golden Oak Ranch; Utah: Kanab; Kanab Movie Fort.

Apple Dumpling Gang, The (1975 Buena Vista) Bill Bixby. LOC: California: Disney's Golden Oak Ranch; Colorado: Deschutes National Forest; Oregon: Bend.

April Morning (1988 The Samuel Goldwyn Company) Tommy Lee Jones. LOC: CANADA: Quebec: Quebec.

Arena (1953 MGM) Gig Young. LOC: Arizona: Tucson Rodeo.

Arizona (1940 Columbia) Jean Arthur. LOC: Arizona: Old Tucson; Cortaro; Double U Guest Ranch, Tucson.

Arizona Bad Man (1935 Kent) Reb Russell. LOC: California: Frank LaSalle Ranch.

Arizona Bound (1941 Monogram) Rough Riders. LOC: California: Kernville; Arizona: Burnt Ranch, Prescott; Granite Dells.

Arizona Bushwhackers (1968 Paramount) Howard Keel. LOC: California: Vasquez Rocks; Paramount Studio backlot.

Arizona Cowboy, The (1950 Republic) Rex Allen. LOC: California: Iverson Ranch.

Arizona Cyclone (1934 Imperial) Wally Wales. LOC: California: Ralph M. Like Studio backlot.

Arizona Cyclone (1941 Universal) Johnny Mack Brown. LOC: California: Iverson Ranch; Corriganville.

Arizona Days (1937 Grand National) Tex Ritter. LOC: California: Brandeis Ranch; Ralph M. Like Studio backlot; Garner Ranch.

Arizona Frontier (1940 Monogram) Tex Ritter. LOC: Arizona: Prescott.

Arizona Gang Busters (1940 PRC) Tim McCoy. LOC: California: Brandeis Ranch.

Arizona Gunfighter, The (1937 Republic) Bob Steele. LOC: California: Jauregui Ranch; Walker Ranch.

Arizona Kid, The (1930 Fox) Warner Baxter. LOC: Utah: Grafton; Zion National Park.

Arizona Kid, The (1939 Republic) Roy Rogers. LOC: California: Iverson Ranch; Republic Studio backlot; Towsley Canyon.

Arizona Legion (1939 RKO) George O'Brien. LOC: California: Iverson Ranch; Corriganville; Burro Flats.

Arizona Mahoney (1936 Paramount) Buster Crabbe. LOC: California: Cedar Lake; Arizona: Mesa.

Arizona Manhunt (1951 Republic) Michael Chapin. LOC: California: Iverson Ranch.

Arizona Nights (1934 Reliable) Jack Perrin. LOC: California: Vasquez Rocks.

Arizona Raiders (1965 Columbia) Audie Murphy. LOC: Arizona: Old Tucson; Cortaro; Apacheland.

Arizona Raiders, The (1936 Paramount) Buster Crabbe. LOC: California: Kernville; Paramount Ranch.

Arizona Ranger, The (1948 RKO) Tim Holt. LOC: California: Jauregui Ranch; Lone Pine.

Arizona Round-Up (1942 Monogram) Tom Keene. LOC: California: Rancho Placeritos; Walker Ranch.

Arizona Stage Coach (1942 Monogram) Range Busters. LOC: California: Corriganville.

Arizona Territory (1950 Monogram) Whip Wilson. LOC: California: Iverson Ranch.

Arizona Terror (1942 Republic) Donald Barry. LOC: California: Burro Flats.

Arizona Terror, The (1931 Tiffany) Ken Maynard. LOC: California: Vasquez Rocks.

Arizona Trail (1943 Universal) Tex Ritter. LOC: California: Corriganville.

Arizona Trails (1935 Art Mix Productions) Bill Patton. LOC: California: Lake Los Angeles; Frank LaSalle Ranch.

Arizona Whirlwind (1944 Monogram) Trail Blazers. LOC: California: Corriganville; Rancho Placeritos.

Arizona Wildcat, The (1939 20th Century Fox) Jane Withers. LOC: California: 20th Century Fox Studio backlot.

Arizonian, The (1935 RKO) Richard Dix. LOC: California: Iverson Ranch; Vasquez Rocks.

Arkansas Judge (1941 Republic) Weaver Brothers and Elviry. LOC: California: Republic Studios backlot.

Arliss (2001) Ty Murray. LOC: California: Anaheim.

Army Girl (1938 Republic) Preston Foster. LOC: California: Lone Pine.

Arrow in the Dust (1954 Allied Artists) Sterling Hayden. LOC: California: Iverson Ranch.

Arrowhead (1953 Paramount) Charlton Heston. LOC: Texas: Brackettville; Fort Clark.

Around the World in 80 Days (1956 United Artists) David Niven. LOC: California: RKO 40 Acres; Iverson Movie Ranch; Newport Beach; Lone Pine; Universal Studio backlot; Arizona: Canelo; Elgin; McNeal; Sonoita; Colorado: Denver & Rio Grande Western Railroad; Durango and Silverton Narrow Gauge Railroad; San Juan Mountains; Silverton; New Mexico: Alamogordo; White Sands Missile Range; BANGLADESH: Barabkunda; Chittagong; Sylhet; Sreemangal; MEXICO: Mexico City; SPAIN: Chinchon, Madrid.

At Gunpoint (1955 Allied Artists) Fred MacMurray. LOC: California: Rancho Placeritos.

Atkins (1984 DEFA/Buftea Studios) Oleg Borissow. LOC: EAST GERMANY: ROMANIA:

Aurora Encounter (1986 New World Pictures) Jack Elam. LOC: Texas: AuroraBig D. Ranch Dallas.

Avenger, The (1931 Columbia) Buck Jones. LOC: California: Vasquez Rocks; Paramount Ranch.

Avenging Angel (2007 RHI Entertainment) Kevin Sorbo. LOC: California: Disney's Golden Oak Ranch; Sable Ranch; Vasquez Rocks; Veluzat Motion Picture Ranch.

Avenging Angel, The (1995 TNT) Tom Berenger. LOC: Utah: Morgan.

Avenging Rider, The (1943 RKO) Tim Holt. LOC: California: Iverson Ranch.

Avenging Waters (1936 Columbia) Ken Maynard. LOC: California: Iverson Ranch; Kernville.

Avenging, The (1981 Doty-Dayton) Michael Horse. LOC: New Mexico: J. W. Eaves Movie Ranch Santa Fe.

Back in the Saddle (1941 Republic) Gene Autry. LOC: California: Iverson Ranch; Chatsworth Train Depot; Antelope Valley (Lake Los Angeles/Palmdale Area); Republic Studio backlot; Los Angeles River.

Back to God's Country (1953 Universal) Rock Hudson. LOC: Colorado: Idaho: Sun Valley.

Back to the Future, Part III (1990 Universal) Michael J. Fox. LOC: California: China Flats; Monrovia; Oxnard; Pacoima; Port Hueneme; Red Hills Ranch; Jamestown, Tuolumne County; South Pasadena; Universal Studios backlot; Arizona: Monument Valley.

Back to the Soil (1934 Columbia) George Sidney. LOC:

Back to the Woods (1937 Columbia) Three Stooges. LOC: California: Franklin Canyon Reservoir (stock footage from Whoops! I'm an Indian).

Back Trail (1948 Monogram) Johnny Mack Brown. LOC: California: Rancho Placeritos; Walker Ranch.

Backlash (1956 Universal) Richard Widmark. LOC: Arizona: Old Tucson; Cortaro; Sonoita; Patagonia.

Backtrack! (1969 Universal) Neville Brand. LOC: California: Jamestown; Universal Studio backlot.

Bad Bascomb (1946 MGM) Wallace Beery. LOC: Wyoming: Jackson Hole; Jenny Lake; Potholes; Square G Ranch.

Bad Company (1972 Paramount) Jim Davis. LOC: Kansas: Wichita.

Bad Day at Black Rock (1955 MGM) Spencer Tracy. LOC: California: MGM backlot; Lone Pine.

Bad Girls (1994 20th Century-Fox) Madeleine Stowe. LOC: California: Red Hills Ranch; Jamestown, Tuolumne County; Sierra Railroad/Red Hills; Texas: Alamo Village Brackettville; Rancho Rio Grande/Moody's Ranch/Sycamore Creek Del Rio.

Bad Jim (1990 21st Century-Fox) James Brolin. LOC: Arizona: Cowtown, Peoria; Phoenix; Prescott; Sedona.

Bad Lands (1939 RKO) Robert Barrat. LOC: California: Fairview Mountain, Apple Valley.

Bad Man from Red Butte (1940 Universal) Johnny Mack Brown. LOC: California: Agoura Ranch; Universal Studio backlot.

Bad Man of Brimstone, The (1937 MGM) Wallace Beery. LOC: California: Red Rock Canyon; Arizona: Grand Canyon National Park; Utah: Kanab Canyon; Johnson Canyon; The Gap; Three Lakes; Zion National Park.

Bad Man of Deadwood (1941 Republic) Roy Rogers. LOC: California: Iverson Ranch; Republic Studio backlot.

Bad Man, The (1930 First National) Walter Huston. LOC: California: Jauregui Ranch; Warner Bros backlot.

Bad Man, The (1941 MGM) Ronald Reagan. LOC: California: Red Rock Canyon; Arizona: Lupton; New Mexico: Gallup.

Bad Men of Missouri (1941 Warner Bros.) Dennis Morgan. LOC: California: Iverson Ranch; Corriganville; Tuolumne County; Columbia; Sonora; Utah: Kanab.

Bad Men of the Border (1945 Universal) Kirby Grant. LOC: California: Iverson Ranch; Corriganville.

Bad Men of the Hills (1942 Columbia) Charles Starrett. LOC: California: Iverson Ranch.

Bad Men of Thunder Gap (1943 PRC) Texas Rangers. LOC: California: Rancho Placeritos; Walker Ranch.

Bad Men of Tombstone (1949 Allied Artists) Barry Sullivan. LOC: California: Iverson Ranch; Brandeis Ranch.

Bad Men's Money (1929 J Charles Davis Prod) Yakima Canutt. LOC: California: Frank LaSalle Ranch; Temecula; Temecula Hotel; Towsley Canyon.

Badge of Marshal Brennan, The (1957 Allied Artists) Jim Davis. LOC: Utah: Kanab Canyon.

Badlanders, The (1958 MGM) Alan Ladd. LOC: Arizona: Yuma Territorial Prison; Old Tucson.

Badlands of Dakota (1941 Universal) Robert Stack. LOC: California: Red Rock Canyon.

Badlands of Montana (1957 20th Century Fox) Rex Reason. LOC: California: Bronson Canyon.

Badman's Country (1958 Warner Bros) George Montgomery. LOC: California: Iverson Ranch; Rancho Placeritos.

Badman's Gold (1951 United Artists) Johnny Carpenter. LOC: California: Corriganville.

Badman's Territory (1946 RKO) Randolph Scott. LOC: California: Agoura Ranch; RKO Encino Ranch.

Bait (1954 Columbia) John Agar. LOC: California: Bronson Canyon.

Baja Oklahoma (1988 HBO) Lesley Ann Warren. LOC: Texas: Fort Worth; Haslett; Justin

Baker's Hawk (1976 Doty Dayton) Clint Walker. LOC: Utah: Provo Canyon.

Ballad of a Gunfighter (1964 Bill Ward) Marty Robbins. LOC: California: Republic Studio backlot; Utah: Kanab.

Ballad of Cable Hogue, The (1970 Warner Bros.) Jason Robards. LOC: Arizona: Apacheland; Nevada: Valley of Fire State Park.

Ballad of Gregorio Cortez, The (1982 PBS) Edward James Olmos. LOC: New Mexico: Chama; Cumbres and Toltec Scenic Railroad; Cerrillos; J. W. Eaves Movie Ranch Santa Fe; Las Vegas

Ballad of Josie, The (1968 Universal) Doris Day. LOC: California: Janss Conejo Ranch; North Ranch; Albertson Ranch.

Ballad of Little Jo, The (1993 Fine Line Features) Suzy Amis. LOC: Montana: Carbon County; Custer National Forest; Red Lodge

Ballad of Lucy Whipple, The (2001 CBS) Glenn Close. LOC: Utah: Park City.

Band of Angels (1957 Warner Bros) Clark Gable. LOC: Louisiana: Geismer.

Bandidas (2006 Europa Corp./Ultra Films/Canal+/TPS Star) Salma Hayek. LOC: MEXICO: Durango: Chocolate, City of Durango; Plaza del Cuarto Centenario; Palacio del Gobierno; Auditorio del Pueblo; Teatro Ricardo Castro; El Chorro railway station, Comarca Lagunera; Ex Hacienda de El Mortero, Suchil; La Joya Ranch; La Perla; Los Alamos; Los Tres Molinos; Pedricena; Rancho El Carmen; Rancho Marley; Ventanas; San Luis Potosí: Guadalcazar/Gruta de las Candelas; La Luz; Real de Catorce; Casa de Moneda; Chapel of Guadalupe; Vanegas; Mexico City: Distrito Federal; Estudios Churubusco Azteca; Palacio de Correos; Universidad Nacional Autonoma de Mexico/Jardin botanico.

Bandido! (1956 United Artists) Robert Mitchum. LOC: MEXICO: Guerrero: Acapulco; Iguala; Taxco; Morelos: Ex Hacienda Cocoyoc, Yautepec; Tepoztlan; Xochitepec.

Bandit King of Texas (1949 Republic) Allan Lane. LOC: California: Iverson Ranch; Republic Studio backlot.

Bandit Queen (1950 Lippert) Barbara Britton. LOC: California: Vasquez Rocks.

Bandit Ranger (1942 RKO) Tim Holt. LOC: California: Corriganville; RKO Encino Ranch.

Bandit Trail, The (1941 RKO) Tim Holt. LOC: California: Iverson Ranch; Brandeis Ranch; RKO Encino Ranch.

Bandits (1991 Estudios Churubusco Azteca S.A./Bandidos Films) Eduardo Toussaint. LOC: MEXICO: Hidalgo: Zempoala, Santiago Tepeyahualco.

Bandits and Ballads (1939 RKO) Ray Whitley. LOC:

Bandits of Dark Canyon (1947 Republic) Allan Lane. LOC: California: Iverson Ranch; Vasquez Rocks.

Bandits of El Dorado (1949 Columbia) Charles Starrett. LOC: California: Iverson Ranch; Columbia Ranch.

Bandits of the Badlands (1945 Republic) Sunset Carson. LOC: California: Iverson Ranch; Republic Studio backlot.
Bandits of the West (1953 Republic) Allan Lane. LOC: California: Iverson Ranch; Burro Flats.
Bandits, The (1967 Conrad-Zacharias) Robert Conrad. LOC: MEXICO: Mexico: Desierto de los Leones; Mexico City: Iztapalapa, Santa Cruz Meyehualco.
Bandolero! (1968 20th Century Fox) James Stewart. LOC: Arizona: Lee's Ferry; Texas: Alamo Village; Brackettville; Del Rio; Utah: Glen Canyon National Recreation Area.
Bang Bang Kid, The (1968 Ajay Films) Guy Madison. LOC: SPAIN: Andalucia: Desierto de Tabernas; Almeria.
Banjo Hackett: Roamin' Free (1976 Columbia-TV) Don Meredith. LOC: California: Goleta, Los Padres National Forest.
Bar 20 (1943 United Artists) William Boyd. LOC: California: Lone Pine; Anchor Ranch.
Bar 20 Justice (1938 Paramount) William Boyd. LOC: California: Kernville; Lone Pine; Paramount Ranch.
Bar 20 Rides Again (1935 Paramount) William Boyd. LOC: California: Lone Pine.
Bar Buckaroos (1940 RKO) Ray Whitley. LOST/MISSING/UNAVAILABLE.
Bar L Ranch (1930 Big 4) Wally Wales. LOST/MISSING.
Bar Z Bad Men (1937 Republic) Johnny Mack Brown. LOC: California: Jauregui Ranch; Walker Ranch; Brandeis Ranch; Ralph M. Like Studio backlot.
Barbarosa (1982 Universal Pictures) Gary Busey. LOC: Texas: Alamo Village; Big Bend National Park; Lajitas Western set.
Barbary Coast (1935 United Artists) Edward G. Robinson. LOC: California: Samuel Goldwyn Studio backlot.
Barbary Coast Gent (1944 MGM) Wallace Beery. LOC: California: Lone Pine; MGM backlot.
Barbed Wire (1952 Columbia) Gene Autry. LOC: California: Pioneertown; Columbia Ranch.
Baron of Arizona, The (1950 Lippert) Vincent Price. LOC: California: Corriganville.
Barquero (1970 United Artists) Lee Van Cleef. LOC: Colorado: Buckskin Joe; Brush Hollow Reservoir.
Barricade (1950 Warner Bros) Dane Clark. LOC: California: Bronson Canyon; Vasquez Rocks.
Barrier, The (1937 Paramount) Leo Carrillo. LOC: Washington: Mt. Baker National Forest; Mt. Rainier.
Battle at Apache Pass, The (1952 Universal) Jeff Chandler. LOC: Utah: Professor Valley; Ida Gulch; Colorado River; Courthouse Wash, Arches National Park.
Battle of Greed (1937 Crescent) Tom Keene. LOC: California: Rancho Placeritos.
Battle of Rogue River (1954 Columbia) George Montgomery. LOC: California:

Iverson Ranch; Norco; Santa Ana River; Columbia Ranch.

Battles of Chief Pontiac, The (1952 Realart) Lex Barker. LOC: South Dakota: Rapid City.

Battling Buckaroo (1932 Kent) Lane Chandler. LOC: California: Lone Pine; Anchor Ranch.

Battling Marshal (1948 Astor) Sunset Carson. LOC: California: Valyermo.

Battling with Buffalo Bill (1931 Universal) Tom Tyler. LOC: California: Towsley Canyon; Walker Ranch.

Bear Island (1979 Columbia) Donald Sutherland. LOC: Alaska: Glaciar Bay; CANADA: British Columbia

Bears and I, The (1974 Buena Vista) Patrick Wayne. LOC: CANADA: Chilko Lake, British Columbia.

Beast of Hollow Mountain, The (1956 United Artists) Guy Madison. LOC: MEXICO: Morelos: Tepoztlán.

Beau Bandit (1930 RKO) Rod La Rocque. LOC: California: Apple Valley; Kemper Campbell Ranch

Beautiful Blonde From Bashful Bend, The (1949 20th Century Fox) Betty Grable. LOC: California: RKO Encino Ranch.

Beauty and the Bandit (1946 Monogram) Duncan Renaldo. LOC: California: Iverson Ranch; Corriganville; Walker Ranch.

Beguiled, The (1971 Universal) Clint Eastwood. LOC: Louisiana: Geismer, Ashland-Belle Helene Plantation; Baton Rouge; Geismer.

Behind Southern Lines (1952 Monogram) Guy Madison. LOC: California: Rancho Placeritos; Walker Ranch.

Belle Le Grand (1951 Republic) John Carroll. LOC: California: Republic Studio backlot.

Belle of the Nineties (1934 Paramount) Mae West. LOC: California: Paramount Ranch.

Belle of the Yukon (1944 International Pictures) Randolph Scott. LOC: California: Cedar Lake; Universal Studio backlot.

Belle Starr (1941 20th Century Fox) Randolph Scott. LOC: California: Iverson Ranch; Sherwood Forest; 20th Century Fox backlot; Missouri: Joplin; Noel.

Belle Starr (1980 CBS) Elizabeth Montgomery. LOC: California: Railtown; Toulumne County; Warner Bros Studio backlot.

Belle Starr's Daughter (1948 20th Century Fox) George Montgomery. LOC: California: Bridgeport; Iverson Ranch; Corriganville.

Bells of Capistrano (1942 Republic) Gene Autry. LOC: California: ?Agoura? Ranch; Republic Studio backlot.

Bells of Coronado (1950 Republic) Roy Rogers. LOC: California: Sable Ranch; Little Rock Dam; Palmdale; Republic Studio backlot.

Bells of Rosarita (1945 Republic) Roy Rogers. LOC: California: Iverson Ranch; Republic Studio backlot.

Bells of San Angelo (1947 Republic) Roy Rogers. LOC: California: Republic Studio backlot; Nevada: Valley of Fire; Red Rock Canyon; Goodsprings.

Bells of San Fernando (1947 Screen Guild) Donald Woods. LOC: California: Beales Cut; Rancho Placeritos.

Below the Border (1942 Monogram) Rough Riders. LOC: California: Rancho Placeritos; Walker Ranch; Bronson Canyon.

Bend of the River (1952 Universal) James Stewart. LOC: California: Universal Studios backlot; Oregon: Mt. Hood; Sandy;River, Snake River Country; Timberline;Washington/Oregon: Columbia River Gorge.

Beneath Western Skies (1944 Republic) Robert Livingston. LOC: California: Corriganville.

Benedict Arnold: A Question of Honor (2003 A&E Television Networks) Aidan Quinn. LOC: IRELAND: Ballykonckan, Valleymount, County Wicklow; County Meath; Dublin, County Dublin; Kilruddery House, Bray, County Wicklow; Poulaphouca, County Wicklow.

Best Man Wins (1948 Columbia) Edgar Buchanan. LOC: California: Columbia Ranch.

Best of the Badmen (1951 RKO) Robert Ryan. LOC: California: Iverson Ranch; RKO Encino Ranch; Utah: Kanab Canyon; Paria; Duck Creek; Strawberry Valley.

Between Fighting Men (1932 World Wide) Ken Maynard. LOC: California: Trem Carr Ranch; Jauregui Ranch.

Between God, the Devil and a Winchester (1972 Unicorn Video) Gilbert Roland. LOC: SPAIN.

Between Men (1935 Superior) Johnny Mack Brown. LOC: California: Lone Pine.

Between the Sand and the Sky (2008 Shorris Film) Dee Wallace. LOC: California: Los Angeles.

Beyond the Last Frontier (1943 Republic) Eddie Dew. LOC: California: Iverson Ranch; Corriganville; Walker Ranch.

Beyond the Law (1930 Syndicate) Robert Frazer. LOC: California: Jauregui Ranch.

Beyond the Law (1934 Columbia) Tim McCoy. LOC: California: Walker Ranch.

Beyond the Law (1968 Roxy Film) Lee Van Cleef. LOC: SPAIN: Almería.

Beyond the Pecos (1945 Universal) Rod Cameron. LOC: California: Corriganville.

Beyond the Prairie, Part 2: The True Story of Laura Ingalls Wilder (2002 CBS) Meredith Monroe. LOC: Texas: Austin; Bastrop; Buda; Driftwood: Uhland.

Beyond the Prairie: The True Story of Laura Ingalls Wilder (1999 CBS) Meredith Monroe. LOC:

Beyond the Purple Hills (1950 Columbia) Gene Autry. LOC: California: Corriganville; Rancho Placeritos; Lone Pine.

Beyond the Rio Grande (1930 Big 4) Jack Perrin. LOST/MISSING.

Beyond the Rockies (1932 RKO) Tom Keene. LOC: California: Trem Carr Ranch;

Lone Pine.

Beyond the Sacramento (1940 Columbia) Bill Elliott. LOC: California: Iverson Ranch; Corriganville.

Big Bear (1998 Alliance Atlantis) Gordon Tootoosis. LOC: CANADA: Saskatchewan: Pasqua First Nations Reserve; Saskatoon; Wilcox; Quebec.

Big Bonanza, The (1944 Republic) Richard Arlen. LOC: California: Iverson Ranch.

Big Boy Rides Again (1935 Beacon) Big Boy Williams. LOC: California: Jauregui Ranch; Walker Ranch.

Big Calibre (1935 Commodore) Bob Steele. LOC: California: Lone Pine.

Big Cat, The (1949 Eagle Lion) Preston Foster. LOC: Utah: Kanab Canyon.

Big City (2007 Miroir Magique!) Vincent Valladon. LOC: BULGARIA: Sofia; CANADA: Alberta: Calgary.

Big Country, The (1958 United Artists) Gregory Peck. LOC: California: Red Rock Canyon; Last Chance Canyon Road; Orvis Cattle Co., Farmington, Stanislaus County; Ione, Amador County; Marysville; Drais Ranch, Stockton.

Big Hand for the Little Lady, A (1966 Warner Bros) Henry Fonda. LOC: California: Warner Bros. backlot; Disney Golden Oak Ranch; Arizona: Flagstaff.

Big Jack (1949 MGM) Wallace Beery) Maryland.

Big Jake (1971 National General) John Wayne. LOC: MEXICO: Durango: Chupaderos; El Arenal; El Saltito waterfall; La Joya Ranch; Rancho Marley; Zacatecas: Sombrerete, Sierra de Organos.

Big Land, The (1957 Warner Bros) Alan Ladd. LOC: California: Tuolumne County.

Big Money Rustlas (2010 Psychopathic Records) Violent J. LOC: California: Paramount Ranch.

Big Show, The (1936 Republic) Gene Autry. LOC: California: Iverson Ranch; Yrigoyen Ranch; Republic Studios backlot; Texas: Dallas State Fair.

Big Sky, The (1952 RKO) Kirk Douglas. LOC: California: 20th Century Fox backlot; Montana: Big Horn (2nd unit Crow buffalo kill); Wyoming: Jackson Hole; near Moran; Snake River; Grand Teton National Park.

Big Sombrero, The (1949 Columbia) Gene Autry. LOC: California: Corriganville; Rancho Placeritos; Vasquez Rocks; Red Rock Canyon; Rancho Maria; Arizona: Starr Pass.

Big Stampede, The (1932 Warner Bros) John Wayne. LOC: California: Providencia Ranch; Miller and Lux Ranch.

Big Steal, The (1949 RKO) Robert Mitchum. LOC: California: Iverson Ranch.

Big Timber (1950 Monogram) Roddy McDowall. LOC: California: Lone Pine.

Big Trail, The (1930 Fox) John Wayne. LOC: California: Sequoia National Park; Arizona: Yuma; Oregon: Utah: Hurricane Bluffs; Wyoming: Jackson Hole.

Big Trees, The (1952 Warner Bros) Kirk Douglas. LOC: California: Orick; Eureka; Redwood Groves.

Billy Jack (1971 Warner Bros) Tom Laughlin. LOC: New Mexico: J. W. Eaves Ranch; Santa Fe; Santa Clara Pueblo; Bandelier National Monument.

Billy the Kid (1930 MGM) Johnny Mack Brown. LOC: California: Porter Ranch, San Fernando Valley; Arizona: Grand Canyon National Park; New Mexico: Gallup; Kit Carson Cave; Utah: Zion National Park.

Billy the Kid (1941 MGM) Robert Taylor. LOC: Arizona: Sedona; Double U Guest Ranch; Sabino Canyon; Arizona/Utah: Monument Valley.

Billy the Kid in Santa Fe (1941 PRC) Bob Steele. LOC: California: Rancho Placeritos; Jauregui Ranch; Walker Ranch.

Billy the Kid in Texas (1940 PRC) Bob Steele. LOC: California: Iverson Ranch; Rancho Placeritos.

Billy the Kid Outlawed (1940 PRC) Bob Steele. LOC: California: Iverson Ranch; Rancho Placeritos; Jauregui Ranch; Walker Ranch.

Billy the Kid Returns (1938 Republic) Roy Rogers. LOC: California: Iverson Ranch; Janss Janss Conejo Ranch; Republic Studio backlot.

Billy the Kid Trapped (1942 PRC) Buster Crabbe. LOC: California: Iverson Ranch; Corriganville; Rancho Placeritos.

Billy the Kid vs. Dracula (1966 Embassy) Chuck Courtney. LOC: California: Corriganville.

Billy the Kid Wanted (1941 PRC) Buster Crabbe. LOC: California: Iverson Ranch; Rancho Placeritos.

Billy the Kid's Fighting Pals (1941 PRC) Bob Steele. LOC: California: Iverson Ranch; Rancho Placeritos.

Billy the Kid's Gun Justice (1940 PRC) Bob Steele. LOC: California: Iverson Ranch; Brandeis Ranch.

Billy the Kid's Range War (1941 PRC) Bob Steele. LOC: California: Iverson Ranch.

Billy the Kid's Round-Up (1941 PRC) Buster Crabbe. LOC: California: Walker Ranch.

Billy the Kid's Smoking Guns (1942 PRC) Buster Crabbe. LOC: California: Corriganville.

Billy Two Hats (1974 United Artists) Gregory Peck. LOC: ISRAEL: Sarco Western International Village (Sarcoville), Tel Aviv; desert between Ashkelon and Beer-Sheba

Bite the Bullet (1975 Columbia) Gene Hackman. LOC: New Mexico: Cumbres and Toltec Scenic Railroad; Chama; Taos; White Sands National Monument; Nevada: Valley of Fire State Park.

Bitter Creek (1954 Allied Artists) William Elliott. LOC: California: Iverson Ranch; Corriganville.

Black Aces (1937 Universal) Buck Jones. LOC: California: Walker Ranch; Kernville.

Black Arrow (1944 Columbia) Mark Roberts. LOC: California: Iverson Ranch; Columbia Ranch.

Black Bandit, The (1938 Universal) Bob Baker. LOC: California: Iverson Ranch;

Jauregui Ranch; Brandeis Ranch.

Black Bart (1948 Universal) Yvonne De Carlo. LOC: California: Iverson Ranch; Corriganville; Utah: Kanab; Paria; Strawberry Valley.

Black Dakotas, The (1954 Columbia) Gary Merrill. LOC: California: Iverson Ranch; Corriganville; Burro Flats; Bronson Canyon.

Black Eagle (1948 Columbia) William Bishop. LOC: California: Iverson Ranch.

Black Eagle of Santa Fe (1966 Rapid-Film) Brad Harris. LOC: SPAIN: Almeria; CZECHOSLOVAKIA: near Prague.

Black Fox (1995 CBS) Christopher Reeve. LOC: CANADA: Alberta: CL Ranch Calgary.

Black Fox: Good Men and Bad (1995 CBS) Christopher Reeve. LOC: CANADA: Alberta: CL Ranch Calgary.

Black Fox: The Price of Peace (1995 CBS) Christopher Reeve. LOC: CANADA: Alberta: CL Ranch Calgary.

Black Gold (1947 Allied Artists) Anthony Quinn. LOC: California: Vasquez Rocks; Kentucky: Churchill Downs.

Black Gold (1963 Warner Bros) Philip Carey. LOC: California: Vasquez Rocks.

Black Hills (1947 Eagle Lion) Eddie Dean. LOC: California: Iverson Ranch; Corriganville.

Black Hills Ambush (1952 Republic) Allan Lane. LOC: California: Iverson Ranch; Corriganville.

Black Hills Express, The (1943 Republic) Donald Barry. LOC: California: Iverson Ranch; Corriganville.

Black Horse Canyon (1954 Universal) Joel McCrea. LOC: California: Universal Studio backlot; Arizona: Bloomquist Ranch, Douglas.

Black Lash, The (1952 Western Adventure) Lash La Rue. LOC: California: Iverson Ranch; Corriganville.

Black Market Rustlers (1943 Monogram) Range Busters. LOC: California: Rancho Placeritos; Jauregui Ranch; Walker Ranch.

Black Patch (1957 Warner Bros) George Montgomery. LOC: California: Rancho Placeritos.

Black Robe (1991 Alliance International) Lothaire Bluteau. LOC: CANADA: Quebec: Lac St. Jean Saguenay Region; Saint-Felix d'Otis; FRANCE: Rouen.

Black Rodeo (1972 Cinerama) Muhammad Ali. LOC: New York: Harlem; Randall's Island.

Black Spurs (1965 Paramount) Rory Calhoun. LOC: California: Iverson Ranch; Corriganville.

Black Whip, The (1956 Regal) Hugh Marlowe. LOC: California: Iverson Ranch; Corriganville.

Blackjack Ketchum, Desperado (1956 Columbia) Howard Duff. LOC: California: Iverson Ranch; Lone Pine.

Blazing Across the Pecos (1948 Columbia) Charles Starrett. LOC: California:

Iverson Ranch; Providencia Ranch; Columbia Ranch.

Blazing Bullets (1951 Monogram) Johnny Mack Brown. LOC: California: Iverson Ranch.

Blazing Forest, The (1952 Paramount) Richard Arlen. LOC: California: Truckee; Feather River.

Blazing Frontier (1943 PRC) Buster Crabbe. LOC: California: Corriganville; Rancho Placeritos.

Blazing Guns (1935 Kent) Reb Russell. LOC: California: Iverson Ranch.

Blazing Guns (1943 Monogram) Trail Blazers. LOC: California: Corriganville; Rancho Placeritos; Walker Ranch.

Blazing Justice (1936 Spectrum) Bill Cody. LOC: California: Brandeis Ranch; Ralph M. Like Studio backlot.

Blazing Saddles (1974 Warner Bros) Gene Wilder. LOC: California: Vasquez Rocks.

Blazing Six Shooters (1940 Columbia) Charles Starrett. LOC: California: Iverson Ranch; ?Agoura? Ranch.

Blazing Sixes (1937 Warner Bros) Dick Foran. LOC: California: ?Agoura? Ranch; ?Burro Flats?; Warner Bros backlot.

Blazing Stewardesses (1975 Independent International) Yvonne De Carlo. LOC: California: Palmdale; Palm Springs.

Blazing Sun, The (1950 Columbia) Gene Autry. LOC: California: Lone Pine.

Blazing the Overland Trail (1956 Columbia) Lee Roberts. LOC: California: Iverson Ranch; Walker Ranch; Rancho Placeritos; Big Bear.

Blazing the Western Trail (1945 Columbia) Charles Starrett. LOC: California: Corriganville; Providencia Ranch; Columbia Ranch.

Blazing Trail, The (1949 Columbia) Charles Starrett. LOC: California: Iverson Ranch; Corriganville; Columbia Ranch.

Blocked Trail, The (1943 Republic) Three Mesquiteers. LOC: California: Iverson Ranch.

Blood Arrow (1958 20th Century Fox) Scott Brady. LOC: California: Iverson Ranch.

Blood For a Silver Dollar (1965 Fono Roma) Montgomery Wood. LOC: ITALY: Rome: Manziana/la casaccia; Mazzano Romano/Caseate di Montegelato; Parco Nazionale dell'Abruzzo.

Blood Money (1974 Harbor Prod) Lee Van Cleef. LOC: SPAIN: Almería, Andalucía; Guadix, Granada; La Calahorra, Granada.

Blood on the Arrow (1964 Allied Artists) Dale Robertson. LOC: Arizona: Superior; Magma Arizona Railroad.

Blood on the Brazos (2007 Sindinero Productions) Todd Jenkins. LOC: Texas: Nemo/Brazos River South of Fort Worth.

Blood on the Moon (1948 RKO) Robert Mitchum. LOC: California: RKO Encino Ranch; Calabasas; Arizona: Sedona; Van Dusen Cabin.

Blood Red (1989 Buena Vista Pictures) Dennis Hopper. LOC: California: Columbia State Historic Park; Jamestown/railway station.

Blood River (1991 CBS) Rick Schroder. LOC: CANADA: Alberta: Calgary Alberta - British Columbia: Ft.Steele.

Blood Trail (1996 Madrugada Ranch) Ty O'Neal. LOC: Texas: Abilene; Buffalo Gap; D-J Tubb Ranch; Larry Guy Ranch; Macy Ranch; Panther Canyon; Merkel; Sweetwater; Snyder; Tuscola.

BloodRayne II: Deliverance (2007 Brightlight Pictures) Nastassia Malte. LOC: CANADA: British Columbia: Bordertown/Western town Maple Ridge, Vancouver.

Blowing Wild (1953 Warner Bros) Gary Cooper. LOC: MEXICO.

Blue (1968 Paramount) Terence Stamp. LOC: Utah: Professor Valley; La Sal; Long Valley; Seven Mile Canyon.

Blue and the Gray, The (1982 Columbia TriStar miniseries) Gregory Peck. LOC: Arkansas: Eureka Springs train scene; Fayetteville; Forth Smith; Van Buren.

Blue Canadian Rockies (1952 Columbia) Gene Autry. LOC: California: Big Bear; Cedar Lake; Columbia Ranch.

Blue Eyes (2007 Walker/Cable Productions) John Castellanos. LOC: Texas: Alamo Village BrackettvilleMontgomery.

Blue Montana Skies (1939 Republic) Gene Autry. LOC: California: Big Bear; Cedar Lake; Wrightwood; Agoura Ranch.

Blue Steel (1934 Monogram) John Wayne. LOC: California: Trem Carr Ranch; Lone Pine.

Blueberry (2004 Ultra Films/Tps Star/120 Films/Tfi Films Productions/Ugc Images/Ajoz Films) Vincent Cassel. LOC: MEXICO: Zacatecas: Sierre de Organos; Chihuahua: Ciudad Juarez; Durango: Coahuila: Torreon; SPAIN: Andalucia: Almería, Tabernas Canyon Negro.

Bob Wills and His Texas Playboys (1944 Warner Bros) Bob Wills. LOC: California.

Bobbie Jo and the Outlaw (1976 American International) Lynda Carter. LOC: New Mexico: Albuquerque; Santa Rosa; Vaughn.

Boiling Point, The (1932 Allied) Hoot Gibson. LOC: California: Lake Sherwood; Los Turas Ranch.

Bold Caballero, The (1937 Republic) Bob Livingston. LOC: California: Iverson Ranch; Republic Studio backlot; Red Rock Canyon.

Bold Frontiersman, The (1948 Republic) Allan Lane. LOC: California: Iverson Ranch; Corriganville.

Bonanza Town (1951 Columbia) Charles Starrett. LOC: California: Iverson Ranch.

Bonanza: The Next Generation (1988 Gaylord Entertainment) John Ireland. LOC: Nevada: Ponderosa Ranch Incline Village, Lake Tahoe; Spooner Lake, Lake Tahoe-Nevada State Park Incline Village, Lake Tahoe; Washoe Valley/Bowers Mansion.

Bonanza: The Return (1993 NBC) Michael Landon, Jr. LOC: California: Tuolumne, Jamestown; San Andreas courthouse; Nevada: Ponderosa Ranch Incline Village, Lake Tahoe.

Bonanza: Under Attack (1995 NBC) Ben Johnson. LOC: Nevada: Ponderosa Ranch.

Boom Goes the Groom (1939 Columbia) Andy Clyde. LOC: Columbia Ranch.

Boom Town (1940 MGM) Clark Gable. LOC: California: Bakersfield; Taft.

Boot Hill Bandits (1942 Monogram) Range Busters. LOC: California: Rancho Placeritos; Walker Ranch.

Boothill Brigade (1937 Republic) Johnny Mack Brown. LOC: California: Jauregui Ranch; Walker Ranch.

Boots and Saddles (1937 Republic) Gene Autry. LOC: California: Lone Pine; Republic Studio backlot.

Boots of Destiny (1937 Grand National) Ken Maynard. LOC: California: Trem Carr Ranch; Jauregui Ranch; Walker Ranch.

Border Badmen (1945 PRC) Buster Crabbe. LOC: California: Corriganville.

Border Bandits (1946 Monogram) Johnny Mack Brown. LOC: California: Rancho Placeritos.

Border Brigands (1935 Universal) Buck Jones. LOC: California: Big Bear.

Border Buckaroos (1943 PRC) Texas Rangers. LOC: California: Corriganville.

Border Caballero (1936 Puritan) Tim McCoy. LOC: California: Trem Carr Ranch; Walker Ranch.

Border Cafe (1937 RKO) Harry Carey. LOC: California: Jauregui Ranch; Vasquez Rocks.

Border City Rustlers (1953 Allied Artists) Guy Madison. LOC: California: Rancho Placeritos.

Border Devils (1932 Atlantic) Harry Carey. LOC: California: Kernville; Palm Springs.

Border Fence (1951 Astor) Walt Wayne. LOC: Texas: San Antonio.

Border Feud (1947 PRC) Lash La Rue. LOC: California: Iverson Ranch.

Border G-Man (1938 RKO) George O'Brien. LOC: California: Jauregui Ranch; Walker Ranch; Abalone Cove near Portuguese Bend

Border Guns (1934 Aywon) Bill Cody. LOC: California: Brandeis Ranch; Ralph M. Like Studio backlot.

Border Law (1931 Columbia) Buck Jones. LOC: California: Paramount Ranch; Providencia Ranch.

Border Legion, The (1930 Paramount) Richard Arlen. LOC: California: Paramount Ranch; Tuolumne County.

Border Legion, The (1940 Republic) Roy Rogers. LOC: California: Burro Flats; Republic Studio backlot.

Border Menace, The (1934 Aywon) Bill Cody. LOC: California: probably Pico Canyon.

Border Outlaws (1950 Eagle Lion) Spade Cooley. LOC: California: Agoura Ranch; French Ranch.

Border Patrol (1943 United Artists) William Boyd. LOC: California: Kernville; Kernville Movie Street; Rancho Placeritos.

Border Patrolman, The (1936 20th Century Fox) George O'Brien. LOC: California: Death Valley; The Inn at Furnace Creek.

Border Phantom (1936 Republic) Bob Steele. LOC: California: Mystery Adobe Ranch; Walker Ranch; Ralph M. Like Studio backlot.

Border Rangers (1951 Lippert) Donald Barry. LOC: California: Iverson Ranch; Corriganville; Rancho Placeritos; Vasquez Rocks.

Border River (1954 Universal) Joel McCrea. LOC: Utah: Professor Valley; Colorado River; Courthouse Wash.

Border Romance (1929 Tiffany) Armida. LOC: California: Paramount Ranch.

Border Roundup (1942 PRC) Buster Crabbe. LOC: California: Corriganville.

Border Saddlemates (1952 Republic) Rex Allen. LOC: California: Iverson Ranch.

Border Shootout (1990 Phoenix Production Partners) Glenn Ford. LOC: California: Eagle Tail Ranch, Newhall Ranch; Universal Studios backlot; Arizona: Old Tucson; Utah: Kanab, Eagle Lane Ranch; Orville Robinson Ranch Fort.

Border Treasure (1950 RKO) Tim Holt. LOC: California: Lone Pine; San Fernando Mission; Anchor Ranch; RKO Encino Ranch.

Border Vengeance (1935 Kent) Reb Russell. LOC: California: Los Angeles Stockyards.

Border Vigilantes (1941 Paramount) William Boyd. LOC: California: Rancho Placeritos; Lone Pine.

Border Wolves (1938 Universal) Bob Baker. LOC: California: Crestline; Lake Gregory; Universal Studio backlot.

Border, The (1982 RKO/Universal Pictures) Charles Bronson. LOC: Texas: El Paso; GUATEMALA: Antigua; Guatemala City.

Borderland (1937 Paramount) William Boyd. LOC: California: Paramount Ranch; Kernville; Kelso Valley.

Borderline (1980 ITC) Charles Bronson. LOC: California: San Diego.

Bordertown Gunfighters (1943 Republic) Bill Elliott. LOC: California: Iverson Ranch; Walker Ranch; Republic Studio backlot.

Bordertown Trail (1944 Republic) Sunset Carson. LOC: California: Iverson Ranch; Republic Studio backlot.

Born Reckless (1959 Warner Bros) Jeff Richards. LOC: California: Saugus.

Born to Battle (1935 Commodore) Tom Tyler. LOC: California: Frank LaSalle Ranch; Jauregui Ranch.

Born to Buck (1968 Casey Tibbs) Narrated by Henry Fonda and Rex Allen. LOC: Montana.

Born to the Saddle (1953 Astor) Chuck Courtney. LOC: California: Lone Pine; Rancho Placeritos.

Born to the West (1937 Paramount) John Wayne. LOC: California: Paramount Ranch.

Borrowed Trouble (1948 United Artists) William Boyd. LOC: California: Lone Pine; Anchorville.

Boss Cowboy (1934 Superior) Buddy Roosevelt. LOC: California: Palmdale.

Boss Nigger (1974 Dimension Prod) Fred Williamson. LOC: New Mexico: J. W. Eaves Ranch.

Boss of Boomtown (1944 Universal) Rod Cameron. LOC: California: Corriganville.

Boss of Bullion City (1941 Universal) Johnny Mack Brown. LOC: California: Iverson Ranch.

Boss of Hangtown Mesa (1942 Universal) Johnny Mack Brown. LOC: California: Corriganville.

Boss of Lonely Valley (1937 Universal) Buck Jones. LOC: California: Kernville; Newhall.

Boss of Rawhide (1943 PRC) Texas Rangers. LOC: California: Corriganville.

Boss Rider of Gun Creek (1936 Universal) Buck Jones. LOC: California: Kernville.

Both Barrels Blazing (1945 Columbia) Charles Starrett. LOC: California: Corriganville; Columbia Ranch.

Bottom of the Bottle, The (1956 20th Century Fox) Joseph Cotton. LOC: Arizona: Old Tucson; Nogales; Santa Cruz Valley.

Bounty (2009 Stage Ham Films) Austin O'Brien. LOC: California: Caravan West Ranch Agua Dulce.

Bounty Hunter, The (1954 Warner Bros) Randolph Scott. LOC: California: Iverson Ranch; Red Rock Canyon

Bounty Hunter, The (1989 Action International) Bo Hopkins. LOC: Oklahoma: Sand Springs.

Bounty Killer, The (1965 Embassy) Rod Cameron. LOC: California: Corriganville; Glenmoor Ranch; Columbia Ranch.

Bounty Man, The (1972 ABC-TV) Clint Walker. LOC: California: Bell Location Ranch.

Bowery Buckaroos (1947 Monogram) Leo Gorcey. LOC: California: Rancho Placeritos; Jauregui Ranch.

Boy From Oklahoma, The (1954 Warner Bros) Will Rogers, Jr. LOC: California: Warner Ranch.

Boy Who Talked to Badgers, The (1975 Buena Vista) Christian Juttner. LOC: CANADA: Alberta.

Boys of Twilight, The (1992 CBS Western Series) Peter Cook. LOC: Utah: Park City.

Boy's Ranch (1946 MGM) James Craig. LOC: Texas.

Brand of Fear (1949 Monogram) Jimmy Wakely. LOC: California: Rancho Placeritos; Walker Ranch.

Brand of Hate, The (1934 Supreme) Bob Steele. LOC: California.
Brand of Shame (1968 B&B Prod) Donna Duzit. LOC:
Brand of the Devil (1944 PRC) Texas Rangers. LOC: California: Corriganville.
Brand of the Outlaws (1936 Superior) Bob Steele. LOC: California: Jauregui Ranch; Walker Ranch; Ralph M Like Studio backlot.
Branded (1931 Columbia) Buck Jones. LOC: California: Kernville; Vasquez Rocks; Paramount Ranch.
Branded (1951 Paramount) Alan Ladd. LOC: California: Rancho Placeritos; Vasquez Rocks; Arizona: Douglas; Portal; Globe; Salt River Canyon; San Simon.
Branded A Bandit (1924 Ben Wilson Productions) Yakima Canutt. LOC: California: Kernville; Isabella.
Branded a Coward (1935 Supreme) Johnny Mack Brown. LOC: California: Kernville; Kernville Movie Street.
Branded Men (1931 Tiffany) Ken Maynard. LOC: California: Vasquez Rocks; Brandeis Ranch.
Brass Legend, The (1956 United Artists) Hugh O'Brian. LOC: California: Iverson Ranch; Corriganville; Rancho Placeritos.
Bravados, The (1958 20th Century Fox) Gregory Peck. LOC: MEXICO: Michoacan: Tarimbaro; Virgen de la Escalera.
Brave Bulls, The (1951 Columbia) Anthony Quinn. LOC: MEXICO: Mexico City, The Plaza bullfighting ring; Guanajuato: San Miguel de Allende.
Brave Warrior (1952 Columbia) Jon Hall. LOC: California: Iverson Ranch; Corriganville; Columbia Ranch.
Bravos, The (1972 Universal-TV) George Peppard. LOC: Arizona: Sedona.
Breakheart Pass (1976 United Artists) Charles Bronson. LOC: Idaho: Lewiston; Camas Prairie Railroad.
Breakout (1975 Columbia) Charles Bronson. LOC: Idaho.
Breed of the Border (1933 Monogram) Bob Steele. LOC: California: Jauregui Ranch.
Breed of the West (1930 Big 4) Wally Wales. LOC: California: Universal Studio backlot.
Bride Comes to Yellow Sky, The (1952 RKO) Robert Preston. LOC: California: Rancho Placeritos.
Brigham (1977 Sunset Films) Maurice Grandmaison. LOC: Arizona: Pipe Springs National Monument; Utah: Kanab; Salt Lake City.
Brigham Young (1940 20th Century Fox) Tyrone Power. LOC: California: Century Ranch; Big Bear Valley; Cedar Lake; Shay Ranch; Holkohom Valley; Lone Pine; Utah: Kanab; Nevada: Jiggs.
Brighty of the Grand Canyon (1967 Feature Film Corp.) Joseph Cotton. LOC: Arizona: Grand Canyon North Rim; Utah: Duck Creek, Cedar Mountain.
Brimstone (1949 Republic) Rod Cameron. LOC: California: Kernville; Republic Studio backlot.

Broadway to Cheyenne (1932 Monogram) Rex Bell. LOC: California: Trem Carr Ranch; Vasquez Rocks.

Brokeback Mountain (2005 Paramount Pictures) Jake Gyllenhaal. LOC: New Mexico: La Mesilla; Wyoming: Grand Teton National Park; CANADA: Alberta: Calgary; Fort Macleod; Kananaskis County.

Broken Arrow (1950 20th Century Fox) James Stewart. LOC: California: Iverson Ranch; Lone Pine; Arizona: Sedona; Oak Creek Canyon.

Broken Chain, The (1993 TNT) Pierce Brosnan. LOC: Virginia: Williamsburg; Yorktown.

Broken Lance (1954 20th Century Fox) Spencer Tracy. LOC: California: Century Ranch; 20th Century Fox Studio backlot; Arizona: Sonoita; Circle Z Ranch, Patagonia.

Broken Land, The (1962 20th Century Fox) Kent Taylor. LOC: Arizona: Apacheland.

Broken Star, The (1956 United Artists) Howard Duff. LOC: Arizona: Old Tucson.

Broken Trail (2004 A Butchers Run Film Productions miniseries) Robert Duvall. LOC: CANADA: Alberta: Bragg Creek; Calgary: Cochrane Creek; Highwood River, near Longview.

Bronco Billy (1980 Warner Bros) Clint Eastwood. LOC: Idaho: Boise; Meridian; Oregon: Ontario.

Bronco Buster (1952 Universal) John Lund. LOC: California: Los Angeles; Arizona: Phoenix; Wyoming: Cheyenne; CANADA: Calgary.

Bronze Buckaroo, The (1939 Sack Amusement) Herb Jeffreys. LOC: California: Victorville, N. B. Murray Dude Ranch.

Brother of the Wind (1973 Sun International) Dick Robinson. LOC: CANADA: Canmore, Alberta.

Brothers Blue (1973 Warner Bros) Jack Palance. LOC: ITALY: Cinecitta.

Brothers in Arms (2005 Destination Films) David Carradine. LOC: California: Disney's Golden Oak Ranch Placerita Canyon, Newhall; Rancho Maria Placerita Canyon, Newhall; Sable Ranch Placerita Canyon, Newhall.

Brothers in the Saddle (1949 RKO) Tim Holt. LOC: California: Garner Ranch; RKO Encino Ranch.

Brothers O'Toole, The (1973 American National Enterprises) John Astin. LOC: Colorado: Buckskin Joe, Canon City.

Brothers of the Frontier (1996 ABC) Doug Abrahams. LOC: CANADA: British Columbia: Bordertown/Western town Maple Ridge, Vancouver.

Brothers of the West (1937 Victory) Tom Tyler. LOC: California: Brandeis Ranch.

Buchanan Rides Alone (1958 Columbia) Randolph Scott. LOC: Arizona: Old Tucson; Sabino Canyon.

Buck and the Magic Bracelet (1999 Gruppo Minerva International) Matt McCoy. LOC: ITALY.

Buck and the Preacher (1972 Columbia) Sidney Poitier. LOC: California: Marysville; MEXICO: Durango: El Saltito waterfall, Nombre de Dios; Villa del Oeste.

Buck at the Edge of the Heaven (1991 Media Creative Entertainment) John Savage. LOC:

Buck Benny Rides Again (1940 Paramount) Jack Benny. LOC: California: Deadman Point; Griffith Park; Juaregui Ranch; Paramount Studios backlot.

Buckaroo Broadcast, A (1938 RKO) Ray Whitley. LOC:

Buckaroo from Powder River (1947 Columbia) Charles Starrett. LOC: California: Walker Ranch; Providencia Ranch.

Buckaroo Sheriff of Texas (1951 Republic) Michael Chapin. LOC: California: Iverson Ranch; Bronson Canyon.

Buckeye and Blue (1988 Buckeye and Blue Productions) Robyn Lively. LOC: Arizona: MescalOld TucsonSabino Canyon Tucson.

Buckskin (1968 Paramount) Barry Sullivan. LOC: California: Vasquez Rocks.

Buckskin Frontier (1943 United Artists) Richard Dix. LOC: California: Kernville; Oklahoma: Cache.

Buckskin Lady, The (1957 United Artists) Patricia Medina. LOC: California: Iverson Ranch; Corriganville.

Buddy Goes West (1981 Alex Cinematografica) Bud Spencer. LOC: SPAIN: Minihollywood/Western town Almería; Rancho Leone/Western set Almería; La Calahorra Railroad east of Guadix, Granada province.

Buffalo Bill (1944 20th Century Fox) Joel McCrea. LOC: Arizona: House Rock Valley; Utah: Paria; Johnson Canyon; Kanab; Montana: Crow Indian Reservation.

Buffalo Bill and the Indians or Sitting Bull's History Lesson (1976 United Artists) Paul Newman. LOC: CANADA: Morley; Stoney Indian Reserve, Alberta.

Buffalo Bill in Tomahawk Territory (1952 United Artists) Clayton Moore. LOC: California: Iverson Ranch; Corriganville.

Buffalo Bill Rides Again (1947 Screen Guild) Richard Arlen. LOC: California: Iverson Ranch.

Buffalo Girls (1995 CBS) Anjelica Huston. LOC: New Mexico: Albuquerque; Tingley Coliseum; Bonanza Creek Ranch Santa Fe; Charles R Ranch Las Vegas; Cook Ranch/Cerro Pelon Ranch, Galisteo; Río Chama at Powder River; Wyoming: Valle Grande: ENGLAND: Bristol.

Buffalo Gun (1961 Globe) Webb Pierce. LOC: California: Corriganville; Rancho Placeritos; Walker Ranch.

Buffalo Rider (1978 Starfire) Rick Guinn. LOC: Utah: Oakley area; Smith Lake; Morehouse Lake, Weber River Canyon.

Buffalo Soldiers (1997 TNT) Danny Glover. LOC: Arizona: Cochise Stronghold National MonumentMescalRain Valley ElginWillcox Playa dry lake.

Buffalo Soldiers, The (1979 NBC-TV) John Beck. LOC: Arizona: Old Tucson; Mescal.

Bugles in the Afternoon (1952 Warner Bros) Ray Milland. LOC: California: Warner Ranch; Utah: Aspen Mirror Lake; Kanab Canyon; Strawberry Valley.

Bull of the West, The (1975 Universal) Lee J. Cobb. LOC: California: Janss Janss Conejo Ranch.

Bulldog Courage (1935 Puritan) Tim McCoy. LOC: California: Brandeis Ranch; Trem Carr Ranch; Towsley Canyon.

Bullet Code (1940 RKO) George O'Brien. LOC: California: Iverson Ranch.

Bullet for a Badman (1964 Universal) Audie Murphy. LOC: California: Universal Studio backlot; Utah: Snow Canyon; Berry Springs; Virgin River; Zion National Park.

Bullet for Billy the Kid, A (1963 A.D.P. Pictures) Gaston Sands. LOST/MISSING'

Bullet Is Waiting, A (1954 Columbia) Jean Simmons. LOC: California: Burro Flats.

Bullets and Ballads (1940 Universal) Armida. LOC: No exteriors.

Bullets and Saddles (1943 Monogram) Range Busters. LOC: California: Corriganville.

Bullets for Bandits (1942 Columbia) Tex Ritter. LOC: California: Corriganville; Agoura Ranch; Universal Studio backlot.

Bullets for Rustlers (1940 Columbia) Charles Starrett. LOC: California: Iverson Ranch; Columbia Ranch.

Bullfighter and the Lady (1951 Republic) Robert Stack. LOC: MEXICO: Mexico City; Querétaro: Xayai; Zacatapec.

Bullwhip (1958 Allied Artists) Guy Madison. LOC: California: Columbia; Tuolumne County; Kenny Ranch, Murphys, Calaveras County.

Burning Hills, The (1956 Warner Bros) Tab Hunter. LOC: California: Warner Ranch; Kernville.

Burrowers, The (2008 Blue Star Pictures) Dough Hutchinson. LOC: New Mexico: Santa Fe.

Bury Me Not on the Lone Prairie (1941 Universal) Johnny Mack Brown. LOC: California: Iverson Ranch.

Bury My Heart at Wounded Knee (2007 HBO) Adam Beach. LOC: CANADA: Alberta: Calgary; Bowvista Farms; Heritage Park Historical Village; Millarfield Farms; Nicholl Ranch; Swinging 7 Ranches; Tsuu T'ina Reserve.

Bus Stop (1956 20th Century Fox) Marilyn Monroe. LOC: Arizona: Phoenix; Idaho: Sun Valley.

Bushwhackers, The (1951 Realart) John Ireland. LOC: California: Ingram Ranch.

Butch and Sundance: The Early Days (1979 20th Century Fox) William Katt. LOC: New Mexico: J. W. Eaves Ranch; El Rancho de las Golondrinas; Chama; Cochiti Rocks; Jemez Springs; Taos Pueblo; Colorado: Alamosa; Conejos; Cumbres and Toltec Scenic Railroad; Ouray; San Juan, San Miguel Counties; Telluride.

Butch Cassidy and the Sundance Kid (1969 20th Century Fox) Paul Newman. LOC: California: Lake Sherwood; Century Ranch; Utah: Grafton; Zion National Park; Snow Canyon; New Mexico: Taos; Chama; Colorado: Durango-Silverton

Narrow Gauge Railroad; Florida: Mesa; MEXICO: Guerrero: Taxco; Morelos: Cuautla area; La Paz; Tepoztlan; Tlayacapan.

Buttermilk Sky (2009 Talmarc Productions/Lost Horses Inc.) Michael Madsen. LOC: New Mexico: Bonanza Creek Ranch Santa Fe.

Buzzy and the Phantom Pinto (1941 Ziehm) Buzzy Henry. LOC: Arizona: Cudia City.

Buzzy Rides the Range (1940 Ziehm) Buzzy Henry. LOC: Arizona: Cudia City.

By Dawn's Early Light (2000 Daniel L. Paulson) Richard Crenna. LOC: CANADA: British Columbia: Wild Horse Town/Western town Kamloops.

Cactus Capers (1942 RKO) Ray Whitley. LOC:

Cactus Caravan (1950 Universal) Tex Williams. LOST/MISSING/UNAVAILABLE.

Cactus Cut-Up (1949 RKO) Leon Errol. LOC:

Cactus Kid, The (1934 Reliable) Jack Perrin. LOC: California: Frank LaSalle Ranch.

Cactus Makes Perfect (1942 Columbia) Three Stooges. LOC: California: Columbia Ranch.

Cahill United States Marshal (1973 Warner Bros) John Wayne. LOC: California: Warner Bros Studio backlot; MEXICO: Durango: La Joya Ranch.

Cain's Way (1970 M.D.A. Associates Inc.) John Carradine. LOC: California: Pioneertown.

Calaboose (1943 United Artists) Noah Beery, Jr. LOC: California: Lone Pine; Hal Roach Studio backlot.

Calamity Jane (1953 Warner Bros) Doris Day. LOC: California: Warner Ranch.

Calamity Jane (1984 CBS) Jane Alexander. LOC: Arizona: MescalOld TucsonPeña Blanca Canyon West of Nogales.

Calamity Jane and Sam Bass (1949 Universal) Howard Duff. LOC: California: Iverson Ranch; Red Rock Canyon; Utah: Kanab Rodeo Grounds; Kanab Canyon.

California (1947 Paramount) Ray Milland. LOC: California: Burro Flats; Iverson Ranch; Saddle Rock Ranch; Arizona: Sedona; Painted Desert; Flagstaff.

California (1963 American International) Jock Mahoney. LOC: California: Iverson Ranch; Republic Studio backlot.

California Conquest (1952 Columbia) Cornel Wilde. LOC: California: Warner Ranch; Kennedy Meadow, Tuolumne County.

California Firebrand (1948 Republic) Monte Hale. LOC: California: Iverson Ranch; Walker Ranch.

California Frontier (1938 Columbia) Buck Jones. LOC: California: Rancho Placeritos; Santa Barbara Mission.

California Gold Rush (1946 Republic) Bill Elliott. LOC: California: Iverson Ranch.

California Gold Rush (1981 NBC) Robert Hays. LOC: Utah: Summit County; Wasatch County.

California Joe (1943 Republic) Don Barry. LOC: California: Iverson Ranch.

California Mail (1929 First National) Ken Maynard. LOC: California: Kernville.
California Mail, The (1936 Warner Bros) Dick Foran. LOC: California: Iverson Ranch.
California or Bust (1941 RKO) Ray Whitley. LOC:
California Passage (1950 Republic) Forrest Tucker. LOC: California: Iverson Ranch.
California Trail, The (1933 Columbia) Buck Jones. LOC: California: Iverson Ranch.
Californian, The (1937 20th Century Fox) Ricardo Cortez. LOC: California: Iverson Ranch; Rancho Placeritos.
Call of the Canyon (1942 Republic) Gene Autry. LOC: California: Iverson Ranch; Bronson Canyon; Lone Pine; ?Agoura? Ranch.
Call of the Coyote (1934 Imperial) Pat Carlyle. LOC: Arizona: Grand Canyon.
Call of the Desert (1930 Syndicate) Tom Tyler. LOC: California: Jauregui Ranch; Walker Ranch.
Call of the Forest (1949 Lippert) Robert Lowery. LOC: California: Chatsworth Train Station.
Call of the Klondike (1950 Monogram) Kirby Grant. LOC: California: Big Bear; Cedar Lake.
Call of the Prairie (1936 Paramount) William Boyd. LOC: California: Kernville; Kernville Movie Street.
Call of the Rockies (1938 Columbia) Charles Starrett. LOC: California: Iverson Ranch.
Call of the Rockies (1938 Columbia) Charles Starrett. LOC: California: Columbia Ranch; Iverson Ranch.
Call of the Rockies (1944 Republic) Sunset Carson. LOC: California: Iverson Ranch; Republic Studio backlot.
Call of the West (1930 Columbia) Dorothy Revier. LOC:
Call of the Wild (1935 United Artists) Clark Gable. LOC: California: RKO Encino Ranch; Mammoth Lakes; Tuolumne County; Feather River; Nevada: Lake Tahoe; Washington: Lake Chelan; Mt. Baker National Forest.
Call of the Wild (1993 RHI Entertainment) Rick Schroder. LOC: CANADA: British Columbia: Bordertown/Western town Maple Ridge, Vancouver.
Call of the Wild (2000 Animal Planet) Nick Mancuso. LOC: CANADA: British Columbia: Bordertown/Western town Maple Ridge, Vancouver.
Call of the Wild: The Dog of the Yukon (1996 Blue Rider Pictures) Rutger Hauer. LOC: CANADA: Quebec.
Call of the Yukon (1938 Republic) Richard Arlen. LOC: Alaska: pre-production shots; no live action.
Call the Mesquiteers (1938 Republic) Three Mesquiteers. LOC: California: Iverson Ranch; Vasquez Rocks; Republic Studio backlot
Callaway Went Thataway (1951 MGM) Fred MacMurray. LOC: California: Iverson

Ranch; Agoura Ranch; MGM backlot.

Calling Wild Bill Elliott (1943 Republic) Bill Elliott. LOC: California: Iverson Ranch; Corriganville; Burro Flats.

Can't Help Singing (1944 Universal) Deanna Durbin. LOC: California: Lake Arrowhead; Universal Studio backlot; Utah: Duck Creek; Strawberry Point; Navajo Lake.

Canadian Mounties vs. Atomic Invaders (1953 Republic) Bill Henry. LOC: California: Big Bear Lake; Republic Studio backlot.

Canadian Pacific (1949 20th Century Fox) Randolph Scott. LOC: CANADA: Lake Louise, Banff National Park.

Canadians, The (1961 20th Century Fox) Robert Ryan. LOC: CANADA: Cypress Hills, Saskatchewan.

Cancel My Reservation (1972 Warner Bros) Bob Hope. LOC: Arizona: Phoenix Airport; Verde River; Blue Point; Carl Hovgard desert mansion; New York: New York City.

Cannibal! The Musical (1991 Cannibal Films Ltd.) Dian Bachar. LOC: Colorado: Black Canyon of the Gunnison Gunnison; Boulder; Buckskin Joe Canon City; Lake City; Ouray.

Canyon Ambush (1952 Monogram) Johnny Mack Brown. LOC: California: Iverson Ranch.

Canyon City (1943 Republic) Don Barry. LOC: California: Iverson Ranch.

Canyon Crossroads (1955 United Artists) Richard Basehart. LOC: Utah: Moab; Professor Valley; Seven Mile Canyon.

Canyon Hawks (1930 Big 4) Wally Wales. LOC: California: Towsley Canyon; Universal Studio backlot.

Canyon of Missing Men, The (1930 Syndicate) Tom Tyler. LOC: California: Jauregui Ranch; Walker Ranch; Cave of Munits, West Hills.

Canyon Passage (1946 Universal) Dana Andrews. LOC: California: Universal Studio backlot; Oregon: Diamond Lake.

Canyon Raiders (1951 Monogram) Whip Wilson. LOC: California: Iverson Ranch.

Canyon River (1956 Allied Artists) George Montgomery. LOC: California: Rancho Placeritos.

Captain John Smith and Pocahontas (1953 United Artists) Anthony Dexter. LOC: California: Bronson Canyon.

Captain Thunder (1930 Warner Bros) Fay Wray. LOC: California: Warner Bros backlot.

Captive of Billy the Kid (1952 Republic) Alan Lane. LOC: California: Iverson Ranch; Corriganville.

Capture of Bigfoot, The (1980 Studio Film Corp.) Stafford Morgan. LOC: Wisconsin: Gleason.

Capture of Grizzly Adams, The (1982 NBC) Dan Haggerty. LOC: Utah: Heber City/Schick-Sunn Movie Town; Park City; Uinta Mountains.

Capture, The (1950 RKO) Lew Ayres. LOC: California: Pioneertown.

Caravan Trail, The (1946 PRC) Eddie Dean. LOC: California: Iverson Ranch.

Cariboo Trail, The (1950 20th Century Fox) Randolph Scott. LOC: California: Bronson Canyon; Republic Studio backlot; Colorado: Gunnison; CANADA: British Columbia.

Carnival Boat (1932 RKO) William Boyd. LOC: California: Sugar Pine.

Carolina (1934 Fox) Janet Gaynor. LOC: California: Colton; Banning House.

Carolina Cannonball (1955 Republic) Judy Canova. LOC: California: Mohave Desert.

Carolina Moon (1940 Republic) Gene Autry. LOC: California: Idyllwild; Keen Camp; Riviera Country Club; 17085 Rancho St., Encino; Republic Studio backlot.

Carrying the Mail (1934 Imperial) Wally Wales. LOC: California: Brandeis Ranch.

Carson City (1952 Warner Bros) Randolph Scott. LOC: California: Iverson Ranch; Bronson Canyon; Bell Ranch.

Carson City Cyclone (1943 Republic) Don Barry. LOC: California: Iverson Ranch; Corriganville; Walker Ranch.

Carson City Kid, The (1940 Republic) Roy Rogers. LOC: California: Iverson Ranch; Burro Flats; Republic Studio backlot.

Carson City Raiders (1948 Republic) Allan Lane. LOC: California: Iverson Ranch.

Caryl of the Mountains (1936 Reliable Pictures) Rin-Tin-Tin. LOC: California: Big Bear.

Casey's Shadow (1978 Columbia) Walter Matthau. LOC: Louisiana: Opelousas; Lafayette; New Mexico: Lincoln National Forest; Ruidoso Downs; Lincoln County; Ruidoso.

Cassidy of Bar 20 (1938 Paramount) William Boyd. LOC: California: Paramount Ranch; Bishop; Lone Pine.

Cast a Long Shadow (1959 United Artists) Audie Murphy. LOC: California: Corriganville; Janss Janss Conejo Ranch; Century Ranch.

Castaway Cowboy, The (1974 Buena Vista) James Garner. LOC: Hawaii: Kauaii.

Cat Ballou (1965 Columbia) Lee Marvin. LOC: California: Columbia Ranch; Colorado: Buckskin Joe, Canon City.

Catlow (1971 MGM) Yul Brynner. LOC: SPAIN: Almerica; Patio de la Escuela des Artes y Oficios; Plaza Vieja; Casa de los Puche; Plaza Bendicho; Cortijo Romero; Balsicas de Alfaro; Dune di Cabo de Gata; Enix; Finca El Romeral; Gador; Rambla Lanujar; Rancho Leone; Texas-Hollywood; Valle del Buho; Valle de los Genoveses.

Cattle Annie and Little Britches (1981 Universal Pictures) Burt Lancaster. LOC: MEXICO: Durango: Chupaderos; El Saltito waterfall.

Cattle Drive (1951 Universal) Joel McCrea. LOC: California: Death Valley; Utah: Paria.

Cattle Empire (1958 20th Century Fox) Joel McCrea. LOC: California: Lone Pine.

Cattle King (1963 MGM) Robert Taylor. LOC: California: Kernville, Dalley Ranch; MGM backlot.

Cattle Queen (1951 United Artists) Maria Hart. LOC: California: Iverson Ranch.

Cattle Queen of Montana (1954 RKO) Barbara Stanwyck. LOC: California: Iverson Ranch; Columbia Ranch; Montana: Glacier National Park.

Cattle Raiders (1938 Columbia) Charles Starrett. LOC: California: French Ranch; Agoura.

Cattle Stampede (1943 PRC) Buster Crabbe. LOC: California: Corriganville.

Cattle Thief, The (1936 Columbia) Ken Maynard. LOC: California: Lone Pine.

Cattle Town (1952 Warner Bros) Dennis Morgan. LOC: California: Warner Ranch.

Caught (1931 Paramount) Richard Arlen. LOC: California: Paramount Ranch.

Cavalcade of the West (1936 Diversion) Hoot Gibson. LOC: California: Vasquez Rocks; Brandeis Ranch.

Cavalier of the West (1931 Atlantic) Harry Carey. LOC: California: Mystery Adobe Ranch; Tec-Art Studio backlot.

Cavalry (1936 Republic) Bob Steele. LOC: California: Kernville; Kernville Movie Street.

Cavalry Scout (1951 Monogram) Rod Cameron. LOC: California: Corriganville; Keen Camp.

Cave of Outlaws (1951 Universal) Macdonald Carey. LOC: California: Iverson Ranch; Vasquez Rocks; Tuolomne County; Universal Studio backlot; Arizona: Colossal Cave; New Mexico: Carlsbad Caverns.

Challenge of the Mackennas, The (1969 Picturmedia) John Ireland. LOC: ITALY: Mazzano Romano/La Selcia, set messicano.

Challenge of the Range (1949 Columbia) Charles Starrett. LOC: California: Iverson Ranch.

Challenge to be Free (1976 Pacific International) Mike Mazurki. LOC: Alaska: CANADA: Yukon.

Champions of Justice (1956 Wrather) Clayton Moore. LOC: California: Iverson Ranch; Corriganville; Ingram Ranch.

Chance: Trail of the Apache (1978 Appaloosa Productions) Christopher Clark. LOC: New Mexico: Chama Valley.

Charge at Feather River, The (1953 Warner Bros) Guy Madison. LOC: California: Vasquez Rocks; Newhall; Santa Ana River, Norco.

Charlie Siringo (1977 Yale Media Design Studios) Steve Railsback. LOC: New Mexico: Las Vegas; Santa Fe.

Charlie, the Lonesome Cougar (1967 Buena Vista) Ron Brown. LOC: Idaho: North Fork of the Clearwater River (River Log Drive) ; Washington: Broughton Log Flume, Underwood; Broughton Lumber Co. Mill; Columbia River Gorge.

Charro! (1969 National General) Elvis Presley. LOC: Arizona: Apacheland.

Chase, The (1966 Columbia) Robert Redford. LOC: California: Chico.

Chato (1972 United Artists) Charles Bronson. LOC: SPAIN: Almeria: Balsicas de

Alfaro; Llano Mellado; Canon Negro; Dune di Cabo de gata; Garganta de Alfaro; Llano Mellado; Las Salinas; La Sartenilla; Rambla Benavides; Rambla Indalecio e canyon cieco laterale; Rambla Lanujar; Rancho Leone; Texas-Hollywood.

Cheatin' Hearts (1993 Trimark Pictures) Kris Kristofferson. LOC: New Mexico: HillsboroTruth of Consequences.

Check Your Guns (1948 Eagle Lion) Eddie Dean. LOC: California: Iverson Ranch.

Cherokee Flash, The (1945 Republic) Sunset Carson. LOC: California: Iverson Ranch; Republic Studio backlot.

Cherokee Kid, The (1996 HBO) James Coburn. LOC: California: Bronson Canyon; Disney's Golden Oak Ranch; Vasquez Rocks.

Cherokee Strip (1940 Paramount) Richard Dix. LOC: California: Iverson Ranch; Kernville; Lone Valley.

Cherokee Strip, The (1937 Warner Bros) Dick Foran. LOC: California: Iverson Ranch; Warner Ranch.

Cherokee Uprising (1950 Monogram) Whip Wilson. LOC: California: Iverson Ranch.

Cheyenne (1929 First National) Ken Maynard. LOC: Wyoming: Cheyenne.

Cheyenne (1947 Warner Bros) Dennis Morgan. LOC: California: Warner Ranch; Arizona: Sedona.

Cheyenne (1995 Halo Pictures) Gary Hudson. LOC: Utah: Arches National Park/Double Arch and cave Moab; Dead Horse Point State Park; Mill Creek Canyon; Moab; Potash Road Moab; Professor Valley Moab.

Cheyenne Autumn (1964 Warner Bros) Richard Widmark. LOC: California: Janss Conejo Ranch; RKO Ranch, Encino; Arizona: Magma Arizona Railroad; Arizona/Utah: Monument Valley; Utah: Fisher Towers; Moab; Professor Valley; San Juan River; Mexican Hat; Park Avenue, Arches National Park; White's Ranch; Colorado: Gunnison.

Cheyenne Cowboy (1949 Universal) Tex Williams. LOC:

Cheyenne Cyclone, The (1931 Kent) Lane Chandler. LOC:

Cheyenne Kid, The (1930 West Coast) Buffalo Bill, Jr. LOST/MISSING.

Cheyenne Kid, The (1933 RKO) Tom Keene. LOC: California: Iverson Ranch; Bronson Canyon; RKO Encino Ranch.

Cheyenne Kid, The (1940 Monogram) Jack Randall. LOC: California: Iverson Ranch; Rancho Placeritos; Walker Ranch.

Cheyenne Rides Again (1937 Victory) Tom Tyler. LOC: California: Brandeis Ranch; Victory Pictures Studio backlot.

Cheyenne Roundup (1943 Universal) Johnny Mack Brown. LOC: California: Iverson Ranch; Universal Studio backlot.

Cheyenne Social Club, The (1970 National General) James Stewart. LOC: New Mexico: J. W. Eaves Ranch; Bonanza Creek Ranch.

Cheyenne Takes Over (1947 Eagle Lion) Lash La Rue. LOC: California: Iverson Ranch.

Cheyenne Tornado (1935 Kent) Reb Russell. LOC: California: Jauregui Ranch; Frank LaSalle Ranch; Towsley Canyon; Universal Studio backlot.

Cheyenne Warrior (1994 The Pacific Trust) Kelly Preston. LOC: California: Big Sky Ranch Simi Valley.

Cheyenne Wildcat (1944 Republic) Bill Elliott. LOC: California: Iverson Ranch; Republic Studio backlot.

Chicago Kid, The (1945 Republic) Don Barry. LOC: California: Iverson Ranch.

Chief Crazy Horse (1955 Universal) Victor Mature. LOC: South Dakota: 777 Bison Ranch; Badlands National Park.

Child Bride of Short Creek (1981 NBC) Christopher Atkins. LOC: Utah: Grafton - St.George.

Children of Sanchez (1978 Carmel Enterprises) Anthony Quinn. LOC: MEXICO: Mexico City; Ocotlan, Tlaxcala: Tepeyanco, Tlaxcala.

China 9, Liberty 37 (1978 Lorimar/Titanus/Compagnia Europes) Warren Oates. LOC: SPAIN: Almería.

Chip of the Flying U (1939 Universal) Johnny Mack Brown. LOC: California: Iverson Ranch; Jauregui Ranch; Universal Studio backlot.

Chisholms, The (1979 Alan Landsburg Prod) Robert Preston. LOC: California: Tuolumne County; Colorado: Bent's Old Fort National Historic Site; Nebraska.

Chisum (1970 Warner Bros) John Wayne. LOC: California: Century Ranch; New Mexico: J. W. Eaves Ranch; MEXICO: Durango: Chupaderos; Rancho Marley.

Christmas Mountain (1981 Osmond International) Mark Miller. LOC: Utah: Heber City/Schick-Sunn Movie Town.

Chuka (1967 Paramount) Rod Taylor. LOC: California: Lake Los Angeles.

Cimarron (1931 RKO) Richard Dix. LOC: California: Harry Quinn Ranch; RKO Encino Ranch.

Cimarron (1960 MGM) Glenn Ford. LOC: California: Century Ranch; Janss Conejo Ranch; Albertson Ranch; MGM backlot; Arizona: Mescal.

Cimarron Kid, The (1952 Universal) Audie Murphy. LOC: California: Tuolumne County; Columbia; Jamestown; Universal Studio backlot.

Circle Canyon (1934 Superior) Buddy Roosevelt. LOC: California: Acton; Palmdale.

Circle of Death (1935 Kent) Montie Montana. LOC: California: Calabasas, Yrigoyen Ranch; Ralph M. Like Studio backlot.

Cisco Kid and the Lady, The (1939 20th Century Fox) Cesar Romero. LOC: California: Lone Pine; 20th Century Fox Backlot.

Cisco Kid Returns, The (1945 Monogram) Duncan Renaldo. LOC: California: Rancho Placeritos; Lake Sherwood; Kernville; San Fernando Mission.

Cisco Kid, The (1931 Fox) Warner Baxter. LOC: California: Iverson Ranch; Arizona: Santa Catalina Mountains.

Cisco Kid, The (1994 TNT) Jimmy Smits. LOC: MEXICO: Zacatecas: Guadalupe; Sombrerete; Hidalgo: Pachuca; San Pedro Tlochataco; Santa Maria Regla.

City of Bad Men (1953 20th Century Fox) Dale Robertson. LOC: California: Vasquez Rocks; Jauregui Ranch; 20th Century Fox Backlot.

City Slickers (1991 Castle Rock International) Billy Crystal. LOC: Colorado: Durango - New Mexico: Abiquiú Ghost Ranch; Nambé Pueblo; Santa Clara Pueblo; Taos; The White Place/Plaza Blanca Abiquiú.

City Slickers II: The Legend of Curly's Gold (1994 Columbia) Billy Crystal. LOC: California: Fillmore; Nevada: Las Vegas; New York: New York; Utah: Dugout Ranch and Indian Creek Canyon, Moab; Fossil Point, Goblin Valley State Park, Professor Valley and Onion Creek, Moab.

Claim, The (2001 Canal+/BBC/Pathé Pictures International) Peter Mullan. LOC: Colorado: Durango and Silverton Narrow Gauge Railroad; CANADA: Alberta: Kananaskis County gold-rush town set; Fortress Mountain Kananaskis County.

Clancy of the Mounted (1933 Universal) Tom Tyler. LOC: California: Universal Studio backlot.

Claws (1977 Alaska Pictures) Myron Healy. LOC: Alaska: Juneau.

Clearing the Range (1931 Allied) Hoot Gibson. LOC: California: Universal Studio backlot; Paramount Ranch; Vasquez Rocks.

Cliff Edwards and His Musical Buckaroos (1941 Warner Bros) Cliff Edwards. LOC:

Climb an Angry Mountain (1972 Warner Bros-TV) Fess Parker. LOC: California: Mt. Shasta.

Cocaine Cowboys (1979 International Harmony) Jack Palance. LOC: New York: Mantauk Point.

Cockeyed Cowboys of Calico County, The (1970 Universal) Dan Blocker. LOC: California: Universal Studio backlot.

Code of Honor (1930 Syndicate) Mahlon Hamilton. LOC: California: Placerita Canyon.

Code of the Cactus (1939 Victory) Tim McCoy. LOC: California: Brandeis Ranch.

Code of the Fearless (1939 Spectrum) Fred Scott. LOC: California: Iverson Ranch; Brandeis Ranch.

Code of the Lawless (1945 Universal) Kirby Grant. LOC: California: Iverson Ranch.

Code of the Mounted (1935 Ambassador) Kermit Maynard. LOC: California: Big Bear; Lake Arrowhead.

Code of the Outlaw (1942 Republic) Three Mesquiteers. LOC: California: Iverson Ranch; ?Agoura? Ranch; Republic Studio backlot.

Code of the Pony Express (1950 Columbia) Jock Mahoney. LOC: California: Pioneertown.

Code of the Prairie (1944 Republic) Sunset Carson. LOC: California: Iverson Ranch; Republic Studio backlot.

Code of the Range (1936 Columbia) Charles Starrett. LOC:

Code of the Rangers (1938 Monogram) Tim McCoy. LOC: California: Walker Ranch.

Code of the Saddle (1947 Monogram) Johnny Mack Brown. LOC: California: Rancho Placeritos; Jauregui Ranch; Walker Ranch.

Code of the Silver Sage (1950 Republic) Allan Lane. LOC: California: Iverson Ranch; Corriganville.

Code of the West (1947 RKO) James Warren. LOC: California: Lone Pine; RKO Encino Ranch.

Cody of the Pony Express (1950 Columbia) Jock Mahoney. LOC: California: Pioneertown.

Cold Mountain (2003 Miramax Films) Nicole Kidman. LOC: South Carolina: Charleston; Virginia: Carter's Grove, Williamsburg military hospital exterior, Richmond river; ROMANIA: Carpathian Mountains mountain scenes, Potigrafu.

Cole Younger, Gunfighter (1958 Allied Artists) Frank Lovejoy. LOC: California: Iverson Ranch; Rancho Placeritos.

Colorado (1940 Republic) Roy Rogers. LOC: California: Vasquez Rocks; Red Rock Canyon; Republic Studio backlot.

Colorado Ambush (1951 Monogram) Johnny Mack Brown. LOC: California: Rancho Placeritos.

Colorado Kid, The (1937 Republic) Bob Steele. LOC: California: Jauregui Ranch; Walker Ranch.

Colorado Pioneers (1945 Republic) Bill Elliott. LOC: California: Iverson Ranch.

Colorado Ranger (1950 Lippert) Jimmy Ellison. LOC: California: Iverson Ranch.

Colorado Serenade (1946 PRC) Eddie Dean. LOC: California: Corriganville; Rancho Placeritos; Walker Ranch.

Colorado Sundown (1952 Republic) Rex Allen. LOC: California: Big Bear; Shay Ranch; Lake Arrowhead.

Colorado Sunset (1939 Republic) Gene Autry. LOC: California: Corriganville; Garner Ranch; Keen Camp; Republic Studio backlot.

Colorado Territory (1949 Warner Bros) Joel McCrea. LOC: California: Warner Ranch; Warner Bros Studio backlot; Arizona: Sedona; Colorado: Durango-Silverton Narrow Gauge Railroad; New Mexico: Gallup.

Colorado Trail, The (1938 Columbia) Charles Starrett. LOC:

Colt 45 (1950 Warner Bros) Randolph Scott. LOC: California: Iverson Ranch; Vasquez Rocks.

Colt Comrades (1943 United Artists) William Boyd. LOC: California: Lone Pine; Lone Pine Train Depot; California Studio backlot.

Colt, The (2005 Hallmark Entertainment) Ryan Merriman. LOC: CANADA: British Columbia: Bordertown/Western town Maple Ridge, Vancouver.

Column South (1953 Universal) Audie Murphy. LOC: California: Apple Valley: Deadman Point, Fairview Valley/Reeves Dry Lake, Apple Valley; Universal Studio backlot.

Comanche (1956 United Artists) Dana Andrews. LOC: MEXICO: Durango: Ex Hacienda La Ferreria de Flores; Cerro de la Cruz Mountains.

Comanche Moon (2008 CBS miniseries) Steve Zahn. LOC: New Mexico: Bonanza Creek Ranch Santa Fe; Cook Ranch/Cerro Pelon Ranch Galisteo; El Rancho de las Golondrinas Santa Fe; Las Vegas; Los Luceros near Española; Pecos River Ranch Pecos; Río Chama; San Cristobal Ranch Galisteo; Santa Clara Pueblo, The White Place/Plaza Blanca Abiquiú; Texas: Rancho Rio Grande/Moody's Ranch Del Rio.

Comanche Station (1960 Columbia) Randolph Scott. LOC: California: Lone Pine.

Comanche Territory (1950 Universal) Macdonald Carey. LOC: Arizona: Sedona.

Comancheros, The (1961 20th Century Fox) John Wayne. LOC: California: 20th Century Fox Studio backlot; Utah: Castle Valley; Colorado River; Professor Valley; Dead Horse Point State Park; Kings Bottom; La Sal Mountains.

Come and Get It (1935 United Artists) Edward Arnold. LOC: Idaho: Clearwater River; North Fork River.

Come On, Cowboys (1937 Republic) Three Mesquiteers. LOC: California: Iverson Ranch; Brandeis Ranch; Republic Studio backlot.

Come On, Danger (1932 RKO) Tom Keene. LOC: California: Towsley Canyon; Jauregui Ranch; RKO Encino Ranch.

Come On, Danger! (1942 RKO) Tim Holt. LOC: California: Iverson Ranch; Corriganville; RKO Encino Ranch.

Come On, Rangers! (1938 Republic) Roy Rogers. LOC: California: Kernville; Republic Studio backlot.

Come On, Tarzan (1932 World Wide) Ken Maynard. LOC: California: French Ranch; Kernville.

Comeback Trail, The (1982 Dynamic Entertainment) Buster Crabbe. LOC: New Mexico: J. W. Eaves Movie Ranch Santa Fe.

Comes a Horseman (1978 United Artists) James Caan. LOC: Arizona: Coconino National Forest; Flagstaff; Colorado: Cañon City; Wet Mountain Valley.

Comin' 'Round the Mountain (1936 Republic) Gene Autry. LOC: California: Agoura Ranch; Lone Pine; Olancha Sand Dunes; Republic Studios backlot.

Comin'at Ya! (1981 Filmways) Tony Anthony. LOC: SPAIN: Cabo de Gata/sand dunes, Almería; Canyon Negro, Tabernas, Almería; Daganzo Western town Madrid; Playa de Mónsul Almería; Río Alberche Aldea del Fresno, Madrid; Texas-Hollywood/Western set Almería; Valle del Búho West of Tabernas, Almería.

Command, The (1954 Warner Bros) Guy Madison. LOC: California: Agoura; Janss Conejo Ranch; Russell Ranch; Warner Ranch.

Conagher (1991 TNT) Sam Elliott. LOC: Colorado: Buckskin Joe, Canon City; Robert Cordova Ranch.

Concentratin' Kid (1930 Universal) Hoot Gibson. LOC: California: Janss Janss Conejo Ranch.

Conflict (1936 Universal) John Wayne. LOC: California: Tuolumne County.

Conquering Horde, The (1931 Paramount) Richard Arlen. LOC: California: Paramount Ranch; Tuolumne County.

Conquerors, The (1932 RKO) Richard Dix. LOC: California: Tuolumne County; Cooperstown, Stanislaus County.

Conquest of Cheyenne (1946 Republic) Bill Elliott. LOC: California: Iverson Ranch.

Conquest of Cochise (1953 Columbia) Robert Stack. LOC: California: Columbia Ranch; Corriganville; Vasquez Rocks; French Ranch.

Convict Cowboy (1995 MGM) Jon Voight. LOC: CANADA: Alberta: Calgary.

Convict Stage (1965 20th Century Fox) Harry Lauter. LOC: California: Vasquez Rocks; Utah: Kanab Movie Ranch; William Mackelprang Ranch Movie Sets.

Convoy (1978 United Artists) Kris Kristofferson. LOC: California: Needles; New Mexico: Albuquerque; Cerrillos; Estancia; Las Vegas; White Sands National Monument.

Coogan's Bluff (1968 Universal) Clint Eastwood. LOC: California: Mojave; New York: New York City.

Copper Canyon (1950 Paramount) Ray Milland. LOC: California: Vasquez Rocks; Arizona: Sedona.

Copper Sky (1957 Regal) Jeff Morrow. LOC: Utah: Johnson Canyon; Kanab Canyon.

Copperhead (2008 Universal TV) Billy Drago. LOC: BULGARIA:.

Corner in Colleens, A (1916 Kay-Bee) Bessie Barriscale. LOC: California: Inceville.

Cornered (1932 Columbia) Tim McCoy. LOC: California: Iverson Ranch; Paramount Ranch.

Coroner Creek (1948 Columbia) Randolph Scott. LOC: California: Iverson Ranch; Lake Sherwood; Goldwyn Studio backlot; Arizona: Sedona; Sedona Western Street.

Corpus Christi Bandits (1945 Republic) Allan Lane. LOC: California: Iverson Ranch; Corriganville.

Corral Cuties (1954 Universal) Tennessee Ernie Ford. LOC:

Corralling a School Marm (1940 RKO) Ray Whitley. LOC:

Cotter (1973 Gold Key) Don Murray. LOC: California: outside of Oxnard.

Count the Clues (1956 Wrather) Clayton Moore. LOC: California: Iverson Ranch; Corriganville; Lone Pine.

Count Three and Pray (1955 Columbia) Van Heflin. LOC: California: Rowland V. Lee Ranch; Columbia Ranch.

Country Beyond, The (1936 20th Century Fox) Paul Kelly. LOC: California: Iverson Ranch; Truckee; Nevada: Lake Tahoe.

Country Western Hoedown (1967 Jam Art) Pee Wee King. LOC:

Courage of Kavik, the Wolf Dog, The (1980 NBC) John Ireland. LOC: Alaska: Hyder, Juneau; Tok; CANADA: Alberta: Banff National Park, British Columbia:

Stewart, Vancouver; Ontario: Batchawana Bay.

Courage of the North (1935 Stage and Screen) John Preston. LOC: California: Big Bear.

Courage of the West (1937 Universal) Bob Baker. LOC: California: Lone Pine; Nevada: Virginia and Truckee Railroad.

Courageous Avenger, The (1935 Supreme) Johnny Mack Brown. LOC: California: Ralph M. Like Studio backlot; Lone Pine.

Court Martial of General George Armstrong Custer, The (1977 Warner Bros-TV) James Olson. LOC: California: Warner Bros. backlot.

Courtin' Trouble (1948 Monogram) Jimmy Wakely. LOC: California: Walker Ranch.

Courtin' Wildcats (1929 Universal) Hoot Gibson. LOC: California: Universal backlot; Fillmore to Saugus.

Covered Wagon Days (1940 Republic) Three Mesquiteers. LOC: California: Iverson Ranch; Burro Flats; Republic Studio backlot.

Covered Wagon Raid (1950 Republic) Allan Lane. LOC: California: Iverson Ranch; Corriganville.

Covered Wagon Trails (1930 Syndicate) Bob Custer. LOC:

Covered Wagon Trails (1940 Monogram) Jack Randall. LOC: California: Walker Ranch.

Cow Camp Ballads (1929 Paramount) Everett Cheethan. LOC:

Cow Country (1953 Allied Artists) Edmond O'Brien. LOC: California: Iverson Ranch; ?Agoura? Ranch; Vasquez Rocks; Rancho Placeritos.

Cow Town (1950 Columbia) Gene Autry. LOC: California: Iverson Ranch; Lone Pine; Columbia Ranch.

Coward of the County (1981 CBS) Kenny Rogers. LOC: Georgia: Crawfordville; Covington.

Cowboy (1958 Columbia) Jack Lemmon. LOC: New Mexico: San Ildefonso Pueblo; Jarrett Ranch, Santa Fe; Lawton.

Cowboy (1983 MGM TV/CBS) James Brolin. LOC: Texas: Maypearl; Waxahachie.

Cowboy and the Ballerina, The (1984 CBS) Lee Majors. LOC:

Cowboy and the Bandit (1935 Syndicate) Rex Lease. LOC: California: Jauregui Ranch; Ralph M. Like Studio backlot.

Cowboy and the Blonde, The (1941 20th Century Fox) Mary Beth Hughes. LOC: California: Riviera Country Club.

Cowboy and the Indians, The (1949 Columbia) Gene Autry. LOC: California: Pioneertown; Columbia Ranch.

Cowboy and the Kid, The (1936 Universal) Buck Jones. LOC: California: Agoura; Lake Malibu; Lake Sherwood.

Cowboy and the Lady, The (1938 United Artists) Gary Cooper. LOC: California: Iverson Ranch; Agoura; Lake Malibu; Russell Ranch; Bishop.

Cowboy and the Outlaw, The (1929 Syndicate) Bob Steele. LOC:

Cowboy and the Prizefighter (1949 Eagle Lion) Jim Bannon. LOC: California: Iverson Ranch; Rancho Placeritos; Agoura Ranch.

Cowboy and the Senorita (1944 Republic) Roy Rogers. LOC: California: Iverson Ranch; Corriganville; Juaregui Ranch; Walker Ranch; Republic Studio backlot.

Cowboy Blues (1946 Columbia) Ken Curtis. LOC: California: Columbia Ranch.

Cowboy Canteen (1944 Columbia) Charles Starrett. LOC: California: Jauregui Ranch; Walker Ranch.

Cowboy Cavalier (1948 Monogram) Jimmy Wakely. LOC: California: Rancho Placeritos; Walker Ranch.

Cowboy Commandos (1943 Monogram) Range Busters. LOC: California: Corriganville.

Cowboy Counsellor, The (1932 Allied) Hoot Gibson. LOC: California: Jauregui Ranch; Trem Carr Ranch; Walker Ranch.

Cowboy from Brooklyn, The (1938 Warner Bros) Dick Powell. LOC: California: Warner Bros. studio backlot.

Cowboy from Lonesome River (1944 Columbia) Charles Starrett. LOC:

Cowboy from Sundown, The (1940 Monogram) Tex Ritter. LOC: California: Rancho Placeritos; Garner Ranch.

Cowboy Holiday (1934 Beacon) Big Boy Williams. LOC: California: Iverson Ranch; Lone Pine.

Cowboy in the Clouds (1943 Columbia) Charles Starrett. LOC: California: Iverson Ranch.

Cowboy Millionaire, The (1935 Fox) George O'Brien. LOC: California: RKO Encino Ranch; Arizona: Phoenix; England: London, Buckingham Palace, Hyde Park, Trafalgar Square, Thames River.

Cowboy Run (2003 American World Pictures) David Hasselhoff. LOC: CANADA: Alberta: Calgary.

Cowboy Serenade (1942 Republic) Gene Autry. LOC: California: Iverson Ranch; Agoura Ranch; Chatsworth Train Station; probably Brown Latigo St Area, Malibu; Saddle Peak Rd; Stunt Rd; Schueren Rd; Topanga Tower Mtwy, Malibu; Schueren Rd Near Tabard Rd Malibu; Republic Studio backlot.

Cowboy Star, The (1936 Columbia) Charles Starrett. LOC: California: Iverson Ranch; Corriganville; Brandeis Ranch.

Cowboy Up (2001 Code Entertainment/Neverland Films/Orchid Productions) Kiefer Sutherland. LOC: California: Santa Maria; Nevada: Las Vegas.

Cowboy Way, The (1994 Universal) Woody Harrelson. LOC: New Mexico: Española; San Marcos area; Santa Fe; New York: New York.

Cowboy, The (1954 Lippert) Elmo Williams. Documentary filmed in various western states

Cowboys & Aliens (2010 Dream Works SKG/Imagine Entertainment) Daniel Craig. LOC: New Mexico: Abiquiú; Lake Abiquiú; Bonanza Creek Ranch, Santa Fe; Diablo Canyon North of Santa Fe; The White Place/Plaza Blanca, Abiquiú;

San Cristobal Ranch, Galisteo.

Cowboys Don't Cry (1988 Atlantis Films Ltd./CBS) Brian Aebly. LOC: CANADA: Alberta: Bruin Inn, St.Albert.

Cowboys from Texas (1939 Republic) Three Mesquiteers. LOC: California: Agoura Ranch; Republic Studios backlot.

Cowboy's Holiday, A (1949 Astor) Art Davis. LOC:

Cowboys, The (1972 Warner Bros) John Wayne. LOC: Colorado: Durango; Buckskin Joe; Pagosa Springs; New Mexico: Sante Fe area; Bonanza Creek Ranch; J. W. Eaves Ranch; Chama; San Cristobal Ranch near Galisteo.

Cow-Catcher's Daughter, The (1931 Mack Sennett) Harry Gribbon. LOC:

Coyote Canyon (1949 Universal) Tex Williams. LOC:

Coyote Trails (1935 Commodore) Tom Tyler. LOC: California: Bronson Canyon; Frank LaSalle Ranch.

Crashing Broadway (1933 Monogram) Rex Bell. LOC: California: Jauregui Ranch.

Crashing Thru (1939 Monogram) James Newill. LOC: California: Big Bear.

Crashing Thru (1949 Monogram) Whip Wilson. LOC: California: Iverson Ranch; Rancho Placeritos.

Crazy Horse (1996 TNT) Michael Greyeyes. LOC: South Dakota: Black Hills.

Crimson Trail, The (1935 Universal) Buck Jones. LOC: California: Iverson Ranch; Bronson Canyon; Kernville.

Cripple Creek (1952 Columbia) George Montgomery. LOC: California: Iverson Ranch; Columbia Ranch.

Crooked River (1950 Lippert) Jimmy Ellison. LOC: California: Iverson Ranch.

Crooked Trail, The (1936 Supreme) Johnny Mack Brown. LOC: California: Vasquez Rocks; Walker Ranch; Ralph M. Like Studio backlot.

Cross Fire (1933 RKO) Tom Keene. LOC: California: Walker Ranch; Lake Sherwood; Vasquez Rocks; RKO Encino Ranch.

Crossed Trails (1948 Monogram) Johnny Mack Brown. LOC: California: Walker Ranch.

Crossfire Trail (2001 TNT) Tom Selleck. LOC: CANADA: Alberta: CL Ranch Calgary.

Crossing, The (2000 A&E Television Networks/Columbia TriStar Television) Jeff Daniels. LOC: CANADA: Alberta; Ontario; Hamilton; Morrisburg; Stouffville.

Cry Blood, Apache (1970 Golden Eagle) Jody McCrea. LOC: California: Sequoia National Forest; Arizona: Eagletail Mountains; Cabeza Prieta Mountains; Coyote Mountains Wilderness; Kofa National Wildlife Reguge; Big Horn Mountains Wilderness.

Cry to the Wind (1979 Sebastian International) Sheldon Woods. LOC:

Culpepper Cattle Company, The (1972 20th Century Fox) Gary Grimes. LOC: New Mexico: J. W. Eaves Ranch, Santa Fe.

Cupid Rides the Range (1939 RKO) Ray Whitley. LOC:

Curse of Demon Mountain (1977 Howco) Joe Don Baker. LOC: Arkansas: Bull

Shoals State Park.

Curse of the Sacred Mountain (2005 Skeleton Creek Productions) Rick Simpson. LOC: New Mexico: Bonanza Creek Ranch Santa Fe.

Curse of the Undead (1958 Universal) Eric Fleming. LOC: California: Universal Studio backlot.

Curtain Call at Cactus Creek (1950 Universal) Donald O'Connor. LOC: California: Universal Studio backlot.

Custer's Last Stand (1936 Stage and Screen) Rex Lease. LOC: California: Iverson Ranch; Ralph M. Like Studio backlot; Vasquez Rocks; D. W. Griffith Ranch.

Cutter's Trail (1970 CBS-TV) John Gavin. LOC: Utah: Kanab Canyon; Kanab Movie Fort; The Gap.

Cyclone Fury (1951 Columbia) Charles Starrett. LOC: California: Iverson Ranch; Corriganville; Columbia Ranch.

Cyclone Kid (1942 Republic) Donald Barry. LOC: California: Iverson Ranch.

Cyclone Kid, The (1931 Big 4) Buzz Barton. LOST/MISSING.

Cyclone of the Saddle (1935 Superior) Rex Lease. LOC: California: Ralph M. Like Studio backlot.

Cyclone on Horseback (1941 RKO) Tim Holt. LOC: California: Corriganville.

Cyclone Prairie Rangers (1944 Columbia) Charles Starrett. LOC: California: Corriganville.

Cyclone Ranger, The (1935 Spectrum) Bill Cody. LOC: California: Iverson Ranch; Agoura; Red Rock Canyon.

Cyclone Tom (1919 Fox) Tom Mix. LOC: California: Bronson Canyon.

Dakota (1945 Republic) John Wayne. LOC: California: Iverson Ranch; Vasquez Rocks; Mammoth Lakes; San Joaquin Valley.

Dakota Incident (1956 Republic) Dale Robertson. LOC: California: Red Rock Canyon; Republic Studio backlot.

Dakota Kid, The (1951 Republic) Michael Chapin. LOC: California: Iverson Ranch.

Dakota Lil (1950 20th Century Fox) Rod Cameron. LOC: California: Bridgeport.

Dallas (1950 Warner Bros) Gary Cooper. LOC: California: Iverson Ranch; Warner Ranch; Warner Bros backlot.

Dalton Gang, The (1949 Lippert) Don Barry. LOC: California: Iverson Ranch.

Dalton Girls, The (1957 United Artists) Merry Anders. LOC: Utah: Kanab; Kanab Movie Fort; Turkey Crossing, Kanab Creek.

Dalton That Got Away (1960 Dalton Films) Mike Connors. LOC: MEXICO: Mexico City area.

Daltons Ride Again, The (1945 Universal) Alan Curtis. LOC: California: Iverson Ranch; ?Agoura Ranch?; Universal Studio backlot;

Daltons vs. Lucky Luke, The (2004 UGC/Paris/Integral Film, Berg/Sogedasa, Barcelona) Til Schweiger. LOC: SPAIN: Rodalquilar AlmeríaTexas-Hollywood/Western town Almería.

Daltons' Women, The (1951 Western Adventure) Lash La Rue. LOC: California: Iverson Ranch.

Dan Candy's Law (1974 American-International) Donald Sutherland. LOC: CANADA: Battleford, Duck Lake, Saskatoon, Saskatchewan.

Dances with Wolves (1990 Tig Production) Kevin Costner. LOC: Georgia: South Dakota: Badlands National Park; Sage Creek Wilderness Area; Belle Fourche River/ranch North of Sturgis; 777 Bison Ranch Rapid City; Triple U Standing Butte Ranch; Fort Pierre; Spearfish Canyon/Little Spearfish Creek; Northern edge of Black Hills National Forest.

Danger Ahead (1940 Monogram) James Newill. LOC: California: Rancho Placeritos; Westlake Blvd; Lake Sherwood.

Danger Trails (1935 Beacon) Big Boy Williams. LOC: California: Lone Pine.

Danger Valley (1937 Monogram) Jack Randall. LOC: California: Red Rock Canyon; Rancho Placeritos.

Dangerous Days of Kiowa Jones (1966 MGM) Robert Horton. LOC: California: Vasquez Rocks.

Dangerous Mission (1954 RKO) Victor Mature. LOC: Montana: Glacier National Park.

Dangerous Nan McGrew (1930 Paramount) Helen Kane. No exteriors.

Dangerous Venture (1947 United Artists) William Boyd. LOC: California: Lone Pine; Anchor Ranch.

Dangers of the Canadian Mounted (1948 Republic) Jim Bannon. LOC: California: Big Bear; Cedar Lake; Republic Studio backlot.

Daniel Boone (1936 RKO) George O'Brien. LOC: California: Cedar Lake; Big Bear.

Daniel Boone, Trail Blazer (1956 Republic) Bruce Bennett. LOC: MEXICO: Mexico City area.

Daredevils of the West (1943 Republic) Allan Lane. LOC: California: Lone Pine; Iverson Ranch; Republic Studio backlot.

Daring Caballero, The (1949 United Artists) Duncan Renaldo. LOC: California: Pioneertown.

Daring Danger (1932 Columbia) Tim McCoy. LOC: California: Jauregui Ranch; Walker Ranch.

Dark Before Dawn (1988 Lazy E Prod.) Doug McClure. LOC: Kansas: Hugoton; Oklahoma: Edmond.

Dark Command (1940 Republic) John Wayne. LOC: California: Agoura Ranch; Lake Sherwood; Republic Studio backlot.

Daughter of the West (1949 Film Classics) Martha Vickers. LOC: California: Iverson Ranch.

Daughters of Joshua Cabe, The (1972 ABC-TV) Buddy Ebsen. LOC: California: Bell Ranch.

Davy Crockett and the River Pirates (1956 Buena Vista) Fess Parker. LOC: Illinois: Cave-In-Rock.

Davy Crockett Indian Scout (1950 United Artists) George Montgomery. LOC: California: Iverson Ranch; Red Rock Canyon.

Davy Crockett, King of the Wild Frontier (1955 Buena Vista) Fess Parker. LOC: California: Janss Janss Conejo Ranch; North Carolina: Tennessee: Nashville; Knoxville.

Davy Crockett: Rainbow in the Thunder (1988 Walt Disney Television) Johnny Cash. LOC: CANADA: British Columbia: Golden Ears Provincial Park.

Dawn at Socorro (1954 Universal) Rory Calhoun. LOC: California: Fairview Valley/Reeves Dry Lake, Apple Valley.

Dawn on the Great Divide (1942 Monogram) Buck Jones. LOC: California: Walker Ranch; Big Bear; Cedar Lake.

Dawn Rider, The (1935 Monogram) John Wayne. LOC: California: Trem Carr Ranch.

Dawn Trail, The (1930 Columbia) Buck Jones. LOC: California: Kernville; Paramount Ranch.

Day Lincoln Was Shot, The (1998 TNT) Rob Morrow,. LOC: New York: New York - Virginia: PetersburgRichmond - Washington D.C.

Day of Fury, A (1956 Universal) Dale Robertson. LOC: California: Universal backlot.

Day of the Bad Man (1958 Universal) Fred MacMurray. LOC: California: Universal Studio backlot.

Day of the Evil Gun (1968 MGM) Glenn Ford. LOC: MEXICO: Coahuila: Bilbao sand dunes; Durango: Chupaderos; El Saltito waterfall; Villa del Oeste.

Day of the Outlaw (1959 United Artists) Robert Ryan. LOC: Oregon: Bend; Cascades and Dutchman Flat.

Day of the Wolves (1973 TVM) Richard Egan. LOC: Arizona: Lake Havasu City.

Days of Buffalo Bill (1946 Republic) Sunset Carson. LOC: California: Iverson Ranch; Republic Studio backlot.

Days of Heaven (1978 Paramount) Richard Gere. LOC: CANADA: Alberta: Raymond.

Days of Jesse James (1939 Republic) Roy Rogers. LOC: California: Iverson Ranch; Mentryville; Frank LaSalle Ranch; Republic Studio backlot; Rancho Placeritos.

Days of Old Cheyenne (1943 Republic) Roy Rogers. LOC: California: Iverson Ranch.

Dead and the Damned, The (2011 Inception Media Group) David A. Lockhart. LOC: California: Jamestown; Sonora; Marin; Oakland.

Dead Birds (2004 Dead Birds Films) Henry Thomas. LOC: Alabama: Mobile.

Dead Don't Dream, The (1948 United Artists) William Boyd. LOC: California: Lone Pine; Anchor Ranch.

Dead Man (1995 Miramax) Johnny Depp. LOC: Arizona: Sedona - Oregon: Applegate RiverRogue RiverSiskiyou.

Dead Man's Bounty (2006 Lions Gate Entertainment) Val Kilmer. LOC: Poland: Chelmska Studios Warsaw.

Dead Man's Gold (1948 Screen Guild) Lash La Rue. LOC: California: Iverson Ranch; Ingram Ranch.

Dead Man's Gulch (1943 Republic) Don Barry. LOC: California: Iverson Ranch; Agoura Ranch.

Dead Man's Revenge (1994 Summersalt Equi-Service Ltd.) Bruce Dern. LOC: Canada.

Dead Man's Trail (1952 Monogram) Johnny Mack Brown. LOC: California: Iverson Ranch.

Dead Man's Walk (1996 ABC miniseries) Jonny Lee Miller. LOC: Texas: CF Ranch Alpine; Lajitas; Long Draw; Terlingua; Red Rock Ranch Van Horn.

Dead Noon (2007 Blue Collar Flicks) Kane Hodder. LOC: California: Los Angeles Montana: Kalispell Wyoming: Cody; Douglas.

Dead or Alive (1944 PRC) Texas Rangers. LOC: California: Corriganville.

Deadline (1948 Astor) Sunset Carson. LOC: California: Valyermo; Pearblossom.

Deadline, The (1931 Columbia) Buck Jones. LOC: California: Bronson Canyon; Paramount Ranch.

Deadly Companions, The (1961 Pathe-American) Maureen O'Hara. LOC: Arizona: Old Tucson.

Deadly Reactor (1989 Action International Pictures) Stuart Whitman. LOC: California: Independence.

Deadly Trackers, The (1973 Warner Bros) Richard Harris. LOC: MEXICO: Durango: Villa del Oeste; Morelos: Ex Hacienda Cocoyoc, Cocoyoc; Ex Hacienda de Coahuixtla, San Pedro Apatlaco; Ex Hacienda San Jose Vista Hermosa near Tequesquitengo; Tlayacapan.

Deadwood '76 (1965 Fairway-International) Arch Hall, Jr. LOC: California: Corriganville; South Dakota: Black Hills National Forest; Badlands National Park.

Deadwood Dick (1940 Columbia) Don Douglas. LOC: California: Iverson Ranch; Rancho Placeritos.

Deadwood Pass (1933 Monarch) Tom Tyler. LOC: California: Lake Sherwood; Towsley Canyon; Frank LaSalle Ranch.

Death Fangs (1934 Imperial) David Sharpe. LOC:

Death Goes North (1939 Warwick Films) Edgar Edwards. LOC: CANADA: Victoria, British Columbia.

Death Hunt (1981 20th Century-Fox) Charles Bronson. LOC: CANADA: Alberta: Banff National Park; Canmore; Drumheller; New Mexico: Sandía Mountains Albuquerque.

Death Keeps Coming (2010 Tarantino Productions) Dee Wallace. LOC: New Mexico: Santa Fe.

Death of a Gunfighter (1969 Universal) Richard Widmark. LOC: California: Disney's Golden Oak Ranch; Universal Studio backlot.

Death Rides a Horse (1967 Produzione Esecutiva Cinematografica) Lee Van Cleef. LOC: SPAIN: La Calhorra, Granada, Andalucia; Tabernas; Bateria de San Felipe; Desierto de Tabernas.

Death Rides the Plains (1943 PRC) Bob Livingston. LOC: California: Iverson Ranch.

Death Rides the Range (1940 Colony) Ken Maynard. LOC: California: Ranch01; Unknown western street; Walker Ranch.

Death Valley (1946 Screen Guild Productions) Robert Lowery. LOC: California: Death Valley, 20 Mule Team Canyon.

Death Valley Gunfighter (1949 Republic) Allan Lane. LOC: California: Iverson Ranch; Republic Studio backlot.

Death Valley Manhunt (1943 Republic) Bill Elliott. LOC: California: Iverson Ranch; Walker Ranch; Republic Studio backlot.

Death Valley Outlaws (1941 Republic) Don Barry. LOC: California: Iverson Ranch.

Death Valley Rangers (1943 Monogram) Trail Blazers. LOC: California: Corriganville; Rancho Placeritos.

Decision at Sundown (1957 Columbia) Randolph Scott. LOC: California: Columbia Ranch; ?Agoura Ranch?.

Decoy, The (2006 Higgins/Kreinbrink Productions) Justin Krienbrink. LOC: Arizona: Gammons Gulch Benson; Mescal; Old Tucson; Sonoita; Willcox.

Deep in the Heart of Texas (1942 Minoco Productions) Van Alexander and His Orchestra. LOC: No exteriors.

Deep in the Heart of Texas (1942 Universal) Johnny Mack Brown. LOC: California: Corriganville; Universal Studio backlot.

Deep Valley (1947 Warner Bros) Dane Clark. LOC: California: Big Bear; Hermosa Beach.

Deerslayer (1943 Republic) Bruce Kellogg. LOC: California: Lake Elsinore.

Deerslayer, The (1957 20th Century Fox) Lex Barker. LOC: California: Bass Lake, Madera County.

Deerslayer, The (1978 NBC TV/Sunn Classics) Steve Forrest. LOC: Utah: Wasatch National Forest; Uinta Mountains.

Defiance (2000 Missouri Trails Productions) Jim Freivogel. LOC: Missouri: Cedar Creek Conference Center, La Charette Trading Post; Moon Athye Farm; The Old Chicken Ranch; Stone Mill Meadow Farm.

Defying the Law (1935 Aywon) Ted Wells. LOC: California: Ralph M. Like Studio backlot.

Demon for Trouble, A (1935 Commodore) Bob Steele. LOC: California: Lone Pine.

Denver and Rio Grande (1952 Paramount) Edmond O'Brien. LOC: Colorado: Durango; Durango-Silverton Narrow Gauge Railroad.

Denver Kid, The (1948 Republic) Allan Lane. LOC: California: Iverson Ranch; Vasquez Rocks.

Deputy Marshal (1949 Lippert) Jon Hall. LOC: California: Iverson Ranch; Corriganville.

Der Scout (1983 DEFA/Studio Mongolkino) Gojko Mitic. LOC: Mongolia.

Desert Bandit (1941 Republic) Don Barry. LOC: California: Iverson Ranch; Walker Ranch.

Desert Death (1935 MGM) Raymond Hatton. LOC: California.

Desert Gold (1936 Paramount) Buster Crabbe. LOC: California: Iverson Ranch; Paramount Ranch; Bodie.

Desert Guns (1936 Beaumont) Conway Tearle. LOC:

Desert Horseman, The (1946 Columbia) Charles Starrett. LOC: California: Iverson Ranch; Columbia Ranch.

Desert Justice (1936 Atlantic) Jack Perrin. LOC: California: Los Angeles Police Academy; Pacoima Dam; intersection of Country Club Drive, N Sunset Canyon Drive, and E. Olive Avenue; Antelope Valley; possibly 7th Street near Union Ave.; Ralph M. Like Studio backlot.

Desert Man (1934 Imperial) Wally Wales. LOC: California: Vincent Train Depot.

Desert Mesa (1935 Victor Adamson) Wally West. LOC: California: Mojave Desert; Utah: Grafton; Robinson Canyon; Zion National Park.

Desert of Lost Men (1951 Republic) Allan Lane. LOC: California: Iverson Ranch.

Desert Passage (1952 RKO) Tim Holt. LOC: California: Iverson Ranch; Walker Ranch; Agoura; Russell Ranch.

Desert Patrol (1938 Republic) Bob Steele. LOC: California: Jauregui Ranch; Walker Ranch.

Desert Phantom (1936 Supreme) Johnny Mack Brown. LOC: California: Brandeis Ranch.

Desert Pursuit (1952 Monogram) Wayne Morris. LOC: California: Lone Pine; Olancha Sand Dunes.

Desert Trail, The (1935 Monogram) John Wayne. LOC: California: Trem Carr Ranch; Jauregui Ranch; Walker Ranch; Hoot Gibson Rodeo Arena.

Desert Vengeance (1931 Columbia) Buck Jones. LOC: California: Porter Ranch; Lone Pine.

Desert Vigilante (1949 Columbia) Charles Starrett. LOC: California: Iverson Ranch; Bronson Canyon; Columbia Ranch.

Desolation Canyon (2006 Hallmark Entertainment) Stacy Keach. LOC: California: Disney's Golden Oak Ranch; Rancho Maria; Vasquez Rocks.

Desperado (1987 Universal) Alex McArthur. LOC: Arizona: Mescal; Monument Valley; Old Tucson; Patagonia; Sonoita Valley/Rosemont Mountains foothills.

Desperado, The (1954 Allied Artists) Wayne Morris. LOC: California: Iverson Ranch; Ingram Ranch.

Desperado: Avalanche at Devil's Ridge (1988 Universal Pictures) Alex McArthur. LOC: New Mexico: Bonanza Creek Ranch Santa Fe; Cook Ranch/Cerro Pelon Ranch Galisteo; J. W. Eaves Movie Ranch Santa Fe; Rio Chama Black Mesa;

Tesuque Pueblo; Zia Pueblo/Gypsum Point.

Desperado: Badlands Justice (1989 Universal) Alex McArthur. LOC: Arizona: Mescal.

Desperado: Sole Survivor/The Outlaw Wars (1989 Universal) Alex McArthur. LOC: Arizona: Box Canyon/Greaterville Road; Mescal; Old Tucson; Patagonia; Rio Rico/Sonoita Creek set, Sonoita.

Desperadoes of Dodge City (1948 Republic) Allan Lane. LOC: California: Iverson Ranch.

Desperadoes of the West (1950 Republic) Richard Powers. LOC: California: Iverson Ranch; Republic Studio backlot.

Desperadoes, The (1943 Columbia) Randolph Scott. LOC: California: Columbia Ranch; Utah: Kanab.

Desperadoes' Outpost (1952 Republic) Allan Lane. LOC: California: Iverson Ranch.

Desperados Are in Town, The (1956 20th Century Fox) Robert Arthur. LOC: California: Ingram Ranch.

Desperate Mission (1971 ABC TV/20th Century Fox) Ricardo Montalban. LOC: MEXICO: Durango: Chupaderos; El Saltito waterfall; Rancho Marley.

Desperate Trail, The (1995 Turner Home Entertainment) Sam Elliott. LOC: New Mexico: Bonanza Creek Ranch Santa FeTesuque Pueblo.

Desperate Trails (1939 Universal) Johnny Mack Brown. LOC: California: Lake Sherwood; Kernville; Sonora; Toulumne County.

Desperate Women (1978 NBC TV) Susan Saint James. LOC: MEXICO: Durango.

Destry (1955 Universal) Audie Murphy. LOC: California: Universal backlot.

Destry Rides Again (1932 Universal) Tom Mix. LOC: California: French Ranch; Lake Sherwood; El Segundo; Towsley Canyon.

Destry Rides Again (1939 Universal) James Stewart. LOC: California: Universal Studio backlot.

Devil and Leroy Bassett, The (1973 Johnson/Pearson Prod.) George Flower. LOC: New Mexico: Pecos; Santa Fe.

Devil and Miss Sarah, The (1971 ABC-TV/Universal) Gene Barry. LOC: Utah: Paria; Glen Canyon National Recreation Area.

Devil Bear, The (1977 Alaska Pictures) Jason Evers. LOC: Alaska: Juneau.

Devil Horse, The (1932 Mascot) Harry Carey. LOC: California: Iverson Ranch; Beale's Cut; Kernville.

Devil on Horseback, The (1936 Grand National) Lili Damita. LOC: California: Republic Studios backlot; Hemet.

Devil Riders (1943 PRC) Buster Crabbe. LOC: California: Iverson Ranch; Rancho Placeritos.

Devil's Bedroom, The (1963 Allied Artists) John Lupton. LOC: Texas.

Devil's Canyon (1935 Sunset) Noah Beery Jr. LOC:

Devil's Canyon (1953 RKO) Dale Robertson. LOC: California: RKO Encino Ranch;

Arizona: Cortaro.

Devil's Doorway (1950 MGM) Robert Taylor. LOC: California: MGM backlot; Colorado: Aspen; Grand Junction.

Devil's Mistress, The (1968 W.G.W.) Joan Stapleton. LOC: New Mexico: Las Cruces.

Devil's Playground, The (1946 United Artists) William Boyd. LOC: California: Lone Pine.

Devil's Saddle Legion, The (1937 Warner Bros) Dick Foran. LOC: California: Lake Sherwood.

Devil's Trail, The (1942 Columbia) William Elliott. LOC: California: Iverson Ranch.

Diamond Jim (1935 Universal) Edward Arnold. LOC: California: San Luis Obispo.

Diamond Trail (1932 Monogram) Rex Bell. LOC: California: Trem Carr Ranch; Walker Ranch.

Dig That Uranium (1955 Monogram) Leo Gorcey. LOC: California: Iverson Ranch; Corriganville.

Ding Dong Williams (1946 RKO Radio) Glenn Vernon. LOC: California: Lake Sherwood.

Dirty Dingus Magee (1970 MGM) Frank Sinatra. LOC: California: MGM backlot; Arizona: Old Tucson; Mescal.

Dirty Little Billy (1972 United Artists) Michael J. Pollard. LOC: Arizona: Golder Ranch, Tucson; Mescal; New Mexico: Lincoln County; Ruidoso.

Disapparearances (2006 Border Run Pictures/Kingdom Country Productions/Moody Street Pictures) Kris Kristofferson. LOC: New Hampshire: Lincoln; Vermont: St. Johnsbury; West Barnet; West Burke.

Distant Drums (1951 Warner Bros) Gary Cooper. LOC: Florida: Silver Springs; St. Augustine.

Distant Trumpet, A (1964 Warner Bros) Troy Donahue. LOC: Arizona: Leupp, Little Colorado River's Grand Falls; New Mexico: Gallup.

Divided Loyalties (1989 History Productions Limited) Tantoo Cardinal. LOC: CANADA.

Django Unchained (2012) Jamie Foxx. LOC: California: Lasky Mesa; Melody Ranch; Lone Pine; Louisiana: Evergreen Plantation, Edgard; Wyoming: Jackson Hole.

Django Strikes (1987 Filmes International/ Reteitalia) Franco Nero. LOC: COLOMBIA.

Doc (1971 United Artists) Stacy Keach Jr. LOC: SPAIN: Almeria: Canon Negro; Dune di Cabo de Gata; Mini-Hollywood; Llano Mellado; Texas-Hollywood; Madrid: La Pedriza/Finca Magdalena/Manzanares El Real.

Doc Holliday: The Man and the Legend (1994 Oceanic Films) Erich Hauser. LOC: New Mexico: Shakespeare/ghost town Lordsburg.

Doc West (2009 De Angelis Group Western Series) Terence Hill. LOC: New Mexico:

Abiquiú Ghost Ranch; Bonanza Creek Ranch Santa Fe; Cerro Pelon Ranch Galisteo; El Rancho de las Golondrinas Santa Fe; Pecos River Ranch; Santa Fe /Scottish Rite Temple; Waldo Canyon; Zia Pueblo.

Dodge City (1939 Warner Bros) Errol Flynn. LOC: California: Warner Ranch; Modesto and Warnerville, Stanislaus County.

Dodge City Trail (1937 Columbia) Charles Starrett. LOC:

Dollar for the Dead (1998 TNT) Emilio Estévez. LOC: SPAIN: Canyon Negro Tabernas, Almería; Fort El Cóndor Almería; Texas-Hollywood/Western town Almería; La Pedriza Manzanares El Real, Madrid.

Domino Kid, The (1957 Columbia) Rory Calhoun. LOC: California: Iverson Ranch; Columbia Ranch.

Don Daredevil Rides Again (1951 Republic) Ken Curtis. LOC: California: Iverson Ranch; Republic Studio backlot.

Don't Fence Me In (1945 Republic) Roy Rogers. LOC: California: Big Bear; Peter Pan Woodland Club House; Republic Studio backlot.

Donner Party, The (2009 Anacapa Entertainment) Crispin Glover. LOC: California: Donner PassLake Tahoe.

Donner Pass: The Road to Survival (1978 NBC TV/ Sun Classics) Robert Fuller. LOC: Arizona: Pipe Springs National Monument; Utah: Kanab Canyon; Kanab Movie Fort; Timpanogos; Tom's Canyon.

Doolins of Oklahoma, The (1949 Columbia) Randolph Scott. LOC: California: Iverson Ranch; Janss Conejo Ranch; Lone Pine; Columbia Ranch.

Doomed at Sundown (1937 Republic) Bob Steele. LOC: California: Iverson Ranch; Walker Ranch; Ralph M. Like Studio backlot.

Doomed Caravan (1941 Paramount) William Boyd. LOC: California: Kernville; Kelso Canyon; Kelso Canyon Abode Town.

Down Dakota Way (1949 Republic) Roy Rogers. LOC: California: Corriganville; Walker Ranch; Republic Studio backlot.

Down in Arkansas (1938 Republic) June Weaver. LOC: California: Big Bear; Lake Arrowhead.

Down in the Valley (2005 Element Films/Class 5 Films) Bruce Dern. LOC: California: Los Angeles.

Down Laredo Way (1953 Republic) Rex Allen. LOC: California: Iverson Ranch; Burro Flats.

Down Liberty Road (1956 Fairbanks) Marshall Thompson. LOC: California: Corriganville

Down Mexico Way (1941 Republic) Gene Autry. LOC: California: Corriganville; Lone Pine; Republic Studio backlot.

Down Missouri Way (1946 PRC) Eddie Dean. LOC: California: San Fernando Valley.

Down Rio Grande Way (1942 Columbia) Charles Starrett. LOC: California: Iverson Ranch; Columbia Ranch.

Down Texas Way (1942 Monogram) Rough Riders. LOC: California: Walker Ranch; Rancho Placeritos.

Down the Wyoming Trail (1939 Monogram) Tex Ritter. LOC: Wyoming: Hansen Ranch and Neilsen Ranch, Jackson; National Elk Refuge; Wilson; Jackson.

Dr. Quinn, Medicine Woman: The Movie (1999 CBS) Jane Seymour. LOC: California: Paramount Ranch; Veluzat Motion Picture Ranch, Saugus.

Dragoon Wells Massacre (1957 Allied Artists) Barry Sullivan. LOC: Utah: Kanab; Kanab Movie Fort; The Gap.

Drango (1957 United Artists) Jeff Chandler. LOC: California: Morrison Ranch; Louisiana: St. Francisville.

Draw! (1984 Home Box Office Premiere Films) Kirk Douglas. LOC: CANADA: Alberta: Fort Edmonton.

Dream Keeper (2003 Hallmark Entertainment/RTL Productions/Sextant Entertainment Group) George Aguilar. LOC: Arizona: Tucson; New Mexico: Abiquiú Ghost Ranch; Jemez Pueblo; Santa Fe; Zia Pueblo; South Dakota: Pine Ridge; CANADA: Alberta: Rosedale, Drumheller; Wayne, Drumheller.

Dream West (1986 Sunn Classics/CBS) Richard Chamberlain. LOC: Arizona: Flagstaff; Grand Canyon National Park; Old Tucson; Sedona; California: Sable Ranch Placerita Canyon, Newhall; Colorado: Central City; Gilpin; Bent's Old Fort La Junta; Otero; Virginia: Wyoming: Cattleman Bridge Jackson Hole.

Drift Fence (1936 Paramount) Buster Crabbe. LOC: California: Big Bear; Universal Studio backlot.

Drifter, The (1932 Willis Kent) William Farnum. LOC: California: Paramount Ranch.

Drifter, The (1944 PRC) Buster Crabbe. LOC: California: Iverson Ranch; Rancho Placeritos.

Driftin' Kid, The (1941 Monogram) Tom Keene. LOC: California: Rancho Placeritos; Walker Ranch.

Driftin' River (1946 PRC) Eddie Dean. LOC: California: Iverson Ranch; Corriganville; Rancho Placeritos; Jauregui Ranch; Walker Ranch.

Drifting Along (1946 Monogram) Johnny Mack Brown. LOC: California: Iverson Ranch; Jauregui Ranch.

Drifting Westward (1939 Monogram) Jack Randall. LOC: California: Rancho Placeritos; Walker Ranch.

Drum Beat (1954 Warner Bros) Alan Ladd. LOC: Arizona: Sedona.

Drum Taps (1933 World Wide) Ken Maynard. LOC: California: Jauregui Ranch; Towsley Canyon.

Drums Across the River (1954 Universal) Audie Murphy. LOC: California: Burro Flats; Barton Flats, San Bernardino National Forest; Red Rock Canyon; Kernville; Universal Studio backlot.

Drums Along the Mohawk (1939 20th Century Fox) Henry Fonda. LOC: Pennsylvania: Cook County; Utah: Aspen Mirror Lake; Duck Creek; Strawberry Point.

Drums in the Deep South (1951 RKO) James Craig. LOC: California: Tuolumne County.

Drums of Destiny (1937 Crescent) Tom Keene. LOC:

Drylanders, The (1963 Columbia) Frances Hyland. LOC: CANADA: Swift Current, Saskatchewan.

Dual: The Lone Drifter (2008 Grizzly Peak Films/Creative Convergence) Michael Worth. LOC: Arizona: Mescal.

Duchess and the Dirtwater Fox, The (1976 20th Century Fox) George Segal. LOC: Colorado: Buckskin Joe, Canon City; Central City; Custer, Gilpin Counties.

Dude Bandit, The (1933 Allied) Hoot Gibson. LOC: California: Jauregui Ranch; Vasquez Rocks.

Dude Cowboy (1941 RKO) Tim Holt. LOC: California: Corriganville; French Ranch; Bronson Canyon; RKO Encino Ranch.

Dude Goes West, The (1948 Allied Artists) Eddie Albert. LOC: California: Iverson Ranch.

Dude Ranch (1931 Paramount) Jack Oakie. LOC: California: Paramount Ranch.

Dude Ranch Harmony (1949 Variety) Dewey Groom. LOC:

Dude Ranger, The (1934 Fox) George O'Brien. LOC: Utah: Bryce Canyon National Park; Eagle Rock, Johnson Canyon, Kanab; Zion National Park; Springdale Church.

Dude Wrangler, The (1930 World Wide) Tom Keene. LOST/MISSING.

Dudes Are Pretty People (1942 United Artists) Jimmy Rogers. LOC: California: Iverson Ranch; Lone Pine.

Dudley-Do Right (1999 Universal Pictures) Brendan Fraser. LOC: CANADA: British Columbia: Aldergrove; Burnaby; Vancouver.

Duel at Apache Wells (1957 Republic) Jim Davis. LOC: California: Iverson Ranch; Red Rock Canyon.

Duel at Diablo (1966 United Artists) James Garner. LOC: Utah: Kanab Canyon; Paria; Kanab Movie Fort; Tom's Canyon.

Duel at Silver Creek (1952 Universal) Audie Murphy. LOC: California: Iverson Ranch; Corriganville; Vasquez Rocks; Universal Studio backlot.

Duel in the Sun (1947 Selznick) Gregory Peck. LOC: California: Corriganville; Lasky Mesa; Tuolumne County; Arizona: High Haven Ranch, Empire Ranch, Sonoita; Starr Pass; Tumacacori Mission.

Dugan of the Badlands (1931 Monogram) Bill Cody. LOST/MISSING.

Durango Kid, The (1940 Columbia) Charles Starrett. LOC: California: Agoura Ranch; Lone Pine; Columbia Ranch.

Durango Valley Raiders (1938 Republic) Bob Steele. LOC: California: Iverson Ranch; Jauregui Ranch; Walker Ranch.

Dust is Dust (1994 The Water Hole Gang, Inc.) Robert Vaughn. LOC: Texas: Luck Ranch/Willieville/Nelson Ranch Spicewood, Austin.

Dynamite Canyon (1941 Monogram) Tom Keene. LOC: California: Kernville; Arizona: Prescott; Watson Lake.

Dynamite Pass (1950 RKO) Tim Holt. LOC: California: Lone Pine.

Dynamite Ranch (1932 World Wide) Ken Maynard. LOC: California: Providencia Ranch; Southern Pacific train tracks outside Corriganville.

Eagle and the Hawk, The (1950 Paramount) John Payne. LOC: Arizona: Sedona.

Eagle's Brood, The (1935 Paramount) William Boyd. LOC: California: Trem Carr Ranch; Kernville; Tuolumne County; Kennedy Meadow; Lone Pine.

Eagle's Wing (1979 Rank Film Distributors) Martin Sheen. LOC: MEXICO: Durango: Suchil, Hacienda de El Mortero.

East Meets West (1995 Kihachi Productions) Hiroyuki Sanada. LOC: New Mexico: Bonanza Creek Ranch Santa Fe; Charles R Ranch Las Vegas; Cook Ranch/Cerro Pelon Ranch Galisteo; J. W. Eaves Movie Ranch Santa Fe; Las Vegas; Valle Grande; Zia Pueblo/Gypsum Point.

Ebenezer Scrooge (1997 Nomadic Pictures) Jack Palance. LOC: CANADA: Alberta: CL Ranch Calgary.

Echo Ranch (1948 Universal) Red River Dave. LOC: Texas: San Antonio.

Edge of Eternity (1959 Columbia) Cornel Wilde. LOC: Arizona: Kingman; Oatman; Grand Canyon National Park.

Education of Little Tree, The (1997 Paramount Pictures) Joseph Ashton. LOC: North Carolina: Cullowohee; Great Smoky Mountains; Tennessee: Blue Ridge Mountains; CANADA: Quebec: Harrington.

Eight Seconds (1994 New Line Cinema) Stephen Baldwin. LOC: California: San Diego; Oregon: Pendleton; Texas: Boerne; Del Rio; Helotes; San Antonio; Seguin.

El Condor (1970 National General) Lee Van Cleef. LOC: SPAIN: Tabernas.

El Diablo (1990 HBO) Anthony Edwards. LOC: Arizona: Old Tucson.

El Diablo Rides (1939 Metropolitan) Bob Steele. LOC: California: Walker Ranch; Jauregui Ranch.

El Dorado (1967 Paramount) John Wayne. LOC: Arizona: Old Tucson; Amado Ranch, Tucson; Avra Valley; Sonoita Creek, Patagonia.

El Dorado Pass (1948 Columbia) Charles Starrett. LOC: Columbia Ranch.

El Paso (1949 Paramount) John Payne. LOC: California: Iverson Ranch; Corriganville.

El Paso Kid, The (1946 Republic) Sunset Carson. LOC: California: Iverson Ranch; Republic Studio backlot.

El Paso Stampede (1953 Republic) Allan Lane. LOC: California: Iverson Ranch.

Electric Horseman, The (1979 Wildwood Prod/Columbia/Universal) Robert Redford. LOC: Nevada: Las Vegas; Utah: Grafton; Snow Canyon; Zion National Park.

Elfego Baca: Six Gun Law (1962 Buena Vista) Robert Loggia. LOC: California: Iverson Ranch.

Emperor of the North (1973 20th Century Fox) Lee Marvin. LOC: Oregon: Cotton Grove.

Empty Holsters (1937 Warner Bros) Dick Foran. LOC: California: Iverson Ranch.

Empty Saddles (1936 Universal) Buck Jones. LOC: California: Garner Ranch; Keen Camp.

End of the Trail (1932 Columbia) Tim McCoy. LOC: Wyoming: Little Wind River Canyon, Wind River Reservation, Lander.

End of the Trail (1936 Columbia) Jack Holt. LOST/MISSING.

Enemy of the Law (1945 PRC) Texas Rangers. LOC: California: Corriganville.

Escape from Fort Bravo (1953 MGM) William Holden. LOC: California: Corriganville; Death Valley; MGM backlot; New Mexico: Gallup.

Escape from Red Rock (1958 20th Century Fox) Brian Donlevy. LOC: California: Iverson Ranch.

Escort West (1959 United Artists) Victor Mature. LOC: California: Iverson Ranch.

Eskimo (1934 MGM) W. S. Van Dyke. LOC: Alaska: Teller.

Even Cowgirls Get the Blues (1993 New Line Cinema) Uma Thurman. LOC: Oregon: Bend; Portland; Sisters; Terrebonne.

Everybody's Dancin'! (1950 Lippert) Spade Cooley. LOC:

Everyman's Law (1936 Supreme) Johnny Mack Brown. LOC: California: Walker Ranch.

Everything That Rises (1998 TNT) Dennis Quaid. LOC: Montana: Livingston

Eye for an Eye, An (1966 Embassy) Robert Lansing. LOC: California: Lone Pine; Olancha Sand Dunes; Dolomite.

Eyes of Texas (1948 Republic) Roy Rogers. LOC: California: Walker Ranch; Republic Studio backlot.

Fabulous Texan, The (1947 Republic) William Elliott. LOC: California: Iverson Ranch; Republic Studio backlot; Arizona: Sedona; Flagstaff.

Face of a Fugitive (1959 Columbia) Fred MacMurray. LOC: California: Railtown; Toulomne County; Corriganville; Columbia Ranch.

Face to the Wind (1972 Warner Bros) Cliff Potts. LOC: New Mexico: Belén; Cuba; Santa Fe National Forest; Sandia Crest.

Fade-In (1968 Paramount) Burt Reynolds. LOC: Utah: Moab; Castle Valley; Professor Valley.

Fairplay (1971 Clyce Properties) Paul Ford. LOC: Texas: Dallas area.

Fair Warning (1931 Fox) George O'Brien. LOC: California: Death Valley.

Falcon Out West, The (1944 RKO Radio) Tom Conway. LOC: California: Corriganville.

Fall of the Alamo, The (1938 National Pictures) Claudia Britton. LOC: Texas: San Antonio, San Josè Mission.

False Colors (1943 United Artists) William Boyd. LOC: California: Lone Pine; California Studio backlot.

False Paradise (1948 United Artists) William Boyd. LOC: California: Lone Pine;

Anchorville.

Fancy Pants (1950 Paramount) Bob Hope. LOC: California: Busch Gardens; Chatsworth Train Tunnel; Lewis Mansion; MGM Studio backlot; New Mexico: Santa Fe.

Fandango (1970 Clover Films) James Whitworth. LOC:

Fangs of the Arctic (1953 Allied Artists) Kirby Grant. LOC: California: Big Bear; Cedar Lake.

Fangs of the Wild (1939 Metropolitan) Dennis Moore. LOC: California: Ranch01; Crestline; Lake Gregory.

Far and Away (1992 Universal Pictures) Tom Cruise. LOC: Montana: Billings - Ireland: Dingle Kerry County.

Far Country, The (1955 Universal) James Stewart. LOC: CANADA: Columbia Ice Fields; Jasper National Park.

Far Frontier, The (1948 Republic) Roy Rogers. LOC: California: Iverson Ranch; Walker Ranch; Vasquez Rocks; Littlerock Dam; Republic Studio backlot.

Far Horizon, The (1955 Paramount) Fred MacMurray. LOC: Wyoming: Cattleman Bridge, Colter Bay, Jackson Lake, Jackson Hole; Snake River.

Far Side of Jericho, The (2006 Mountainair Films/Further Productions) Patrick Bergin. LOC: New Mexico: Bonanza Creek Ranch; Cerrillos Waldo Canyon; Cook Ranch/Cerro Pelon Ranch Galisteo; Diablo Canyon North of Santa Fe; J.W.Eaves Movie Ranch Santa Fe; Madrid; Nambé Pueblo; Zia Pueblo/Gypsum Point.

Fargo (1952 Monogram) Bill Elliott. LOC: California: Iverson Ranch; Corriganville.

Fargo Express (1933 Fox) Ken Maynard. LOC: California: Iverson Ranch.

Fargo Kid, The (1940 RKO) Tim Holt. LOC: California: Iverson Ranch; Utah: Kanab; Paria.

Fargo Phantom, The (1950 Universal) Tex Williams. LOC:

Faro Nell, or In Old Californy (1929 Christie) Louise Fazenda. LOC: California: Antelope Valley.

Fast Bullets (1936 Reliable) Tom Tyler. LOC: California: Frank LaSalle Ranch.

Fast on the Draw (1950 Lippert) Russell Hayden. LOC: California: Iverson Ranch.

Fastest Guitar Alive, The (1967 MGM) Roy Orbison. LOC: California: MGM backlot; North Ranch.

Fastest Gun Alive, The (1956 MGM) Glenn Ford. LOC: California: Red Rock Canyon; MGM backlot.

Female Bunch, The (1969 Dalia Prod/Gilbreth) Russ Tamblyn. LOC: California: Spahn Ranch; Utah: Capitol Reef National Park; Hanksville.

Fence Riders (1950 Monogram) Whip Wilson. LOC: California: Iverson Ranch; Rancho Placeritos; Walker Ranch.

Ferocious Pal (1934 Principal) Kazan the Wonder Dog. LOC: California: Iverson Ranch; Ralph M. Like Studio backlot.

Feud Maker, The (1938 Republic) Bob Steele. LOC: California: Brandeis Ranch;

Rancho Placeritos; Walker Ranch.

Feud of the Range (1939 Metropolitan) Bob Steele. LOC: California: Ralph M. Like Studio backlot; Utah: Kanab; Johnson Canyon.

Feud of the Trail, The (1937 Victory) Tom Tyler. LOC: California: Brandeis Ranch.

Feud of the West (1936 Grand National) Hoot Gibson. LOC: California: Walker Ranch; Vasquez Rocks.

Feud, The (1977 Singing Cowboy Films) Jeff Goldin. LOC: California: Vasquez Rocks.

Feudin' Rhythm (1949 Columbia) Kirby Grant. LOC: California: Corriganville.

Feudin', Fussin', and A-Fightin' (1948 Universal) Donald O'Connor. LOC: California: Universal backlot.

Fiddlin' Buckaroo, The (1933 Universal) Ken Maynard. LOC: California: Lone Pine; Mount Whitney.

Fiend Who Walked the West, The (1958 20th Century Fox) Hugh O'Brian. LOC: California: Century Ranch; 20th Century Fox backlot

Fiesta (1947 MGM) Esther Williams. LOC: MEXICO: Jalisco: Guadalajara; Queretaro: Mexico City; Puebla; Tlaxcala: Plaza de Toros Jorge el Ranchero Aguilar.

Fight Before Christmas, A (1994 Rialto Film) Terence Hill. LOC: New Mexico: Abiquiú Reservoir; Bonanza Creek Ranch Santa Fe; J.W.Eaves Movie Ranch Santa Fe; Tent Rocks Cochiti Pueblo; Valle Grande; Zia Pueblo/Gypsum Point.

Fight for Love, A (1919 Universal) Harry Carey. LOC: California: Big Bear.

Fight of the Wild Stallions (1947 Universal) Narrated by Ben Grauer. LOC: Wyoming: Red Desert.

Fighter, The (1952 United Artists) Richard Conte. LOC: Texas: El Paso; MEXICO: Mexico City; Michoacan: Lake Patzcuaro and Patzcuaro Island, Janitzio

Fightin' Thru (1930 Tiffany) Ken Maynard. LOC: California: Warner Bros backlot; Walker Ranch.

Fighting Bill Carson (1945 PRC) Buster Crabbe. LOC: California: Corriganville.

Fighting Bill Fargo (1942 Universal) Johnny Mack Brown. LOC: California: Iverson Ranch; Agoura Ranch; Universal Studio backlot;

Fighting Buckaroo, The (1943 Columbia) Charles Starrett. LOC: California: Iverson Ranch.

Fighting Caballero (1935 Superior) Rex Lease. LOC: California: Ralph M. Like Studio backlot.

Fighting Caravans (1931 Paramount) Gary Cooper. LOC: California: Paramount Ranch; Tuolumne County; Phoenix Lake; Dardanelle.

Fighting Champ, The (1932 Monogram) Bob Steele. LOC: California: Jauregui Ranch; Walker Ranch.

Fighting Code, The (1933 Columbia) Buck Jones. LOC: California: Bronson Canyon.

Fighting Cowboy, The (1933 Superior) Buffalo Bill Jr. LOC: California: Victor Valley.

Fighting Deputy, The (1937 Spectrum) Fred Scott. LOC: California: Brandeis Ranch.

Fighting Fool, The (1932 Columbia) Tim McCoy. LOC: California: Trem Carr Ranch.

Fighting for Justice (1932 Columbia) Tim McCoy. LOC: California: Trem Carr Ranch; Walker Ranch.

Fighting Frontier (1943 RKO) Tim Holt. LOC: California: Iverson Ranch; RKO Encino Ranch.

Fighting Frontiersman, The (1946 Columbia) Charles Starrett. LOC: California: Iverson Ranch; Columbia Ranch.

Fighting Gringo, The (1939 RKO) George O'Brien. LOC: California: Iverson Ranch; Brandeis Ranch; RKO Encino Ranch.

Fighting Hero (1935 Commodore) Tom Tyler. LOC: California: Frank LaSalle Ranch.

Fighting Kentuckian, The (1949 Republic) John Wayne. LOC: California: Agoura Ranch; Sherwood Forest; Republic Studio backlot.

Fighting Lawman, The (1953 Allied Artists) Wayne Morris. LOC: California: Corriganville.

Fighting Legion, The (1930 Universal) Ken Maynard. LOC: California: Lake Sherwood; Paramount Ranch; Lone Pine.

Fighting Mad (1939 Monogram) James Newill. LOC: California: Big Bear.

Fighting Mad (1956 Border) Joe Robinson. LOC: SCOTLAND.

Fighting Man of the Plains (1949 20th Century Fox) Randolph Scott. LOC: California: Columbia Ranch.

Fighting Marshal, The (1931 Columbia) Tim McCoy. LOC: California: Trem Carr Ranch.

Fighting Mustang (1948 Astor) Sunset Carson. LOC: California: Oliver Drake Ranch, Pearblossom.

Fighting Parson, The (1930 Hal Roach) Harry Langdon. LOC: California.

Fighting Parson, The (1933 Allied) Hoot Gibson. LOC: California: Jauregui Ranch; Trem Carr Ranch; Towsley Canyon.

Fighting Pioneers (1935 Resolute) Rex Bell. LOC: California: Russell Ranch.

Fighting Ranger, The (1934 Columbia) Buck Jones. LOC: California: Kernville; Lone Pine.

Fighting Ranger, The (1948 Monogram) Johnny Mack Brown. LOC: California: Rancho Placeritos; Walker Ranch.

Fighting Redhead, The (1949 Eagle Lion) Jim Bannon. LOC: California: Iverson Ranch; Rancho Placeritos; Agoura Ranch.

Fighting Renegade, The (1939 Victory) Tim McCoy. LOC: California: Corriganville

Fighting Shadows (1935 Columbia) Tim McCoy. LOC: California: Big Bear; Wrightwood.

Fighting Sheriff, The (1931 Columbia) Buck Jones. LOC: California: Iverson Ranch; Agoura; Paramount Ranch.

Fighting Stallion, The (1950 Eagle Lion) Bill Edwards. LOC: California: Rancho Placeritos; Rancho Maria.

Fighting Texan, The (1937 Ambassador) Kermit Maynard. LOC: California: Iverson Ranch; Jauregui Ranch; Walker Ranch, Vasquez Rocks.

Fighting Texans, The (1933 Monogram) Rex Bell. LOC: California: Jauregui Ranch; Walker Ranch.

Fighting Through (1934 Kent) Reb Russell. LOC: California: Iverson Ranch.

Fighting to Live (1934 Principal) Reb Russell. LOC: California: Red Rock Canyon.

Fighting Trooper, The (1934 Ambassador) Kermit Maynard. LOC: California: Lake Arrowhead; Camp Seeley; Crestline.

Fighting Valley (1943 PRC) Texas Rangers. LOC: California: Corriganville.

Fighting Vigilantes, The (1947 Eagle Lion) Lash LaRue. LOC: California: Iverson Ranch.

Fighting with Buffalo Bill (1926 Universal) Wallace MacDonald. LOC: California: Lasky Mesa.

Fighting with Kit Carson (1933 Mascot) Johnny Mack Brown. LOC: California: Iverson Ranch; Russell Ranch.

Fire Creek (1968 Warner Bros) James Stewart. LOC: California: North Ranch; Arizona: Sedona.

Firebrand Jordan (1930 Big 4) Lane Chandler. LOC: California: Kernville; The Mountain Inn and other main street businesses, Kernville.

Firebrand, The (1962 20th Century Fox) Kent Taylor. LOC: California: Lone Pine.

Firebrands of Arizona (1944 Republic) Sunset Carson. LOC: California: Iverson Ranch; Corriganville; Republic Studio backlot.

First Texan, The (1956 Allied Artists) Joel McCrea. LOC: California: Janss Conejo Ranch; Warner Ranch.

First Traveling Saleslady, The (1956 RKO) Ginger Rogers. LOC: California: Lone Pine.

Fish Hawk (1981 Avco Embassy Pictures) Will Samson. LOC: CANADA: Ontario: Kleinburg.

Fistful of Rawhide (1970 Rebel Arts) Patricia Moore. LOC:

Five Bad Men (1935 Sunset) Noah Beery, Jr. LOST/MISSING.

Five Bloody Graves (1970 Independent- International) Scott Brady. LOC: Utah: Capitol Reef National Park.

Five Bold Women (1960 Citation) Jeff Morrow. LOC: Texas: Brackettville.

Five Card Stud (1968 Paramount) Dean Martin. LOC: MEXICO: Durango: Chupaderos.

Five Giants from Texas (1966 Miro Cinematografica/Balcazar) Guy Madison. LOC: SPAIN: Barcelona.

Five Guns to Tombstone (1961 United Artists) James Brown. LOC: California:

Corriganville; Iverson Ranch.

Five Guns West (1955 American Releasing Corp) John Lund. LOC: California: Iverson Ranch; Ingram Ranch.

Flame of Barbary Coast (1945 Republic) John Wayne. LOC: California: Mammoth Lakes; Villa Leon; Malibu Beach; Republic Studio backlot.

Flame of the West (1945 Monogram) Johnny Mack Brown. LOC: California: Walker Ranch; Russell Ranch.

Flaming Bullets (1945 PRC) Texas Rangers. LOC: California: Corriganville.

Flaming Feather (1952 Paramount) Sterling Hayden. LOC: California: Iverson Ranch; Arizona: Sedona; Montezuma Castle.

Flaming Frontier (1958 20th Century Fox) Bruce Bennett. LOC: California: Bronson Canyon; Canada.

Flaming Frontiers (1938 Universal) Johnny Mack Brown. LOC: California: Kernville; Universal Studio backlot.

Flaming Guns (1932 Universal) Tom Mix. LOC: California: Lone Pine; Brandt Ranch; Antelope Valley.

Flaming Lead (1939 Colony) Ken Maynard. LOC: California: Walker Ranch; Jauregui Ranch; Kernville.

Flaming Star (1960 20th Century Fox) Elvis Presley. LOC: California: Janss Conejo Ranch; Century Ranch.

Flap (1970 Warner Bros) Anthony Quinn. LOC: New Mexico: Madrid; Albuquerque; San Ildefonso Pueblo; Santa Clara Pueblo; Puye Cliffs; Santo Domingo; Santa Fe.

Flashing Guns (1947 Monogram) Johnny Mack Brown. LOC: California: Iverson Ranch; Rancho Placeritos.

Flesh and the Spur (1956 American International) John Agar. LOC: California: Iverson Ranch; Rancho Placeritos.

Flicka (2006 20th Century Fox) Alison Lohman. LOC: Wyoming: Eaton's Ranch Wolf; Polo Ranch Big Horn; Sheridan.

Flying Lariats (1931 Big 4) Wally Wales. LOC: California: Universal backlot; Sonora.

Follow the River (1995 Signboard Hill Productions) Sheryl Lee. LOC: North Carolina: Sapphire.

Fool's Gold (1947 United Artists) William Boyd. LOC: California: Kernville.

Fools' Parade (1971 Columbia) James Stewart. LOC: West Virginia: Moundsville.

For the Service (1936 Universal) Buck Jones. LOC: California: Red Rock Canyon.

Forbidden Trail (1932 Columbia) Buck Jones. LOC: California: Paramount Ranch.

Forbidden Trails (1941 Monogram) Rough Riders. LOC: California: Walker Ranch; Jauregui Ranch; Rancho Placeritos.

Forbidden Valley (1938 Universal) Noah Beery, Jr. LOC: California: Tuolumne County; Columbia; Mammoth Lakes.

Forest Rangers, The (1942 Paramount) Fred MacMurray. LOC: California: Big Bear; Paramount Ranch; San Lorenzo Valley; Santa Cruz Mountains; Montana: Missoula; Oregon: Lakeview.

Forest Warrior (1996 Turner Entertainment) Chuck Norris. LOC: Oregon: Hood River; Lost Lake; Mount Hood; Parkdale; ENGLAND: Berry Pomeroy/Berry Pomeroy Church.

Forlorn River (1937 Paramount) Buster Crabbe. LOC: California: Kernville; Kernville Movie Street.

Fort Apache (1948 RKO) John Wayne. LOC: California: Corriganville; Arizona/Utah: Monument Valley; Utah: San Juan River; Mexican Hat; Dead Horse Point State Park; Goosenecks State Park.

Fort Bowie (1958 United Artists) Ben Johnson. LOC: Utah: Kanab Canyon; Kanab Movie Fort; Johnson Canyon; William Mackelprang Ranch Movie Sets.

Fort Courageous (1965 20th Century Fox) Donald Barry. LOC: Utah: Kanab; Kanab Movie Fort.

Fort Defiance (1951 United Artists) Dane Clark. LOC: California: Rancho Placeritos; New Mexico: Gallup.

Fort Dobbs (1958 Warner Bros) Clint Walker. LOC: Utah: Moab; Castle Valley; Professor Valley; Kanab; Kanab Movie Fort; Paria; Aspen Mirror Lake; Duck Creek.

Fort Dodge Stampede (1951 Republic) Allan Lane. LOC: California: Iverson Ranch.

Fort Massacre (1958 United Artists) Joel McCrea. LOC: New Mexico: Gallup; Twin Lakes; Manuelito Canyon; cliff dwelling 2.7 miles east of Arizona/New Mexico border along state highway 118 on north side

Fort Osage (1952 Monogram) Rod Cameron. LOC: California: Corriganville; Rancho Placeritos; Keen Camp; Garner Ranch.

Fort Savage Raiders (1951 Columbia) Charles Starrett. LOC: California: Corriganville; Columbia Ranch.

Fort Ti (1953 Columbia) George Montgomery. LOC: California: Corriganville; Sherwood Forest; Lake Sherwood; Agoura Ranch; Columbia Ranch.

Fort Utah (1967 Paramount) John Ireland. LOC: California: Albertson Ranch; Vasquez Rocks; Paramount Studio backlot.

Fort Vengeance (1953 Allied Artists) James Craig. LOC: California: Iverson Ranch; Corriganville.

Fort Worth (1951 Warner Bros) Randolph Scott. LOC: California: Iverson Ranch; Warner Ranch; Tuolumne County.

Fort Yuma (1955 United Artists) Peter Graves. LOC: Utah: Kanab; Kanab Movie Fort; Turkey Crossing, Kanab Creek.

Forty Graves for Forty Guns (1971 Box Office International) Robert Padilla. LOC: New Mexico: Picuris Pueblo.

Forty Guns (1957 20th Century Fox) Barry Sullivan. LOC: California: 20th Century Fox Studio backlot; Janss Janss Conejo Ranch.

Forty Guns to Apache Pass (1967 Columbia) Audie Murphy. LOC: California: Russell Ranch/Albertson Ranch/Glenmoore Cattle Ranch; North Ranch; Red Rock Canyon; Lake Los Angeles.

Forty Thieves (1944 United Artists) William Boyd. LOC: California: Kernville; Kern River Suspension Bridge; California Studio backlot.

Forty-Five Calibre Echo (1932 Homer Prod) Jack Perrin) LOST/MISSING

Forty-Niners, The (1932 Freuler) Tom Tyler. LOC: California: Trem Carr Ranch.

Forty-Niners, The (1954 Allied Artists) William Elliott. LOC: California: Iverson Ranch; Corriganville.

Four Eyes and Six-Guns (1992 Turner Pictures) Judge Reinhold. LOC: Arizona: Bisbee; Mescal; Old Tucson.

Four Faces West (1948 United Artists) Joel McCrea. LOC: New Mexico: Gallup; El Morro National Monument; San Rafael; White Sands National Monument.

Four Fast Guns (1960 Universal) James Craig. LOC: Arizona: Apacheland.

Four For Texas (1963 Warner Bros) Frank Sinatra. LOC: California: Red Rock Canyon.

Four Guns to the Border (1954 Universal) Rory Calhoun. LOC: California: Berry/Bell Ranch; Fairview Valley/Reeves Dry Lake, Apple Valley; Universal Studio backlot.

Four Rode Out (1969 ADA Films/Sagittarious Productions) Pernell Roberts. LOC: SPAIN: Almería.

Fourth Horseman, The (1932 Universal) Tom Mix. LOC: California: Iverson Ranch; Universal backlot, Six Points.

Foxfire (1955 Universal) Hume Cronyn. LOC: Arizona: Kingman; Oatman; Grand Canyon National Park.

Frank and Jesse (1994 Trimark Pictures) Robert Lowe. LOC: Arkansas: ArKansas and Missouri Railroad; Chester; Eureka Springs and North ArKansas Railroad; Fayetteville; Fort Smith.

Freckles (1960 20th Century Fox) Martin West. LOC: California: Big Bear.

Freighters of Destiny (1931 RKO) Tom Keene. LOC: California: Iverson Ranch; Jauregui Ranch; Trem Carr Ranch; Lone Pine.

Frenchie (1951 Universal) Joel McCrea. LOC: California: Bishop; Mammoth Lakes.

Friendly Persuasion (1956 Allied Artists) Gary Cooper. LOC: California: M and T Ranch, Butte County; Chico; Oroville.

Frisco Kid (1935 Warner Bros) James Cagney. LOC: California: San Francisco.

Frisco Kid, The (1979 Warner Bros) Gene Wilder. LOC: California: Santa Barbara Mission; Arizona: Mescal; Colorado: Larimer, Weld Counties.

Frisco Sal (1945 Universal) Turhan Bey. LOC: California: French Ranch.

Frisco Tornado (1950 Republic) Allan Lane. LOC: California: Iverson Ranch; Corriganville.

From Broadway to Cheyenne (1932 Monogram) Rex Bell. LOC: California: Trem Carr Ranch.

From Hell to Texas (1958 20th Century Fox) Don Murray. LOC: California: Lone Pine; Dolomite; Mammoth Lakes; Hot Springs.

From Noon Till Three (1976 United Artists) Charles Bronson. LOC: California: Thousand Oaks; Warner Bros. backlot.

Frontier Agent (1948 Monogram) Johnny Mack Brown. LOC: California: Walker Ranch.

Frontier Badmen (1943 Universal) Robert Paige. LOC: California: Walker Ranch; Rancho Placeritos.

Frontier Crusader (1940 PRC) Tim McCoy. LOC: California: Iverson Ranch; Rancho Placeritos.

Frontier Days (1934 Spectrum) Bill Cody. LOC: California: Lone Pine; Universal Studio backlot.

Frontier Days (1945 Warner Bros) Robert Shayne. LOC:

Frontier Feud (1945 Monogram) Johnny Mack Brown. LOC: California: Walker Ranch; Rancho Placeritos.

Frontier Frolic (1946 Universal) Bob Wills. LOC:

Frontier Fugitives (1945 PRC) Texas Rangers. LOC: California: Iverson Ranch; Corriganville.

Frontier Fury (1943 Columbia) Charles Starrett. LOC: California: Walker Ranch.

Frontier Gal (1945 Universal) Yvonne De Carlo. LOC: California: Kernville; Lake Mary; Mammoth Lakes.

Frontier Gambler (1956 Associated Releasing Corp) Kent Taylor. LOC: California: Jauregui Ranch.

Frontier Gun (1958 20th Century Fox) John Agar. LOC: California: 20th Century Fox backlot.

Frontier Gun Law (1946 Columbia) Charles Starrett. LOC:

Frontier Investigator (1949 Republic) Allan Lane. LOC: California: Iverson Ranch.

Frontier Justice (1936 Grand National) Hoot Gibson. LOC: California: Kernville.

Frontier Law (1943 Universal) Russell Hayden. LOC: California: Corriganville.

Frontier Marshal (1934 Fox) George O'Brien. LOST/MISSING.

Frontier Marshal (1939 20th Century Fox) Randolph Scott. LOC: California: Lone Pine; 20th Century Fox Backlot.

Frontier Outlaws (1944 PRC) Buster Crabbe. LOC: California: Corriganville.

Frontier Outpost (1950 Columbia) Charles Starrett. LOC: California: Corriganville.

Frontier Phantom, The (1952 Western Adventure) Lash LaRue. LOC: California: Iverson Ranch.

Frontier Pony Express (1939 Republic) Roy Rogers. LOC: California: Iverson Ranch; Towsley Canyon; Agoura; Republic Studio backlot.

Frontier Revenge (1948 Screen Guild) Lash LaRue. LOC: California: Iverson Ranch; Corriganville.

Frontier Scout (1938 Grand National) George Houston. LOC: California: Kernville.

Frontier Town (1938 Grand National) Tex Ritter. LOC: California: Kernville.

Frontier Uprising (1961 United Artists) Jim Davis. LOC: California: Iverson Ranch.

Frontier Vengeance (1940 Republic) Donald Barry. LOC: California: Iverson Ranch; Burro Flats.

Frontier Woman (1956 Top Pictures) Cindy Carson) Mississippi.

Frontiers of '49 (1939 Columbia) Bill Elliott. LOC: California: Iverson Ranch.

Frontiersmen, The (1938 Paramount) William Boyd. LOC: California: Rancho Placeritos; Tahquitz Lodge; Garner Ranch; Keen Camp; Kernville.

Fugitive from Sonora (1943 Republic) Donald Barry. LOC: California: Iverson Ranch; Corriganville.

Fugitive of the Plains (1943 PRC) Buster Crabbe. LOC: California: Corriganville; Rancho Placeritos.

Fugitive Sheriff, The (1936 Columbia) Ken Maynard. LOC: California: Trem Carr Ranch; Iverson Ranch.

Fugitive Valley (1941 Monogram) Range Busters. LOC: California: Corriganville.

Fugitive, The (1933 Monogram) Rex Bell. LOC: California: Walker Ranch; Jauregui Ranch.

Fugitive, The (1947 RKO) Henry Fonda. LOC: MEXICO: Guerrero: Acapulco; Morelos: Cuernavaca; Taxco; Tepoztlan; Puebla: Cholula; Veracruz: Perote.

Furies, The (1950 Paramount) Barbara Stanwyck. LOC: Arizona: Patagonia; Empire Ranch; High Haven Ranch, Sonoita; Starr Pass.

Further Adventures of the Wilderness Family, The (1978 Pacific International) Robert Logan. LOC: Utah: Uinta National Forest.

Fury and the Woman (1937 Rialto Productions Corp.) William Gargan. LOC: CANADA: Victoria, British Columbia.

Fury at Furnace Creek (1948 20th Century Fox) Victor Mature. LOC: Utah: Hurricane; Johnson Canyon; Johnson Canyon Buffalo Bill fort; Paria; Zion National Park; 20th Century Fox backlot.

Fury at Gunsight Pass (1956 Columbia) David Brian. LOC: California: Vasquez Rocks; Columbia Ranch.

Fury at Showdown (1957 United Artists) John Derek. LOC: California: Iverson Ranch; 20th Century Fox backlot.

Fury in Paradise (1955 Gibraltar) Peter M. Thompson. LOC: MEXICO: Morelos: Hacienda Vista Hermosa, Tequesquitengo.

Fuzzy Settles Down (1944 PRC) Buster Crabbe. LOC: California: Iverson Ranch; Corriganville.

Gal Who Took the West, The (1949 Universal) Yvonne DeCarlo. LOC: California: Calabasas: Clarence Brown Ranch; Pasadena City Hall; Universal Studio backlot; Arizona: Cortaro.

Gallant Defender (1935 Columbia) Charles Starrett. LOC: California: Trem Carr Ranch.

Gallant Fool, The (1933 Monogram) Bob Steele. LOC: California:

Gallant Legion, The (1948 Republic) William Elliott. LOC: California: Iverson Ranch; Bronson Canyon; Vasquez Rocks; Republic Studio backlot.

Galloping Dynamite (1937 Ambassador) Kermit Maynard. LOC: California: Iverson Ranch; Jauregui Ranch; Vasquez Rocks.

Galloping Kid, The (1932 Imperial) Robert Emmett Tansey. LOST/MISSING

Galloping Romeo (1933 Monogram) Bob Steele. LOC: California: Trem Carr Ranch; Lake Sherwood.

Galloping Thru (1931 Monogram) Tom Tyler) LOST/MISSING

Galloping Thunder (1946 Columbia) Charles Starrett. LOC: California: Iverson Ranch; Providencia Ranch; Columbia Ranch.

Gambler from Natchez, The (1954 20th Century Fox) Dale Robertson. LOC: California: L. A. County Arboretum.

Gambler Returns, The: The Luck of the Draw (1991 CBS) Kenny Rogers. LOC: California: Big Sky Ranch; Disney's Golden Oak Ranch.

Gambler V: Playing for Keeps (1994 CBS) Kenny Rogers. LOC: Texas: Alamo Village; Big Bend National Park; Big Bend Ranch State Park; El Camino Del Rio between Lajitas and Presidio; Crow Town/Mexican set; Galveston/The Grand 1894 Opera House; Houston; Lajitas /Mexican set; Mission San José State and National Historic Site San Antonio; Rancho Rio Grande/Moody's Ranch Del Rio; Texas State Railroad; Rusk-Palestine; Uvalde; Villa de la Mina Terlingua.

Gambler Wore a Gun, The (1961 United Artists) Jim Davis. LOC: California: Iverson Ranch; Corriganville.

Gambler, the Girl and the Gunslinger, The (2009 The Hallmark Channel) Dean Cain. LOC: CANADA: British Columbia: Vancouver.

Gambling Terror, The (1937 Republic) Johnny Mack Brown. LOC: California: Iverson Ranch; Walker Ranch; Ralph M. Like Studio backlot.

Gangs of Sonora (1941 Republic) Three Mesquiteers. LOC: California: Iverson Ranch; Rancho Placeritos; Burro Flats.

Gangster's Den (1945 PRC) Buster Crabbe. LOC: California: Corriganville.

Gangsters of the Frontier (1944 PRC) Tex Ritter. LOC: California: Corriganville.

Garden of Evil (1954 20th Century Fox) Gary Cooper. LOC: MEXICO: Guanajuato: Cerro de la Bufa; Cerro del Hormiguero; Marfil; Church of San Jose and Senor Santiago; Guerrero: Los Concheros River; Michoacan: Rio Cupatitzio; San Juan Parangaricutiro, near Paricutin Volcano, Uruapan; Morelos: Tepoztlan.

Gas House Kids Go West (1947 Pathe) Carl Alfalfa Switzer. LOC: California: Hidden Valley ranch; Forest Lawn Drive, Burbank.

Gatling Gun, The (1972 Ellman Enterprises) Guy Stockwell. LOC: New Mexico:

Abiquiu Ghost Ranch; J. W. Eaves Ranch, Santa Fe.

Gaucho Serenade (1940 Republic) Gene Autry. LOC: California: Idllywild; Lake Hemet; Fillmore to Valencia Railroad; Republic Studio backlot.

Gauchos of El Dorado (1941 Republic) Three Mesquiteers. LOC: California: Iverson Ranch; Corriganville; Walker Ranch; Kernville.

Gay Amigo, The (1949 United Artists) Duncan Renaldo. LOC: California: Iverson Ranch; Rancho Placeritos.

Gay Buckaroo, The (1932 Allied) Hoot Gibson. LOC: California: Walker Ranch; Jauregui Ranch; Lake Sherwood.

Gay Caballero, The (1932 Fox) George O'Brien) LOST/MISSING

Gay Caballero, The (1940 20th Century Fox) Cesar Romero. LOC: California: Lone Pine; Anchor Ranch; 20th Century Fox backlot.

Gay Cavalier, The (1946 Monogram) Gilbert Roland. LOC: California: Iverson Ranch.

Gay Desperado, The (1936 United Artists) Ida Lupino. LOC: Arizona: Tucson; Saguaro National Monument; San Xavier Del Bac Mission.

Gay Ranchero, The (1948 Republic) Roy Rogers. LOC: California: Walker Ranch; Conejo Airport; Janss Conejo Ranch; Republic Studio backlot.

Gene Autry and the Mounties (1951 Columbia) Gene Autry. LOC: California: Corriganville; Cedar Lake; Big Bear; Columbia Ranch.

General Spanky (1936 MGM) Spanky McFarland. LOC: California: Hal Roach Ranch; Sacramento River; MGM backlot.

General Sutter (1999 Fasnacht & Partner AG) Hannes Schmidhauser. Arizona; California: Coloma; Los Angeles; Pasadena; Yosemite National Park; Idaho: Yellowstone National Park; Nevada; Oregon; GERMANY: Kandern, Baden-Württemberg; SWITZERLAND: Basel Kanton Basel Stadt; Bergün Kanton Graubünden; Burgdorf Kanton Bern; Liestal Kanton Basel Land; Riehen Kanton Basel Stadt; Rünenberg Kanton Basel Land; Sissach Kanton Basel Land.

Gentle Annie (1944 MGM) Marjorie Main. LOC: California: Agoura Ranch; MGM backlot.

Gentleman from Arizona, The (1939 Monogram) John King. LOC: Arizona: Phoenix; Gila Bend.

Gentleman from California, The (see **The Californian**) (1937 Principal) Ricardo Cortez. LOC: California: French Ranch; Rancho Placeritos.

Gentleman from Texas, The (1946 Monogram) Johnny Mack Brown. LOC: California: Rancho Placeritos.

Gentlemen with Guns (1946 PRC) Buster Crabbe. LOC: California: Corriganville.

George Washington (1984 MGM/UA Television) Barry Bostwick. Pennsylvania: Philadellphia: Independence National Historick Park, Mount Pleasant Mansion, Fairmount Park; Valley Forge National Historical Park; Virginia: Colonial Williamsburg; Fort Belvoir.

Geronimo (1940 Paramount) Preston Foster. LOC: California: Iverson Ranch;

Paramount Ranch; Texas: Fort Bliss.

Geronimo (1962 United Artists) Chuck Connors. LOC: MEXICO: Durango: Ex Hacienda de Tapias; Gomez Palacio; Zacatecas: Sierra de Organos.

Geronimo (1993 TNT) Joseph Runningfox. LOC: Arizona: Chiricahua MountainsLazy K Ranch CortaroOld TucsonSabino CanyonSanta Rita Mountains.

Geronimo: An American Legend (1993 Geronimo Columbia Pictures) Gene Hackman. LOC: New Mexico: J.W. Eaves Ranch/Mexican set Santa Fe; Utah: Professor Valley, Onion Creek Moab; Dead Horse State Park, Shafer Trail Moab; Potash Moab; Needles Overlook; Bates Ranch; Lawson Ranch; Ruby Ranch Road area.

Getaway, The (1972 National General) Steve McQueen. LOC: Texas: El Paso; San Antonio; San Marcos; New Braunfels; Alabama: Huntsville.

Gettysburg (1993 TNT) Martin Sheen) Pennsylvania: Adams CountyCashtownGettysburg National Military ParkYingling Farm.

Ghost City (1932 Monogram) Bill Cody. LOC: California: Trem Carr Ranch.

Ghost Guns (1944 Monogram) Johnny Mack Brown. LOC: California: Iverson Ranch; Walker Ranch.

Ghost of Crossbones Canyon, The (1952 Monogram) Guy Madison. LOC: California: Iverson Ranch; Rancho Placeritos.

Ghost of Hidden Valley (1946 PRC) Buster Crabbe. LOC: California: Rancho Placeritos; Walker Ranch.

Ghost of Zorro (1949 Republic) Clayton Moore. LOC: California: Iverson Ranch; Republic Studio backlot.

Ghost Patrol (1936 Puritan) Tim McCoy. LOC: California: Brandeis Ranch.

Ghost Rider, The (1935 Superior) Rex Lease. LOC: California: Iverson Ranch.

Ghost Rider, The (1943 Monogram) Johnny Mack Brown. LOC: California: Walker Ranch.

Ghost Rock (2004 Lions Gate Films) Gary Busey. LOC: Arizona: MescalOld Tucson/Phillips Ranch.

Ghost Town (1936 Commodore) Harry Carey. LOC: California: Brandeis Ranch; Ralph M. Like Studio backlot.

Ghost Town (1956 United Artists) Kent Taylor. LOC: California: Utah: Johnson Canyon; The Gap.

Ghost Town (1988 Empire/Trans World Ent.) Franc Luz. LOC: Arizona: Mescal.

Ghost Town Gold (1936 Republic) Three Mesquiteers. LOC: California: Iverson Ranch; Brandeis Ranch; Republic Studio backlot.

Ghost Town Law (1942 Monogram) Rough Riders. LOC: California: Walker Ranch; Rancho Placeritos.

Ghost Town Renegades (1947 PRC) Lash LaRue. LOC: California: Iverson Ranch; Rancho Placeritos.

Ghost Town Riders (1938 Universal) Bob Baker. LOC: California: Iverson Ranch; Brandeis Ranch.

Ghost Town: The Movie (2008 Lions Gate Films/Fireshoe Productions) Herbert Cowboy Coward. LOC: North Carolina: Canton; Cherokee; Harmon Den; Ghost Town in the Sky Theme Park, Maggie Valley.

Ghost Valley (1932 RKO) Tom Keene. LOC: California: Hornitos; Paramount Ranch; Bronson Canyon.

Ghost Valley Raiders (1940 Republic) Donald Barry. LOC: California: Iverson Ranch; Corriganville; Republic Studio backlot.

Giant (1956 Warner Bros) James Dean. LOC: California: Statler Hotel, Los Angeles; Texas: Evans Ranch, Marfa; Valentine; Virginia: near Charlottesville.

Giant from the Unknown (1958 Astor) Ed Kemmer. LOC: California: Big Bear; Cedar Lake; Fawnskin.

Giant of Thunder Mountain, The (1991 American Happenings) Jack Elam. LOC: California: Yosemite National Park.

Ginger Snaps Back: The Beginning (2004 Lions Gate Films) Katharine Isabelle. LOC: CANADA: Alberta: Fort Edmonton Park.

Girl and the Gambler, The (1939 RKO) Tim Holt. LOC: California: Vasquez Rocks.

Girl Crazy (1932 RKO) Wheeler & Woolsey. LOC: California: RKO Encino Ranch.

Girl Crazy (1943 MGM) Mickey Rooney. LOC: California: Palm Springs area.

Girl from Alaska, The (1942 Republic) Ray Middleton. LOC: California: Mammoth Lakes.

Girl from God's Country (1940 Republic) Chester Morris. LOC: California: Mammoth Lakes.

Girl from Gunsight, The (1949 Universal) Tex Williams. LOST/MISSING/UNAVAILABLE.

Girl from San Lorenzo, The (1950 United Artists) Duncan Renaldo. LOC: California: Pioneertown.

Girl in the Woods (1958 Republic) Forrest Tucker) Pacific Northwest.

Girl of the Golden West, The (1930 First National) Ann Harding. LOC:

Girl of the Golden West, The (1938 MGM) Jeanette MacDonald. LOC: California: Saddle Rock Ranch.

Girl of the Ozarks (1936 Paramount) Leif Erickson. LOC: California: Paramount Ranch; Big Bear; Cedar Lake; I. S. Ranch, Big Bear Valley.

Girl of the Rio (1932 RKO) Dolores Del Rio. LOC:

Girl Rush (1944 RKO) Wally Brown. LOC: California: Corriganville; RKO Encino Ranch.

Girl Trouble (1933 Karmel) Jack Perrin. LOC: California: Trem Carr Ranch.

Git Along Little Doggies (1937 Republic) Gene Autry. LOC: California: Kernville; Iverson Ranch; Republic Studios backlot.

Glory (1989 TriStar Pictures) Denzel Washington) Georgia: Jeckyll Island; Savannah; Massachusetts: Boston: African-American National Historic Site; Ipswich: Appleton Farm; Sturbridge: Old Sturbridge Village.

Glory Glory (2000 Peakviewing Productions/Tanmarsh Communications) Amanda Donohoe. South Africa: GautengJohannesburg.

Glory Guys, The (1965 United Artists) Tom Tryon. LOC: California: Paramount Studios Western Street; MEXICO: Durango: Casa Blanca; Rancho Marley.

Glory Trail, The (1936 Crescent) Tom Keene. LOC: California: Iverson Ranch.

Go West (1925 MGM) Buster Keaton. LOC: California: Downtown Los Angeles; Santa Fe Depot; Metro Studio backlot; Arizona: Tap Duncan's Valley Ranch, Kingman; Hackberry.

Go West (1940 MGM) The Marx Brothers. LOC: California: Tuolumne County; Red Rock Canyon; MGM backlot.

Go West, Young Girl (1978 Columbia-TV) Karen Valentine. LOC: Arizona: Old Tucson; Sabino Canyon.

Go West, Young Lady (1941 Columbia) Glenn Ford. LOC: California: Iverson Ranch; Columbia Ranch.

God's Country (1946 Screen Guild) Robert Lowery. LOC: California: Benbow Lake, Garberville; Humboldt County.

God's Country and the Man (1931 Syndicate) Tom Tyler. LOC: California: Trem Carr Ranch.

God's Country and the Man (1937 Monogram) Tom Keene. LOC: California: Mammoth Lakes.

God's Country and the Woman (1937 Warner Bros) George Brent. LOC: Washington: Mt. St. Helens; Spirit Lake; Longview.

Godchild, The (1974 MGM-TV) Jack Palance. LOC: California: Vasquez Rocks; Red Rock Canyon; Arizona: Old Tucson.

Gods and Generals (2003 TNT) Robert Duvall. LOC: Maryland: Antietam Battlefield Sharpsburg; Baltimore: Hagerstown; Middletown; Virginia: Leesburg: Lexington Virginia Military Institute; Washington & Lee University; Staunton; Winchester; West Virginia: Harper's Ferry.

Goin' South (1978 Paramount) Jack Nicholson. LOC: MEXICO: Durango: La Joya Ranch; Rancho Marley.

Gold (1932 Majestic) Jack Hoxie. LOC: California: Walker Ranch; Trem Carr Ranch.

Gold Ghost, The (1934 Educational) Buster Keaton. LOC: California: Trem Carr Ranch.

Gold is Where You Find It (1938 Warner Bros) George Brent. LOC: California: Weaverville.

Gold is Where You Lose It (1944 Columbia) Andy Clyde. LOC:

Gold Mine in the Sky (1938 Republic) Gene Autry. LOC: California: Lake Hemet; Idyllwild; Keen Camp; Garner Ranch; Lang Train Depot; Republic Studio backlot.

Gold of the Seven Saints (1961 Warner Bros) Clint Walker. LOC: California: Warner Bros. Backlot; Utah: Fisher Towers; Professor Valley; Arches National Park;

Dead Horse Point State Park.

Gold Raiders (1951 United Artists) George O'Brien. LOC: California: Iverson Ranch.

Gold Strike (1950 Universal) Tex Williams. LOC:

Golden Girl (1951 20th Century Fox) Mitzi Gaynor. LOC: California: 20th Century Fox backlot.

Golden Stallion, The (1949 Republic) Roy Rogers. LOC: California: Iverson Ranch; Jauregui Ranch; Republic Studio backlot.

Golden Trail, The (1940 Monogram) Tex Ritter. LOC: California: Rancho Placeritos; Vasquez Rocks.

Golden West, The (1932 Fox) George O'Brien. LOC: California: Vasquez Rocks; Arizona: Kohl Ranch, Payson; Sedona.

Goldrush: A Real Life Alaskan Adventure (1998 Walt Disney) Alyssa Milano. LOC: CANADA: British Columbia: Vancouver.

Goldtown Ghost Raiders (1953 Columbia) Gene Autry. LOC: California: Lone Pine; Anchor Ranch; Columbia Ranch.

Gone with the West (1975 International Cine) James Caan. LOC: California: Monogram Studio backlot; Vasquez Rocks.

Gone with the Wind (1939 Selznick) Clark Gable. LOC: California: Chico; Lasky Mesa; RKO 40 acres; Big Bear; Busch Gardens.

Good Day for a Hanging (1959 Columbia) Fred MacMurray. LOC: California: Tuolumne County; Columbia Ranch.

Good Day to Die, A (1995 CBS) Sidney Poitiers. LOC: CANADA: Alberta: Stoney Indian Reserve.

Good Guys and the Bad Guys, The (1969 Warner Bros) Robert Mitchum. LOC: New Mexico: Chama; Cumbres and Toltec Scenic Railroad.

Good Morning Sheriff (1930 Educational) Lloyd Hamilton. LOC: California: Chatsworth; possibly Universal Studio backlot.

Good Night For Justice (2011 Hallmark Channel) Luke Perry. LOC: CANADA: Bordertown, British Columbia.

Good Old Boys, The (1995 TNT) Tommy Lee Jones. LOC: Texas: Alamo Village Brackettville; CF Ranch Alpine; Fort Davis National Park; Rancho Rio Grande /Moody's Ranch/Western town and Pinto Creek Del Rio.

Goofs and Saddles (1937 Columbia) Three Stooges. LOC: California: Providencia Ranch.

Gordon of Ghost City (1933 Universal) Buck Jones. LOC: California: Bronson Canyon; Bodie; Universal Studio backlot.

Gore Vidal's Billy the Kid (1989 Von Zerneck Sertner Films Productions) Val Kilmer. LOC: Arizona: Old TucsonHelvetia ghost townSedona Red Rock Crossing.

Grand Canyon (1949 Screen Guild) Richard Arlen. LOC: Arizona: Grand Canyon National Park.

Grand Canyon Trail (1948 Republic) Roy Rogers. LOC: California: Iverson Ranch;

Red Rock Canyon; Griffith Park; Republic Studio backlot.

Grand Duel, The (1972 Corona) Lee Van Cleef. ITALY.

Great Adventure, The (1976 Pacific International) Jack Palance. LOC: SPAIN: Daganzo, Madrid; MEXICO: Avandaro, Valle de Bravo, Estado de México.

Great Adventures of Wild Bill Hickock, The (1938 Columbia) Bill Elliott. LOC: California: Bronson Canyon; Big Bear; Columbia Ranch; Utah: Eagle Gate, Cave Lake, Three Lakes, Kanab.

Great Alaskan Mystery, The (1944 Universal) Milburn Stone. LOC: California: Iverson Ranch; Lewis Mansion; Universal Studio backlot.

Great American Cowboy, The (1974 American National Ent) Phil Lyne. LOC: Wyoming: Cheyenne.

Great Bank Robbery, The (1969 Warner Bros) Clint Walker. LOC: California: Tuolumne County; Jamestown; Red Hills.

Great Day in the Morning (1956 RKO) Robert Stack. LOC: Colorado: Silverton; Molas Pass.

Great Divide, The (1929 First National) Ian Keith. LOC: Utah: Grafton.

Great Gundown, The (1977 AVCO Embassy) Robert Padilla. LOC: New Mexico: Chama.

Great Jesse James Raid, The (1953 Lippert) Willard Parker. LOC: California: Bronson Canyon; Rancho Placeritos.

Great Locomotive Chase, The (1956 Buena Vista) Fess Parker) Georgia: Tallulah Falls Railway, Clayton.

Great Man's Lady, The (1942 Paramount) Joel McCrea. LOC: California: Joel McCrea's Ranch, Thousand Oaks; 225 N Lima St, Sierra Madre; Paramount Ranch.

Great Meadow, The (1931 MGM) Johnny Mack Brown. LOC: California: Lake Sherwood; Russell Ranch; Tuolumne County.

Great Missouri Raid, The (1951 Paramount) Wendell Corey. LOC: California: Jamestown, Tuolumne County.

Great Northfield, Minnesota Raid, The (1971 Universal) Cliff Robertson. LOC: Oregon: Jacksonville.

Great Scout and Cathouse Thursday, The (1976 American International) Lee Marvin. LOC: MEXICO: Durango: Villa del Oeste.

Great Sioux Massacre, The (1965 Columbia) Joseph Cotton. LOC: Arizona: Old Tucson; Vail.

Great Sioux Uprising, The (1953 Universal) Jeff Chandler. LOC: Oregon: Pendleton; Umatilla Indian Reservation.

Great Stagecoach Robbery (1945 Republic) Bill Elliott. LOC: California: Iverson Ranch.

Great Train Robbery, The (1941 Republic) Bob Steele. LOC: California: Iverson Ranch; Red Rock Canyon; Tuolumne County; O'Neil Reservoir; Jamestown.

Green Grass of Wyoming (1948 20th Century Fox) Robert Arthur. LOC: Utah:

MacDonald Ranch, Glendale; Kanab; Duck Creek; Strawberry Valley; Panguitch Lake; Smithsonian Butte area above Grafton.

Grey Owl (1999 Buena Vista) Pierce Brosnan. LOC: CANADA: Quebec: Wakefield.

Greyeagle (1977 American International) Ben Johnson. LOC: Montana: Gates of the Mountain; Helena.

Grim Prairie Tales: Hit the Trail...to Terror (1990 East-West Film Partners) James Earl Jones. LOC:

Grizzly (1976 Film Ventures Intl) Christopher George. LOC:

Grizzly Adams and the Legend of Dark Mountain (1999 Joda Productions/Sheldon/Post Company) Tom Tayback. LOC:

Grizzly and the Treasure, The (1974 Gold Key) Andrew Gordon. LOC:

Grizzly Mountain (1997 Mega Communications/Napor Kids) Dan Haggerty. LOC: Oregon: Eugene: Grants Pass.

Groom Wore Spurs, The (1951 Universal) Ginger Rogers. LOC: California: Neil McCarthy estate, Hidden Valley.

Guardian of the Wilderness (1977 Sunn Classics) Denver Pyle. LOC: California: Yosemite National Park; Utah: Capitol, Kamas, Park City.

Guilty Trails (1938 Universal) Bob Baker. LOC: California: Walker Ranch; Jauregui Ranch; Rancho Placeritos.

Gun and the Pulpit, The (1974 ABC TV) Marjoe Gortner. LOC: Arizona: Old Tucson; Mescal.

Gun Battle at Monterey (1957 Allied Artists) Sterling Hayden. LOC: California: Red Rock Canyon.

Gun Belt (1953 United Artists) George Montgomery. LOC: California: Iverson Ranch; Agoura Ranch; Columbia Ranch.

Gun Brothers (1956 United Artists) Buster Crabbe. LOC: California: Corriganville.

Gun Code (1940 PRC) Tim McCoy. LOC: California: Iverson Ranch; Rancho Placeritos.

Gun Duel in Durango (1957 United Artists) George Montgomery. LOC: California: Iverson Ranch; Corriganville.

Gun Fever (1958 United Artists) Mark Stevens. LOC: California: Iverson Ranch; Ingram Ranch; Berry/Bell Ranch.

Gun Fight (1961 United Artists) James Brown. LOC: California: Iverson Ranch; Corriganville; probably San Gabriel Mountains.

Gun for a Coward (1957 Universal) Fred MacMurray. LOC: California: Universal Studio backlot; Vasquez Rocks.

Gun Fury (1953 Columbia) Rock Hudson. LOC: Arizona: Sedona.

Gun Glory (1957 MGM) Stewart Granger. LOC: California: Bronson Canyon; Garberville; MGM backlot.

Gun Grit (1936 Atlantic) Jack Perrin. LOC: California: Brandeis Ranch; Ralph M. Like Studio north entrance; 1504 N. Commonwealth Ave.; Chatsworth Train Station.

Gun Hawk, The (1963 Allied Artists) Rory Calhoun. LOC: California: Bronson Canyon; Republic Studio backlot.

Gun Justice (1933 Universal) Ken Maynard. LOC: California: Kernville.

Gun Law (1933 Majestic) Jack Hoxie. LOC: California: Iverson Ranch; Frank LaSalle Ranch; Frank Straubinger Ranch.

Gun Law (1938 RKO) George O'Brien. LOC: California: Corriganville; Cougar Buttes area, Luzerne Valley.

Gun Law Justice (1949 Monogram) Jimmy Wakely. LOC: California: Walker Ranch.

Gun Lords of Stirrup Basin (1937 Republic) Bob Steele. LOC: California: Walker Ranch; Jauregui Ranch; Ralph M. Like Studio backlot.

Gun Packer (1938 Monogram) Jack Randall. LOC: California: Kernville.

Gun Play (1935 Beacon) Big Boy Williams. LOC: California: Agoura.

Gun Ranger, The (1936 Republic) Bob Steele. LOC: California: Ralph M. Like Studio backlot; Walker Ranch; Jauregui Ranch.

Gun Riders, The (1969 Independent International) Scott Brady. LOC: Utah: Kanab.

Gun Runner (1949 Monogram) Jimmy Wakely. LOC: California: Walker Ranch.

Gun Smoke (1931 Paramount) Richard Arlen. LOC: California: Paramount Ranch; Bronson Canyon; Northridge Train Station.

Gun Smoke (1945 Monogram) Richard Arlen. LOC: California: Iverson Ranch; Walker Ranch.

Gun Smugglers (1948 RKO) Tim Holt. LOC: California: Lone Pine.

Gun Street (1961 United Artists) James Brown. LOC: California: Iverson Ranch; Corriganville.

Gun Talk (1947 Monogram) Johnny Mack Brown. LOC: California: Iverson Ranch.

Gun That Won the West, The (1955 Columbia) Dennis Morgan. LOC: California: Iverson Ranch.

Gun the Man Down (1956 United Artists) James Arness. LOC: California: Ingram Ranch.

Gun to Gun (1944 Warner Bros) Robert Shayne. LOC:

Gun Town (1946 Universal) Kirby Grant. LOC: California: Iverson Ranch; Red Rock Canyon.

Gundown at Sandoval (1963 Buena Vista) Tom Tryon. LOC: California: Disney Studio backlot; Texas: Frio Town.

Gundown, The (2009 Silver Bullet Film) Peter Coyote. LOC: Arizona: Gammons Gulch Benson.

Gunfight at Black Horse Canyon (1962 Revue) Dale Robertson. LOC: California: Vasquez Rocks.

Gunfight at Comanche Creek (1963 Allied Artists) Audie Murphy. LOC: California: Iverson Ranch; Paramount Studio backlot.

Gunfight at Dodge City, The (1959 United Artists) Joel McCrea. LOC: California:

Corriganville; Rancho Placeritos; Tuolumne County.

Gunfight at La Mesa (2010 Lions Gate Films) Dan Braun. LOC: New Mexico: La MesaLas CrucesMesilla.

Gunfight at the O.K. Corral (1957 Paramount) Burt Lancaster. LOC: California: Paramount Studio backlot; Arizona: Quarter Circle U Ranch; Old Tucson; Elgin; Sonoita; Rio Rico.

Gunfight in Abilene (1967 Universal) Bobby Darrin. LOC: California: Universal Studio backlot.

Gunfight, A (1971 Paramount) Kirk Douglas. LOC: New Mexico: J. W. Eaves Ranch.

Gunfighter (1998 Plaster City Productions) Martin Sheen. LOC: Nevada: Elko-Lovelock.

Gunfighter, The (1950 20th Century Fox) Gregory Peck. LOC: California: Lone Pine; Olancha Sand Dunes; Century Ranch; 20th Century Fox Studio backlot.

Gunfighter's Moon (1995 Rysher Entertainment) Lance Henriksen. LOC: CANADA: British Columbia: Vancouver: Maple Ridge: Bordertown.

Gunfighter's Pledge, A (2008 The Hallmark Channel) Luke Perry. LOC: California: Big Sky Ranch; Sable Ranch.

Gunfighters of Abilene (1960 United Artists) Buster Crabbe. LOC: California: Iverson Ranch; Rancho Placeritos.

Gunfighters of the Northwest (1953 Columbia) Jock Mahoney. LOC: California: Cedar Lake.

Gunfighters, The (1947 Columbia) Randolph Scott. LOC: California: Columbia Ranch; Jauregui Ranch; Rancho Placeritos; Vasquez Rocks; Arizona: Sedona.

Gunfighters, The (1987 Columbia TriStar/Jeff King Productions) George Kennedy. LOC: CANADA: Alberta.

Gunfire (1935 Resolute) Rex Bell. LOC: California: Brandeis Ranch; Trem Carr Ranch.

Gunfire (1950 Lippert) Donald Barry. LOC: California: Iverson Ranch; Rancho Placeritos; Vasquez Rocks.

Gunfire at Indian Gap (1958 Republic) Vera Ralston. LOC: California: Lone Pine.

Gunless (2010 Alliance Films) Sienna Guillory. LOC: CANADA: British Columbia: Fort Langley National Historic Site; Elkink Ranch.

Gunman from Bodie, The (1941 Monogram) Rough Riders. LOC: California: Jauregui Ranch; Rancho Placeritos.

Gunman, The (1952 Monogram) Whip Wilson. LOC: California: Iverson Ranch.

Gunman's Code (1946 Universal) Kirby Grant. LOC: California: Iverson Ranch.

Gunman's Walk (1958 Columbia) Van Heflin. LOC: California: Columbia Ranch; Arizona: Sonoita; Rain Valley; Patagonia; Elgin; San Rafael Valley.

Gunmen from Laredo (1959 Columbia) Jim Davis. LOC: California: Corriganville; Columbia Ranch; Bronson Canyon; Iverson Ranch.

Gunmen of Abilene (1950 Republic) Allan Lane. LOC: California: Iverson Ranch.

Gunning for Justice (1948 Monogram) Johnny Mack Brown. LOC: California: Walker Ranch.

Gunning for Vengeance (1946 Columbia) Charles Starrett. LOC: California: Iverson Ranch; Columbia Ranch.

Gun Play (1935 Beacon Productions) Guinn Big Boy Williams. LOC: California: Agoura Ranch.

Gunplay (1951 RKO) Tim Holt. LOC: California: Iverson Ranch; Jauregui Ranch.

Gunpoint (1966 Universal) Audie Murphy. LOC: California: Universal Studio backlot; Bell Location Ranch; Utah: Snow Canyon; St. George; Silver Reef.

Guns Along the Bravo (2001 Skeleton Creek Productions) Rick Simpson. LOC: New Mexico: J.W. Eaves Ranch Santa Fe.

Guns and Guitars (1936 Republic) Gene Autry. LOC: California: Garner Ranch.

Guns for San Sebastian (1968 MGM) Anthony Quinn. LOC: MEXICO: Durango: Chupaderos; El Saltito waterfall; Gomez Palacio; Rancho Marley; Guanajuato: Atotonilco; San Miguel de Allende; Zacatecas: Sierra de Organos.

Guns in the Dark (1937 Republic) Johnny Mack Brown. LOC: California: Brandeis Ranch; Rancho Placeritos.

Guns of a Stranger (1973 Universal) Marty Robbins. LOC: Arizona: Old Tucson.

Guns of Diablo (1964 MGM-TV) Charles Bronson. LOC: California: MGM backlot.

Guns of Fort Petticoat, The (1957 Columbia) Audie Murphy. LOC: California: Iverson Ranch; Arizona: Amado; Old Tucson.

Guns of Hate (1948 RKO) Tim Holt. LOC: California: Lone Pine; RKO Encino Ranch.

Guns of Honor (1994 TuckerGurl) Martin Sheen) South Africa: GautengMagaliesberg.

Guns of the Law (1944 PRC) Texas Rangers. LOC: California: Corriganville.

Guns of the Pecos (1937 Warner Bros) Dick Foran. LOC: California: Iverson Ranch; Jauregui Ranch.

Guns of the Timberland (1960 Warner Bros) Alan Ladd. LOC: California: Plumas County, Quincy; Blairsden Depot; Graeagle; Clio tresle over Williow Creek; Maybe; Vinton; Warner Bros backlot.

Gunsight Ridge (1957 United Artists) Joel McCrea. LOC: California: Janss Conejo Ranch; Bell Ranch; Arizona: Old Tucson; Patagonia; Sonoita.

Gunslinger (1956 American Releasing Corp) John Ireland. LOC: California: Ingram Ranch.

Gunslingers (1950 Monogram) Whip Wilson. LOC: California: Iverson Ranch; Walker Ranch; Rancho Placeritos.

Gunsmoke (1953 Universal) Audie Murphy. LOC: California: Big Bear; Jauregui Ranch; Universal Studio backlot.

Gunsmoke III: To the Last Man (1991 CBS) James Arness. LOC: Arizona: Circle Z Ranch/Sonoita Creek PatagoniaMescalOld TucsonSan Rafael Ranch San Rafael ValleySonoita.

Gunsmoke in Tucson (1958 Allied Artists) Mark Stevens. LOC: California: Iverson Ranch; Rancho Placeritos; Sable Ranch; Arizona: Old Tucson.

Gunsmoke IV: The Long Ride (1993 CBS) James Arness. LOC: New Mexico: Bonanza Creek Ranch Santa FeCook Ranch/Cerro Pelon Ranch GalisteoPuye CliffsSanta Clara PuebloValle Grande.

Gunsmoke Mesa (1944 PRC) Texas Rangers. LOC: California: Corriganville.

Gunsmoke on the Guadalupe (1935 Kent) Rocky Camron. LOC: California: Ralph M. Like Studio backlot.

Gunsmoke Ranch (1937 Republic) Three Mesquiteers. LOC: California: Red Rock Canyon; Lone Pine; Republic Studio backlot.

Gunsmoke Trail (1938 Monogram) Jack Randall. LOC: California: Iverson Ranch; Brandeis Ranch.

Gunsmoke: One Man's Justice (1994 CBS) James Arness. LOC: Arizona: Circle Z Ranch Ranch; Sonoita Creek ; Patagonia; Mescal; Old Tucson.

Gunsmoke: Return to Dodge (1987 CBS) James Arness. LOC: CANADA: Alberta: Calgary; Canmore.

Gunsmoke: The Last Apache (1990 CBS) James Arness. LOC: Texas: Alamo Village Brackettville; Big Bend Ranch State Park; Rancho Rio Grande/Moody's Ranch Del Rio.

Gypsy Colt (1954 MGM) Narrated by Art Baker. LOC: California: Red Rock Canyon; Rosamond Dry Lake; Colorado: Aspen; Grand Junction.

Hail to the Rangers (1943 Columbia) Charles Starrett. LOC: California: Iverson Ranch.

Hair-Trigger Casey (1936 Atlantic) Jack Perrin. LOC: California: Jauregui Ranch; Ralph M. Like Studio backlot; Frank LaSalle Ranch.

Half Way to Hell (1961 Victor Adamson) Al Adamson. LOC: Utah: Capitol Reef National Park.

Half-Breed, The (1952 RKO) Robert Young. LOC: California: RKO Encino Ranch; Arizona: Sedona; Red Rock Crossing.

Half-Pint Molly (1931 Pathe) Tom Tyler. LOC:

Hallelujah Trail, The (1965 United Artists) Burt Lancaster. LOC: Arizona: Lupton; California: Paramount Studio Western Street; New Mexico: Gallup; Fort Russell built 25 miles north of Gallup; Shiprock; Tohatchi.

Halliday Brand, The (1957 United Artists) Joseph Cotton. LOC: California: Iverson Ranch; Rancho Placeritos .

Hands Across the Border (1943 Republic) Roy Rogers. LOC: California: Lone Pine; Republic Studio backlot.

Hands Across the Rockies (1941 Columbia) Bill Elliott. LOC: California: Iverson Ranch; Columbia Ranch.

Hang 'Em High (1968 United Artists) Clint Eastwood. LOC: California: MGM backlot #3; New Mexico: Las Cruces; White Sands National Monument.

Hanged Man, The (1974 ABC-TV) Steve Forrest. LOC: California: Red Rock Canyon; Arizona: Old Tucson; Mescal.

Hanging of Jake Ellis, The (1969 Great Empire Films) Charles Napier. LOC: California: Corriganville.

Hanging Tree, The (1959 Warner Bros) Gary Cooper. LOC: Washington: Yakima; Naches.

Hangman, The (1959 Paramount) Robert Taylor. LOC: Arizona: Old Tucson.

Hangman's Knot (1952 Columbia) Randolph Scott. LOC: California: Iverson Ranch; Corriganville; Lone Pine.

Hannah Lee (1953 Realart) John Ireland. LOC: California: Iverson Ranch.

Hannie Caulder (1971 Paramount) Raquel Welch. LOC: SPAIN: Costa Del Sol; Almeria.

Hard Bounty (1995 Sunset Films International) Matt McCoy. LOC: Arizona: Old Tucson.

Hard Ground (2003 Hallmark Entertainment) Burt Reynolds. LOC: California: Blue Cloud Ranch; Rene Veluzat Ranch; Arizona: Lake Havasu City.

Hard Hombre, The (1931 Allied Artists) Hoot Gibson. LOC: California: California Studio backlot; Vasquez Rocks; Walker Ranch.

Hard Man, The (1957 Columbia) Guy Madison. LOC: California: Corriganville; French Ranch; Columbia Ranch.

Hard on the Trail (1971 Brentwood International) Lash LaRue. LOC: California: Spahn Ranch; Bell Ranch.

Hard Ride, The (2008 Talmarc Productions) Thadd Turner. LOC: New Mexico: Bonanza Creek Ranch Santa Fe.

Hard Rock Harrigan (1935 Fox) George O'Brien. LOC: California: Indio; Parker Dam; Colorado River Aqueduct; Coachella Tunnel.

Hardcase (1972 ABC-TV) Clint Walker. LOC: MEXICO: Morelos: Cuernavaca.

Harlem on the Prairie (1937 Jeb Buell Prod) Herb Jeffries. LOC: California: Iverson Ranch.

Harlem Rides the Range (1939 Hollywood Pictures) Herb Jeffries. LOC: California: Fairview Mountain; N. B. Murray Dude Ranch.

Harmony Trail (1944 Mattox) Ken Maynard. LOC: California: Corriganville.

Harry Tracy – Desperado (1982 IMC/Isram) Bruce Dern. LOC: CANADA: Alberta: Calgary; British Columbia: Mt.Seymour Regional Park;

Harvey Girls, The (1946 MGM) Judy Garland. LOC: California: Iverson Ranch; MGM backlot; Arizona/Utah: Monument Valley.

Haunted Gold (1932 Warner Bros) John Wayne. LOC: California: Providencia Ranch; Warner Bros Studio backlot.

Haunted Mine, The (1946 Monogram) Johnny Mack Brown. LOC: California: Walker Ranch.

Haunted Ranch (1943 Monogram) John King. LOC: California: Jauregui Ranch; Rancho Placeritos.

Haunted Trails (1949 Monogram) Whip Wilson. LOC: California: Iverson Ranch;

Palmdale.

Haunted, The (1977 A. B. Enterprises/International) Aldo Ray. LOC: Arizona: Superstition Mountains; Apache Junction.

Hawaiian Buckaroo (1938 20th Century Fox) Smith Ballew. LOC: California: French Ranch; Russell Ranch.

Hawk of Powder River, The (1948 Eagle Lion) Eddie Dean. LOC: California: Iverson Ranch.

Hawk of the Wilderness (1938 Republic) Bruce Bennett. LOC: California: Iverson Ranch; Lake Sherwood; Bronson Canyon; Mammoth Lakes.

Hawk of Wild River, The (1952 Columbia) Charles Starrett. LOC: California: Iverson Ranch; Columbia Ranch.

Hawken's Breed (1987 Charles B.Pierce/Garrison Productions) Peter Fonda. LOC: Tennessee: Lakes Park area Dover.

Hawkeye (1994 Stephen J.Cannell Productions Western Series) Duncan Fraser. LOC: CANADA: British Columbia: Bordertown/Western town Maple Ridge, VancouverDistrict Watershed, North Vancouver.

Hawmps! (1976 Mulberry Square) James Hampton. LOC: California: Buttercup Valley; Arizona: Old Tucson; Texas Canyon.

He Rides Tall (1964 Universal) Tony Young. LOC: California: Janss Conejo Ranch.

Headin' for Trouble (1931 Big 4) Bob Custer. LOC: California: Jauregui Ranch; Ralph M. Like Studio backlot.

Headin' East (1937 Columbia) Buck Jones. LOC: New York: New York City.

Headin' for the Rio Grande (1936 Grand National) Tex Ritter. LOC: California: Garner Valley; Keen Camp; Ralph M. Like Studio backlot.

Headin' North (1930 Tiffany) Bob Steele. LOC: California.

Heading West (1946 Columbia) Charles Starrett. LOC: California: Iverson Ranch; Columbia Ranch.

Heart of Arizona (1938 Paramount) William Boyd. LOC: California: Lone Pine.

Heart of the Golden West (1942 Republic) Roy Rogers. LOC: California: Jauregui Ranch; Kernville; Mammoth Lakes; Republic Studio backlot.

Heart of the North (1938 Warner Bros) Dick Foran. LOC: California: Big Bear; Cedar Lake; Sequoia National Park.

Heart of the Rio Grande (1942 Republic) Gene Autry. LOC: California: Bronson Canyon; Agoura Ranch; Iverson Ranch; Chatsworth Train Station; Republic Studio backlot.

Heart of the Rockies (1937 Republic) Three Mesquiteers. LOC: California: San Jacinto Mountains; Lake Hemet; Tahquitz Lodge; Tahquitz Mountains.

Heart of the Rockies (1951 Republic) Roy Rogers. LOC: California: Iverson Ranch; Walker Ranch; Republic Studio backlot.

Heart of the West (1936 Paramount) William Boyd. LOC: California: Kernville; Kernville Movie Street.

Heartland (1979 Wilderness Women Prod/Filmhaus) Rip Torn. LOC: Montana: Garneill; Horlowton; White Sulphur Springs.

Hearts and Hoofs (1930 Pathe) Cornelius Keefe. LOC:

Hearts of the West (1975 MGM) Jeff Bridges. LOC: California: Vasquez Rocks; Harold Lloyd Estate; Malibu; various Los Angeles locations; Warner Bros. backlot.

Heathens and Thieves (2012 Orofino) Andrew Simpson. LOC: California: Scott Valley; Yreka.

Heaven Only Knows (1947 United Artists) Robert Cummings. LOC: California: Goldwyn Studio backlot.

Heaven with a Barbed Wire Fence (1939 20th Century Fox) Glenn Ford. LOC: California: Janss Janss Conejo Ranch; Newhall.

Heaven with a Gun (1969 MGM) Glenn Ford. LOC: Arizona: Old Tucson; Patagonia; Sonoita; San Rafael Valley; New Mexico: Santa Fe.

Heaven's Gate (1980 United Artists) Kris Kristofferson. LOC: Idaho: Wallace Northern Pacific Depot - Montana: ButteGlacier National ParkKalispell.

Heir to Trouble (1935 Columbia) Ken Maynard. LOC: California: Iverson Ranch; Kernville.

Heldorado (1946 Republic) Roy Rogers. LOC: California: Iverson Ranch; Chatsworth Train Depot; Republic Studio backlot; Nevada: Las Vegas; Hoover Dam; Lake Mead; Valley of Fire State Park; Red Rock Canyon.

Hell Bent for Leather (1960 Universal) Audie Murphy. LOC: California: Lone Pine; Dolomite; Universal Studio backlot.

Hell Canyon Outlaws (1957 Republic) Dale Robertson. LOC: California: Corriganville.

Hell Fire Austin (1932 Tiffany) Ken Maynard. LOC: California: Lone Pine; Lone Pine Train Depot; Hoot Gibson Rodeo Arena.

Hell to Pay (2005 HTB Productions) James Drury. LOC: California: Disney's Golden Oak Ranch; Sable Ranch; Albertson Ranch/Western town; Janss Janss Conejo Ranch stock footage.

Hell's Heroes (1929 Universal) Charles Bickford. LOC: California: Red Rock Canyon; Bodie; Panamint Valley; Universal Studio backlot.

Hell's Outpost (1954 Republic) Rod Cameron. LOC: California: Iverson Ranch; Towsley Canyon; Republic Studio backlot.

Hell's Valley (1931 Big 4) Wally Wales. LOST/MISSING.

Helldorado (1934 20th Century Fox) Richard Arlen. LOST/MISSING.

Heller in Pink Tights (1960 Paramount) Anthony Quinn. LOC: California: Bronson Canyon; Arizona: Old Tucson; San Xavier Del Bac Mission; Sabino Canyon; Arivaca; Sonoita.

Hellfire (1949 Republic) William Elliott. LOC: California: Iverson Ranch; Arizona: Sedona.

Hellgate (1952 Lippert) Sterling Hayden. LOC: California: Corriganville; Bronson

Canyon.

Hello Trouble (1932 Columbia) Buck Jones. LOC: California: Bronson Canyon.

Hell's Crossroads (1957 Republic) Stephen McNalley. LOC: California: Iverson Ranch; Republic Studio backlot.

Here Comes the Cavalry (1941 Warner Bros) Richard Travis. LOC: Texas: Fort Bliss.

Heritage of the Desert (1932 Paramount) Randolph Scott. LOC: California: Paramount Ranch; Red Rock Canyon.

Heritage of the Desert (1939 Paramount) Donald Woods. LOC: California: Kernville.

Heroes of the Alamo (1937 Columbia) Rex Lease. LOC: California: Rancho Placeritos; Walker Ranch.

Heroes of the Hills (1938 Republic) Three Mesquiteers. LOC: California: Brandeis Ranch; Corriganville; Lang Train Station; Republic Studio backlot.

Heroes of the Range (1936 Columbia) Ken Maynard. LOC: California: Trem Carr Ranch; Kernville.

Heroes of the Saddle (1940 Republic) Three Mesquiteers. LOC: California: Iverson Ranch; Agoura Ranch; Republic Studio backlot.

Heroes of the West (1932 Universal) Noah Beery, Jr. LOC: California: Agoura Ranch; Bronson Canyon; Universal Studio backlot.

Hi, Gaucho! (1935 RKO) John Carroll. LOC: California: Holman Ranch, Calabasas; RKO Encino Ranch.

Hiawatha (1952 United Artists) Vince Edwards. LOC: California: Madera County.

Hiawatha (1984 CBS International) Yvonne Bryceland. LOC:

Hidalgo (2004 Buena Vista) Viggo Mortensen. LOC: California: Cuddeback Dry Lake/Ridgecrest; Dumont Dunes; Oklahoma: Blackjack Mountain; South Dakota: Buffalo Gap/Black Hills National Forest; Hot Spring/Black Hills National Forest; Montana: Blackfeet Indian Reservation; Browning; Kalispell Glacier National Park; MOROCCO.

Hidden Danger (1948 Monogram) Johnny Mack Brown. LOC: California: Rancho Placeritos.

Hidden Gold (1932 Universal) Tom Mix. LOC: California: Garner Ranch; Lake Hemet.

Hidden Gold (1940 Paramount) William Boyd. LOC: California: Rancho Placeritos; Lake Sherwood; Kernville.

Hidden Guns (1956 Republic) Richard Arlen. LOC: California: Corriganville; Ingram Ranch.

Hidden Valley (1932 Monogram) Bob Steele. LOC: California: Lone Pine.

Hidden Valley Days (1948 Universal) Red River Dave. LOST/MISSING. LOC: Texas: San Antonio.

Hidden Valley Outlaws (1944 Republic) Bill Elliott. LOC: California: Iverson Ranch; Corriganville; Republic Studio backlot.

High Country, The (1981 CFDC) Timothy Bottoms. LOC: CANADA: Alberta: Banff National Park; Canmore; British Columbia: Invermere.

High Hell (1958 Paramount) John Derek. LOC: SWITZERLAND: Bern; Jungfrau.

High Lonesome (1950 Eagle Lion) John Barrymore, Jr. LOC: Texas: Antelope Springs; Brite Ranch; Capote Mountains near Marfa.

High Noon (1952 Columbia United Artists) Gary Cooper. LOC: California: Iverson Ranch; Columbia Ranch; Columbia and Tuolumne City, Tuolumne County; Warnerville.

High Noon (2000 Rosemont Productions/TBS Superstation) Tom Skerritt. LOC: CANADA: Alberta: CL Ranch Calgary.

High Noon, Part II: The Return of Will Kane (1980 CBS) Lee Majors. LOC: Arizona: Old Tucson - California: Tuolumne County.

High Plains Drifter (1973 Universal) Clint Eastwood. LOC: California: Mono Lake.

High Plains Invaders (2009 Castel Film Romania) Costantin Barbulescu. LOC: ROMANIA.

Hills of Oklahoma (1950 Republic) Rex Allen. LOC: California: Iverson Ranch; Republic Studio backlot.

Hills of Old Wyoming (1937 Paramount) William Boyd. LOC: California: Kernville.

Hills of Utah (1951 Columbia) Gene Autry. LOC: California: Iverson Ranch; Agoura Ranch; Corriganville.

Hills Run Red, The (1966 Dino De Laurentiis) Thomas Hunter. LOC: ITALY: Dinocitta; SPAIN: Madrid: Colmenar Viejo, La Pedria, Manzanares el Real.

Hi-Lo Country, The (1998 Universal Pictures) Woody Harrelson. LOC: New Mexico: Cook Ranch/Cerro Pelon Ranch Galisteo; Española; Las Vegas; San José.

Hired Gun, The (1957 MGM) Rory Calhoun. LOC: California: Lone Pine; MGM backlot.

Hired Gun, The (1961 Joseph Brenner Assoc.) Don Borisenko. LOC: CANADA: Ontario: Klienberg.

Hired Hand, The (1971 Universal) Peter Fonda. LOC: New Mexico: Cabezón; Chama; White Sands National Monument.

His Big Minute (1929 Educational) Lloyd Hamilton. LOC:

His Brother's Ghost (1945 PRC) Buster Crabbe. LOC: California: Corriganville.

His Fighting Blood (1935 Ambassador) Kermit Maynard. LOC: California: Big Bear.

Hit the Saddle (1937 Republic) Three Mesquiteers. LOC: California: Iverson Ranch; Brandeis Ranch; Red Rock Canyon; Republic Studio backlot.

Hittin' the Trail (1937 Grand National) Tex Ritter. LOC: California: Kernville; Kernville Movie Street.

Hi-Yo Silver (1940 Republic) Lee Powell. LOC: California: Iverson Ranch; Lone Pine.

Hoedown (1950 Columbia) Eddy Arnold. LOC: California: Columbia Ranch.

Hold 'er Sheriff (1931 Mack Sennett) Marjorie Beebe. LOC:

Hollister (1989 CBS) Brian Bloom. LOC: New Mexico: Abiquiú Ghost Ranch; Bonanza Creek Ranch; Carson National Forest near Abiquiú; Chama; Cook Ranch/Cerro Pelon Ranch; Cumbres and Toltec Scenic Railroad; J.W. Eaves Movie Ranch; Santa Clara Pueblo; Zia Pueblo/Gypsum Point.

Hollywood Barn Dance (1947 Screen Guild) Ernest Tubb. LOC:

Hollywood Cowboy (1937 RKO) George O'Brien. LOC: California: Brandeis Ranch; Lone Pine.

Hollywood Round-Up (1937 Columbia) Buck Jones. LOC: California: Iverson Ranch; Brandeis Ranch; Rancho Placeritos; Bronson Canyon; Vasquez Rocks.

Holy Terror, A (1931 Fox) George O' Brien. LOC: California: Providencia Ranch.

Hombre (1967 20th Century Fox) Paul Newman. LOC: California: Bell Ranch; Arizona: Old Tucson; Helvetia Mine; Nevada: Jean.

Home from the Hill (1960 MGM) Robert Mitchum. LOC: Texas: Brackettville; Mississippi: Oxford.

Home in Oklahoma (1946 Republic) Roy Rogers. LOC: California: Republic Studio backlot; Oklahoma: Flying L Ranch, Davis; Davis Train Depot.

Home in San Antone (1949 Columbia) Roy Acuff. LOC: California: Iverson Ranch.

Home in Wyomin' (1942 Republic) Gene Autry. LOC: California: Agoura Ranch; Republic Studio backlot.

Home on the Prairie (1939 Republic) Gene Autry. LOC: California: Jauregui Ranch.

Home on the Range (1935 Paramount) Randolph Scott. LOC: California: Lake Malibu; Century Ranch.

Home on the Range (1946 Republic) Monte Hale. LOC: California: Iverson Ranch; Chatsworth Lake; Republic Studio backlot.

Homesteaders of Paradise Valley (1947 Republic) Allen Lane. LOC: California: Iverson Ranch; Burro Flats.

Homesteaders, The (1953 Allied Artists) Bill Elliott. LOC: California: Iverson Ranch; Corriganville; Burro Flats.

Hondo (1954 Warner Bros) John Wayne. LOC: Utah: Snow Canyon; MEXICO: Chihuahua: San Francisco de Conchos; Church of San Francisco de Asis; Cerro de la Cruz; Cerro de la Mesa; Vado de las babisas; Rio Conchos.

Hondo and the Apaches (1967 MGM) Ralph Taeger. LOC: California: Lake Los Angeles; MGM backlot.

Honeychile (1951 Republic) Judy Canova. LOC: California: Bishop; Republic Studio backlot.

Honeysuckle Rose (1980 Warner Bros) Willie Nelson. LOC: Texas: Austin; Padre Island National Seashore.

Honkers, The (1972 United Artists) James Coburn. LOC: New Mexico: Carlsbad.

Honky Tonk (1941 MGM) Clark Gable. LOC: California: MGM backlot.

Honor of the Mounted (1932 Monogram) Tom Tyler. LOC: California: Trem Carr Ranch; Walker Ranch; Lake Sherwood.

Honor of the Range (1934 Universal) Ken Maynard. LOC: California: Bronson Canyon; Towsley Canyon; Ralph M. Like Studio.

Honor of the West (1939 Universal) Bob Baker. LOC: California: Kernville.

Hooper (1978 Warner Bros) Burt Reynolds. LOC: California: Warner Bros backlot; Alabama: Birmingham; Tuscaloosa.

Hop-Along Cassidy (1935 Paramount) William Boyd. LOC: California: Lone Pine.

Hopalong Cassidy Returns (1936 Paramount) William Boyd. LOC: California: Kernville; Kernville Movie Street.

Hopalong Rides Again (1937 Paramount) William Boyd. LOC: California: Lone Pine.

Hope Ranch (2002 Animal Planet) Bruce Boxleitner. LOC: California: Greenfield Ranch; JMJ Ranch; Peter Pitchess Detention Center.

Hoppy Serves a Writ (1943 United Artists) William Boyd. LOC: California: Kernville; California Studio backlot.

Hoppy's Holiday (1947 United Artists) William Boyd. LOC: California: Providencia Ranch; Rancho Placeritos.

Horizons West (1952 Universal) Robert Ryan. LOC: California: Jauregui Ranch; Universal Studio backlot.

Horse (1965 Film-Makers' Cooperative) Tosh Carillo. LOC:

Horse Crazy (2001 Pure Entertainment) Dally Christensen. LOC: Arizona: Littlefield; Utah: Snow Canyon State Park, St.George.

Horse Soldiers, The (1959 United Artists) John Wayne. LOC: California: MGM backlot; Mississippi: Natchez; Louisiana: Alexandria.

Horse Whisperer, The (1997 Buena Vista) Robert Redford. LOC: Montana: Livingston.

Horsemen of the Sierras (1949 Columbia) Charles Starrett. LOC: California: Iverson Ranch; Columbia Ranch.

Horses' Collars (1935 Columbia) Three Stooges. LOC: No Exterior Locations

Hostile Country (1950 Lippert) Jimmy Ellison. LOC: California: Iverson Ranch.

Hostile Guns (1967 Paramount) George Montgomery. LOC: California: Columbia Ranch; Iverson Ranch; Vasquez Rocks.

Hot Lead (1951 RKO) Tim Holt. LOC: California: Iverson Ranch; Walker Ranch; Jauregui Ranch.

Hot Lead and Cold Feet (1978 Buena Vista) Jim Dale. LOC: Oregon: Bend.

Hot Spur (1968 Olympic Intl) James Arena. LOC: California.

Hour of the Gun (1967 United Artists) James Garner. LOC: MEXICO: Coahuila: Torreón; Durango: La Goma railway station, Ciudad Lerdo; Comarca Lagunera; Ro Nazas; Torrecillas; Comarca Lagunera; Guanajuato: San Miguel de Allende; Morelos.

Houston: The Legend of Texas (1986 CBS) Sam Elliott. LOC: Texas: Bracketville: Alamo Village; Houston: Sam Houston Park; Rancho Rio Grande; Moody's Ranch; Del Rio Round Top/Winedale Historical Farm.

How the West Was Fun (1994 ABC) Mary-Kate Olsen. LOC: CANADA: Alberta: Rafter Six Ranch North of Calgary.

How the West Was Won (1963 MGM) Carroll Baker. LOC: California: Corriganville; Lone Pine; Convict Lake; Scotia; Arizona: Oatman; Magma Arizona Railroad; Arizona/Utah: Monument Valley; Colorado: Delta; Gunnison River; Molas Pass; Kentucky: Ohio and Cumberland Rivers; Paducah; South Dakota: Black Hills; Custer State Park; Rapid City; Illinois: Ohio River; Battery Rock.

Howards of Virginia, The (1940 Columbia) Cary Grant. LOC: California: Fulton; San Lorenzo Valley; Virginia: Williamsburg.

Hud (1963 Paramount) Paul Newman. LOC: Texas: Henderson Ranch, Claude.

Hudson's Bay (1941 20th Century Fox) Paul Muni. LOC: Idaho: McCall.

Human Targets (1932 Big 4) Buzz Barton. LOC: California: Ralph M. Like Studio backlot.

Hunley, The (1999 TNT) Armand Assante. LOC: South Carolina: Charleston

Hunted Men (1930 Syndicate) Bob Steele. LOC: California: Jauregui Ranch.

Hurricane Horseman (1931 Kent) Lane Chandler. LOC: California: Iverson Ranch; Towsley Canyon; Tec-Art Studio backlot.

Hurricane Smith (1941 Republic) Ray Middleton. LOC: Republic Studio backlot.

I Do Not Forgive .. I Kill! (1968 United Picture/Trebol Film) James Philbrook. LOC: SPAIN: Andalucia: Desierto de Tabernas; Almeria.

I Killed Geronimo (1950 Eagle Lion) James Ellison. LOC: California: Vasquez Rocks.

I Killed Wild Bill Hickock (1956 The Wheeler Company) John Carpenter. LOC: California: Iverson Ranch.

I Shot Billy the Kid (1950 Lippert) Don Barry. LOC: California: Iverson Ranch; Vasquez Rocks; Rancho Placeritos.

I Shot Jesse James (1949 Screen Guild) John Ireland. LOC: California: Iverson Ranch.

I Take This Woman (1931 Paramount) Gary Cooper. LOC: California: Paramount Ranch.

I Will Fight No More Forever (1975 David Wolper Prod-TV) James Whitmore. LOC: MEXICO: Durango: Hilalgo: Tula; Morelos: Cuernavaca; Laguna de Zempoala; Tres Marias.

Ice Palace (1960 Warner Bros) Richard Burton. LOC: Arkansas: Petersburg.

Idaho (1943 Republic) Roy Rogers. LOC: California: Kernville; Republic Studio backlot.

Idaho Kid, The (1936 Colony) Rex Bell. LOC: California: Brandeis Ranch; Jauregui Ranch.

Idaho Red (1929 FBO) Tom Tyler. LOC:

I'm from the City (1938 RKO) Joe Penner. LOC: California: Corriganville.

In Caliente (1935 Warner Bros) Dolores Del Rio. LOC: MEXICO: Baja California Norte: Hotel Agua Caliente, Tijuana.

In Early Arizona (1938 Columbia) Bill Elliott. LOC: California: Iverson Ranch; Rancho Placeritos.

In Line of Duty (1931 Monogram) Noah Beery. LOC: California.

In Old Amarillo (1951 Republic) Roy Rogers. LOC: California: El Mirage; Republic Studio backlot.

In Old Arizona (1929 Fox) Warner Baxter. LOC: California: Mission San Juan Capistrano; Deadman Point; Utah: Zion National Park; Grafton.

In Old Caliente (1939 Republic) Roy Rogers. LOC: California: Iverson Ranch; Agoura Ranch; Leo Carrillo State Beach.

In Old California (1929 Audible) Tom Keene. LOC:

In Old California (1942 Republic) John Wayne. LOC: California: Kernville; Big Tujunga; Republic Studio backlot.

In Old Cheyenne (1931 World Wide) Rex Lease. LOC: California: Bronson Canyon.

In Old Cheyenne (1941 Republic) Roy Rogers. LOC: California: Iverson Ranch; Republic Studio backlot.

In Old Colorado (1941 Paramount) William Boyd. LOC: California: Lone Pine.

In Old Mexico (1938 Paramount) William Boyd. LOC: California: Kelso Valley; Paramount Ranch.

In Old Montana (1939 Spectrum) Fred Scott. LOC: California: Jauregui Ranch; Walker Ranch.

In Old Monterey (1939 Republic) Gene Autry. LOC: California: Iverson Ranch; Lone Pine; Consumers Rock and Gravel Company; Republic Studio backlot.

In Old New Mexico (1945 Monogram) Duncan Renaldo. LOC: California: Corriganville; San Fernando Mission.

In Old Oklahoma (1943 Republic) John Wayne. LOC: California: Bakersfield; Modesto; Taft; Utah: Kanab; Paria; Zion National Park.

In Old Sacramento (1946 Republic) Bill Elliott. LOC: California: Iverson Ranch; Kernville; Tuolumne County; Kennedy Meadow.

In Old Santa Fe (1934 Mascot) Ken Maynard. LOC: California: Paradise Springs; Antelope Valley.

In Pursuit of Honor (1995 HBO) Don Johnson. LOC: AUSTRALIA.

Incendiary Blonde (1945 Paramount) Betty Hutton. LOC: California: Paramount Ranch; Arizona: Tucson.

Incident at Oglala (1992 Spanish Fork Motion Picture) Norman Zigrossi. LOC: Iowa: Cedar Rapids; Kansas: Leavenworth/United States Federal Penitentiary; South Dakota: Oglala, Pine Ridge Indian Reservation.

Incident at Phantom Hill (1966 Universal) Robert Fuller. LOC: California: Lake Los Angeles; Piute Butte; Piru Creek; Universal Studio backlot.

Incredible Rocky Mountain Race, The (1977 Sunn Classic) Forrest Tucker. LOC: Arizona: Old Tucson.

Independence (1987 Sunn Classics) Anthony Zerbe. LOC: New Mexico: J.W.Eaves

Movie Ranch Santa Fe.

Indian Agent (1948 RKO) Tim Holt. LOC: California: Lone Pine.

Indian Fighter, The (1955 United Artists) Kirk Douglas. LOC: Oregon: Bend.

Indian Paint (1965 Crown International) Johnny Crawford. LOC: Texas: Cleburne; Grand Prairie; Mansfield.

Indian Territory (1950 Columbia) Gene Autry. LOC: California: Corriganville; Pioneertown.

Indian Uprising (1952 Columbia) George Montgomery. LOC: California: Iverson Ranch; Corriganville; Bronson Canyon; Columbia Ranch; Arizona: Sedona.

Indians Are Coming, The (1930 Universal) Tim McCoy. LOC: California: Universal backlot.

Inside Straight (1951 MGM) David Brian. LOC: California: MGM Studios backlot.

Into the Badlands (1991 Ogiens/Kane Productions, Inc.) Bruce Dern. LOC: New Mexico: Bonanza Creek Ranch; Cook Ranch/Cerro Pelon Ranch; J.W.Eaves Movie Ranch/Mexican set; Nambé Pueblo; Zia Pueblo/Gypsum Point.

Into the West (2005 TNT miniseries) Irene Bedard. LOC: New Mexico: Bonanza Creek Ranch; Bonito Lake; Lincoln National Forest; Cook Ranch/Cerro Pelon Ranch; Diablo Canyon; El Rancho de las Golondrinas; Fort Stanton Lincoln County; J.W. Eaves Movie Ranch; Los Alamos/American Springs; Santa Fe National Forest; Millennium Mines; San Cristobal Ranch; Santa Fe/Old Main Prison; The White Place Abiquiú; CANADA: CL Ranch; Drumhelle/badlands; Lonview.

Invaders, The (1929 Syndicate) Bob Steele. LOC:

Invitation to a Gunfighter (1964 United Artists) Yul Brynner. LOC: California: Universal backlot.

Irish Gringo, The (1935 Keith Productions) Pat Carlyle. LOC: California: Brandeis Ranch.

Iron Mistress, The (1952 Warner Bros) Alan Ladd. LOC: California: Warner Ranch.

Iron Mountain Trail (1953 Republic) Rex Allen. LOC: California: Burro Flats.

Iron Sheriff, The (1957 United Artists) Sterling Hayden. LOC: California: Iverson Ranch; Corriganville.

Iron Will (1994 Buena Vista) Mackenzie Astin. LOC: Maine: Bingham; Minnesota: Brookston; Cloquet; Duluth: City Hall; Kerrick; Lutsen Mountain Ski Area; Two Harbors; Wisconsin: Oliver; Superior.

Iroquois Trail, The (1950 United Artists) George Montgomery. LOC: California: Big Bear; Cedar Lake.

It Happened Out West (1937 Principal) Paul Kelly. LOC: California: Red Rock Canyon.

It's a Big Country: An American Anthology (1952 MGM) Ethel Barrymore. LOC: California: Massachusetts: Boston.

Ivory-Handled Gun, The (1935 Universal) Buck Jones. LOC: California: Jauregui

Ranch; Vasquez Rocks.

J. W. Coop (1972 Columbia) Cliff Robertson. LOC: California: Angels Camp; Inglewood Forum; Oakdale; Porterville; Red Bluff; Sonora; Springville; Woodlake; Oklahoma: McAlester State Prison; New York: Madison Square Garden.

Jack Bull, The (1999 HBO) John Cusack. LOC: CANADA: Alberta: CL Ranch Calgary.

Jack London's Tales of Klondike (1981 CBC) Robert Carradine) Canada.

Jack McCall, Desperado (1953 Columbia) George Montgomery. LOC: California: Corriganville; Rancho Placeritos.

Jack Slade (1953 Allied Artists) Mark Stevens. LOC: California: Iverson Ranch; Burro Flats; Tuolumne County.

Jackals (1985 M.F.G.Enterprises, Inc.) Jameson Parker. LOC: Arizona: Mescal.

Jackass Mail (1942 MGM) Wallace Beery. LOC: California: Iverson Ranch; Keen Camp; Idyllwild; San Jacinto Mountains.

James A. Michener's Texas (1994 Republic) Maria Conchita Alonso. LOC: Texas: Alamo Village; Amistad Recreation Area; Devil's River Ranch; Rancho Rio Grande/Moody's Ranch Del Rio.

James Brothers of Missouri, The (1950 Republic) Keith Richards. LOC: California: Iverson Ranch; Republic Studio backlot; Corriganville.

Jaws of Justice (1933 Principal) Jack Perrin. LOC: California: Big Bear Lake Dam; Lake Tahoe.

Jayhawkers, The (1959 Paramount) Jeff Chandler. LOC: California: Bronson Canyon; Janss Janss Conejo Ranch; Paramount Studio backlot.

Jeepers Creepers (1939 Republic) Leon Weaver. LOC: California: Lake Hemet; Keen Camp.

Jeep-Herders (1945 Planet Pictures) June Carlson. LOC: California: Main Hospital, Veterans Administration Facility, West Los Angeles; Agoura Ranch; unidentified Train Depot; unidentified oil wills.

Jeremiah Johnson (1972 Warner Bros) Robert Redford. LOC: Utah: Leeds; St. George; Snow Canyon; Ivins Bench; Timpanogos; Vernal; Zion National Park.

Jericho (2001 Black Knight Productions) Mark Valley. LOC: Colorado: Cumbres and Toltec Scenic Railroad; Los Pinos; New Mexico: Chama/Cumbres and Toltec Scenic Railroad; Texas: Alamo Village; Rancho Rio Grande/Moody's Ranch/Lonesome Dove set and Pinto Creek Del Rio.

Jesse James (1939 20th Century Fox) Tyrone Power. LOC: California: 20th Century Fox Studio backlot; Missouri: Pineville; Lake of the Ozarks, Noel; Neosho; Elk River.

Jesse James at Bay (1941 Republic) Roy Rogers. LOC: California: Iverson Ranch; Vasquez Rocks; Republic Studio backlot.

Jesse James Meets Frankenstein's Daughter (1966 Embassy) John Lupton. LOC: California: Corriganville.

Jesse James Rides Again (1947 Republic) Clayton Moore. LOC: California: Iverson Ranch; Republic Studio backlot.

Jesse James vs. the Daltons (1954 Columbia) Brett King. LOC: California: Rowland V. Lee Ranch; Columbia Ranch.

Jesse James, Jr. (1942 Republic) Don Barry. LOC: California: Iverson Ranch; Agoura Ranch.

Jesse James' Women (1954 United Artists) Donald Barry. LOC: Mississippi: Silver Creek.

Jessi's Girls (1975 Manson Prod) Sondra Currie. LOC: Utah: Capitol Reef National Park.

Jesuit Joe (1991 Duckster / Ciné Cinq / Canal +;) Peter Tarter. LOC: CANADA: British Columbia: BaskervilleWells.

Jiggs and Maggie Out West (1950 Monogram) Joe Yule. LOC: California: Iverson Ranch; Rancho Placeritos.

Joaquín Murrieta (1965 Warner Bros) Jeffrey Hunter. LOC: SPAIN: Colmenar Viejo.

Joe Dakota (1957 Universal) Jock Mahoney. LOC: California: Janss Janss Conejo Ranch; Universal Studio backlot.

Joe Kidd (1972 Universal) Clint Eastwood. LOC: California: Lone Pine; Bishop; The Buttermilks; Arizona: Old Tucson.

Joe Navidad (1967 Producers Releasing Organization) Jeffrey Hunter. LOC: SPAIN: Colmenar Viejo.

Joe Panther (1976 Artclass) Brian Keith. LOC: Florida; Miami; Micosuke Village; Wakulla Springs.

Johnny Concho (1956 United Artists) Frank Sinatra. LOC: California: Iverson Ranch; Corriganville; Rancho Placeritos.

Johnny Firecloud (1975 Entertainment Ventures) Victor Mohica. LOC: California: Piru.

Johnny Guitar (1954 Republic) Sterling Hayden. LOC: Arizona: Sedona.

Johnny Reno (1966 Paramount) Dana Andrews. LOC: California: Vasquez Rocks; Paramount Studio backlot.

Johnny Shiloh (1963 Buena Vista) Brian Keith. LOC: California: Disney's Golden Oak Ranch; Disney Studio backlot.

Johnny Tiger (1966 Universal) Chad Everett. LOC: Arizona: Old Tucson; Florida: Wekiwa Springs, Apopka.

Johnson County War, The (2001 The Hallmark Channel) Tom Berenger. LOC: CANADA: Alberta: CL Ranch Calgary; Kananaskis County; Longview.

Jonah Hex (2009 Warner Bros) Josh Brolin. LOC: California: Los Angeles; Santa Clarita; LOUISIANA: Bayou Gauche; Crow Pointe; Fort Pike; New Orleans; Raceland Plantation; Rosedown Plantation, St. Francisville.

Jonathan of the Bears (1994 Viva/Project Camp J.V.) Franco Nero. LOC: RUSSIA: Alabimo.

John Nesbitt's Passing Parade: The Amazing Mr. Nordill (1947 MGM) Leon

Ames. LOC: No exteriors.

Jory (1972 Avco-Embassy) John Marley. LOC: MEXICO: Coahuila: Torreon; Durango: El Saltito waterfall; Rancho Marley; Rio Tunal; Villa del Oeste.

Joseph Smith, Prophet of the Restoration (2005 The Church of Jesus Christ of Latter-day-Saints) Nathan Mitchell. LOC: Utah: Cove Fort Historic Site.

Joshua (1976 Lone Star Prod) Fred Williamson. LOC: Utah: Arches National Park; Valley of the Gods.

Journey through Rosebud (1972 Avco/Embassy) Robert Forster. LOC: South Dakota: Rosebud Indian Reservation.

Journey to Shiloh (1968 Universal) James Caan. LOC: California: Janss Janss Conejo Ranch; Lake Los Angeles; Universal Studio backlot.

Journeyman, The (2001 Harbinger Pictures/Eleven Pictures) Brad Hunt. LOC: Texas: Big Bend Ranch State Park; CF Ranch/mission set; Alpine; Crow Town/Mexican set; Lajitas/Mexican set; Terlingua/cemetery.

Juarez (1939 Warner Bros) Paul Muni. LOC: California: Iverson Ranch; Warner Ranch.

Jubal (1956 Columbia) Glenn Ford. LOC: Wyoming: Jackson Hole; Triangle X Dude Ranch; Togwotee Pass; Brooks Lake Lodge.

Jubilee Trail (1954 Republic) Vera Ralston. LOC: California: Red Rock Canyon; Republic Studio backlot.

Judgement Book, The (1935 Beaumont) Conway Tearle. LOST/MISSING

Junction City (1952 Columbia) Charles Starrett. LOC: California: Columbia Ranch.

Junior Bonner (1972 Cinerama Releasing Corp) Steve McQueen. LOC: Arizona: Prescott.

Justice of the Range (1935 Columbia) Tim McCoy. LOC: California: Jauregui Ranch; Paramount Ranch.

Justice of the West (1956 Wrather) Clayton Moore. LOC: California: Iverson Ranch; Corriganville; Tuolumne County; Columbia.

Kangaroo (1952 20th Century Fox) Peter Lawford. LOC: AUSTRALIA: Queensland.

Kangaroo Kid, The (1950 United Artists) Jock Mahoney. LOC: AUSTRALIA: Denison St., Sofala, New South Wales.

Kansan, The (1943 United Artists) Richard Dix. LOC: California: Kernville; California Studio backlot.

Kansas Cyclone (1941 Republic) Don Barry. LOC: California: Iverson Ranch.

Kansas Pacific (1953 Allied Artists) Sterling Hayden. LOC: California: Iverson Ranch; Tuolumne County.

Kansas Raiders (1950 Universal) Audie Murphy. LOC: California: Garner Ranch; Universal Studio backlot.

Kansas Territory (1952 Monogram) Bill Elliott. LOC: California: Iverson Ranch; Ingram Ranch; Red Rock Canyon.

Kansas Terrors, The (1939 Republic) Three Mesquiteers. LOC: California: Iverson

Ranch; Burro Flats; Republic Studio backlot.

Kate Bliss and the Ticker-Tape Kid (1978 Aaron Spelling) Suzanne Pleshette. LOC: California: Tuolumne County.

Keep Shooting (1942 RKO) Ray Whitley. LOC:

Keep the Change (1992 Turner Pictures) William Petersen. LOC: Montana: LivingstonParadise Valley.

Kelly (1981 Paramount/Famous Players Film Corporation) Robert Logan. LOC: CANADA: Alberta: Calgary; Canmore; British Columbia: Yoho National Park.

Kenny Rogers as The Gambler (1980 CBS Western Series) Kenny Rogers. LOC: Arizona: Old Tucson; California: Sierra Railroad.

Kenny Rogers as The Gambler, Part III: The Legend Continues (1987 CBS) Kenny Rogers. LOC: California: Rancho Maria; New Mexico: Cook Ranch/Cerro Pelon Ranch; El Rancho de las Golondrinas; J.W. Eaves Movie Ranch/Western town and Mexican set.

Kenny Rogers as The Gambler: The Adventure Continues (1983 CBS) Kenny Rogers. LOC: Arizona: Apacheland; Carefree; Phoenix; Peña Blanca Canyon West of Nogales; Sedona; California: Tuolumne County.

Kentuckian, The (1955 United Artists) Burt Lancaster. LOC: Kentucky; Owensboro; Tennessee.

Kentucky Rifle (1956 Howco Productions) Lance Fuller. LOC: California: Vasquez Rocks.

Kid and the Gunfighter, The (1985 Saga Films International) Chuck Biller. LOC: PHILIPPINES.

Kid and the Killers, The (1974 Cinema Shares) Jon Cypher. LOC: COLUMBIA.

Kid Blue (1973 20th Century Fox) Dennis Hopper. LOC: MEXICO: Durango: Chupaderos.

Kid Colter (1984 Wind River Productions) Janine Turner. LOC: Washington: Port Angeles; Port Towsend.

Kid Courageous (1935 Commodore) Bob Steele. LOC: California: Kernville;.

Kid from Amarillo, The (1951 Columbia) Charles Starrett. LOC: California: Iverson Ranch; Columbia Ranch.

Kid from Arizona, The (1931 Cosmos) Jack Perrin. LOST/MISSING.

Kid from Broken Gun, The (1952 Columbia) Charles Starrett. LOC: California: Columbia Ranch; Iverson Ranch.

Kid from Gower Gulch, The (1949 Friedgen) Spade Cooley. LOC: California: Pearblossom; Ridgecrest.

Kid from Santa Fe, The (1940 Monogram) Jack Randall. LOC: California: Walker Ranch.

Kid from Texas, The (1939 MGM) Dennis O'Keefe. LOC: California: Encino.

Kid from Texas, The (1950 Universal) Audie Murphy. LOC: California: Garner Ranch; Idyllwild; Universal Studio backlot.

Kid Ranger, The (1936 Superior) Bob Steele. LOC: California: Lebec; Ralph M.

Like Studio backlot.

Kid Rides Again, The (1943 PRC) Buster Crabbe. LOC: California: Corriganville; Rancho Placeritos.

Kid's Last Ride, The (1941 Monogram) Range Busters. LOC: California: Walker Ranch; Jauregui Ranch; Rancho Placeritos.

King and Four Queens, The (1956 United Artists) Clark Gable. LOC: Utah: Snow Canyon.

King of Dodge City (1941 Columbia) Bill Elliott. LOC: California: Iverson Ranch; Rancho Placeritos.

King of Texas (2002 TNT) Patrick Stewart. LOC: MEXICO: Durango: Canon de las Flores; La Perla; Rancho Marley; Hildalgo: Pachuca; Tlaxcala: Hacienda San Pedro Tenexac, Terrenate.

King of the Arena (1933 Universal) Ken Maynard. LOC: California: Towsley Canyon; Vasquez Rocks.

King of the Bandits (1947 Monogram) Gilbert Roland. LOC: California: Iverson Ranch; Rancho Placeritos.

King of the Bullwhip (1951 Western Adventures) Lash LaRue. LOC: California: Iverson Ranch.

King of the Cowboys (1943 Republic) Roy Rogers. LOC: California: Iverson Ranch; Gaviota train trestle; Republic Studio backlot.

King of the Forest Rangers (1946 Republic) Larry Thompson. LOC: California: Big Bear; Republic Studio backlot.

King of the Grizzlies (1970 Walt Disney) John Yesno. LOC: CANADA: Banff National Park; Moraine Lake; Kananaskis Forest; Kananaskis River; Takakkaw Falls; Yoho National Park.

King of the Lumberjacks (1940 Warner Bros) John Payne. LOC: California: Big Bear.

King of the Mounties (1942 Republic) Allan Lane. LOC: California: Iverson Ranch; Big Bear; Cedar Lake; Republic Studio backlot.

King of the Pecos (1936 Republic) John Wayne. LOC: California: Trem Carr Ranch; Lone Pine.

King of the Royal Mounted (1936 20th Century Fox) Robert Kent. LOC: California: Cedar Lake; Mammoth Lakes.

King of the Royal Mounted (1940 Republic) Allan Lane. LOC: California: Big Bear; Cedar Lake.

King of the Sierras (1938 Grand National) Hobart Bosworth. LOC: Arizona: Fredonia; Sedona.

King of the Stallions (1942 Monogram) Chief Thunder Cloud. LOC: California: Bronson Canyon; Monogram Studio backlot; Crater Canyon.

King of the Texas Rangers (1941 Republic) Sammy Baugh. LOC: California: Iverson Ranch; Corriganville; Lake Sherwood; Morris Dam; Adams Airport; Platt Ranch; Santa Susana Pass Train Cut and Tunnel; Republic Studio backlot;

near the intersection of old San Gabriel Canyon Road and San Gabriel Canyon Road; San Pedro Harbor.

King of the Wild Horses (1933 Columbia) William Janney. LOC: Arizona: Red Rock Crossing, Sedona.

King of the Wild Horses (1947 Columbia) Preston Foster. LOC: California: Iverson Ranch.

King of the Wild Stallions (1959 Allied Artists) George Montgomery. LOC: California: Bronson Canyon; Vasquez Rocks; Monogram Studio backlot.

Kings of the Sun (1963 United Artists) Yul Brynner. MEXICO: Sinaloa: Mazatlan; Yucatan: Chichén Itzá.

Kino, the Padre on Horseback (1977 Key International) Richard Egan. LOC: Arizona: Cave Creek; Tucson area.

Kiss of Fire (1955 Universal) Jack Palance. LOC: Nevada: Valley of Fire State Park; Red Rock Canyon; Willow Springs; Mt. Charleston.

Kissing Bandit, The (1948 MGM) Frank Sinatra. LOC: California: Tuolumne County; Kennedy Meadow; Murphys; MGM backlot.

Kit Carson (1940 United Artists) Dana Andrews. LOC: California: Iverson Ranch; Rabbit Dry Lake; Arizona: Tsegi Canyon; Arizona/Utah: Monument Valley; Utah: San Juan River; Mexican Hat.

Klondike (1932 Monogram) Thelma Todd. LOC: California: Clover Field, Santa Monica.

Klondike Annie (1936 Paramount) Mae West) No Exterior Locations

Klondike Fever (1980 Jack London Story CFL) Rod Steiger. LOC: CANADA: British Columbia: Barkerville; Fraser Canyon; Harrison Lake; Three Valley Gap; Vancouver; Wells; Yukon.

Klondike Kate (1943 Columbia) Ann Savage. LOC: California: Columbia Ranch.

Knife for the Ladies, A (1973 Bryanston) Jack Elam. LOC: Arizona: Old Tucson.

Knight of the Plains (1938 Spectrum) Fred Scott. LOC: California: Brandeis Ranch.

Knights of the Range (1940 Paramount) Russell Hayden. LOC: California: Lone Pine; Mammoth Lakes.

Konga, The Wild Stallion (1939 Columbia) Rochelle Hudson. LOC: California.

Kootenai Brown (1991 National Film Board of Canada/British Columbia Film Commission/Crescent Entertainment) Tom Burlinson. LOC: CANADA: Alberta: Waterton Lakes National Park; British Columbia: Barkerville; Vancouver.

Kung Fu: The Movie (1986 CBS) David Carradine. LOC: California: Disney Golden Oak Ranch.

Lady for a Night (1942 Republic) Joan Blondell. LOC: California: Agoura Ranch; Republic Studio backlot.

Lady from Cheyenne, The (1941 Universal) Loretta Young. LOC: California: Mojave Train Depot; Universal Studio backlot.

Lady from Louisiana (1941 Republic) John Wayne. LOC: California: Rowland V.

Lee Ranch.

Lady from Texas, The (1951 Universal) Howard Duff. LOC: California: Jauregui Ranch; Universal Studio backlot.

Lady Gambles, The (1949 Universal) Barbara Stanwyck. LOC: Nevada: Lake Mead; Boulder Dam.

Lady Takes a Chance, A (1943 RKO) John Wayne. LOC: California: Hidden Valley; New York: New York.

Lakota Woman: Siege at Wounded Knee (1994 TNT) Irene Bedard. LOC: South Dakota: Triple U/Standing Butte Ranch; Fort Pierre.

Land Beyond the Law (1937 Warner Bros) Dick Foran. LOC: California: Iverson Ranch; Burro Flats; Warner Ranch.

Land of Fighting Men (1938 Monogram) Jack Randall. LOC: California: Iverson Ranch; Brandeis Ranch.

Land of Hunted Men (1943 Monogram) Range Busters. LOC: California: Corriganville.

Land of Missing Men, The (1930 Tiffany) Bob Steele. LOC: California: Vasquez Rocks.

Land of the Lawless (1947 Monogram) Johnny Mack Brown. LOC: California: Walker Ranch; Rancho Placeritos.

Land of the Open Range (1942 RKO) Tim Holt. LOC: California: Corriganville; Burro Flats.

Land of the Outlaws (1944 Monogram) Johnny Mack Brown. LOC: California: Rancho Placeritos; Walker Ranch.

Land of the Six Guns (1940 Monogram) Jack Randall. LOC: California: Rancho Placeritos; Walker Ranch; Bronson Canyon.

Land of Wanted Men (1931 Monogram) Bill Cody. LOC: California: Trem Carr Ranch.

Landrush (1946 Columbia) Charles Starrett. LOC: California: Iverson Ranch; Providencia Ranch; Columbia Ranch.

Laramie (1949 Columbia) Charles Starrett. LOC: California: Iverson Ranch; Corriganville.

Laramie Kid, The (1935 Commodore) Tom Tyler. LOC: California: Mentryville; Frank LaSalle Ranch; Pico Canyon.

Laramie Mountains (1952 Columbia) Charles Starrett. LOC: California: Iverson Ranch; Corriganville.

Laramie Trail, The (1944 Republic) Bob Livingston. LOC: California: Iverson Ranch.

Lariats and Sixshooters (1931 Cosmos) Jack Perrin) LOST/MISSING

Las Vegas Story, The (1952 RKO) Victor Mature. LOC: Nevada: Las Vegas.

Lasca of the Rio Grande (1931 Universal) Leo Carrillo. LOC: California: Tuolumne County.

Lash, The (1930 First National) Richard Barthelmess. LOC: California: Russell

Ranch.

Last Bandit, The (1949 Republic) William Elliott. LOC: California: Iverson Ranch; Brandeis Ranch; Vasquez Rocks; Red Rock Canyon; Soledad Canyon; Lang Train Station; Republic Studio backlot.

Last Challenge, The (1967 MGM) Glenn Ford. LOC: California: Lake Los Angeles area; Arizona: Old Tucson; Sabino Canyon.

Last Command, The (1955 Republic) Sterling Hayden. LOC: California: Republic Studio backlot; Universal Studio backlot; Texas: Brackettville.

Last Confederate, The: The Story of Robert Adams (2004 Solar Filmworks/Thinkfilm Strongbow Pictures) Julian Adams. LOC: North Carolina: Wilmington; South Carolina: Columbia Wavering Place Plantation, U.S. Route 378.

Last Cowboy, The (2003 The Hallmark Channel) Lance Henriksen. LOC: California: Del Mar; Santa Ynez.

Last Day, The (1975 Paramount-TV) Richard Widmark. LOC: California: Paramount backlot.

Last Days of Boot Hill (1947 Columbia) Charles Starrett. LOC: California: Corriganville; Providencia Ranch.

Last Days of Frank and Jessie James, The (1986 Joseph Cates Productions) Kris Kristofferson) Tennessee: Tennessee Valley Railroad Chattanooga.

Last Escape of Billy the Kid, The (1978 US Filmco of Delaware) Jack Elam. LOC: Pennsylvania: Dilworthtown; New Mexico: Lincoln.

Last Frontier Uprising (1947 Republic) Monte Hale. LOC: California: Iverson Ranch; Agoura Ranch.

Last Frontier, The (1932 RKO) Lon Chaney Jr. LOC: California: Kernville; Kernville Movie Street.

Last Frontier, The (1955 Columbia) Victor Mature. LOC: MEXICO: Mexico: Amecameca; Salazar.

Last Gun, The (1964 British Lion) Cameron Mitchell. LOC: ITALY: Camposecco Plateau.

Last Gunfighter, The (1961 Brenner) Don Borisenko. LOC: CANADA.

Last Hard Men, The (1976 20th Century Fox) Charlton Heston. LOC: Arizona: Old Tucson; Pena Blanca Canyon; Rio Rico.

Last Horseman, The (1944 Columbia) Russell Hayden. LOC: California: Walker Ranch.

Last Horseman, The (2009 Talmarc Productions) Buck Taylor. LOC: New Mexico: Bonanza Creek Ranch.

Last Hunt, The (1956 MGM) Robert Taylor. LOC: South Dakota: Sylvan Lake; Badlands; Black Hills; Custer State Park.

Last Man Standing (1996 Ancora vivo New Line Cinema/Lone Wolf) Bruce Willis. LOC: California: Veluzat Motion Picture Ranch; New Mexico: Cook Ranch/Cerro Pelon Ranch; Texas: El Paso.

Last Musketeer, The (1952 Republic) Rex Allen. LOC: California: Vasquez Rocks; Lake Los Angeles.

Last of a Breed (1997 episode—series Walker, Texas Ranger CBS) Chuck Norris. LOC: New Mexico: Bonanza Creek Ranch; Cook Ranch/Cerro Pelon Ranch; Diablo Canyon; El Rancho de las Golondrinas; The White Place/Plaza Blanca Abiquiú.

Last of His Tribe, The (1992 HBO) Jon Voight. LOC: California: Oakland; Red Hills Ranch, Jamestown; Sacramento; San Francisco; Washington: Bellingham.

Last of the Bad Men (1957 Allied Artists) George Montgomery. LOC: California: Iverson Ranch; Rancho Placeritos.

Last of the Clintons, The (1935 Ajay Films) Harry Carey. LOC: California: Brandeis Ranch.

Last of the Comanches (1953 Columbia) Broderick Crawford. LOC: California: Buttercup Valley; Columbia Ranch.

Last of the Desperados (1955 Associated) James Craig. LOC: California: Corriganville; Ingram Ranch; Walker Ranch; Rancho Placeritos.

Last of the Dogmen (1996 Chargeurs) Tom Berenger. LOC: CANADA: Alberta: Banff National Park; Canmore; British Columbia: Yoho National Park; MEXICO: Morelos: Cuernavaca; Los Laguna de Zampoala.

Last of the Duanes, The (1930 Fox) George O'Brien. LOC: Arizona: Sedona; Oak Creek Canyon.

Last of the Duanes, The (1941 20th Century Fox) George Montgomery. LOC: California: Lone Pine.

Last of the Fast Guns, The (1958 Universal) Jock Mahoney. LOC: California: Universal Studio backlot; MEXICO: Morelos: Tepoztlan; Taxco; Vilchis Ranch.

Last of the Mohicans (1977 NBC-TV) Steve Forrest. LOC: Arizona: Pipe Springs National Monument; Utah: Duck Creek; Strawberry Valley.

Last of the Mohicans, The (1932 Mascot) Harry Carey. LOC: California: Lake Sherwood; Lake Malibu; Russell Ranch; Kernville.

Last of the Mohicans, The (1936 United Artists) Randolph Scott. LOC: California: Iverson Ranch; Lake Sherwood; Big Bear; Cedar Lake; Kernville.

Last of the Mohicans, The (1992 20th Century-Fox) Daniel-Day Lewis. LOC: North Carolina: Asheville; Blue Ridge Mountains Blueridge Parkway; Greenknob Overlook; Massacre Valley; Burke County; Chimney Rock Park Hickory Nuts Falls; Inspiration Point; Dupont Plant Falls; Lake James Linville Access Area; North Cove; Pisgah National Forest Dupont Plant Falls; Linville Falls; Nolichucky River; Table Rock Mountain; Toecane District; Weaverville Reems Creek.

Last of the Pony Riders (1953 Columbia) Gene Autry. LOC: California: Columbia Ranch; Pioneertown.

Last of the Redmen, The (1947 Columbia) Jon Hall. LOC: California: Corriganville; Lake Sherwood; Mt. Wilson; Providencia Ranch.

Last of the Warrens (1936 Supreme) Bob Steele. LOC: California: Walker Ranch; Jauregui Ranch; Ralph M. Like Studio backlot.
Last of the Wild Horses (1948 Screen Guild) James Ellison. LOC: California: Columbia; Touloume County; Oregon: Jacksonville.
Last Outlaw, The (1936 RKO) Harry Carey. LOC: California: Iverson Ranch.
Last Outlaw, The (1980 Pegasus Productions/7 Network miniseries) John Jarratt. LOC: AUSTRALIA: New South Wales: Forbes; Victoria: Seymour.
Last Outlaw, The (1993 HBO) Mickey Rourke. LOC: New Mexico: Abiquiú Ghost Ranch; Cook Ranch/Cerro Pelon Ranch; Diablo Canyon; Nambé Pueblo; Río Chama; The White Place/Plaza Blanca; Abiquiú; Zia Pueblo/Gypsum Point.
Last Outpost, The (1951 Paramount) Ronald Reagan. LOC: Arizona: Old Tucson; San Xavier Del Bac Mission.
Last Picture Show, The (1971 Columbia) Ben Johnson. LOC: Texas: Archer City.
Last Posse, The (1953 Columbia) Broderick Crawford. LOC: California: Lone Pine.
Last Rebel, The (1971 Sterling World) Joe Namath. LOC: ITALY.
Last Ride of the Dalton Gang, The (1979 NBC-TV) Cliff Potts. LOC: California: Bronson Canyon; Tuolumne County; Columbia State Historic Park.
Last Ride, The (2009 Schiwago Film) Pierre Brice) AUSTRALIA: South Australia: Flinders Ranges; Lake Gairddner; Port Augusta; Port Wakefield; Parachilna.
Last Rites of Ransom Pride, The (2009 Calgary Nomadic Pictures) Kris Kristofferson. LOC: CANADA: Alberta: Calgary/Currie Barracks; Drumheller/badlands; Longview; British Columbia: Vancouver.
Last Roundup, The (1934 Paramount) Randolph Scott. LOC: California: Paramount Ranch; Calabasas.
Last Round-Up, The (1947 Columbia) Gene Autry. LOC: California: Corriganville; Tuolumne County; Arizona: Old Tucson; Rattlesnake Pass; San Xavier Del Bac Mission.
Last Stagecoach West (1957 Republic) Jim Davis. LOC: California: Iverson Ranch; Vasquez Rocks; Towsley Canyon; Republic Studio backlot.
Last Stand at Saber River (1996 TNT) Tom Selleck. LOC: New Mexico: Bonanza Creek Ranch Santa FeCharles R Ranch Las VegasSanta Clara Pueblo, Valle Grande.
Last Stand, The (1938 Universal) Bob Baker. LOC: California: Jauregui Ranch; Beale's Cut; Lake Gregory; Universal Studio backlot.
Last Sunset, The (1961 Universal) Rock Hudson. LOC: MEXICO: Aguascalientes: Jesus Maria; Rancho La Presa; Presa Abelardo Rodriguez; Las Paias Viejas; El Pedregal; ex Hacienda de San Ignacio Milpillas, ex Hacienda de Santa Maria de Gallardo; Rancho San Luis Gonzaga; El Llano; Jalisco: Cienega de Mata de Lagos de Moreno.
Last Trail, The (1933 Fox) George O'Brien. LOC: California: French Ranch.
Last Train from Gun Hill (1959 Paramount) Kirk Douglas. LOC: California: Rancho Placeritos; Paramount Studio backlot; Arizona: Sonoita; Circle Z Ranch,

Patagonia.

Last Wagon, The (1956 20th Century Fox) Richard Widmark. LOC: Arizona: Sedona.

Laughing Boy (1934 MGM) Ramon Navarro. LOC: Arizona: Cameron; Painted Desert.

Law and Jake Wade, The (1958 MGM) Robert Taylor. LOC: California: Lone Pine; Bishop; Death Valley.

Law and Lawless (1932 Majestic) Jack Hoxie. LOC: California: Iverson Ranch; French Ranch; Tec-Art Studio backlot.

Law and Lead (1936 Colony) Rex Bell. LOC: California: Brandeis Ranch; Lone Pine.

Law and Order (1932 Universal) Walter Huston. LOC: California: Vasquez Rocks; Universal Studio backlot.

Law and Order (1940 Universal) Johnny Mack Brown. LOC: California: Iverson Ranch.

Law and Order (1942 PRC) Buster Crabbe. LOC: California: Corriganville.

Law and Order (1953 Universal) Ronald Reagan. LOC: California: Red Rock Canyon; Universal Studio backlot.

Law Beyond the Range (1935 Columbia) Tim McCoy. LOC: California: Paramount Ranch.

Law Comes to Gunsight, The (1947 Monogram) Johnny Mack Brown. LOC: California: Walker Ranch; Rancho Placeritos.

Law Comes to Texas, The (1939 Columbia) William Elliott. LOC: California: Iverson Ranch.

Law Commands, The (1937 Crescent) Tom Keene. LOC: California: Rancho Placeritos.

Law for Tombstone (1937 Universal) Buck Jones. LOC: California: Agoura; Kernville.

Law Men (1944 Monogram) Johnny Mack Brown. LOC: California: Rancho Placeritos.

Law of the 45s, The (1935 First Division) Big Boy Williams. LOC: California: Frank LaSalle Ranch; Ralph M. Like Studio backlot.

Law of the Badlands (1945 Warner Bros) Robert Shayne. LOC:

Law of the Badlands (1951 RKO) Tim Holt. LOC: California: Iverson Ranch; Agoura.

Law of the Barbary Coast (1949 Columbia) Gloria Henry. LOC: No exteriors.

Law of the Canyon (1947 Columbia) Charles Starrett. LOC: California: Iverson Ranch; Columbia Ranch.

Law of the Golden West (1949 Republic) Monte Hale. LOC: California: Iverson Ranch.

Law of the Land (1976 Quinn Martin Prod-TV) Jim Davis. LOC: California: Tuolumne County.

Law of the Lash (1947 PRC) Lash LaRue. LOC: California: Corriganville; Iverson Ranch; Rancho Placeritos.
Law of the Lawless (1964 Paramount) Dale Robertson. LOC: California: Iverson Ranch; Paramount backlot.
Law of the North (1932 Monogram) Bill Cody. LOC: California: Trem Carr Ranch; Walker Ranch.
Law of the Northwest (1943 Columbia) Charles Starrett. LOC: California: Big Bear; Bartlett Lake.
Law of the Pampas (1939 Paramount) William Boyd. LOC: California: Lone Pine; Anchor Ranch; Mt. Witney Portal Road.
Law of the Panhandle (1950 Monogram) Johnny Mack Brown. LOC: California: Iverson Ranch; Walker Ranch.
Law of the Plains (1938 Columbia) Charles Starrett. LOC:
Law of the Range (1941 Universal) Johnny Mack Brown. LOC: California: Iverson Ranch; Brandeis Ranch; Universal Studio backlot.
Law of the Ranger (1937 Columbia) Bob Allen. LOC: California: Corriganville.
Law of the Rio Grande (1931 Syndicate) Bob Custer. LOC: California: Jauregui Ranch; Towsley Canyon; Trem Carr Ranch.
Law of the Saddle (1943 PRC) Bob Livingston. LOC: California: Corriganville.
Law of the Texan (1938 Columbia) Buck Jones. LOC: California: Iverson Ranch; Corriganville; Burro Flats.
Law of the Timber (1941 PRC) Marjorie Reynolds. LOC: California: Big Bear.
Law of the Valley (1944 Monogram) Johnny Mack Brown. LOC: California: Walker Ranch.
Law of the West (1932 World Wide) Bob Steele. LOC: California: Frank LaSalle Ranch.
Law of the West (1949 Monogram) Johnny Mack Brown. LOC: California: Walker Ranch.
Law of the Wild, The (1934 Mascot) Bob Custer. LOC: California: Iverson Ranch; Frank Straubinger Ranch.
Law of the Wolf (1941 Ziehm) Dennis Moore. LOC: California: Lake Arrowhead.
Law Rides Again, The (1943 Monogram) Trail Blazers. LOC: California: Corriganville; Rancho Placeritos; Walker Ranch.
Law Rides, The (1936 Superior) Bob Steele. LOC: California: Walker Ranch.
Law vs. Billy the Kid, The (1954 Columbia) Scott Brady. LOC: California: Rancho Placeritos; Agoura Ranch; Walker Ranch.
Law West of Tombstone, The (1938 RKO) Harry Carey. LOC: California: RKO Encino Ranch.
Lawless Border (1935 Spectrum) Bill Cody. LOC:
Lawless Breed (1946 Universal) Kirby Grant. LOC: California: Iverson Ranch.
Lawless Breed, The (1953 Universal) Rock Hudson. LOC: California: Jauregui Ranch; Circle J Ranch; Vasquez Rocks; Universal Studio backlot.

Lawless Code (1949 Monogram) Jimmy Wakely. LOC: California: Walker Ranch.

Lawless Cowboys (1951 Monogram) Whip Wilson. LOC: California: Iverson Ranch.

Lawless Eighties, The (1957 Republic) Buster Crabbe. LOC: California: Iverson Ranch; Towsley Canyon; Republic Studio backlot.

Lawless Empire (1945 Columbia) Charles Starrett. LOC: California: Walker Ranch; Columbia Ranch.

Lawless Frontier, The (1934 Monogram) John Wayne. LOC: California: Trem Carr Ranch; Red Rock Canyon; Kernville.

Lawless Land (1936 Republic) Johnny Mack Brown. LOC: California: Ralph M. Like Studio backlot; Republic Studios backlot; Walker Ranch.

Lawless Nineties, The (1936 Republic) John Wayne. LOC: California: Trem Carr Ranch.

Lawless Plainsmen (1942 Columbia) Charles Starrett. LOC: California: Iverson Ranch; Brandeis Ranch; Columbia Ranch.

Lawless Range (1935 Republic) John Wayne. LOC: California: Lone Pine; Vasquez Rocks; Trem Carr Ranch.

Lawless Rider, The (1954 United Artists) John Carpenter. LOC: California: Iverson Ranch; Corriganville; Ingram Ranch.

Lawless Riders (1935 Columbia) Ken Maynard. LOC: California: Iverson Ranch; Trem Carr Ranch; Lone Pine.

Lawless Street, A (1955 Columbia) Randolph Scott. LOC: California: Columbia Ranch; French Ranch.

Lawless Valley (1932 Kent) Lane Chandler. LOC: California: Chatsworth Manor; Chatsworth Lake.

Lawless Valley (1938 RKO) George O'Brien. LOC: California: Corriganville; RKO Encino Ranch.

Lawless, The (1950 Paramount) Macdonald Carey. LOC: California: Grass Valley, Marysville.

Lawless, The (1956 Wrather) Clayton Moore. LOC: California: Iverson Ranch; Corriganville; Ingram Ranch; Rancho Placeritos.

Lawman (1971 United Artists) Burt Lancaster. LOC: MEXICO: Durango: Chupaderos; El Saltito waterfall; Rancho Marley; Zacatecas: Sierra de Organos.

Lawman is Born, A (1937 Republic) Johnny Mack Brown. LOC: California: Walker Ranch; Rancho Placeritos.

Lawmen (1944 Monogram) Johnny Mack Brown. LOC: California: Iverson Ranch; Walker Ranch.

Lay That Rifle Down (1955 Republic) Judy Canova. LOC: California: Iverson Ranch; Republic Studio backlot.

Leadville Gunslinger (1952 Republic) Allan Lane. LOC: California: Iverson Ranch; Burro Flats.

Leather Burners (1943 United Artists) William Boyd. LOC: California: Bronson Canyon; Lone Pine; possibly Keeler Train Depot; California Studio backlot.

Left for Dead (2007 Finding Films/Sophia Productions) Maria Alche. LOC: ARGENTINA.

Left-Handed Gun, The (1958 Warner Bros) Paul Newman. LOC: California: Janss Janss Conejo Ranch; Warner Bros Studio backlot; Warner Ranch.

Left-Handed Law (1937 Universal) Buck Jones. LOC: California: Walker Ranch.

Legacy of the Incas, The (1966 Orbita) Guy Madison. LOC: BULGARIA: Belogradtschik National Park; Kraija Maja reservoir; Nataschalo; Neguschewo; Prebodna Cave; Robotana; Sofia; Peru: Machu Picchu; Cuzco; SPAIN: Aranjuez, Madrid.

Legend (1995 UPN) Richard Dean Anderson. LOC: Arizona: MescalOld Tucson.

Legend of Butch & Sundance, The (2004 NBC) David Clayton Rogers. LOC: CANADA: Alberta: Calgary.

Legend of Custer, The (1968 20th Century Fox) Wayne Maunder. LOC: California: Century Ranch; Bell/Berry Ranch.

Legend of Death Valley (1977 American National Ent) Robert Dawson. LOC:

Legend of Earl Durand, The (1974 Howco) Peter Haskell. LOC: Wyoming: Pinedale; Jackson: Bridger Teton National Forest.

Legend of God's Gun, The (2007 Indian Pictures) Robert Bones. LOC: California: Bodfish; Bronson Canyon; Calico Ghost Town; Death Valley Junction; Joshua Tree National Park; Paramount Ranch; Pioneertown; Rainbow National Landmark; Silver City Ghost Town; Vasquez Rocks.

Legend of Grizzly Adams, The (1990 Bull on the Run Productions) Gene Edwards. LOC: Arizona: Old Tucson

Legend of Jake Kincaid (2002 Dirt Road Productions) Alan Autry. LOC: California: Fresno; North Fork/Old Town; San Joaquin Valley.

Legend of Lobo, The (1962 Buena Vista) Rex Allen. LOC: Arizona: Sedona.

Legend of Nigger Charlie, The (1972 Paramount) Fred Williamson. LOC: New Mexico: J. W. Eaves Ranch; Virginia: Shirley Plantation.

Legend of the Boy and the Eagle (1967 Buena Vista) Frank DeKova. LOC: Arizona: Canyon de Chelly; Flagstaff; Sedona; New Mexico: Zuni; Utah: Glen Canyon.

Legend of the Golden Gun (1979 NBC) Jeff Osterhage. LOC: California: Bronson Canyon.

Legend of the Lone Ranger, The (1949 Apex) Clayton Moore. LOC: California: Bronson Canyon; Iverson Ranch.

Legend of the Lone Ranger, The (1981 Universal Pictures) Klinton Spilsbury. LOC: Arizona: Monument Valley; California: Bronson Canyon; Vasquez Rocks; Nevada: Valley of Fire State Park; New Mexico: Abiquiú Ghost Ranch; Bonanza Creek Ranch; Cumbres & Toltec Scenic Railroad; El Rancho de las Golondrinas; J.W. Eaves Movie Ranch; The White Place/Plaza Blanca Abiquiú.

Legend of the Lost (1957 United Artists) John Wayne. LOC: LIBYA: Leptis Magna.

Legend of the Phantom Rider, The (2000 A Seed Production) Robert McRay. LOC: Arizona: Dragoon Mountains; Mescal; Willcox dry lake.

Legend of Tom Dooley, The (1959 Columbia) Michael Landon. LOC: California: Iverson Ranch.

Legend of Walks Far Woman, The (1982 NBC) Raquel Welch. LOC: Montana: Billings; Hardin; Red Lodge.

Legend of Wolf Mountain, The (1992 Majestic Entertainment) Bo Hopkins. LOC: Utah: Salt Lake City area.

Legend of Zorro, The (2005 Columbia Pictures) Antonio Banderas. LOC: MEXICO: San Luis Potosí: Ex Hacienda Gogorron, Villa de Reyes; Minas Ventura and Canon Ventura; Rancho Cortez; Ex Hacienda La Muralla; Salinas de Hidalgo; Ipina building; Villa de Reyes; NEW ZEALAND: Wellington.

Legends of the Fall (1994 TriStar Pictures) Brad Pitt. LOC: CANADA: Alberta: Calgary; Ghost River; Morley; Stoney Indian Reservation; British Columbia: Gastown Vancouver; JAMAICA.

Legion of the Lawless (1940 RKO) George O'Brien. LOC: California: Corriganville; Jauregui Ranch; RKO Encino Ranch.

Let Freedom Ring (1939 MGM) Nelson Eddy. LOC: California: Garner Ranch; Keen Camp; Arizona: Santa Catalina Mountains.

Let's Sing a Western Song (1947 Universal) The Gordonaires. LOC:

Life and Legend of Buffalo Jones, The (1976 Starfire Filmes) Rick Guinn. LOC: UTAH: Bridal Veil Falls, Provo Canyon.

Life and Times of Grizzly Adams, The (1974 Sunn Classics) Dan Haggerty. LOC: Utah: Heber City, Kamas, Mirror Lake.

Life and Times of Judge Roy Bean, The (1972 National General) Paul Newman. LOC: Arizona: Old Tucson; Mescal.

Life in the Raw (1933 Fox) George O'Brien. LOC: California: Lone Pine; Hesperia.

Light in the Forest, The (1958 Buena Vista) Fess Parker) Tennessee: Great Smoky Mountains. and around Gatlinburg.

Light of the Western Stars, The (1940 Paramount) Russell Hayden. LOC: California: Lone Pine.

Light of Western Stars, The (1930 Paramount) Richard Arlen. LOC: California: Paramount Ranch; Lone Pine.

Lightnin' (1930 Fox) Joel McCrea. LOC: Nevada: Reno; Lake Tahoe.

Lightnin' Bill Carson (1936 Puritan) Tim McCoy. LOC: California: Walker Ranch; Trem Carr Ranch.

Lightnin' Crandall (1937 Republic) Bob Steele. LOC: California: Walker Ranch; Jauregui Ranch; Kernville.

Lightnin' Smith Returns (1931 Syndicate) Buddy Roosevelt) LOST/MISSING

Lightning Bill (1934 Superior) Buffalo Bill Jr. LOC: California.

Lightning Carson Rides Again (1938 Victory) Tim McCoy. LOC: California: Brandeis Ranch.

Lightning Guns (1950 Columbia) Charles Starrett. LOC: California: Iverson Ranch.

Lightning Jack (1993 Buena Vista) Paul Hogan. LOC: Arizona: Cork Screw Canyon/Antelope Canyon, Page; Mescal; Monument Valley; Old Tucson; Colorado: Buckskin Joe; Red Rock Canyon; New Mexico: Bonanza Creek Ranch; Carson National Forest near Abiquiú; Cook Ranch/Cerro Pelon Ranch; Santa Fe National Forest near Los Alamos; The White Place/Plaza Blanca Abiquiú; Utah: Arches National Park; Halls Crossing; Professor Valley and Onion Creek; Valley of the Gods; Mexican Hat.

Lightning Raiders (1946 PRC) Buster Crabbe. LOC: California: Corriganville.

Lightning Range (1934 Superior) Buddy Roosevelt. LOC: California: Ranch01.

Lightning Strikes West (1940 Colony) Ken Maynard. LOC: California: Walker Ranch; Jauregui Ranch.

Lightning Triggers (1935 Kent) Reb Russell. LOC: California: Frank LaSalle Ranch; Towsley Canyon; Ralph M. Like Studio backlot.

Lightning Warrior (1931 Mascot) Frankie Darro. LOC: California: Iverson Ranch; Bronson Canyon; Kernville; Kernville Movie Street.

Lights of Old Santa Fe (1944 Republic) Roy Rogers. LOC: California: French Ranch; Kernville; Republic Studio backlot.

Linda and Abilene (1969 United Pictures) Sharon Matt. LOC: California: Spahn Ranch.

Lion and the Horse, The (1952 Warner Bros) Steve Cochran. LOC: Utah: Kanab Canyon; Three Lakes; Zion National Park.

Lion's Den, The (1936 Puritan) Tim McCoy. LOC: California: Brandeis Ranch; Jauregui Ranch; Chatsworth Train Depot.

Little Big Horn (1951 Lippert) Lloyd Bridges. LOC: California: Iverson Ranch.

Little Big Man (1970 National General) Dustin Hoffman. LOC: California: North Ranch; Montana: Billings; Cheyenne and Crow Indian Reservations; Custer Battlefield National Monument; Nevada City; Virginia City; CANADA: CL Ranch, Calgary, Alberta; Morley, Alberta.

Little House on the Prairie (2005 ABC miniseries) Erin Cottrell. LOC: CANADA: Alberta: Cochrane.

Little House: Bless All the Dear Children (1984 NBC) Melissa Gilbert. LOC: California: Big Sky Ranch; Arizona: Old Tucson; Mescal.

Little House: Look Back to Yesterday (1983 NBC) Michael London. LOC: California: Big Sky Ranch; USC.

Little House: The Last Farewell (1984 NBC) Michael Landon. LOC: California: Big Sky Ranch.

Little Joe, the Wrangler (1942 Universal) Johnny Mack Brown. LOC: California: Corriganville.

Little Moon and Jud McGraw (1979 Cougar Prod) James Caan. LOC: Nevada: Las Vegas area.

Little Ranger, The (1938 MGM) Little Rascals. LOC: California:

Little Shepherd of Kingdom Come (1961 20th Century Fox) Jimmie Rodgers.

LOC: California: Big Bear; Hitchcock Ranch; 20th Century Fox backlot.

Little Treasure (1985 TriStar Pictures) Burt Lancaster. LOC: New Mexico: Las Vegas; MEXICO: Durango: La Joya Ranch; Morelos.

Littlest Cowboy, The (2003 Tycoon Studios) Matthew Stagi. LOC: Arizona: Gammons Gulch Benson.

Littlest Rebel, The (1935 20th Century Fox) Shirley Temple. LOC: California: 20th Century Fox backlot.

Llano Kid, The (1939 Paramount) Tito Guizar. LOC: California: Iverson Ranch; Lone Pine; Anchor Ranch.

Loaded Pistols (1949 Columbia) Gene Autry. LOC: California: Iverson Ranch; Corriganville; Lone Pine; Columbia Ranch.

Local Bad Man, The (1932 Allied) Hoot Gibson. LOC: California: Paramount Ranch; Chatsworth Train Station; Walker Ranch.

Lone Avenger, The (1933 World Wide) Ken Maynard. LOC: California: Trem Carr Ranch.

Lone Bandit, The (1934 Empire) Lane Chandler. LOC: California: Newhall.

Lone Cowboy (1933 Paramount) Jackie Cooper. LOC: California: Tuolumne County; Sonora; Knight's Ferry; Warnerville.

Lone Defender, The (1930 Mascot) Rin-Tin-Tin. LOC: California: Tec-Art Studio backlot; Providencia Ranch; Bronson Canyon.

Lone Gun, The (1954 United Artists) George Montgomery. LOC: California: Iverson Ranch; Agoura.

Lone Hand Texan, The (1947 Columbia) Charles Starrett. LOC: California: Corriganville; Columbia Ranch.

Lone Hand, The (1953 Universal) Joel McCrea. LOC: California: Universal Studio backlot; Colorado: Durango-Silverton Narrow Gauge Railroad, Durango; Molas Lake.

Lone Justice 2 (1995 Triboro Entertainment Group) Brad Johnson. LOC: Texas: Luck Ranch/Willieville/Nelson Ranch Spicewood, Austin.

Lone Justice 3 (1996 Triboro Entertainment Group) Brad Johnson. LOC: Texas: Luck Ranch, Willieville; Nelson Ranch, Spicewood; Austin.

Lone Prairie, The (1942 Columbia) Russell Hayden. LOC: California: Iverson Ranch; Corriganville; Agoura.

Lone Ranger and the Lost City of Gold, The (1958 United Artists) Clayton Moore. LOC: Arizona: Old Tucson; San Xavier Del Bac Mission; Cortaro.

Lone Ranger Rides Again, The (1939 Republic) Robert Livingston. LOC: California: Iverson Ranch; Bronson Canyon; Red Rock Canyon; Kernville; Republic Studio backlot.

Lone Ranger, The (1938 Republic) Lee Powell. LOC: California: Iverson Ranch; Lone Pine; Republic Studio backlot.

Lone Ranger, The (1956 Warner Bros) Clayton Moore. LOC: California: Iverson Ranch; Corriganville; Rancho Placeritos; Bronson Canyon; French Ranch;

Utah: Kanab Canyon; Johnson Canyon.

Lone Ranger, The (2003 TNT) Chad Michael Murray. LOC: California: Melody Ranch NewhallLake Piru.

Lone Rider (2008 RHI Entertainment) Lou Diamond Phillips. LOC: California: Disney's Golden Oak Ranch.

Lone Rider Ambushed, The (1941 PRC) George Houston. LOC: California: Walker Ranch.

Lone Rider and the Bandit, The (1942 PRC) George Houston. LOC: California: Walker Ranch; Jauregui Ranch.

Lone Rider Crosses the Rio, The (1941 PRC) George Houston. LOC: California: Iverson Ranch; Corriganville; Rancho Placeritos.

Lone Rider Fights Back, The (1941 PRC) George Houston. LOC: California: Walker Ranch; Jauregui Ranch; Rancho Placeritos.

Lone Rider in Cheyenne, The (1942 PRC) George Houston. LOC: California: Iverson Ranch; Rancho Placeritos.

Lone Rider in Frontier Fury, The (1941 PRC) George Houston. LOC: California: Corriganville; Brandeis Ranch.

Lone Rider in Ghost Town, The (1941 PRC) George Houston. LOC: California: Iverson Ranch.

Lone Rider in Texas Justice, The (1942 PRC) George Houston. LOC: California: Iverson Ranch; Corriganville.

Lone Rider Rides On, The (1941 PRC) George Houston. LOC: California: Corriganville.

Lone Rider, The (1930 Columbia) Buck Jones. LOC: California: Kernville.

Lone Rider, The (1934 Imperial) Wally Wales. LOC: California: Palmdale.

Lone Star (1952 MGM) Clark Gable. LOC: California: MGM backlot; Colorado: Towaoc; Bayfield; Pine River.

Lone Star Law Men (1941 Monogram) Tom Keene. LOC: California: Walker Ranch; Rancho Placeritos.

Lone Star Moonlight (1946 Columbia) Ken Curtis. LOC: California: Columbia Ranch.

Lone Star Pioneers (1939 Columbia) Bill Elliott. LOC: California: Iverson Ranch.

Lone Star Raiders (1940 Republic) Three Mesquiteers. LOC: California: Iverson Ranch; Chatsworth Train Depot; Red Rock Canyon; Republic Studio backlot.

Lone Star Ranger (1942 20th Century Fox) John Kimbrough. LOC: California: Lone Pine.

Lone Star Ranger, The (1930 Fox) George O'Brien. LOC: Arizona: Monument Valley; Tuba City; Winslow; Utah: Rainbow Bridge.

Lone Star Trail, The (1943 Universal) Johnny Mack Brown. LOC: California: Corriganville; Universal Studio backlot.

Lone Star Vigilantes, The (1942 Columbia) Bill Elliott. LOC: California: Iverson Ranch; Corriganville; Burro Flats; Agoura.

Lone Texan (1959 20th Century Fox) Willard Parker. LOC: California: Iverson Ranch; 20th Century Fox backlot.

Lone Texas Ranger (1945 Republic) Bill Elliott. LOC: California: Iverson Ranch; Republic Studio backlot.

Lone Trail, The (1932 Syndicate) Rex Lease. LOC: California: Big Bear.

Lonely Are the Brave (1962 Universal) Kirk Douglas. LOC: New Mexico: Albuquerque; Tijeras Canyon; Sandia Mountains.

Lonely Man, The (1957 Paramount) Jack Palance. LOC: California: Iverson Ranch; Vasquez Rocks.

Lonely Trail, The (1936 Republic) John Wayne. LOC: California: Mentryville; Pico Canyon; Republic Studio backlot.

Lonesome Cowboys (1968 Factory Films) Julian Burroughs. LOC: Arizona: Old Tucson; Rancho Linda Guest Ranch, Oracle.

Lonesome Dove (1989 CBS) Robert Duvall. LOC: New Mexico: Abiquiú; Black Lake Angel Fire; Bonanza Creek Ranch; Cook Ranch/Cerro Pelon Ranch; J. W. Eaves Movie Ranch; San Ildefonso Pueblo; Santo Domingo Pueblo; Tent Rocks Cochiti Pueblo; Texas: Alamo Village; Rancho Rio Grande/Moody's Ranch, Del Rio; Luck Ranch/Willie-ville/Nelson Ranch Spicewood, Austin.

Lonesome Trail (1945 Monogram) Jimmy Wakely. LOC: California: Walker Ranch; Rancho Placeritos.

Lonesome Trail, The (1930 Syndicate) Charles Delaney. LOC:

Lonesome Trail, The (1955 Lippert) Wayne Morris. LOC: California: Paramount Ranch.

Long Gun of New Mexico (2008 Voices Productions) Ray Lopeman. LOC: New Mexico: Deming; Double E Ranch Gila; Pinos Altos Silver City; Rafter Zs Ranch Silver City; Steins Ghost Town.

Long Ride Home, The (2003 Constellation Entertainment) Randy Travis. LOC: California: Paramount Ranch; Veluzat Motion Picture Ranch.

Long Riders, The (1980 United Artists) David Carradine. LOC: California: Burbank Studios; Columbia; Warnerville area, Stanislaus County; Georgia; Texas: Texas State Railroad, Rusk; Palestine.

Long Rope, The (1961 20th Century Fox) Hugh Marlowe. LOC: California: Rancho Placeritos.

Long, Long Trail, The (1929 Universal) Hoot Gibson. LOC: California: French Ranch; Lake Sherwood; Salinas.

Longarm (1988 Universal) Daphne Ashbrook. LOC: New Mexico: Abiquiú Ghost Ranch; Cook Ranch/Cerro Pelon Ranch; J. W. Eaves Movie Ranch; Río Chama.

Longhorn, The (1951 Monogram) William Elliott. LOC: California: Iverson Ranch.

Longhouse Tales, The (2006 AOL Television) Tom Jackson. LOC: CANADA.

Look Out Sister (1949 Ascor) Louis Jordan. LOC: California: Valyermo Ranch.

Los Locos (1997 Polygram Film Productions) Mario Van Peebles. LOC: Arizona: Mescal; Tumacacori Mission; Willcox Playa dry lake.

Loser's End (1934 Reliable) Jack Perrin. LOC: California: Frank LaSalle Ranch.

Lost Canyon (1942 United Artists) William Boyd. LOC: California: Kernville; California Studio backlot.

Lost in Alaska (1952 Universal) Abbott & Costello. LOC: California: Universal Studio backlot.

Lost Ranch (1937 Victory) Tom Tyler. LOC: California: Brandeis Ranch.

Lost Trail, The (1945 Monogram) Johnny Mack Brown. LOC: California: Walker Ranch.

Louis L'Amour's Down the Long Hills (1986 ABC) Bruce Boxleitner. LOC: Utah: Heber Valley; Heber City.

Love Begins (2011 RHI Entertainment) Wes Brown. LOC: California: Melody Ranch.

Love Comes Softly (2003 The Hallmark Channel) Katherine Heigl. LOC: California: Coloma; El Dorado County; Lotus; Paramount Ranch.

Love Finds a Home (2009 The Hallmark Channel) Sarah Jones. LOC: California: Rancho Placeritos; Sable Ranch; Disney's Golden Oak Ranch.

Love Me Tender (1956 20th Century Fox) Elvis Presley. LOC: California: Century Ranch.

Love Ranch (2009 Capitol Films) Joe Pesci. LOC: California: Donner Pass; Nevada: Reno; New Mexico: Albuquerque.

Love Takes Wing (2009 RHI Entertainment) Sarah Jones. LOC: California: Melody Ranch; Sable Ranch.

Love's Abiding Joy (2006 RHI Entertainment) Erin Cottrell. LOC: California: Big Sky Ranch; Disney's Golden Oak Ranch.

Love's Christmas Journey (2011 Mediapool Prod) Natalie Hall. LOC: California: Melody Ranch

Love's Enduring Promise (2004 The Hallmark Channel) January Jones. LOC: California: Big Sky Ranch; Paramount Ranch.

Love's Long Journey (2005 The Hallmark Channel) Erin Cottrell. LOC: California: Big Sky Ranch; Disney's Golden Oak Ranch.

Love's Unending Legacy (2007 The Hallmark Channel) Erin Cottrell. LOC: California: Big Sky Ranch; Disney's Golden Oak Ranch; Paramount Ranch.

Love's Unfolding Dream (2007 RHI Entertainment) Erin Cottrell. LOC: California: Big Sky Ranch; Disney's Golden Oak Ranch; Paramount Ranch.

Lovin' Molly (1974 Columbia) Anthony Perkins. LOC: Texas: Bastrop.

Luck of Roaring Camp, The (1937 Monogram) Owen Davis, Jr. LOC: California: Iverson Ranch; Rancho Placeritos.

Lucky Cisco Kid (1940 20th Century Fox) Cesar Romero. LOC: California: Iverson Ranch; Burro Flats; 20th Century Fox backlot.

Lucky Country/Dark Frontier (2009 The South Australian Film Corporation) Aden Young. LOC: AUSTRALIA.

Lucky Cowboy (1944 Paramount) Eddie Dew. LOC:

IVERSON MOVIE RANCH
Above: Garden of the Gods **Below:** Western Street

BRANDEIS RANCH
Western Town

Above: BUCKSKIN JOE
Below: WILLIAM MACKELPRANG RANCH (JOHNSON CANYON) MOVIE SETS

CORRIGANVILLE MOVIE RANCH
Above: Fort Apache **Below:** "The Man From Colorado" western street

Above: Kernville Western Movie Street
Below: Jack Ingram Western Town

**Above: Trem Carr Ranch Western Street
Below: Rancho Placeritos (Monogram Ranch) Western Street**

Above: RKO Studio Western Street (silent days)
Below: RKO Encino Ranch Western Street

JANSS CONEJO RANCH Western Sets

Lucky Larkin (1930 Universal) Ken Maynard. LOC:

Lucky Larrigan (1932 Monogram) Rex Bell. LOC: California: Midwick Country Club; Glendale Train Station; Trem Carr Ranch.

Lucky Luke (2009 UGC YM) Jean Dujardin. LOC: ARGENTINA: Jujuy; Salta; San Juan; Uspallata.

Lucky Terror (1936 Grand National) Hoot Gibson. LOC: California: Iverson Ranch; Lone Pine; Ralph M. Like Studio backlot.

Lucky Texan, The (1934 Monogram) John Wayne. LOC: California: Jauregui Ranch; Trem Carr Ranch.

Lumberjack (1944 United Artists) William Boyd. LOC: California: Iverson Ranch; Jauregui Ranch; Cedar Lake; California Studio backlot.

Lure of the Wasteland (1939 Al Lane Pictures) Grant Withers. LOC: Utah: Kanab.

Lust for Gold (1949 Columbia) Glenn Ford. LOC: California: Columbia Ranch; Arizona: Superstition Mountains.

Lust in the Dust (1984 A Fox Run Prod./New World) Divine. LOC: New Mexico: Bonanza Creek Ranch; J.W. Eaves Movie Ranch/Mexican set; The White Place, Abiquiú.

Lust to Kill, A (1960 Production Associates) Jim Davis. LOC: California: Valyermo Ranch; Oliver Drake Ranch; Piute Butte.

Lusty Men, The (1952 RKO) Robert Mitchum. LOC: California: Livermore; Arizona: Tucson; Oregon: Pendleton; Washington: Spokane; Texas: San Angelo.

Macahans, The (1976 MGM-TV) James Arness. LOC: California: Franklin Canyon Reservoir; Colorado: Bent's Old Fort National Historic Site; Utah: Kanab Canyon; Kanab Movie Fort; Johnson Canyon Movie Set; Robinson Ranch; Duck Creek.

Machismo: 40 Graves for 40 Guns (1971 Boxoffice International) Robert Padilla. LOC: California: Corriganville; Yosemite.

Macho Callahan (1970 Avco/Embassy) David Janssen. LOC: MEXICO: Durango: Ex Hacienda La Ferreria de Flores; Sierra de Durango; Morelos: Ex Hacienda de Coahuixtla; San Pedro Apatlaco, Ayala.

Macintosh and T. J. (1976 Penland) Clay O'Brien. LOC: Texas: Dickens; Four Sixes Ranch, Guthrie; Lubbock.

MacKenna's Gold (1969 Columbia) Gregory Peck. LOC: California: Palmdale; Arizona: Canyon de Chelley; Lee's Ferry; Utah: Snow Canyon; Coral Pink Sand Dunes; Glen Canyon National Recreation Area; Kanab Canyon; Paria; Oregon: Medford; Rogue River; Grant's Pass.

Mad at the Moon (1992 Republic Picture Productions) Mary Stuart Masterson. LOC: California: Paramount Ranch, Agoura.

Mad, Mad Wagon Party (2010 Delta Corp) George Kennedy. LOC: California: Modesto; Sonora; Arizona: Old Tucson; Sierrita Mountains; Ironwood Forest National Monument.

Magnificent Matador, The (1955 20th Century Fox) Anthony Quinn. LOC:

MEXICO: Mexico: Mexico City, El Toreo bullfighting ring; matador Carlos Arruza's ranch just outside Mexico City.

Magnificent Seven Ride!, The (1972 United Artists) Lee Van Cleef. LOC: California: Lake Los Angeles; Vasquez Rocks; Universal Studio backlot.

Magnificent Seven, The (1960 United Artists) Yul Brynner. LOC: MEXICO: Durango: Santiago Papasquiaro; Morelos: Amatlan; Santiago Tepetlapa; Santo Domingo Ocotitlan; Tepoztlan; Tlayacapan; Mexico: Mexico City: Estudios Churubusco Azteca.

Magnificent Seven: The Series, The (1998 MGM) Michael Biehn. LOC: Arizona: Cochise Stronghold National Monument West side; Mescal; Willcox Playa dry lake; California: Melody Ranch; Veluzat Motion Picture Ranch.

Mail Order Bride (1964 MGM) Buddy Ebsen. LOC: California: MGM backlot; Kennedy Meadows, Tuolomne County.

Mail Order Bride (2008 The Hallmark Channel) Greg Evigan. LOC: CANADA: British Columbia: Bordertown/Western town Maple Ridge, Vancouver.

Major Dundee (1965 Columbia) Charlton Heston. LOC: MEXICO: Durango: Chupaderos; El Saltito waterfall; Ex Hacienda de Tapias; Morcillo; Mexico: La Marquesa National Park; San Juan Teoitihuacan; Guerrero: Guerrero Desert; Rio Mezcala; Hidalgo: Pachuca; Morelos: Cuautla; Jonacatepec; ex Hacienda Pantitlan San Nicolas; Oaxtepec; Rio Tehuixtla; Tequesquitengo; Tlayacapan; Zacatepec; Nuevo Leon: Vista Hermosa; Monterrey.

Make Haste to Live (1954 Republic) Stephen McNally. LOC: New Mexico: Taos.

Man Alone, A (1955 Republic) Ray Milland. LOC: California: Republic Studios backlot; Utah: Snow Canyon.

Man and Boy (1971 J Cornelius Crean Films) Bill Cosby. LOC: Arizona: Carefree.

Man Behind the Gun, The (1953 Warner Bros) Randolph Scott. LOC: California: Iverson Ranch; Corriganville; Berry Ranch.

Man Called Gannon, A (1969 Universal) James Franciosa. LOC: California: Jamestown, Tuolumne County; Warnerville, Stanislaus County.

Man Called Horse, A (1970 National General) Richard Harris. LOC: South Dakota: Custer State Park; MEXICO: Durango: Santa Barbara; Sierra de Durango.

Man from Arizona, The (1932 Monogram) Rex Bell. LOST/MISSING

Man from Bitter Ridge, The (1955 Universal) Lex Barker. LOC: California: Skeleton Canyon/Mecca; Universal Studio backlot.

Man from Cheyenne (1942 Republic) Roy Rogers. LOC: California: Iverson Ranch; Jauregui Ranch; Burro Flats; Red Rock Canyon; Republic Studio backlot.

Man from Colorado, The (1948 Columbia) Glenn Ford. LOC: California: Iverson Ranch; Corriganville.

Man from Dakota, The (1940 MGM) Wallace Beery. LOC: California: Lake Sherwood; Kernville.

Man from Death Valley, The (1931 Monogram) Tom Tyler. LOC: California: Bodie.

Man from Del Rio (1956 United Artists) Anthony Quinn. LOC: California: Rancho Placeritos.

Man from Galveston, The (1964 Warner Bros) Jeffrey Hunter. LOC: California: Warner Ranch.

Man from God's Country (1958 Allied Artists) George Montgomery. LOC: California: Iverson Ranch; Corriganville; Vasquez Rocks.

Man from Guntown, The (1935 Puritan) Tim McCoy. LOC: California: Jauregui Ranch; Ralph M. Like Studio backlot.

Man from Hell, The (1934 Kent) Reb Russell. LOC: California: Bronson Canyon.

Man from Hell's Edges, The (1932 World Wide) Bob Steele. LOC: California: Jauregui Ranch; Garner Ranch; Trem Carr Ranch.

Man from Laramie, The (1955 Columbia) James Stewart. LOC: New Mexico: Jarrett Ranch, Santa Fe; Sandia Crest; Tesuque Pueblo; Taos.

Man from Montana (1941 Universal) Johnny Mack Brown. LOC: California: Agoura; Jauregui Ranch.

Man from Monterey, The (1933 Warner Bros) John Wayne. LOC: California: Providencia Ranch; Warner Bros Studio backlot.

Man from Montreal (1939 Universal) Richard Arlen. LOC: California: Cedar Lake; Big Bear.

Man from Music Mountain (1938 Republic) Gene Autry. LOC: California: Jauregui Ranch; Iverson Ranch; Republic Studios backlot.

Man from Music Mountain (1943 Republic) Roy Rogers. LOC: California: Kernville; Lone Pine; Mammoth Lakes; Republic Studio backlot.

Man from New Mexico, The (1932 Monogram) Tom Tyler. LOC: California: Trem Carr Ranch.

Man from Oklahoma (1945 Republic) Roy Rogers. LOC: California: Iverson Ranch; Vasquez Rocks; Republic Studio backlot.

Man from Rainbow Valley (1946 Republic) Monte Hale. LOC: California: Iverson Ranch; Chatsworth Lake; Val Steve Ranch, 14134 Riverside Drive, Van Nuys.

Man from Snowy River, The (1982 Cambridge Productions Inc./Snowy River Investment Pty. Ldt.) Kirk Douglas. LOC: AUSTRALIA: Victoria: Mansfield; Merrijig; Melbourne Studios, Melbourne.

Man from Sonora (1951 Monogram) Johnny Mack Brown. LOC: California: Iverson Ranch; Corriganville.

Man from Sundown, The (1939 Columbia) Charles Starrett. LOC: California: Columbia Ranch.

Man from Texas, The (1939 Monogram) Tex Ritter. LOC: California: Newhall.

Man from Texas, The (1947 Eagle-Lion) James Craig. LOC: California: Iverson Ranch; Rancho Placeritos.

Man from the Alamo, The (1953 Universal) Glenn Ford. LOC: California: Russell Ranch; Oak Park; Walker Ranch; Jauregui Ranch; Rancho Placeritos; Universal Studio backlot.

Man from the Black Hills (1952 Monogram) Johnny Mack Brown. LOC: California: Iverson Ranch.

Man from the Rio Grande, The (1943 Republic) Donald Barry. LOC: California: Iverson Ranch; Republic Studio backlot; Burro Flats.

Man from Thunder River, The (1943 Republic) William Elliott. LOC: California: Iverson Ranch; Corriganville.

Man from Tumbleweeds, The (1940 Columbia) William Elliott. LOC: California: Iverson Ranch; Columbia Ranch; Morrison Ranch.

Man from Utah, The (1934 Monogram) John Wayne. LOC: California: Trem Carr Ranch; Kernville.

Man From Wyoming, A (1930 Paramount) Gary Cooper. LOC: California: Paramount Ranch.

Man in the Saddle (1951 Columbia) Randolph Scott. LOC: California: Iverson Ranch; French Ranch; Lone Pine; Portal Pond, Mt Whitney Portal Road; Columbia Ranch.

Man in the Shadow (1958 Universal) Jeff Chandler. LOC: California: Conejo Valley; Universal Studio backlot.

Man of Action (1933 Columbia) Tim McCoy. LOC: California: Jauregui Ranch; Trem Carr Ranch.

Man of Conquest (1939 Republic) Richard Dix. LOC: California: Iverson Ranch; Sonora; Salt Spring Valley Reservoir, Stockton.

Man of the East (1971 Jadran Film) Terence Hill. LOC: Colorado: Durango-Silverton Narrow Gauge Railroad; ITALY: De Laurentiis Studio; Manziana; Topr Caldara; YUGOSLAVIA/CROATIA: Plitvice Lakes.

Man of the Forest (1933 Paramount) Randolph Scott. LOC: California: Paramount Ranch; Big Bear; Cedar Lake; Bear Valley.

Man of the West (1958 United Artists) Gary Cooper. LOC: California: Rancho Placeritos; Janss Janss Conejo Ranch; Red Rock Canyon; Tuolumne County; Jamestown.

Man or Gun (1958 Republic) Macdonald Carey. LOC: California: Republic Studio backlot.

Man to Man (1922 Universal) Harry Carey. LOC: California: Agoura Ranch; Arizona: Benson.

Man Trailer, The (1934 Columbia) Buck Jones. LOC: California: Iverson Ranch; Vasquez Rocks; Paramount Ranch; Kernville.

Man Who Came Back, The (2008 Gudegast Productions) Armand Assante. LOC: Texas: Alamo Village; Magnolia Liendo Plantation; Montgomery.

Man Who Loved Cat Dancing, The (1973 MGM) Burt Reynolds. LOC: Arizona: Ajo; Cornelia; Gila Bend; Rio Rico; Utah: Hurricane; Snow Canyon State Park; Paria; near Washington Dam; Virgin on the Virgin River.

Man Who Shot Liberty Valance, The (1962 Paramount) John Wayne. LOC: California: Janss Janss Conejo Ranch.

Man with the Gun (1955 United Artists) Robert Mitchum. LOC: California: 20th Century Fox backlot.

Man with the Steel Whip (1954 Republic) Richard Simmons. LOC: California: Iverson Ranch; Republic Studio backlot.

Man Without a Star (1955 Universal) Kirk Douglas. LOC: California: Ingram Ranch; Janss Janss Conejo Ranch; Agoura Ranch; Universal Studio backlot.

Man's Country (1938 Monogram) Jack Randall. LOC: California: Walker Ranch; Rancho Placeritos; Lone Pine.

Man's Land, A (1932 Allied) Hoot Gibson. LOC: California: Jauregui Ranch; Trem Carr Ranch.

Manhunt, The (1985 Fulvia Films/Samuel Goldwyn Company) John Ethan Wayne. LOC: Arizona: Navajo Bridge; Page; Lake Powell; San Rafael Ranch; San Rafael Valley; Sonoita; Tombstone; Tucson Rodeo Arena.

Manitou's Shoe (2001 Seven Pictures) Michael Bully Herbig. LOC: SPAIN: Canyon Negro Tabernas, Almería; Nueva Frontera/Mexican set Tabernas, Almería; Texas-Hollywood/Western town Almería; Valle del Búho West of Tabernas, Almería.

Many Rivers to Cross (1955 MGM) Robert Taylor. LOC: California: Cloverdale and Preston, Sonoma County.

Mara of the Wilderness (1965 Allied Artists) Adam West. LOC: Oregon: Deshutes National Forest.

Marauders, The (1947 United Artists) William Boyd. LOC: California: Iverson Ranch.

Marauders, The (1955 MGM) Dan Duryea. LOC: California: Bronson Canyon; Painted Canyon, Box Canyon, Mecca.

Mark of the Gun (1969 Emerson) Ross Hagen. LOC: California: Bell Location Ranch; San Bernardino Mountains.

Mark of the Lash (1948 Screen Guild) Lash LaRue. LOC: California: Ingram Ranch; Iverson Ranch.

Mark of the Renegade (1951 Universal) Ricardo Montalban. LOC: California: San Fernando Mission; Universal backlot.

Mark of the Spur (1932 Big 4) Bob Custer. LOC: California: Ralph M. Like Studio; Saugus Train Depot; Saugus.

Mark of Zorro, The (1940 20th Century Fox) Tyrone Power. LOC: California: Warner Ranch.

Mark of Zorro, The (1974 20th Century Fox-TV) Frank Langella. LOC: Arizona: Old Tucson; San Xavier Del Bac Mission.

Marked for Murder (1944 PRC) Texas Rangers. LOC: California: Corriganville.

Marked Trails (1944 Monogram) Hoot Gibson. LOC: California: Walker Ranch.

Marksman, The (1953 Allied Artists) Wayne Morris. LOC: California: Iverson Ranch.

Marshal of Amarillo (1948 Republic) Allan Lane. LOC: California: Iverson Ranch;

Republic Studio backlot.

Marshal of Cedar Rock (1953 Republic) Allan Lane. LOC: California: Iverson Ranch; Burro Flats; Republic Studio backlot.

Marshal of Cripple Creek (1947 Republic) Allan Lane. LOC: California: Iverson Ranch.

Marshal of Gunsmoke (1944 Universal) Tex Ritter. LOC: California: Corriganville; Universal Studio backlot.

Marshal of Heldorado (1950 Lippert) Russell Hayden. LOC: California: Iverson Ranch.

Marshal of Laredo (1945 Republic) Bill Elliott. LOC: California: Iverson Ranch.

Marshal of Mesa City, The (1939 RKO) George O'Brien. LOC: California: Corriganville; RKO Encino Ranch.

Marshal of Reno (1944 Republic) Bill Elliott. LOC: California: Iverson Ranch; Corriganville.

Marshal's Daughter, The (1953 United Artists) Hoot Gibson. LOC: California: Iverson Ranch; Corriganville; Walker Ranch; Vasquez Rocks.

Mask of Zorro, The (1998 TriStar Pictures) Antonio Banderas. LOC: MEXICO: Hidalgo: Atotonilco de Tula; ex Hacienda Santa Maria Regla; carretera No. 105; ex Hacienda de Santago Tetlapayac; Sonora: San Carlos; Tlaxcala: ex Hacienda de San Blas, Lopez Mateos.

Masked Raiders (1949 RKO) Tim Holt. LOC: California: Corriganville; Garner Ranch; Lone Pine.

Masked Rider, The (1941 Universal) Johnny Mack Brown. LOC: California: Iverson Ranch.

Mason of the Mounted (1932 Monogram) Bill Cody. LOC: California: Trem Carr Ranch.

Masquerade (1956 Wrather) Clayton Moore. LOC: California: Iverson Ranch; Corriganville; Lone Pine.

Massacre (1956 20th Century Fox) Dane Clark. LOC: MEXICO: Morelos: Cuernavaca area; Mexico City.

Massacre at Sand Creek (1956 Columbia-TV) John Derek. LOC: California: Corriganville.

Massacre Canyon (1954 Columbia) Phil Carey. LOC: California: Corriganville; Bronson Canyon; Burro Flats; Vasquez Rocks.

Massacre River (1949 Allied Artists) Rory Calhoun. LOC: California: Iverson Ranch; Arizona: Canyon de Chelly; Chinle.

Master Gunfighter, The (1975 Billy Jack Enterprises) Tom Laughlin. LOC: California: Monterey.

Masterson of Kansas (1954 Columbia) George Montgomery. LOC: California: Iverson Ranch; Corriganville; Ingram Ranch; Bronson Canyon; Columbia Ranch.

Match-Making Marshal, The (1955 Allied Artists) Guy Madison. LOC: California: Cedar Lake.

Maverick (1994 Warner Bros) Mel Gibson. LOC: California: Big Pine; El Mirage; Lone Pine; Manzanar; Yosemite National Park; Arizona: Lee's Ferry balanced rocks; Marble Canyon; Oregon: Columbia River Gorge; Utah: Warm Creek Glen Canyon National Recreation Area.

Maverick Queen, The (1956 Republic) Barbara Stanwyck. LOC: Colorado: Silverton; Royal Gorge; Durango-Silverton Narrow Gauge Railroad.

Maverick, The (1952 Allied Artists) William Elliott. LOC: California: Iverson Ranch.

McCabe and Mrs. Miller (1971 Warner Bros) Warren Beatty. LOC: CANADA: Vancouver, British Columbia.

McKenna of the Mounted (1932 Columbia) Buck Jones. LOC: California: Big Bear; San Bernardino Mountains; CANADA: British Columbia.

McLeod's Daughters (1996 Millennium Pictures Pty. Limited) Jack Thompson. LOC: AUSTRALIA: South Australia: Barossa Valley; Gawler 30 miles North of Adelaide; Light Regional District; Two Wells.

McLintock! (1963 United Artists) John Wayne. LOC: Arizona: Old Tucson; San Rafael Valley; Fairbank

McMasters . . . Tougher Than the West Itself, The (1969 Jayjen) Burl Ives. LOC: Arizona: Wolf Hole; Kaibab Mountains; Virgin Mountains; Paiute Wilderness Area; New Mexico: Madrid; Tesuque Pueblo; San Ildefonso Pueblo; Santa Fe.

McMasters, The (1970 Chevron) Burl Ives. LOC: New Mexico: McKee Ranch near Santa Fe; Madrid; San Ildefonso Pueblo; Tesuque Pueblo.

Mean as Hell (2003 Wild Bill at Batrston Station LLC) Steve Cormier. LOC: New Mexico: Bonanza Creek Ranch Santa Fe.

Meanest Men in the West, The (1978 NBC-TV) Charles Bronson. LOC: California: Vasquez Rocks; Universal Studio backlot.

Medico of Painted Springs, The (1941 Columbia) Charles Starrett. LOC: California: Columbia Ranch.

Meeksville Ghost, The (2001 Peakviewing/Tanmarsh Communications) Judge Reinhold. LOC: SOUTH AFRICA.

Meet Me in Las Vegas (1956 MGM) Dan Dailey. LOC: Nevada: Las Vegas.

Meet the Stars #7: Meet Roy Rogers (1941 Republic) Roy Rogers. LOC:

Melody of the Plains (1937 Spectrum) Fred Scott. LOC: California: Walker Ranch; Jauregui Ranch.

Melody Ranch (1940 Republic) Gene Autry. LOC: California: Mammoth Lakes; Lake Mary; Lone Pine; Republic Studio backlot.

Melody Trail (1935 Republic) Gene Autry. LOC: California: Garner Ranch; Idyllwild; Oregon: Pendleton.

Men of America (1932 RKO) William Boyd. LOC: California: Iverson Ranch; Santa Susana Pass Road.

Men of Texas (1942 Universal) Robert Stack. LOC: California: Iverson Ranch.

Men of the North (1930 MGM) Gilbert Roland. LOC: California: Big Bear.

Men of the Plains (1936 Colony) Rex Bell. LOC: California: Brandeis Ranch.

Men of the Timberland (1941 Universal) Richard Arlen. LOC: California: Lone Pine.

Men with Steel Faces (1940 Mascot) Gene Autry. LOC: California: Iverson Ranch; Agoura Ranch; Bronson Canyon.

Men Without Law (1930 Columbia) Buck Jones. LOC: California: Providencia Ranch.

Merry Mavericks (1951 Columbia) Three Stooges. LOC: California: Columbia Ranch.

Mesquite Buckaroo (1939 Metropolitan) Bob Steele. LOC: California: unknown location; Arizona: Arizona State Fairgrounds.

Mexicali Kid, The (1938 Monogram) Jack Randall. LOC: California: Rancho Placeritos; Lake Los Angeles; Red Rock Canyon.

Mexicali Rose (1940 Republic) Gene Autry. LOC: California: Corriganville; Rancho Placeritos; Victorville; Republic Studio backlot.

Mexican Gold (2009 Walker/Cable Productions) John Castellanos. LOC: Texas: Alamo Village Brackettville.

Mexican Hayride (1948 Universal) Abbott & Costello. LOC: California: Iverson Ranch; Calabasas.

Mexican Spitfire Out West (1940 RKO) Lupe Velez. LOC: California: RKO Culver City Studio.

Mexicana (1945 Republic) Tito Guizar. LOC: Stock footage of Mexico; No Exterior Locations.

Mi Amigo (2002 Azalea Film Corp.) Ed Bruce. LOC: Alabama: Mobile.

Mi Querido Tom Mix [My Darling Tom Mix] (1991 Gobierno del Estado de Zacatecas/Instituto Mexicano de Cinematografía) Ana Ofelia Murguía. LOC: Zacatecas: Jerez; Sombrerete.

Michigan Kid (1947 Universal) Jon Hall. LOC: California: Kernville.

Mild West, The (1933 Vitaphone) Janet Reade. LOC: No exteriors. Stock footage of exteriors.

Mine with the Iron Door, The (1936 Columbia) Richard Arlen. LOC: California: Deadman Point, North Verde Ranch/Kemper Campbell Ranch, Old Town Victorville and Train Depot, Upper Desert Knolls Area, Upper Narrows.

Miracle at Sage Creek (2005 Talmarc Productions) David Carradine. LOC: Arizona: Gammons Gulch; Mescal; Old Tucson.

Miracle Down Under (1987 Entertainment Media) John Waters. LOC: AUSTRALIA: Victoria: Melbourne.

Miracle in the Wilderness (1991 TNT) Kris Kristofferson. LOC: New Mexico: El Porvenir; Hermit's Peak; Johnson Mesa; Santa Fe National Forest near Las Vegas.

Miracle of the Hills, The (1959 20th Century Fox) Rex Reason. LOC:

Miracle Rider, The (1935 Mascot) Tom Mix. LOC: California: Iverson Ranch; Mystery Adobe Ranch; Agoura; Woodland Hills; Lone Pine; Mascot Studio backlot.

Misfits, The (1961 United Artists) Clark Gable. LOC: Nevada: Dayton; Reno; Pyramid Lake.

Missing, The (2003 Revolution Studios/Imagine Entertainment) Cate Blanchett. LOC: New Mexico: Abiquiú Ghost Ranch; Bandelier National Monument; Cook Ranch/Cerro Pelon Ranch; El Rancho de las Golondrinas; Río Chama Black Mesa; The Valles Caldera National Preserve; Zia Pueblo/Gypsum Point.

Mississippi Gambler, The (1953 Universal) Tyrone Power. LOC: California: Corriganville; Universal Studio backlot.

Missouri Breaks, The (1976 United Artists) Marlon Brando. LOC: Colorado: Buckskin Joes; Montana: Red Lodge; Billings; Nevada City; Virginia City; New Mexico: Cumbres and Toltec Scenic Railroad.

Missouri Outlaw, A (1941 Republic) Don Barry. LOC: California: Iverson Ranch.

Missouri Traveler, The (1958 Buena Vista) Brandon DeWilde. LOC: California: Rowland V. Lee Ranch; Warner Bros backlot.

Missourians, The (1950 Republic) Monte Hale. LOC: California: Iverson Ranch.

M'Liss (1936 RKO) Anne Shirley. LOC: California: RKO Encino Ranch.

Mohawk (1956 20th Century Fox) Scott Brady. LOC: California: Corriganville.

Mojave Firebrand (1944 Republic) Bill Elliott. LOC: California: Iverson Ranch; Corriganville.

Molly and Lawless John (1972 Producers Distributing Corp) Sam Elliott. LOC: New Mexico: Cerrillos; Nambè Pueblo; Puyè Cliffs; Las Cruces; Mesilla; White Sands National Monument.

Molly Cures a Cowboy (1940 RKO) Ray Whitley. LOC:

Money, Women and Guns (1959 Universal) Jock Mahoney. LOC: California: Lone Pine.

Montana (1950 Warner Bros) Errol Flynn. LOC: California: Warner Ranch.

Montana (1990 HBO) Richard Crenna. LOC: Montana: Bozeman.

Montana Belle (1952 RKO) Jane Russell. LOC: California: Republic Studio backlot; Colorado: Royal Gorge; Durango.

Montana Desperado (1951 Monogram) Johnny Mack Brown. LOC: California: Iverson Ranch.

Montana Incident (1952 Monogram) Whip Wilson. LOC: California: Iverson Ranch.

Montana Kid, The (1931 Monogram) Bill Cody. LOC: California: Walker Ranch; Jauregui Ranch; Trem Carr Ranch.

Montana Moon (1930 MGM) Johnny Mack Brown. LOC: California: San Jacinto Mountains.

Montana Sky (2007 Lifetime Television/Mandalay Entertainment) Ashley Williams. LOC: CANADA: Alberta: Calgary; Okotoks.

Montana Territory (1952 Columbia) Lon McCallister. LOC: California: Iverson Ranch.

Monte Walsh (1970 National General) Lee Marvin. LOC: Arizona: Old Tucson; Mescal; Circle Z Ranch, Patagonia; Elgin.
Monte Walsh (2003 TNT) Tom Selleck. LOC: CANADA: Alberta: CL Ranch; Calgary; Longview; Redwater/railway line Edmonton.
Montezuma's Lost Gold (1978 Gold Key Entertainment) Miles Hinshaw. LOC: California: Buttercup Valley; Arizona: Yuma Territorial Prison.
Mooching through Georgia (1939 Columbia) Buster Keaton. LOC: California: Columbia Ranch.
Moon over Las Vegas (1944 Universal) Anne Gwynne. LOC: Nevada: Las Vegas.
Moon over Montana (1946 Monogram) Jimmy Wakely. LOC: California: Walker Ranch; Rancho Placeritos.
Moonlight and Cactus (1932 Educational) Tom Patricola. LOC:
Moonlight and Cactus (1944 Universal) Leo Carrillo. LOC: California: Universal backlot.
Moonlight on the Prairie (1935 Warner Bros) Dick Foran. LOC: California: Lone Pine; June Lake.
Moonlight on the Range (1937 Spectrum) Fred Scott. LOC: California: Walker Ranch.
Moonlighter, The (1953 Warner Bros) Barbara Stanwyck. LOC: California: Corriganville; Agoura; Vasquez Rocks; Tuolumne County.
More Dead Than Alive (1969 United Artists) Clint Walker. LOC: California: Vasquez Rocks; Bronson Canyon; Warner Bros backlot.
More Than Magic (1956 Wrather) Clayton Moore. LOC: California: Iverson Ranch; Corriganville; Lone Pine; Utah: Kanab.
More Wild, Wild West (1980 CBS) Robert Conrad. LOC: Arizona: Lazy K Ranch Cortaro; Old Tucson.
Mormon Conquest, The (1939 Security National Pictures) Tom Wynn. LOC: Arizona: Grand Canyon North Rim; House Rock Valley; Utah: Bryce Canyon National Park; Kanab Canyon; Zion National Park.
Mother Lode (1982 Agamennon Films) Charlton Heston. LOC: CANADA: British Columbia: Vancouver.
Mountain Justice (1930 Universal) Ken Maynard. LOC: California: Universal Studio backlot.
Mountain Men, The (1980 Columbia Pictures) Charlton Heston. LOC: Arizona: Old Tucson; Wyoming: Triangle X Guest Ranch, Jackson Hole; Yellowstone National Park.
Mountain Rhythm (1939 Republic) Gene Autry. LOC: California: Iverson Ranch: Jauregui Ranch; Republic Studio backlot; Barney Oldfield Resort.
Mountain Rhythm (1943 Republic) Weaver Brothers. LOC: California: Republic Studios Backlot; McKinley Home for Boys and Girls, Canoga Park.
Mounted Fury (1931 Sono Art-World) John Bowers. LOST/MISSING
Mounted Stranger, The (1930 Universal) Hoot Gibson. LOC: California: Palmdale;

Mojave Desert.

Mr. Horn (1979 Lorimar-TV) David Carradine. LOC: MEXICO: Baja California Norte: Tecate.

Mrs. Mike (1949 Nassour) Dick Powell. LOC: California: Big Bear Lake; Cedar Lake; Agoura Ranch.

Mule Train (1950 Columbia) Gene Autry. LOC: California: Iverson Ranch; Corriganville; Lone Pine.

Murder on the Yukon (1940 Monogram) James Newill. LOC: California: Big Bear.

Musical Bandit, The (1941 RKO) Ray Whitley. LOC:

Mustachioed Bandit Meets His End, The (2007 SDI Media) Cazimir Milostan. California: San Dimas; Utah: Kanab Movie Ranch; Paria Canyon; William Mackelprang Ranch Movie Sets.

Mustang (1959 United Artists) Jack Buetel. LOC: California: Spahn Ranch.

Mustang (1973 Buena Vista) Flavio Martinez. LOC: New Mexico: Belen.

Mustang Country (1976 Universal) Joel McCrea. LOC: CANADA: Banff National Park.

Mutiny at Fort Sharp (1966 Walter Manley Enterprises) Broderick Crawford. LOC: SPAIN: Hoyo de Manzanares, Madrid; La Pedriza, Madrid.

My Darling Clementine (1946 20th Century Fox) Henry Fonda. LOC: Arizona: Monument Valley.

My Friend Flicka (1943 20th Century Fox) Roddy McDowall. LOC: California: Century Ranch; Utah: Duck Creek; Strawberry Valley; Navajo Lake; Cedar Breaks National Monument.

My Friend Irma Goes West (1950 Paramount) John Lund. LOC: California: Paramount Studio backlot; Nevada: Las Vegas; New Mexico: Albuquerque Santa Fe Train Station.

My Heroes Have Always Been Cowboys (1991 Samuel Goldwyn Company) Scott Glenn. LOC: Oklahoma: Guthrie, Logan County.

My Little Chickadee (1940 Universal) Mae West. LOC: California: Rancho Placeritos; Tuolumne County.

My Name is Legend (1975 Film Center) Duke Kelly. LOC: Kansas: Medicine Lodge; Quincy.

My Outlaw Brother (1951 Eagle Lion) Mickey Rooney. LOC: MEXICO: Mexico City area.

My Pal the King (1932 Universal) Tom Mix. LOC: California: Universal backlot.

My Pal Trigger (1946 Republic) Roy Rogers. LOC: California: Iverson Ranch; Walker Ranch; Kentucky Park Farms; Hidden Valley; Bishop; Republic Studio backlot.

Mysterious Avenger, The (1936 Columbia) Charles Starrett. LOC: California: Columbia Ranch.

Mysterious Desperado, The (1949 RKO) Tim Holt. LOC: California: Iverson Ranch; Corriganville; San Fernando Mission; Lone Pine.

Mysterious Rider, The (1933 Paramount) Kent Taylor. LOC: California: Paramount Ranch.

Mysterious Rider, The (1938 Paramount) Douglas Dumbrille. LOC: Arizona: Gleason; Saguaro National Monument; San Xavier Del Bac Mission.

Mysterious Rider, The (1942 PRC) Buster Crabbe. LOC: California: Corriganville; Rancho Placeritos.

Mystery Man (1944 United Artists) William Boyd. LOC: California: Lone Pine; California Studio backlot.

Mystery Mountain (1934 Mascot) Ken Maynard. LOC: California: Iverson Ranch; Bronson Canyon.

Mystery of the Hooded Horsemen, The (1937 Grand National) Tex Ritter. LOC: California: Kernville; Kernville Movie Street.

Mystery Ranch (1932 Fox) George O'Brien. LOC: Arizona: Sedona.

Mystery Ranch (1934 Reliable) Tom Tyler. LOC: California: Agoura Ranch.

Mystery Range (1937 Victory) Tom Tyler. LOC: California: Brandeis Ranch.

Mystery Trooper, The (1931 Syndicate) Robert Frazer. LOC: California: Towsley Canyon; Ralph M. Like Studio backlot.

Mystic Warrior, The (1984 ABC miniseries) Nick Ramus. LOC: California: Thousand Oaks.

Naked Alibi (1954 Universal) Sterling Hayden. LOC: MEXICO: Tijuana.

Naked Dawn, The (1955 Universal) Arthur Kennedy. LOC: California: Corriganville; Chatsworth Train Depot.

Naked Gun, The (1956 American Film Releasing Corp) Willard Parker. LOC: California: Corriganville.

Naked Hills, The (1956 Allied Artists) David Wayne. LOC: California: Iverson Ranch; Corriganville.

Naked in the Sun (1957 Allied Artists) James Craig) Florida.

Naked Spur, The (1953 MGM) James Stewart. LOC: Colorado: Durango; Animas River.

Nakia (1974 Columbia-TV) Robert Forster. LOC: New Mexico: Albuquerque.

Nashville Rebel (1966 American International) Waylon Jennings. LOC: Tennessee: Nashville; Ryman Auditorium.

Nate and the Colonel (2003 Ace Entertainment/Canyon Press) Paul Winters. LOC:

Navajo (1952 Lippert) Francis Kee Teller) Arizona/Utah: Monument Valley.

Navajo Kid (1945 PRC) Bob Steele. LOC: California: Corriganville.

Navajo Run (1964 American International) Johnny Seven. LOC: California: Janss Janss Conejo Ranch.

Navajo Trail Raiders (1949 Republic) Allan Lane. LOC: California: Iverson Ranch; Bronson Canyon; Burro Flats.

Navajo Trail, The (1945 Monogram) Johnny Mack Brown. LOC: California: Walker Ranch.

Near the Rainbow's End (1930 Tiffany) Bob Steele. LOC: California: Jauregui

Ranch.

Near the Trail's End (1931 Tiffany) Bob Steele. LOC: California: Jauregui Ranch; Trem Carr Ranch.

Neath Western Skies (1929 Syndicate) Tom Tyler. LOC: California: Jauregui Ranch.

Nebraskan, The (1953 Columbia) Phil Carey. LOC: California: Corriganville; Burro Flats.

Ned Blessing: The Story of My Life and Times (1993 CBS Western Series) Brad Johnson. LOC: Texas: Luck Ranch/Willieville/Nelson Ranch Spicewood, Austin.

Ned Kelly (2003 The Australian Film Commission/AFFC/Studio Canal/WTA /Working Title Films) Heath Ledger) LOC: AUSTRALIA: Victoria: Ballarat; Broadford Melbourne; Clunes; Little River Earth Sanctuary; Glenfern; Hepburn Springs.

Nevada (1935 Paramount) Buster Crabbe. LOC: California: Big Bear; Cedar Lake; Shay Ranch; Paramount Ranch.

Nevada (1944 RKO) Robert Mitchum. LOC: California: Lone Pine; RKO Encino Ranch.

Nevada Badmen (1951 Monogram) Whip Wilson. LOC: California: Iverson Ranch.

Nevada Buckaroo, The (1931 Tiffany) Bob Steele. LOC: California: Walker Ranch; Lake Sherwood; Towsley Canyon; Ralph M. Like Studio backlot.

Nevada City (1941 Republic) Roy Rogers. LOC: California: Jauregui Ranch; Lang; Railroad Scenes on Track along the Soledad Canyon Road; Republic Studio backlot.

Nevada Cyclone (1934 Reliable) Fred Humes. LOC: California: Frank LaSalle Ranch.

Nevada Smith (1966 Paramount) Steve McQueen. LOC: California: Lone Pine; Dolomite; Laws; Mammoth Lakes; Hot Springs; Paramount Studio backlot; Louisiana.

Nevada Smith (1975 NBC-TV/MGM) Lorne Greene. LOC: MEXICO: Durango.

Nevada Trail (1949 Universal) Tex Williams. LOC:

Nevadan, The (1950 Columbia) Randolph Scott. LOC: California: Iverson Ranch; Lone Pine; Columbia Ranch.

Never a Dull Moment (1950 RKO) Fred MacMurray. LOC: California: Jauregui Ranch.

Never Cry Wolf (1983 Buena Vista) Charles Martin Smith. LOC: Alaska: Skagway; CANADA: British Columbia: Atlin; YUKON: Dawson City.

New Frontier (1939 Republic) Three Mesquiteers. LOC: California: Brandeis Ranch; Republic Studio backlot.

New Frontier, The (1935 Republic) John Wayne. LOC: California: Trem Carr Ranch; Kernville; Lone Pine.

New Lion of Sonora, The (1970 NBC-TV) Leif Erikson. LOC: Arizona: Old Tucson;

Pilot for TV series High Chaparral.

New Maverick, The (1978 Warner Bros-TV) James Garner. LOC: Arizona: Old Tucson; San Manuel Arizona Railroad; San Rafael Ranch.

New Mexico (1951 United Artists) Lew Ayres. LOC: California: Iverson Ranch; Corriganville; New Mexico: Gallup; Acoma Pueblo.

New World, The (2005 The New World-Il nuovo mondo New Line Cinema) Colin Farrell. LOC: Virginia: Chickahomini River; ENGLAND: East Molesey/Hampton Court Palace Surrey; Hatfield Hertfordshire; Oxford Oxfordshire.

Night of the Grizzly, The (1966 Paramount) Clint Walker. LOC: California: Cedar Lake.

Night of the Lepus (1972 MGM) Rory Calhoun. LOC: Arizona: Old Tucson; Mescal.

Night on the Range, A (1929 Fox) Tim McCoy. LOC:

Night Passage (1957 Universal) James Stewart. LOC: Colorado: Durango; Durango-Silverton Narrow Gauge Railroad; Silverton; Red Mountain City; Mayflower Mine; Molas Lake.

Night Raiders (1952 Monogram) Whip Wilson. LOC: California: Iverson Ranch.

Night Rider (1962 Parallel) Johnny Cash. LOC: no exteriors.

Night Rider, The (1932 Atlantic) Harry Carey. LOC: California: Chatsworth Manor; Chatsworth Lake; Tec-Art Studio backlot.

Night Rider, The (1979 ABC-TV/Universal) David Selby. LOC: California: Jamestown; Louisiana: Baton Rouge.

Night Riders of Montana (1951 Republic) Allan Lane. LOC: California: Iverson Ranch.

Night Riders, The (1939 Republic) Three Mesquiteers. LOC: California: Agoura Ranch; Republic Studio backlot.

Night Stage to Galveston (1952 Columbia) Gene Autry. LOC: California: Iverson Ranch.

Night Time in Nevada (1948 Republic) Roy Rogers. LOC: California: Antelope Valley; railroad scenes were done on track running from Castaic to Fillmore along Highway 126; Republic Studio backlot.

Nikki, Wild Dog of the North (1961 Buena Vista) Jean Coutu. LOC: CANADA: Alberta: Kananaskis Country; Banff National Park; Canmore.

Nine Lives of Elfego Baca, The (1958 Buena Vista) Robert Loggia. LOC: California: Iverson Ranch; New Mexico: Abiquiu Ghost Ranch; Cerrillos; Tesuque Pueblo.

No Man's Land (1984 NBC) Stella Stevens. LOC: California: Paramount Ranch Agoura.

No Man's Range (1935 Commodore) Bob Steele. LOC: California: Kernville.

No More West (1934 RKO) Bert Lahr. LOC: No exteriors.

No Name on the Bullet (1959 Universal) Audie Murphy. LOC: California: Universal Studio backlot.

Nob Hill (1945 20th Century Fox) George Raft. LOC: California: 20th Century Fox backlot.

Noon Wine (1966 ABC) Jason Robards. LOC: California: Morrison Ranch.

Noose for a Gunman (1960 United Artists) Jim Davis. LOC: California: Iverson Ranch; Corriganville.

North and South III: Heaven and Hell (1994 ABC) James Read. LOC: Texas: Alamo Village BrackettvilleConnally Ranch South of San Antonio.

North and South, Book I (1985 ABC) Patrick Swayze. LOC: Arkansas: Camden-Reader; California: Disney's Golden Oak Ranch; Louisiana: St. Francisville/Greenwood Plantation; Mississippi: Natchez/Stanton Hall; Washington/Jefferson Military College; South Carolina: Charleston; Mount Pleasant/Boone Hall Plantation.

North and South, Book II (1986 ABC) Patrick Swayze. LOC: Arkansas: Camden.

North Beach and Rawhide (1985 CBS) William Shatner. LOC: California.

North from the Lone Star (1941 Columbia) Bill Elliott. LOC: California: Iverson Ranch.

North of Arizona (1935 Reliable) Jack Perrin. LOC: California: Frank LaSalle Ranch.

North of Nome (1936 Columbia) Jack Holt. LOC: California: San Diego.

North of the Border (1946 Screen Guild) Russell Hayden. LOC: California: Iverson Ranch; Corriganville.

North of the Great Divide (1950 Republic) Roy Rogers. LOC: California: Big Bear; Republic Studio backlot.

North of the Rio Grande (1937 Paramount) William Boyd. LOC: California: Columbia; Tuolumne County; Red Hills.

North of the Rockies (1942 Columbia) Bill Elliott. LOC: California: Iverson Ranch; Big Bear; Lake Arrowhead; Baldwin Dry Lake.

North of the Yukon (1939 Columbia) Charles Starrett. LOC: California: Cedar Lake.

North Star, The (1996 AFCL Productions/M6 Film/Federal Films/Regency Enterprises/Urania Film/Nordic Screen/Canal +) James Caan) CANADA: NORWAY: Maridalen; Oslo; Orre Beach; Stavanger.

North to Alaska (1960 20th Century Fox) John Wayne. LOC: California: Cedar Lake; Lone Pine; Hot Springs; Mammoth Lakes.

North to the Klondike (1942 Universal) Broderick Crawford. LOC: California: Big Bear.

North West Mounted Police (1940 Paramount) Gary Cooper. LOC: California: Big Bear; Shay Ranch; Paramount Ranch; Arizona: Flagstaff.

Northern Frontier (1935 Ambassador) Kermit Maynard. LOC: California: Crestline; Camp Seeley.

Northern Patrol (1953 Allied Artists) Kirby Grant. LOC: California: Big Bear; Cedar Lake.

Northern Pursuit (1943 Warner Bros) Errol Flynn. LOC: Idaho: Sun Valley.

Northwest Outpost (1947 Republic) Nelson Eddy. LOC: California: Republic Studio backlot.

Northwest Passage (1940 MGM) Spencer Tracy. LOC: Idaho; McCall; Lake Payette.

Northwest Rangers (1942 MGM) James Craig. LOC: California: Big Bear; Idyllwild.

Northwest Stampede (1948 Eagle Lion) James Craig. LOC: CANADA: Calgary; Banff National Park; Lake Louise.

Northwest Territory (1951 Monogram) Kirby Grant. LOC: California: Big Bear; Cedar Lake.

Northwest Trail (1945 Screen Guild) Bob Steele. LOC: California: Big Bear; Cedar Lake; Lake Arrowhead.

Not Above Suspicion (1956 Wrather) Clayton Moore. LOC: California: Iverson Ranch; Corriganville; Tuolumne County.

Not Exactly Gentlemen/Three Rogues (1931 Fox) Victor McLaglen. LOC: California.

O, My Darling Clementine (1943 Republic) Frank Albertson. LOC: California: Republic Studio backlot.

O'Malley of the Mounted (1936 20th Century Fox) George O'Brien. LOC: California: Palmdale; Sequoia National Park; Palm Springs.

O'Malley Rides Alone (1930 Syndicate) Bob Custer. LOC: California: Big Bear, Lake Arrowhead.

Oath of Vengeance (1944 PRC) Buster Crabbe. LOC: California: Corriganville; Rancho Placeritos.

Oblivion (1994 Full Moon Entertainment) Richard Joseph Paul. LOC: ROMANIA: Bucharest.

Oblivion 2 : Backlash (1996 Full Moon Entertainment) Richard Joseph Paul. LOC: ROMANIA: Bucharest.

Of Human Hearts (1938 MGM) James Stewart. LOC: California: Lake Arrowhead.

Of Mice and Men (1940 United Artists) Burgess Meredith. LOC: California: Agoura Ranch.

Oh! Susanna (1936 Republic) Gene Autry. LOC: California: Iverson Ranch; Kernville; Lone Pine; Lang Railroad Depot, Saugus; Republic Studio backlot.

Oh, Susanna (1951 Republic) Rod Cameron. LOC: California: Corriganville; Utah: Aspen Mirror Lake; Strawberry Valley; Kanab.

Oil Raider, The (1934 Mayfair) Buster Crabbe. LOC: California: El Rey Hotel, San Fernando; San Fernando Freight Depot.

Oklahoma Annie (1952 Republic) Judy Canova. LOC: California: Corriganville.

Oklahoma Badlands (1948 Republic) Allan Lane. LOC: California: Iverson Ranch; Corriganville.

Oklahoma Blues (1948 Monogram) Jimmy Wakely. LOC: California: Walker

Ranch.

Oklahoma Bob Albright and His Rodeo Do Flappers (1929 Vitaphone) Oklahoma Bob Albright. LOC:

Oklahoma Crude (1973 Columbia) George C. Scott. LOC: California: Tuolumne County; Jamestown; Stockton.

Oklahoma Cyclone (1930 Tiffany) Bob Steele. LOC: California.

Oklahoma Frontier (1939 Universal) Johnny Mack Brown. LOC: California: Agoura.

Oklahoma Jim (1931 Monogram) Bill Cody. LOC: California: Ralph M. Like Studio backlot.

Oklahoma Justice (1951 Monogram) Johnny Mack Brown. LOC: California: Iverson Ranch.

Oklahoma Kid, The (1939 Warner Bros) James Cagney. LOC: California: Iverson Ranch; Warner Ranch; Apple Valley.

Oklahoma Outlaws (1943 Warner Bros) Robert Shayne. LOC: Iverson Movie Ranch.

Oklahoma Passage (1989 Oklahoma Educational Television Authority) Jeannette Nolan. LOC: Oklahoma.

Oklahoma Raiders (1944 Universal) Tex Ritter. LOC: California: Corriganville; Universal Studio backlot.

Oklahoma Renegades (1940 Republic) Three Mesquiteers. LOC: California: Iverson Ranch.

Oklahoma Territory (1960 United Artists) Bill Williams. LOC: California: Iverson Ranch; Rancho Placeritos.

Oklahoma Terror (1939 Monogram) Jack Randall. LOC: California: Walker Ranch; Kernville; Kernville Movie Street; Wofford Ranch.

Oklahoma Woman, The (1956 American Releasing Corp) Richard Denning. LOC: California: Ingram Ranch.

Oklahoma! (1955 20th Century Fox) Gordon MacRae. LOC: Arizona: San Rafael Valley; Elgin.

Oklahoman, The (1957 Allied Artists) Joel McCrea. LOC: California: Rancho Placeritos; Janss Janss Conejo Ranch.

Old Barn Dance, The (1938 Republic) Gene Autry. LOC: California: Kernville; Kelso Canyon; Lone Pine; Republic Studio backlot.

Old Chisholm Trail, The (1942 Universal) Johnny Mack Brown. LOC: California: Agoura; Universal Studio backlot.

Old Corral, The (1936 Republic) Gene Autry. LOC: California: Iverson Ranch; Kernville; Republic Studio backlot.

Old Frontier, The (1950 Republic) Monte Hale. LOC: California: Iverson Ranch.

Old Gringo (1989 Columbia Pictures) Gregory Peck. LOC: MEXICO: Hidalgo: Hacienda de Santa Maria Regla; Ometusco; Pachuca; Taxquillo; Venta de Cruz; Coahuila: Torreón; Zacatecas: Zempoala Morelos.

Old Homestead, The (1935 Liberty) Mary Carlisle. LOC: California.

Old Los Angeles (1948 Republic) William Elliott. LOC: California: Iverson Ranch; Republic Studio backlot.

Old Louisiana (1937 Crescent) Tom Keene. LOC: Missouri: Saint Louis.

Old Oklahoma Plains (1952 Republic) Rex Allen. LOC: California: Iverson Ranch; Lone Pine.

Old Overland Trail (1953 Republic) Rex Allen. LOC: California: Burro Flats; Lone Pine.

Old Texas Trail, The (1944 Universal) Rod Cameron. LOC: California: Iverson Ranch; Corriganville.

Old West, The (1952 Columbia) Gene Autry. LOC: California: Corriganville; Kernville; Columbia Ranch.

Old Wyoming Trail, The (1937 Columbia) Charles Starrett. LOC: California: Iverson Ranch; Walker Ranch; Jauregui Ranch.

Old Yeller (1958 Buena Vista) Fess Parker. LOC: California: Iverson Ranch; Sherwood Forest.

Ole Rex (1961 Universal) Billy E. Hughes. LOC: Texas: Wichita Falls.

Omaha Trail, The (1942 MGM) James Craig. LOC: California: Corriganville; Tuolumne County; Sonora; MGM Lot 3

On the Great White Trail (1938 Grand National) James Newill. LOC: California: Big Bear.

On the Old Spanish Trail (1947 Republic) Roy Rogers. LOC: California: Walker Ranch; Lake Sherwood; Morrison Ranch; Kernville; Republic Studio backlot.

On Top of Old Smoky (1953 Columbia) Gene Autry. LOC: California: Columbia Ranch; Pioneertown.

Once Upon a Horse (1958 Universal) Rowan & Martin. LOC: California: Janss Janss Conejo Ranch; Universal Studio backlot.

Once Upon a Texas Train (1988 CBS) Willie Nelson. LOC: Arizona: Mescal; Old Tucson; Nevada: White Pine County.

One Desire (1955 Universal) Rock Hudson,. LOC: California: Universal backlot.

One Foot in Hell (1960 20th Century Fox) Alan Ladd. LOC: California: Iverson Ranch.

One Little Indian (1973 Buena Vista) James Garner. LOC: Utah: Kanab Canyon; Kanab Movie Fort; Coral Pink Sand Dunes; Paria.

One Man Justice (1937 Columbia) Charles Starrett. LOC: California: Columbia Ranch.

One Man Law (1931 Columbia) Buck Jones. LOC: California: Walker Ranch.

One Man's Hero (1999 Hool/Macdonald Productions/Producciones San Patricia/Filmax/Silver Lion Films) Tom Berenger. LOC: MEXICO: Coahuíla: Bilbao sand dunes; Viesca; La Angostura; Durango: Canon de los Delgados; ex Hacienda La Ferreria de Flores; Morelos: Xochitepec; Puebla: Puebla; Zacatecas: Xochitepec.

One Man's Law (1940 Republic) Don Barry. LOC: California: Iverson Ranch.

One Mask Too Many (1956 Wrather) Clayton Moore. LOC: California: Iverson Ranch; Corriganville; Lone Pine.

One More Mountain (1994 ABC) Chris Cooper. LOC: CANADA: Alberta: CL Ranch Calgary.

One More Train to Rob (1971 Universal) George Peppard. LOC: California: Universal backlot.

One Way Trail, The (1931 Columbia) Tim McCoy. LOC: California: Trem Carr Ranch.

One-Eyed Horse (2008 One-Eyed Horse Productions) Mark Redfield. LOC: Maryland: Jessup.

One-Eyed Jacks (1961 Paramount) Marlon Brando. LOC: California: Warner Ranch; Death Valley; Monterey.

Only Good Indian, The (2009 Savage Pictures) Wes Studi. LOC: Kansas: Fort Larned National Historic Site; Monument Rocks/Chalk Pyramids, Gove County; Missouri: Ha Ha Tonka State Park.

Only the Brave (1930 Paramount) Gary Cooper. LOC: California: Paramount Ranch.

Only the Valiant (1951 Warner Bros) Gregory Peck. LOC: California: Warner Ranch; New Mexico: Gallup.

Open Range (1927 Paramount) Lane Chandler. LOC: California: Lasky Ranch; Utah: Zion National Park

Open Range (2003 Touchstone Pictures/Tig Productions) Kevin Costner. LOC: CANADA: Alberta: Calgary; Longview; Morley; Stoney Indian Reservation.

Oregon Passage (1958 Allied Artists) John Ericson. LOC: Oregon: Bend; Deschutes National Forest.

Oregon Trail (1945 Republic) Sunset Carson. LOC: California: Iverson Ranch; Republic Studio backlot.

Oregon Trail Scouts (1947 Republic) Allan Lane. LOC: California: Walker Ranch.

Oregon Trail, The (1936 Republic) John Wayne. LOC: California: Lone Pine.

Oregon Trail, The (1939 Universal) Johnny Mack Brown. LOC: California: Kernville; Kernville Movie Street.

Oregon Trail, The (1959 20th Century Fox) Fred MacMurray. LOC: California: Iverson Ranch.

Oregon Trail, The (1977 Universal-TV) Rod Taylor. LOC: California: Newhall; Arizona: Sedona; Flagstaff.

Orphan of the Pecos (1937 Victory) Tom Tyler. LOC: California: Brandeis Ranch.

Out California Way (1946 Republic) Monte Hale. LOC: California: Iverson Ranch; Val Steve Ranch, 14134 Riverside Drive, Van Nuys; Chatsworth Lake; Los Angeles River on Republic Studio backlot; Republic Studio front lot.

Out West (1947 Columbia) Three Stooges. LOC: California: Columbia Ranch.

Out West with the Hardys (1938 MGM) Lewis Stone. LOC: California: Agoura

Ranch; MGM backlot.

Out West with the Peppers (1940 Columbia) Edith Fellows. LOC: California: Chatsworth Train Station; Columbia Ranch.

Outback (1988 International Film Management/Burrowes Film Group) Jeff Fahey. LOC: AUSTRALIA: New South Wales: Balltrees; Kangaroobie; Orange; Scone; Sidney.

Outcast of Black Mesa (1950 Columbia) Charles Starrett. LOC: California: Iverson Ranch; Columbia Ranch.

Outcast, The (1954 Republic) John Derek. LOC: California: Republic Studio backlot; Colorado: Cañon City.

Outcasts of Poker Flat, The (1937 RKO) Preston Foster. LOC: California: Iverson Ranch; RKO Encino Ranch; Walker Ranch.

Outcasts of Poker Flat, The (1952 20th Century Fox) Dale Robertson. LOC: Colorado: Durango; La Plata Canyon.

Outcasts of the Trail (1949 Republic) Monte Hale. LOC: California: Iverson Ranch.

Outlaw Brand (1948 Monogram) Jimmy Wakely. LOC: California: Rancho Placeritos.

Outlaw Country (1949 Screen Guild) Lash LaRue. LOC: California: Iverson Ranch.

Outlaw Deputy, The (1935 Puritan) Tim McCoy. LOC: California: Iverson Ranch; Walker Ranch.

Outlaw Express (1938 Universal) Bob Baker. LOC: California: Iverson Ranch; Walker Ranch; Rancho Placeritos.

Outlaw Gold (1950 Monogram) Johnny Mack Brown. LOC: California: Iverson Ranch.

Outlaw Josey Wales, The (1976 Warner Bros) Clint Eastwood. LOC: California: Oroville; Arizona: Mescal; Utah: Kanab Canyon, Paria; Coral Pink Sand Dunes; Glen Canyon National Recreation Area.

Outlaw Justice (1932 Majestic) Jack Hoxie. LOC: California: Iverson Ranch.

Outlaw Justice (2000 Once Upon a Time Films) Willie Nelson. LOC: SPAIN: Rancho Leone Tabernas; Texas-Hollywood/Western town and Mexican set Tabernas; Valle del Búho West of Tabernas, Almería.

Outlaw Queen (1957 Globe) Andrea King. LOC: California: Corriganville.

Outlaw Roundup (1944 PRC) Texas Rangers. LOC: California: Corriganville.

Outlaw Rule (1935 Kent) Reb Russell. LOC: California: Trem Carr Ranch; Ralph M. Like Studio backlot; Bell Ranch.

Outlaw Stallion, The (1954 Columbia) Phil Carey. LOC: California: Iverson Ranch; Corriganville; Burro Flats; Santa Susana Road.

Outlaw Tamer (1934 Empire) Lane Chandler. LOC: California: Frank LaSalle Ranch; Towsley Canyon; Ralph M. Like Studio backlot.

Outlaw Trail (1944 Monogram) Trail Blazers. LOC: California: Rancho Placeritos;

Corriganville.

Outlaw Trail: The Treasure of Butch Cassidy (2006 KOAN) Brian Wimmer. LOC: Utah: Bryce Canyon National ParkCirclevilleHeber Valley Railroad/Heber CityKanabProvo Canyon/Bridal Vail Falls.

Outlaw Treasure (1955 American Releasing Corp) John Forbes. LOC: California: Corriganville.

Outlaw Women (1952 Lippert) Marie Windsor. LOC: California: Iverson Ranch; Rancho Placeritos.

Outlaw, The (1943 United Artists) Jack Buetel. LOC: California: Vasquez Rocks; Red Rock Canyon; Arizona: Moenkopi, Tuba City.

Outlaw's Daughter, The (1954 20th Century Fox) Jim Davis. LOC: Arizona: Sedona; Utah: Kanab.

Outlaw's Paradise (1939 Victory) Tim McCoy. LOC: California: Brandeis Ranch; Walker Ranch; Ralph M. Like Studio backlot.

Outlaw's Son (1954 Allied Artists) Guy Madison. LOC: California: Rancho Placeritos.

Outlaw's Son (1957 United Artists) Dane Clark. LOC: California: Iverson Ranch; Walker Ranch; Jauregui Ranch; Rancho Placeritos.

Outlawed Guns (1935 Universal) Buck Jones. LOC: California: Kernville.

Outlaws (1986 Fuorilegge CBS Western Series) Rod Taylor. LOC: California; Texas: Houston.

Outlaw's Highway (1934 Trop Productions) Jack King. LOC: California: Ralph M. Like Studio backlot; Agoura Ranch.

Outlaws is Coming, The (1965 Columbia) The Three Stooges. LOC: California: Columbia Ranch; Russell Ranch; Wyoming: B-Bar-B Buffalo Ranch, Gilette.

Outlaws of Boulder Pass (1942 PRC) George Houston. LOC: California: Iverson Ranch.

Outlaws of Pine Ridge (1942 Republic) Don Barry. LOC: California: Iverson Ranch; Corriganville.

Outlaws of Red River (1967 Fenix) George Montgomery. LOC: SPAIN: Manzanares El Real; Embalse de Santillana; Golden City; La Pedriza/Fince Magdalena.

Outlaws of Santa Fe (1944 Republic) Don Barry. LOC: California: Iverson Ranch; Walker Ranch; Republic Studio backlot.

Outlaws of Sonora (1938 Republic) Three Mesquiteers. LOC: California: Iverson Ranch; Republic Studio backlot.

Outlaws of Stampede Pass (1943 Monogram) Johnny Mack Brown. LOC: California: Iverson Ranch; Rancho Placeritos.

Outlaws of Texas (1950 Monogram) Whip Wilson. LOC: California: Iverson Ranch.

Outlaws of the Cherokee Trail (1941 Republic) Three Mesquiteers. LOC: California: Walker Ranch; Burro Flats.

Outlaws of the Desert (1941 Paramount) William Boyd. LOC: California: Lone Pine; Olancha Sand Dunes; RKO 40 Acres; Keeler Train Depot.

Outlaws of the Panhandle (1941 Columbia) Charles Starrett. LOC: California: Iverson Ranch.

Outlaws of the Plains (1946 PRC) Buster Crabbe. LOC: California: Corriganville.

Outlaws of the Prairie (1937 Columbia) Charles Starrett. LOC: California: Holman Ranch, Calabasas; Columbia Ranch.

Outlaws of the Range (1936 Spectrum) Bill Cody. LOC: California: Straubinger Ranch; Ralph M. Like Studio exterior.

Outlaws of the Rio Grande (1941 PRC) Tim McCoy. LOC: California: Brandeis Ranch.

Outlaws of the Rockies (1945 Columbia) Charles Starrett. LOC: California: Iverson Ranch; Corriganville; Columbia Ranch.

Outlaws: Legend of O.B. Taggart, The (1994 Harstadt/Lund Productions) Mickey Rooney. LOC: New Mexico: Bonanza Creek Ranch Santa FeTesuque Pueblo.

Outpost of the Mounties (1939 Columbia) Charles Starrett. LOC: California: Lake Arrowhead; Totem Point; Big Bear; Cedar Lake.

Outrage, The (1964 MGM) Paul Newman. LOC: California: Bell Ranch; Tuolumne County; Arizona: Saguaro National Monument; Rancho Romero.

Outride the Devil: A Morning with Doc Holliday (2007 Greene HD Productions) Kit Hussey. LOC: Texas: Arlington.

Outriders, The (1950 MGM) Joel McCrea. LOC: California: MGM backlot; Utah: Kanab; Paria; Coral Pink Sand Dunes; Aspen Mirror Lake; Duck Creek; Navajo Lake; Strawberry Valley.

Outsider, The (1994 Morningstar Entertainment) Grainger Hines. LOC: California: Polsa Rosa Ranch; Rancho Maria; Sable Ranch.

Outsider, The (2002 Hallmark Entertainment) Tim Daly) Australia: Queensland: Gold Coast.

Over the Border (1950 Monogram) Johnny Mack Brown. LOC: California: Iverson Ranch.

Over the Hill Gang Rides Again, The (1970 Thomas/Spelling) Walter Brennan. LOC: California: Paramount Studio backlot.

Over the Hill Gang, The (1969 Thomas/Spelling) Walter Brennan. LOC: California: Russell Ranch; Paramount Studio backlot.

Over the Santa Fe Trail (1947 Columbia) Ken Curtis. LOC: California: Iverson Ranch; Columbia Ranch.

Overland Bound (1930 Syndicate) Jack Perrin. LOST/MISSING

Overland Express, The (1938 Columbia) Buck Jones. LOC: California: Iverson Ranch; Red Rock Canyon; Kernville.

Overland Mail (1939 Monogram) Jack Randall. LOC: California: Rancho Placeritos; Walker Ranch; Lake Los Angeles.

Overland Mail (1942 Universal) Lon Chaney, Jr. LOC: California: Kernville; Universal Studio backlot.

Overland Mail Robbery (1943 Republic) Bill Elliott. LOC: California: Iverson

Ranch; Corriganville.

Overland Pacific (1954 United Artists) Jock Mahoney. LOC: California: Corriganville; Burro Flats.

Overland Riders (1946 PRC) Buster Crabbe. LOC: California: Corriganville.

Overland Stage Raiders (1938 Republic) Three Mesquiteers. LOC: California: Iverson Ranch; Conejo Valley Airport; Santa Clara River and railroad along Hwy 126 near Castaic; Republic Studio backlot.

Overland Stagecoach (1942 PRC) Bob Livingston. LOC: California: Iverson Ranch.

Overland Telegraph (1951 RKO) Tim Holt. LOC: California: Iverson Ranch; Walker Ranch; Jauregui Ranch.

Overland to Deadwood (1942 Columbia) Charles Starrett. LOC: California: Iverson Ranch.

Overland Trails (1948 Monogram) Johnny Mack Brown. LOC: California: Iverson Ranch.

Overland with Kit Carson (1939 Columbia) Bill Elliott. LOC: California: Red Rock Canyon; Utah: Cave Lake; Kanab; Zion National Park; Kaibab Forest; St. George.

Overlanders, The (1946 Universal International/J. Arthur Rank) Chips Rafferty. LOC: AUSTRALIA: Queensland; Northern Territory.

Ox-Bow Incident, The (1943 20th Century Fox) Henry Fonda. LOC: California: Iverson Ranch; 20th Century Fox backlot; Lone Pine.

Pack Train (1953 Columbia) Gene Autry. LOC: California: Iverson Ranch; Lone Pine; Columbia Ranch.

Paint Your Wagon (1969 Paramount) Clint Eastwood. LOC: California: Big Bear; Oregon: Baker.

Painted Desert (1938 RKO) George O'Brien. LOC: California: Brandeis Ranch; Red Rock Canyon; RKO Encino Ranch.

Painted Desert, The (1931 RKO/Pathe) William Boyd. LOC: California: Paramount Ranch; Arizona: Painted Desert; Dinosaur Canyon; Tuba City.

Painted Hills, The (1951 MGM) Paul Kelly. LOC: California: Tuolumne County.

Painted Stallion, The (1937 Republic) Ray Corrigan. LOC: California: Iverson Ranch; Bronson Canyon; Kernville; Lake Sherwood; Red Rock Canyon; Lasky Mesa; Republic Studio backlot; Utah: Snow Canyon.

Painted Trail, The (1938 Monogram) Tom Keene. LOC: California: Walker Ranch; Rancho Placeritos; Lake Sherwood.

Pair of Aces (1990 CBS) Willie Nelson. LOC: Texas: Austin; Georgetown.

Pal from Texas, The (1939 Metropolitan) Bob Steele. LOC: California.

Pale Rider (1985 Warner Bros) Clint Eastwood. LOC: California: Tuolumne County; Idaho: Boulder Creek; Sawtooth National Forest; Silver Creek; Sun Valley; Vienna Mine.

Paleface, The (1948 Paramount) Bob Hope. LOC: California: Iverson Ranch; Paramount Ranch; China Flats; Janss Conejo Ranch Airport; Paramount Studio backlot.

Palm Springs (1936 Paramount) Smith Ballew. LOC: California: Palmdale.

Palo Pinto Gold (2008 Cottonwood Entertainment) Trenton Willmon. LOC: Texas: Boerne; Enchanted Springs Ranch.

Palominas (2010 Talmarc Productions) Chris Browning. LOC: New Mexico: Bonanza Creek Ranch Santa Fe.

Palomino (1950 Columbia) Jerome Courtland. LOC: California: Oliver Drake Ranch; Berry/Bell Ranch; Chatsworth Lake and Manor.

Pals of the Golden West (1951 Republic) Roy Rogers. LOC: California: El Mirage; Republic Studio backlot.

Pals of the Pecos (1941 Republic) Three Mesquiteers. LOC: California: Iverson Ranch.

Pals of the Prairie (1929 FBO) Buzz Barton. LOC:

Pals of the Prairie (1933 Imperial) Buffalo Bill, Jr. LOC: California: Ralph M. Like Studio backlot; Lake Chatsworth Manor; Encino Rancho; Pierre Domec's Adobe ruins, Chatsworth Lake.

Pals of the Range (1935 Superior) Rex Lease. LOC: California: Iverson Ranch; Ralph M. Like Studio backlot.

Pals of the Saddle (1938 Republic) Three Mesquiteers. LOC: California: Corriganville; Red Rock Canyon; Saltdale; Republic Studio backlot.

Pals of the Silver Sage (1940 Monogram) Tex Ritter. LOC: California: Lebec; Tejon Ranch.

Pals of the West (1934 Imperial) Wally Wales. LOC: California: Brandeis Ranch.

Panamint's Bad Man (1938 20th Century Fox) Smith Ballew. LOC: California: Agoura; Vasquez Rocks; Columbia Ranch.

Pancho Villa (1973 Sun International) Telly Savalas. LOC: SPAIN: Daganzo; Colmenar Viejo; La Calahorra.

Pancho Villa Returns (1950 Hispano Continental Films) Leo Carrillo. LOC: MEXICO.

Panhandle (1948 Allied Artists) Rod Cameron. LOC: California: Rancho Placeritos; Lone Pine.

Panhandle Trail (1942 PRC) Buster Crabbe. LOC: California: Rancho Placeritos; Corriganville.

Parade of the West (1930 Universal) Ken Maynard. LOC: California: Universal Studio backlot.

Paradise Canyon (1935 Monogram) John Wayne. LOC: California: Hoot Gibson Ranch; Placerita Canyon and Aqueduct; Trem Carr Ranch.

Paradise Trail, The (1979 Mark IV Pictures) Burt Douglas. LOC: New Mexico: Charma.

Paradise Valley (1934 Imperial) Sam Pierce. LOC:

Pardners (1956 Paramount) Martin & Lewis. LOC: California: Iverson Ranch; Rancho Placeritos; Arizona: Tucson.

Pardon My Gun (1930 Pathe) Tom Keene. LOC: California: Lone Pine; Anchor Ranch; Lone Pine Train Depot.

Pardon My Gun (1942 Columbia) Charles Starrett. LOC: California: Iverson Ranch.

Park Avenue Logger (1937 RKO) George O'Brien. LOC: California: Crestline; Eureka; Hollywood Legion Stadium; Oregon: Grants Pass.

Paroled—to Die (1938 Republic) Bob Steele. LOC: California: Iverson Ranch; Jauregui Ranch; Rancho Placeritos.

Parson and the Outlaw, The (1957 Columbia) Anthony Dexter,. LOC: California: Rancho Placeritos; Yosemite National Park.

Parson of Panamint, The (1941 Paramount) Charlie Ruggles. LOC: California: 20th Century Fox backlot; Panamint Mountains.

Partners (1931 RKO) Tom Keene. LOC: California: Kernville; Paramount Ranch.

Partners of the Plains (1938 Paramount) William Boyd. LOC: California: Paramount Ranch; Kernville; Keen Camp; San Jacinto National Forest; Hemet Dam.

Partners of the Sunset (1948 Monogram) Jimmy Wakely. LOC: California: Walker Ranch; Rancho Placeritos.

Partners of the Trail (1931 Monogram) Tom Tyler) LOST/MISSING

Partners of the Trail (1944 Monogram) Johnny Mack Brown. LOC: California: Walker Ranch; Rancho Placeritos.

Passage West (1951 Paramount) John Payne. LOC: California: Iverson Ranch; Corriganville; Muroc Dry Lake.

Passion (1954 RKO) Cornel Wilde. LOC: California: Warner Ranch; Tuolumne County; Kennedy Meadow.

Pat Garrett and Billy the Kid (1973 MGM) James Coburn. LOC: MEXICO: Durango: Casa Blanca; Chupaderos; El Arenal; Rancho Marley.

Pathfinder, The (1953 Columbia) George Montgomery. LOC: California: Walker Ranch.

Pathfinder, The (1996 Leather Stockings Productions) Kevin Dillon. LOC: CANADA: Ontario: Fort Erie; St. Marie Among the Hurons, Midland.

Pathfinder, The (2007 Vinland Productions Canada Inc.) Karl Urban. LOC: CANADA: British Columbia: Vancouver.

Paths of Hate (1964 Ultimate/Hesperia/Cineurope) Rod Cameron. LOC: SPAIN: Hoya de Manzanares.

Patriot, The (2000 Columbia Pictures) Mel Gibson. LOC: South Carolina: Botany Bay Plantation Edisto Island; Brattonsville; Charleston; Chester Darby Farm; Cypress Garden; Fort Lawn; Georgetown; Lowrys; Rock Hill; York.

Pawnee (1957 Republic) George Montgomery. LOC: California: Silver Lakes, Corona; Santa Ana River, Corona. Heavy use of stock footage throughout the film.

Payment in Blood (1968 Columbia) Guy Madison. LOC: ITALY.

Peace for a Gunfighter (1965 Crown Intl) Burt Berger. LOC: Arizona: Salt River Valley area.

Peacemakers (2003 Michael R.Joyce Productions/USA Cable Entertainment) Tom Berenger. LOC: CANADA: British Columbia: Bordertown/Western town Maple Ridge, Vancouver; Kettle Valley Steam Railway.

Pecos Kid, The (1936 Commodore) Fred Kohler Jr. LOC: California: Ralph M. Like Studio backlot; Brandeis Ranch; Frank LaSalle Ranch.

Pecos River (1951 Columbia) Charles Starrett. LOC: California: Iverson Ranch; Corriganville.

Perilous Journey, A (1953 Republic) Vera Ralston. LOC: California: Republic Studios backlot.

Perils of the Royal Mounted (1942 Columbia) Robert Stevens. LOC: California: Big Bear; Iverson Ranch; Corriganville; Kernville; Columbia Ranch; Rancho Placeritos.

Perils of the Wilderness (1956 Columbia) Dennis Moore. LOC: California: Big Bear.

Persuader, The (1957 Allied Artists) William Talman. LOC: California: Rancho Placeritos.

Peter Lundy and the Medicine Hat Stallion (1977 NBC-TV) Leif Garrett. LOC: New Mexico: San Ildefonso Pueblo; Valle Grande.

Phantom Cowboy, The (1935 Aywon) Ted Wells. LOC: California: Ralph M. Like Studio backlot; Placerita Canyon.

Phantom Cowboy, The (1941 Republic) Don Barry. LOC: California: Iverson Ranch; Agoura.

Phantom Empire, The (1935 Mascot) Gene Autry. LOC: California: Chatsworth Park; Bronson Canyon; Agoura Ranch; Griffith Park Observatory.

Phantom Gold (1938 Columbia) Jack Luden. LOC: California: Bronson Canyon; Red Rock Canyon.

Phantom of the Desert (1930 Syndicate) Jack Perrin. LOC: California: Frank LaSalle Ranch; Towsley Canyon.

Phantom of the Plains (1945 Republic) Bill Elliott. LOC: California: Iverson Ranch.

Phantom of the Range, The (1936 Victory) Tom Tyler. LOC: California: Lone Pine; Brandeis Ranch.

Phantom of the West, The (1930 Mascot) Tom Tyler. LOC: California: North Verde Ranch/Kemper Campbell Ranch, Victorville/Apple Valley; Kernville; Tec-Art Studio backlot.

Phantom Patrol (1936 Ambassador) Kermit Maynard. LOC: California: Malibou Lake

Phantom Plainsmen, The (1942 Republic) Three Mesquiteers. LOC: California: Iverson Ranch; Bronson Canyon; Lone Pine.

Phantom Rancher (1940 Colony) Ken Maynard. LOC: California: Brandeis Ranch; Jauregui Ranch; Walker Ranch.

Phantom Ranger (1938 Monogram) Tim McCoy. LOC: California: Iverson Ranch;

Brandeis Ranch.

Phantom Rider, The (1936 Universal) Buck Jones. LOC: California: Walker Ranch; Agoura.

Phantom Rider, The (1946 Republic) Robert Kent. LOC: California: Iverson Ranch; Corriganville; Republic Studio backlot.

Phantom Stage, The (1939 Universal) Bob Baker. LOC: California: Kernville.

Phantom Stagecoach, The (1957 Columbia) William Bishop. LOC: California: Iverson Ranch; Columbia Ranch.

Phantom Stallion (1954 Republic) Rex Allen. LOC: California: Republic Studio backlot; Burro Flats.

Phantom Thunderbolt (1933 World Wide) Ken Maynard. LOC: California: Paramount Ranch; Towsley Canyon.

Phantom Trails (1955 Allied Artists) Guy Madison. LOC: California: Iverson Ranch.

Phantom Valley (1948 Columbia) Charles Starrett. LOC: California: Iverson Ranch; Providencia Ranch; Columbia Ranch.

Pharao's Army (1995 Sinkhole Productions) Kris Kristofferson) Kentucky.

Pierre of the Plains (1942 MGM) John Carroll. LOC: California: Tuolumne County; Sonora; MGM backlot.

Pillars of the Sky (1956 Universal) Jeff Chandler. LOC: Oregon: La Grande.

Pinto Bandit, The (1944 PRC) Texas Rangers. LOC: California: Corriganville.

Pinto Canyon (1940 Metropolitan) Bob Steele. LOC: California: Walker Ranch; Rancho Placeritos.

Pinto Kid, The (1941 Columbia) Charles Starrett. LOC: California: Iverson Ranch.

Pinto Rustlers (1936 Reliable) Tom Tyler. LOC: California: Brandeis Ranch; Towsley Canyon.

Pioneer Days (1940 Monogram) Jack Randall. LOC: California: Iverson Ranch; Rancho Placeritos.

Pioneer Justice (1947 PRC) Lash LaRue. LOC: California: Iverson Ranch; Rancho Placeritos.

Pioneer Marshal (1949 Republic) Monte Hale. LOC: California: Iverson Ranch; Red Rock Canyon.

Pioneer Trail (1938 Columbia) Jack Luden. LOC: California: Iverson Ranch; Rancho Placeritos; Walker Ranch.

Pioneer Woman (1973 ABC-TV) Joanna Pettet. LOC: CANADA: Alberta; Twin Butte, Waterton Lake.

Pioneers of the Frontier (1940 Columbia) Bill Elliott. LOC: California: Iverson Ranch; Columbia Ranch.

Pioneers of the West (1940 Republic) Three Mesquiteers. LOC: California: Iverson Ranch.

Pioneers, The (1941 Monogram) Tex Ritter. LOC: California: Walker Ranch.

Pirates of Monterey (1947 Universal) Rod Cameron. LOC: California: Bronson

Canyon.

Pirates of the Prairie (1942 RKO) Tim Holt. LOC: California: Jauregui Ranch; Walker Ranch; RKO Encino Ranch.

Pirates on Horseback (1941 Paramount) William Boyd. LOC: California: Jauregui Ranch; Rancho Placeritos; Lone Pine.

Pistol Harvest (1951 RKO) Tim Holt. LOC: California: Iverson Ranch; Walker Ranch; Jauregui Ranch.

Pistol Packin' Mama (1943 Republic) Ruth Terry. LOC: California: Republic Studio backlot.

Pistol Packin' Nitwits (1945 Columbia) El Brendel. LOC: California: Columbia Ranch.

Place Called Glory, A (1966 Embassy) Lex Barker) Spain; Esplugas Western Village; Balcázar, Barcelona.

Plainsman and the Lady (1946 Republic) William Elliott. LOC: California: Iverson Ranch; Lone Pine; Mammoth Lakes; Arizona: Monument Valley; House Rock Valley.

Plainsman, The (1936 Paramount) Gary Cooper. LOC: California: Iverson Ranch; Kern River; Montana: Birney; Beecher's Island; Wyoming: Laramie.

Plainsman, The (1966 Universal) Don Murray. LOC: California: Janss Janss Conejo Ranch; Universal Studio backlot; Utah: Kanab Movie Fort; Kanab Canyon; Paria; The Gap; Kimball Valley.

Plainsong (1982 Ed Stabile Prod.) Jessica Nelson. LOC: New Jersey.

Pleasure Treasure (1951 Columbia) Andy Clyde. LOC:

Plunder of the Sun (1953 Warner Bros) Glenn Ford. LOC: AUSTRIA: Schloss Laxenburg.

Plunderers of Painted Flats (1959 Republic) John Carroll. LOC: California: Iverson Ranch.

Plunderers, The (1948 Republic) Rod Cameron. LOC: California: Iverson Ranch; Vasquez Rocks; Kernville; Republic Studio backlot.

Plunderers, The (1960 Allied Artists) Jeff Chandler. LOC: California: Iverson Ranch; Corriganville; Vasquez Rocks; Ingram Ranch.

Pocahontas. The Legend (1995 P.F.A.Films) Sandrine Holt. LOC: CANADA: Ontario: Midland.

Pocatello Kid, The (1931 Tiffany) Ken Maynard. LOC: California: Vasquez Rocks; Trem Carr Ranch; Antelope Valley.

Pocket Money (1972 National General) Lee Marvin. LOC: Arizona: Old Tucson; New Mexico: Santa Fe; Truchas.

Points West (1929 Universal) Hoot Gibson. LOC: California: Lone Pine.

Poker Alice (1987 CBS) Elizabeth Taylor. LOC: Arizona: Old Tucson.

Pony Express (1953 Paramount) Charlton Heston. LOC: California: Paramount Studio backlot; Utah: Johnson Canyon, Kanab Movie Fort; The Gap; Turkey Crossing, Kanab Creek; Paria.

Pony Express Days (1940 Warner Bros) George Reeves. LOC: California: Burro Flats; Warner Ranch.

Pony Express Rider (1976 Doty Dayton) Stewart Peterson. LOC: Texas: Kerrville; Montana: Nevada City; Virginia City.

Pony Post (1940 Universal) Johnny Mack Brown. LOC: California: Iverson Ranch; Agoura; Universal Studio backlot.

Pony Soldier (1952 20th Century Fox) Tyrone Power. LOC: Arizona: Sedona.

Posse (1975 Paramount) Kirk Douglas. LOC: Arizona: Old Tucson; Sabino Canyon; Florence.

Posse (1993 Polygram Film Productions) Mario Van Peebles. LOC: California: Arboretum; Arizona: Mescal; Old Tucson; Sabino Canyon; Sonoita Valley/Rosemont Mountains foothills Western town; Willcox Playa dry lake.

Posse from Hell (1961 Universal) Audie Murphy. LOC: California: Century Ranch; Lone Pine; Olancha Sand Dunes; Universal Studio backlot.

Potluck Pards (1934 Reliable) Wally Wales. LOC: California: Mentryville; Pico Canyon.

Pow Wow Highway (1988 Handmade Films) A.Martinez. LOC: New Mexico: Nambé Reservation; Santa Fe/plaza; Montana: Lame Deer Northern Cheyenne Reservation; South Dakota: Pine Ridge Oglala Sioux Reservation; Wyoming: Sheridan.

Powder River (1953 20th Century Fox) Rory Calhoun. LOC: California: 20th Century Fox backlot; Montana: Flathead River; Glacier National Park.

Powder River Gunfire (1948 Universal) Keene Duncan. LOC: Texas: San Antonio area.

Powder River Rustlers (1949 Republic) Allan Lane. LOC: California: Iverson Ranch; Corriganville.

Powderkeg (1971 Filmways) Rod Taylor. LOC: New Mexico: Bonanza Creek Ranch, Santa Fe; Sandia Mountains; Arizona: Magma Arizona Railroad.

Powdersmoke Range (1935 RKO) Harry Carey. LOC: California: Kernville; RKO Encino Ranch.

Prairie Badmen (1946 PRC) Buster Crabbe. LOC: California: Corriganville.

Prairie Express (1947 Monogram) Johnny Mack Brown. LOC: California: Iverson Ranch; Rancho Placeritos.

Prairie Fever (2008 RHI Entertainment) Kevin Sorbo. LOC: California: Disney's Golden Oak Ranch; Paramount Ranch; Big Sky Ranch.

Prairie Gunsmoke (1942 Columbia) Bill Elliott. LOC: California: Iverson Ranch.

Prairie Justice (1938 Universal) Bob Baker. LOC: California: Walker Ranch; Jauregui Ranch; Rancho Placeritos.

Prairie Law (1940 RKO) George O'Brien. LOC: California: ?Agoura Ranch?; RKO Encino Ranch.

Prairie Moon (1938 Republic) Gene Autry. LOC: California: Iverson Ranch; Brandeis Ranch.

Prairie Outlaws (1948 Eagle Lion) Eddie Dean. LOC: California: Iverson Ranch.

Prairie Pals (1942 PRC) Frontier Marshal. LOC: California: Iverson Ranch; Rancho Placeritos.

Prairie Papas (1938 RKO) Ray Whitley. LOST/MISSING/UNAVAILABLE

Prairie Pioneers (1941 Republic) Three Mesquiteers. LOC: California: Iverson Ranch; Corriganville.

Prairie Pirates (1949 Universal) Tex Williams. LOST/MISSING/UNAVAILABLE

Prairie Raiders (1947 Columbia) Charles Starrett. LOC: California: Corriganville.

Prairie Roundup (1951 Columbia) Charles Starrett. LOC: California: Iverson Ranch.

Prairie Rustlers (1945 PRC) Buster Crabbe. LOC: California: Iverson Ranch; Corriganville.

Prairie Schooners (1940 Columbia) Bill Elliott. LOC: California: Iverson Ranch; Columbia Ranch.

Prairie Spooners (1941 RKO) Ray Whitley) LOST/MISSING/UNAVAILABLE

Prairie Stranger (1941 Columbia) Charles Starrett. LOC: Columbia Ranch.

Prairie Thunder (1937 Warner Bros) Dick Foran. LOC: California: Iverson Ranch.

Prescott Kid, The (1934 Columbia) Tim McCoy. LOC: California: Paramount Ranch.

Pride of the Plains (1944 Republic) Robert Livingston. LOC: California: Iverson Ranch.

Pride of the West (1938 Paramount) William Boyd. LOC: California: Paramount Ranch; Lone Pine.

Prince of the Plains (1949 Republic) Monte Hale. LOC: California: Iverson Ranch.

Prison Farm (1938 Paramount) Lloyd Nolan. LOC: California: Big Bear; Crestline.

Prisoner of Shark Island, The (1936 20th Century Fox) Warner Baxter. LOC: Maryland.

Professional Gun, A (1968 Producers Releasing Organization) Franco Nero) Spain.

Professionals, The (1966 Columbia) Burt Lancaster. LOC: California: Death Valley; Resolution Canyon; Mecca; Nevada: Valley of Fire State Park.

Promise the Moon (1997 CBC) Henry Czerny. LOC: CANADA.

Proposition, The (2005 Film Consortium) Guy Pearce. LOC: AUSTRALIA: Queensland: Winton.

Proud and the Damned, The (1972 Columbia) Chuck Connors. LOC: SPAIN.

Proud Men (1987 Von Zernack-Samuels Prod.) Charlton Heston. LOC: California: Sable Ranch.

Proud Ones, The (1956 20th Century Fox) Robert Ryan. LOC: California: 20th Century Fox backlot; Arizona: Sonoita.

Proud Rebel, The (1958 Buena Vista) Alan Ladd. LOC: Utah: Johnson Canyon Movie Set; Aspen Mirror Lake; Cedar Mountain.

Public Cowboy No. 1 (1937 Republic) Gene Autry. LOC: California: Paulson Packing Company; Kernville; Republic Studio backlot.

Pueblo Terror, The (1931 Cosmos) Buffalo Bill, Jr. LOC: California: Beale's Cut; Jauregui Ranch; Newhall Train Depot; Town of Newhall.

Pure Country (1992 Warner Bros) Rory Calhoun. LOC: Texas: Forth Worth May-pearl Terrell.

Purgatory (1999 TNT) Sam Shepard. LOC: California: Melody Ranch; Barstow area; Warner Bros backlot.

Purple Hills, The (1961 20th Century Fox) Gene Nelson. LOC: Arizona: Apacheland.

Purple Vigilantes, The (1938 Republic) Three Mesquiteers. LOC: California: Iverson Ranch; Republic Studio backlot

Pursued (1947 Warner Bros) Robert Mitchum. LOC: California: Warner Ranch; Arizona: Lupton; New Mexico: Gallup.

Quantez (1957 Universal) Fred MacMurray. LOC: California: Deadman Point, Luzerne Valley; Fairview Valley/Reeves Dry Lake, Apple Valley; Arizona: Sonoita.

Quantrill's Raiders (1958 Allied Artists) Steve Cochran. LOC: California: Iverson Ranch.

Queen of the Yukon (1940 Monogram) Charles Bickford. LOC: California: Big Bear; Cedar Lake.

Quest, The (1976 Columbia-TV) Kurt Russell. LOC: Arizona: Old Tucson.

Quick and the Dead, The (1987 HBO) Sam Elliott. LOC: Arizona: Flagstaff; Sedona; Wupatki National Monument.

Quick and the Dead, The (1995 TriStar Pictures) Sharon Stone. LOC: Arizona: Mescal; Elgin area.

Quick and the Undead, The (2006 Nott Entertainment) Clint Glenn. LOC: California: Santa Clarita - Texas: Tehuacana.

Quick Gun, The (1964 Columbia) Audie Murphy. LOC: California: Iverson Ranch; Bell Ranch.

Quick on the Trigger (1948 Columbia) Charles Starrett. LOC: California: Columbia Ranch; Iverson Ranch.

Quick Trigger Lee (1931 Big 4) Bob Custer. LOC: California: Jauregui Ranch; Ralph M. Like Studio backlot.

Quiet Gun, The (1957 20th Century Fox) Jim Davis. LOC: California: Corriganville.

Quigley Down Under (1990 Carabina Quigley Pathé Entertainment) Tom Selleck. LOC: AUSTRALIA: Northern Territory: Alice Springs; Victoria: Apollo Bay; Glebe; Melbourne; Warrnambool.

Quincannon, Frontier Scout (1956 United Artists) Tony Martin. LOC: Arizona: Pipe Springs National Monument; Utah: Kanab; Kanab Movie Fort; Aspen Mirror Lake; Strawberry Point.

Rachel and the Stranger (1948 RKO) Loretta Young. LOC: Oregon: Eugene.

Racing Blood (1954 20th Century Fox) Bill Williams. LOC:

Racketeer Round-Up (1934 Beaumont) Black King. LOC: California: Highland Springs Guest Ranch, Beaumont.

Racketeers of the Range (1939 RKO) George O'Brien. LOC: California: Corriganville; Brandeis Ranch; Ravenna Train Depot; RKO Encino Ranch.

Rage at Dawn (1955 RKO) Randolph Scott. LOC: California: Tuolumne County; Knight's Ferry; Columbia; Salt Springs Valley, Calaveras County.

Ragtime Cowboy Joe (1940 Universal) Johnny Mack Brown. LOC: California: Agoura.

Raid, The (1954 20th Century Fox) Van Heflin. LOC: California: Sherwood Forest; 20th Century Fox backlot.

Raiders of Ghost City (1944 Universal) Dennis Moore. LOC: California: Iverson Ranch; Universal Studio backlot.

Raiders of Old California (1957 Republic) Jim Davis. LOC: Utah: Kanab Canyon.

Raiders of Red Gap (1943 PRC) Robert Livingston. LOC: California: Corriganville.

Raiders of San Joaquin (1943 Universal) Johnny Mack Brown. LOC: California: Corriganville; Universal Studio backlot.

Raiders of Sunset Pass (1943 Republic) Eddie Dew. LOC: California: Iverson Ranch; Corriganville.

Raiders of the Border (1944 Monogram) Johnny Mack Brown. LOC: California: Walker Ranch.

Raiders of the Range (1942 Republic) Three Mesquiteers. LOC: California: Iverson Ranch; Corriganville; Walker Ranch.

Raiders of the South (1947 Monogram) Johnny Mack Brown. LOC: California: Iverson Ranch.

Raiders of the West (1942 PRC) Frontier Marshal. LOC: California: Iverson Ranch.

Raiders of Tomahawk Creek (1950 Columbia) Charles Starrett. LOC: California: Iverson Ranch.

Raiders, The (1952 Universal) Richard Conte. LOC: California: Iverson Ranch; Universal Studio backlot.

Raiders, The (1964 Universal) Robert Culp. LOC: California: Tuolumne County; Universal Studio backlot.

Rails into Laramie (1954 Universal) John Payne. LOC: California: Universal Studio backlot; Railway Spur between Lone Pine and Mojave.

Rainbow Over Texas (1946 Republic) Roy Rogers. LOC: California: Kentucky Park Farms; Vasquez Rocks; Republic Studio backlot.

Rainbow Over the Range (1940 Monogram) Tex Ritter. LOC: Arizona: Prescott; Granite Dell; Watson Lake.

Rainbow Over the Rockies (1947 Monogram) Jimmy Wakely. LOC: California: Janss Conejo Ranch; Kernville.

Rainbow Ranch (1933 Monogram) Rex Bell. LOC: California: Jauregui Ranch; Trem Carr Ranch; Newhall Train Depot.

Rainbow Riders (1934 Astor) Jack Perrin. LOC: California: Ranch01; Newhall Train Depot.

Rainbow Trail, The (1932 Fox) George O'Brien. LOC: Arizona: Grand Canyon National Park.

Rainbow Valley (1935 Monogram) John Wayne. LOC: California: Trem Carr Ranch; Walker Ranch; Kernville.

Rainbow's End (1935 First Division) Hoot Gibson. LOC: California: Agoura Ranch; Hoot Gibson Rodea Arena; Chatsworth Train Station; Mystery Adobe Ranch.

Rainmaker, The (1957 Paramount) Burt Lancaster) Utah: Kanab.

Raintree County (1957 MGM) Elizabeth Taylor) Kentucky: Danville; Mississippi: Natchez.

Ramona (1936 20th Century Fox) Loretta Young. LOC: California: Mesa Grande Indian Reservation; Warner Hot Springs.

Rampage at Apache Wells (1966 Columbia) Stewart Granger. LOC: CROATIA: Krka Falls, Krka National Park; YUGOSLAVIA: Cetina River; Perucko Reservoir.

Ramrod (1947 United Artists) Joel McCrea. LOC: Utah: Grafton; Kanab; Johnson Canyon; Kolob; Virgin River; Zion National Park.

Ramsbottom Rides Again (1956 British Lion) Jack Hylton. LOC: UNITED KINGDOM.

Ranch House Blues (1930 Pathe) Mildred Harris. LOC: California.

Rancho Deluxe (1974 United Artists) Jeff Bridges. LOC: Montana: Livingston.

Rancho Grande (1940 Republic) Gene Autry. LOC: California: Iverson Ranch; Bronson Canyon; Chatsworth Train Tunnel; Chatsworth Train Depot; Republic Studio backlot.

Rancho Notorious (1952 RKO) Marlene Dietrich. LOC: California: Iverson Ranch; Vasquez Rocks; Columbia Ranch; Republic Studio backlot.

Randy Rides Alone (1934 Monogram) John Wayne. LOC: California: Trem Carr Ranch; Kernville.

Range Beyond the Blue (1947 PRC) Eddie Dean. LOC: California: Iverson Ranch.

Range Busters, The (1940 Monogram) Range Busters. LOC: California: Iverson Ranch; Corriganville; Rancho Placeritos

Range Defenders (1937 Republic) Three Mesquiteers. LOC: California: Kernville; Republic Studio backlot.

Range Feud, The (1931 Columbia) Buck Jones. LOC: California: RKO Encino Ranch; Walker Ranch; Vasquez Rocks.

Range Justice (1949 Monogram) Johnny Mack Brown. LOC: California: Walker Ranch.

Range Land (1949 Monogram) Whip Wilson. LOC: California: Walker Ranch.

Range Law (1931 Tiffany) Ken Maynard. LOC: California: Towsley Canyon; Warner Bros Studio backlot; Vasquez Rocks.

Range Law (1944 Monogram) Johnny Mack Brown. LOC: California: Walker Ranch; Rancho Placeritos.

Range Renegades (1948 Monogram) Jimmy Wakely. LOC: California: Walker Ranch.

Range Riders (1934 Superior) Buddy Roosevelt. LOC: California: Acton; Acton Train Depot; Ralph M. Like Studio backlot.

Range War (1939 Paramount) William Boyd. LOC: California: Lone Pine; Anchor Ranch; Rancho Placeritos.

Range Warfare (1935 Kent) Wally Wales. LOC: California: Frank Straubinger Ranch; Ralph M. Like Studio backlot; Santa Susanna Mtns.

Ranger and the Lady, The (1940 Republic) Roy Rogers. LOC: California: Lake Sherwood; Republic Studio backlot.

Ranger Courage (1937 Columbia) Bob Allen. LOC: California: Iverson Ranch; Burro Flats.

Ranger of Cherokee Strip (1949 Republic) Monte Hale. LOC: California: Iverson Ranch.

Ranger, the Cook and a Hole in the Sky, The (1995 ABC) Sam Elliott. LOC: Montana: Darby; Hamilton; Ravalli County; CANADA: British Columbia: Bordertown/Western town, Maple Ridge, Vancouver.

Ranger's Code (1933 Monogram) Bob Steele) LOST/MISSING

Ranger's Round-Up, The (1938 Spectrum) Fred Scott. LOC: California: Walker Ranch.

Rangers of Fortune (1940 Paramount) Fred MacMurray. LOC: California: Deadman Point, Luzerne Valley.

Rangers Ride, The (1948 Monogram) Jimmy Wakely. LOC: California: Walker Ranch.

Rangers Step In, The (1937 Columbia) Bob Allen. LOC: California: Walker Ranch; Jauregui Ranch; Rancho Placeritos.

Rangers Take Over, The (1942 PRC) Texas Rangers. LOC: California: Iverson Ranch.

Rangle River (1936 Columbia) Victor Jory) AUSTRALIA: New South Wales.

Rare Breed, The (1966 Universal) James Stewart. LOC: California: Jamestown; Railtown; Tuolumne County; Mecca; Universal Studio backlot.

Raton Pass (1951 Warner Bros) Dennis Morgan. LOC: California: Warner Ranch; New Mexico: Gallup.

Ravenous (1999 Twentieth Century-Fox Film) Robert Carlyle. LOC: MEXICO: Durango; SLOVAKIA: Tatranska National Park; Tatra Mountains.

Raw Edge (1956 Universal) Rory Calhoun. LOC: California: Tahquitz Mountains; Garner Ranch.

Raw Timber (1937 Crescent) Tom Keene. LOC:

Rawhide (1938 20th Century Fox) Smith Ballew. LOC: California: RKO Encino Ranch.

Rawhide (1951 20th Century Fox) Tyrone Power. LOC: California: Lone Pine.

Rawhide Mail (1934 Reliable) Jack Perrin. LOC: California: Agoura Ranch; Ralph

M. Like Studio backlot.

Rawhide Rangers (1941 Universal) Johnny Mack Brown. LOC: California: Iverson Ranch; Universal Studio backlot.

Rawhide Romance (1934 Superior) Buffalo Bill, Jr. LOC: California: Ranch01.

Rawhide Terror, The (1934 Security) Art Mix. LOC: California: Frank LaSalle Ranch.

Rawhide Years, The (1956 Universal) Tony Curtis. LOC: California: Lone Pine; Universal Studio backlot.

Ready to Ride (1950 Universal) Tex Williams. LOST/MISSING/UNAVAILABLE

Reason to Live, A Reason to Die, A (1974 K-Tel International) James Coburn. LOC: SPAIN: Almería: Fort Bowie; Mini Hollywood; Gergal; For Bravo; Fuerte El Condor.

Rebel City (1953 Allied Artists) Bill Elliott. LOC: California: Iverson Ranch.

Rebel in Town (1956 United Artists) John Payne. LOC: California: Ingram Ranch; Janss Conejo Ranch.

Rebellion (1936 Crescent) Tom Keene. LOC: California: Iverson Ranch.

Reckless Buckaroo, The (1935 Crescent) Bill Cody. LOC: California: Antelope Valley; Lake Los Angeles.

Reckless Ranger (1937 Columbia) Bob Allen. LOC: California: Iverson Ranch; Brandeis Ranch; Walker Ranch; Jauregui Ranch; Burro Flats.

Reckless Rider, The (1932 Kent) Lane Chandle) LOST/MISSING

Red Badge of Courage, The (1951 MGM) Audie Murphy. LOC: California: Clarence Brown Ranch; Chico; John Huston Ranch.

Red Badge of Courage, The (1974 NBC/20th Century Fox) Richard Thomas. LOC: Arizona: Old Tucson, Patagonia, Rio Rico.

Red Bells (1982 Mosfilm/Vides International/Conacitez) Franco Nero. LOC: MEXICO: Chihuahua: Casa de Janos; Barranco del Cobre; Parral; Sonora: Bavispe; Bacanora; Sierra Madre Occidental; Sierra del Tigre; Morelos: Hacienda Coahuixtla, Apatlaco.

Red Blood of Courage (1935 Ambassador) Kermit Maynard. LOC: California: Big Bear.

Red Canyon (1949 Universal) Howard Duff. LOC: California: Universal Studio backlot; Utah: Kanab Rodeo Grounds; Kanab Canyon; Paria Canyon; Aspen Mirror Lake; Duck Creek.

Red Desert (1949 Lippert) Donald Barry. LOC: California: Iverson Ranch; Red Rock Canyon.

Red Earth, White Earth (1989 Chris/Rose Productions) Timothy Daly. LOC: CANADA: Quebec.

Red Fork Range (1931 Big 4) Wally Wales. LOC: California: Calabasas.

Red Mountain (1951 Paramount) Alan Ladd. LOC: California: Iverson Ranch; Arizona: Lupton; New Mexico: Gallup.

Red Pony, The (1949 Republic) Robert Mitchum. LOC: California: Agoura Ranch.

Red Pony, The (1973 Universal-TV) Henry Fonda. LOC: California: Tuolumne County; Jamestown.

Red Rider, The (1934 Universal) Buck Jones. LOC: California: Agoura; Lake Sherwood.

Red River (1948 United Artists) John Wayne. LOC: California: Iverson Ranch; Arizona: Elgin; Rain Valley; Sonoita Creek; San Pedro River.

Red River (1988 Metro-Goldwyn-Mayer/United Artists) James Arness. LOC: Arizona: Circle Z Ranch/Sonoita Creek; Patagonia; Elgin area; Old Tucson; San Rafael Valley; Sonoita; Verde River.

Red River Range (1938 Republic) Three Mesquiteers. LOC: California: Iverson Ranch; Corriganville; Red Rock Canyon; Republic Studio backlot.

Red River Renegades (1946 Republic) Sunset Carson. LOC: California: Iverson Ranch; Republic Studio backlot.

Red River Robin Hood (1943 RKO) Tim Holt. LOC: California: Iverson Ranch; Corriganville.

Red River Shore (1953 Republic) Rex Allen. LOC: California: Burro Flats.

Red River Valley (1936 Republic) Gene Autry. LOC: California: Iverson Ranch; Trem Carr Ranch; Kernville; Republic Studio backlot; Arizona: Yuma; Yuma Territorial Prison; Nevada: Boulder Dam; Laguna Dam.

Red River Valley (1941 Republic) Roy Rogers. LOC: California: Iverson Ranch; Walker Ranch; Republic Studio backlot.

Red Rope, The (1937 Republic) Bob Steele. LOC: California: Iverson Ranch; Brandeis Ranch.

Red Skies of Montana (1952 20th Century Fox) Richard Widmark. LOC: Montana: Missoula.

Red Stallion in the Rockies (1949 Eagle Lion) Jim Davis. LOC: Colorado: Glenwood Springs; Rocky Mountains.

Red Stallion, The (1947 Eagle Lion) Robert Paige. LOC: California: Iverson Ranch; Dunsmuir; Mt. Shasta City.

Red Sun (1972 National General) Charles Bronson. LOC: SPAIN: Almería; La Calahorra.

Red Sundown (1956 Universal) Rory Calhoun. LOC: California: Janss Janss Conejo Ranch; Universal Studio backlot.

Red Tomahawk (1967 Paramount) Howard Keel. LOC: California: North Ranch; Paramount Studio backlot.

Red, White and Black, The (1970 Horschman Northern) Robert Doqui. LOC: Texas: Fort Davis.

Redemption: A Mile from Hell (2009 Entertainment 7/Gallery Films/Cas-Mor Productions) Dustin Leighton. LOC: Arizona.

Redhead and the Cowboy, The (1951 Paramount) Glenn Ford. LOC: California: Rancho Placeritos; Arizona: Sedona.

Redhead from Wyoming, The (1953 Universal) Maureen O'Hara. LOC: California:

Agoura; Universal Studio backlot.

Red-Headed Stranger (1986 Alive Films) Willie Nelson. LOC: Texas: Luck Ranch/Willieville/Nelson Ranch Spicewood, Austin.

Redskin (1929 Paramount) Richard Dix. LOC: Arizona: Canyon de Chelly; New Mexico: Acoma Pueblo.

Redwood Forest Trail (1950 Republic) Rex Allen. LOC: California: Big Bear; Rowland V Lee Ranch; Republic Studio backlot.

Relentless (1948 Columbia) Robert Young. LOC: California: Corriganville; Columbia Ranch; Arizona: Sedona; Sedona Western Street; Starr Pass; Cortaro.

Relentless (1977 CBS-TV) Will Sampson. LOC: Arizona: Camp Verde; Cottonwood.

Renegade Girl (1946 Screen Guild) Alan Curtis. LOC: California: Corriganville; Agoura Ranch.

Renegade Ranger, The (1938 RKO) George O'Brien. LOC: California: Iverson Ranch; RKO Encino Ranch.

Renegade Trail, The (1939 Paramount) William Boyd. LOC: California: Rancho Placeritos; Lone Pine; Lone Pine Train Station.

Renegade, The (1943 PRC) Buster Crabbe. LOC: California: Rancho Placeritos.

Renegades of Sonora (1948 Republic) Allan Lane. LOC: California: Iverson Ranch; Lone Pine.

Renegades of the Rio Grande (1945 Universal) Rod Cameron. LOC: California: Corriganville; Universal Studio backlot.

Renegades of the Sage (1949 Columbia) Charles Starrett. LOC: California: Iverson Ranch; Corriganville.

Renegades of the West (1932 RKO) Tom Keene. LOC: California: Trem Carr Ranch.

Renegades, The (1946 Columbia) Evelyn Keyes. LOC: California: Iverson Ranch; Corriganville; Lake Sherwood.

Renfrew of the Royal Mounted (1937 Grand National) James Newill. LOC: California: Big Bear; Kernville River; Lake Sherwood.

Reno (1939 RKO) Richard Dix. LOC: Still shots of Reno provided by Reno Chamber of Commerce.

Reprisal! (1956 Columbia) Guy Madison. LOC: California: Columbia Ranch; Arizona: Old Tucson; Kingsley Ranch, Arivaca Junction.

Requiem for a Gunfighter (1965 Embassy) Rod Cameron. LOC: California: Iverson Ranch.

Restless Breed, The (1957 20th Century Fox) Scott Brady. LOC: California: Antelope Valley.

Retribution Road (2009) John Castellanos. LOC: Texas: Alamo Village.

Return of a Man Called Horse, The (1976 United Artists) Richard Harris. LOC: Arizona: Tucson; South Dakota: Custer State Park; MEXICO: Morelos: Cuernevaca; Nayarit: Islas Marias; Sonora: Nogales; UNITED KINGDOM.

Return of Daniel Boone, The (1941 Columbia) Bill Elliott. LOC: California: Lone Pine.

Return of Desperado, The (1988 Universal Pictures) Alex McArthur. LOC: New Mexico: Bonanza Creek Ranch; Cook Ranch/Cerro Pelon Ranch; J.W. Eaves Movie Ranch.

Return of Frank James, The (1940 20th Century Fox) Henry Fonda. LOC: California: Bishop; Convict Lake; Tuolumne County; 20th Century Fox Studio backlot.

Return of Jack Slade, The (1955 Allied Artists) John Ericson. LOC: California: Lone Pine; Columbia, Tuolumne County.

Return of Jesse James, The (1950 Lippert) John Ireland. LOC: California: Rancho Placeritos; Walker Ranch.

Return of Josey Wales, The (1986 Reel Movies International) Michael Parks. LOC: Texas: Alamo Village.

Return of Rin Tin Tin (1947 PRC) Donald Woods. LOC: California: Santa Ynez Mission.

Return of Sabata, The (1972 United Artists) Lee Van Cleef. LOC: ITALY: Rome: Dino De Laurentiis Studio backlot.

Return of the Bad Men (1948 RKO) Robert Ryan. LOC: California: Iverson Ranch; Jauregui Ranch; Fillmore-Saugus Railroad.

Return of the Cisco Kid, The (1939 20th Century Fox) Warner Baxter. LOC: California: Vasquez Rocks; Arizona: Sabino Canyon, Tucson.

Return of the Durango Kid, The (1945 Columbia) Charles Starrett. LOC: California: Corriganville; Columbia Ranch.

Return of the Frontiersman (1950 Warner Bros) Gordon MacRae. LOC: California: Warner Ranch.

Return of the Gunfighter (1967 MGM-TV) Robert Taylor. LOC: Arizona: Old Tucson; Andrada Ranch, Tucson; Amado.

Return of the Lash (1947 PRC) Lash LaRue. LOC: California: Iverson Ranch.

Return of the Rangers (1943 PRC) Texas Rangers. LOC: California: Corriganville.

Return of the Seven (1966 United Artists) Yul Brynner. LOC: SPAIN: Madrid; Nuevo Baztán; Alicante.

Return of the Texan (1952 20th Century Fox) Dale Robertson. LOC: California: Janet Gaynor Ranch, Granada Hills; 20th Century Fox Studio backlot; Texas: San Antonio.

Return of Wild Bill, The (1940 Columbia) Bill Elliott. LOC: California: Iverson Ranch; Corriganville; Columbia Ranch.

Return of Wildfire, The (1948 Screen Guild) Richard Arlen. LOC: California: Vasquez Rocks.

Return to Lonesome Dove (1993 CBS) Jon Voight. LOC: Montana: Billings; Butte; Nevada City.

Return to Snowy River (1988 Walt Disney Pictures) Tom Burlinson. LOC: AUS-

TRALIA: Victoria: Mansfield.

Return to Warbow (1958 Columbia) Phil Carey. LOC: California: Iverson Ranch; Corriganville.

Returning, The (1983 Willow Films) Susan Strasberg. LOC: Utah: Salt Lake City.

Revenge Rider, The (1935 Columbia) Tim McCoy. LOC: California: Jauregui Ranch.

Revengers, The (1972 National General) William Holden. LOC: MEXICO: Chihuahua: Parral; Coahuila: Bilbao sand dunes; El Durazno; Morelos: Lagunas de Zempoala; Tres Marias; Sonora: Bavispe.

Reverend Colt, The (1971 R. M. Films) Guy Madison. LOC: SPAIN: Colmenar Viejo.

Revolt at Fort Laramie (1957 United Artists) John Dehner. LOC: Utah: Aspen Mirror Lake; Duck Creek; Kanab; Kanab Movie Fort; Strawberry Valley.

Revolution (1985 Goldcrest Films International) Al Pacino. LOC: ENGLAND: Burrator Reservoir, Dartmoor Devon; Ely Cambridgeshire; Norfolk.

Reward, The (1965 20th Century Fox) Max von Sydow. LOC: California: Death Valley; Arizona: Old Tucson; Nevada: Rhyolite.

Rhythm of the Rio Grande (1940 Monogram) Tex Ritter. LOC: California: Rancho Placeritos; Lake Los Angeles; Palmdale.

Rhythm of the Saddle (1938 Republic) Gene Autry. LOC: California: Iverson Ranch; Republic Studio backlot.

Rhythm on the Range (1936 Paramount) Bing Crosby. LOC: California: Lone Pine; New York: Madison Square Garden.

Rhythm Round-Up (1945 Columbia) Ken Curtis. LOC: California: Columbia Ranch.

Ricochet Romance (1954 Universal) Marjorie Main. LOC: California: Universal Studio backlot.

Riddle Ranch (1935 Beaumont) David Worth. LOC: California: Highland Springs Guest Ranch, Beaumont; Ralph M. Like Studio backlot.

Ride 'Em Cowboy (1942 Universal) Abbott & Costello. LOC: California: Iverson Ranch; Sable Ranch; B-Bar A in Solemint Canyon; Victorville; Alameda Street, Los Angeles.

Ride 'Em Cowgirl (1939 Grand National) Dorothy Page. LOC: California: Brandeis Ranch; Arizona: Mesa.

Ride 'Em Cowboy (1930 Pathe) Thelma White. LOC:

Ride 'Em Cowboy (1936 Universal) Buck Jones. LOC:

Ride 'Em Cowgirl (1939 Grand National) Dorothy Page. LOC: California: Brandeis Ranch.

Ride a Crooked Trail (1958 Universal) Audie Murphy. LOC: California:Universal Studio backlot; Janss Janss Conejo Ranch.

Ride a Northbound Horse (1969 Buena Vista) Carroll O'Connor. LOC: California: Janss Conejo Ranch.

Ride a Violent Mile (1957 20th Century Fox) John Agar. LOC: Utah: Kanab.

Ride a Wild Stud (1969 Gold Star) Hale Williams. LOC: Nevada: Las Vegas area.

Ride Back, The (1957 United Artists) Anthony Quinn. LOC: California: Rancho Placeritos; Janss Conejo Ranch.

Ride Beyond Vengeance (1966 Columbia) Chuck Connors. LOC: California: Lake Los Angeles; RKO Culver City backlot.

Ride Clear of Diablo (1954 Universal) Audie Murphy. LOC: California: Burro Flats; Fairview Valley/Reeves Dry Lake, Apple Valley; Universal Studio backlot.

Ride Him, Cowboy (1932 Warner Bros) John Wayne. LOC: California: Warner Bros Studio backlot; Providencia Ranch.

Ride in the Whirlwind (1965 Jack H. Harris Ent.) Jack Nicholson. LOC: Utah: Kanab; Paria; Kimball Valley.

Ride Lonesome (1959 Columbia) Randolph Scott. LOC: California: Lone Pine; Olancha Sand Dunes.

Ride On, Vaquero (1941 20th Century Fox) Cesar Romero. LOC: California: Vasquez Rocks; 20th Century Fox backlot.

Ride or Die (2005 Warning Films, Inc.) Sarah Kozer. LOC: California.

Ride Out for Revenge (1957 United Artists) Rory Calhoun. LOC: California: Rancho Placeritos; Janss Janss Conejo Ranch.

Ride the High Country (1962 MGM) Randolph Scott. LOC: California: Bronson Canyon; Century Ranch; Mammoth Lakes; MGM backlot.

Ride the Man Down (1953 Republic) Rod Cameron. LOC: California: Republic Studio backlot; Utah: Kanab Canyon; Coral Pink Sand Dunes.

Ride the Wind (1966 NBC-TV) Lorne Greene. LOC: California: Red Rock Canyon; Vasquez Rocks.

Ride to Hangman's Tree (1967 Universal) Jack Lord. LOC: Utah: Kanab; Paria; Strawberry Valley, Strawberry Point.

Ride with the Devil (1999 Universal Pictures) Tobey Maguire. LOC: Kansas: Fort Osage; Kansas City; Lexington; Pattonsburg.

Ride, Ranger, Ride (1936 Republic) Gene Autry. LOC: California: Calabasas; Republic Studio backlot.

Ride, Ryder, Ride (1949 Eagle-Lion) Jim Bannon. LOC: California: Iverson Ranch; Agoura Ranch; Rancho Placeritos.

Ride, Tenderfoot, Ride (1940 Republic) Gene Autry. LOC: California: Lake Hemet; Agoura Ranch; Glendale Grand Central Air Terminal; Chatsworth Train Depot; Antelope Valley; Chatsworth Lake; Republic Studio backlot.

Ride, The (1997 World Wide Pictures) Michael Biehn. LOC: Arizona: Saguaro Lake Ranch; Mesa; Illinois: Chicago.

Ride, Vaquero! (1953 MGM) Robert Taylor. LOC: California: MGM backlot; Utah: Kanab Canyon; The Gap.

Rider from Tucson (1950 RKO) Tim Holt. LOC: California: Lone Pine.

Rider of Death Valley, The (1932 Universal) Tom Mix. LOC: California: Calabasas; Sand Hills; Univeral Studio backlot; Arizona: Yuma; Ballance Ranch, near Somerton; Black Butte; Telegraph Pass.

Rider of the Law, The (1935 Commodore) Bob Steele. LOC: California: Ralph M. Like Studio backlot; Frank LaSalle Ranch; Towsley Canyon.

Rider of the Plains, A (1931 Syndicate) Tom Tyler. LOC: California: Pioneer Church; Ralph M. Like Studio backlot.

Rider on a Dead Horse (1962 Phoenix) John Vivyan. LOC: Arizona: Apacheland.

Riders from Nowhere (1940 Monogram) Jack Randall. LOC: California: Walker Ranch; Rancho Placeritos.

Riders in the Sky (1949 Columbia) Gene Autry. LOC: California: Iverson Ranch; Pioneertown; Columbia Ranch.

Riders in the Storm (1995 Filmhaus) Bo Hopkins. LOC: Arizona: Tucson.

Riders of Black Mountain (1940 PDC) Tim McCoy. LOC: California: Iverson Ranch.

Riders of Black River (1939 Columbia) Charles Starrett. LOC: California: Agoura.

Riders of Death Valley (1941 Universal) Buck Jones. LOC: California: Iverson Ranch; Red Rock Canyon; Kernville; Universal Studio backlot.

Riders of Destiny (1933 Monogram) John Wayne. LOC: California: Trem Carr Ranch; Antelope Valley.

Riders of Pasco Basin (1940 Universal) Johnny Mack Brown. LOC: California: Agoura; Universal Studio backlot.

Riders of the Badlands (1941 Columbia) Charles Starrett,. LOC: California: Iverson Ranch.

Riders of the Black Hills (1938 Republic) Three Mesquiteers. LOC: California: Iverson Ranch; Corriganville; Vasquez Rocks; Republic Studio backlot.

Riders of the Cactus (1931 Big 4) Wally Wales. LOC: California: Universal backlot; Sonora; Columbia.

Riders of the Dawn (1937 Monogram) Jack Randall. LOC: California: Trem Carr Ranch; Lone Pine; Owens Dry Lake.

Riders of the Dawn (1945 Monogram) Jimmy Wakely. LOC: California: Walker Ranch.

Riders of the Deadline (1943 United Artists) William Boyd. LOC: California: Lone Pine; Anchor Ranch; California Studio backlot.

Riders of the Desert (1932 World Wide) Bob Steele. LOC: California: Trem Carr Ranch; Frank LaSalle Ranch; Towsley Canyon.

Riders of the Dusk (1949 Monogram) Whip Wilson. LOC: California: Iverson Ranch; Walker Ranch.

Riders of the Frontier (1939 Monogram) Tex Ritter. LOC: California: Lone Pine; Rancho Placeritos.

Riders of the Golden Gulch (1932 West Coast) Buffalo Bill, Jr. LOST/MISSING

Riders of the Lone Star (1947 Columbia) Charles Starrett. LOC: California: Corriganville; Providencia Ranch; Columbia Ranch.

Riders of the North (1931 Syndicate) Bob Custer. LOC: California: Big Bear; Lake Sherwood.

Riders of the Northland (1942 Columbia) Charles Starrett. LOC: California: Iverson Ranch.

Riders of the Northwest Mounted (1943 Columbia) Russell Hayden. LOC: California: Cedar Lake.

Riders of the Pony Express (1949 Kayson/Screencraft) Ken Curtis. LOC: California: Corriganville; Antelope Valley.

Riders of the Purple Sage (1931 Fox) George O'Brien. LOC: Arizona: Sedona; Flagstaff.

Riders of the Purple Sage (1941 20th Century Fox) George Montgomery. LOC: California: Lone Pine; Anchor Ranch; 20th Century Fox backlot.

Riders of the Purple Sage (1996 TNT) Ed Harris. LOC: Utah: Dugout Ranch and Indian Creek Moab; Mill Creek Canyon Moab; Pucker Pass/Long Valley Moab; Ten Mile Moab.

Riders of the Range (1950 RKO) Tim Holt. LOC: California: Garner Ranch; RKO Encino Ranch.

Riders of the Rio (1931 Round-Up Pictures) Lane Chandler) LOST/MISSING

Riders of the Rio Grande (1943 Republic) Three Mesquiteers. LOC: California: Iverson Ranch.

Riders of the Rockies (1937 Grand National) Tex Ritter. LOC: California: Brandeis Ranch; Idyllwild and Area; Keen Camp.

Riders of the Sage (1939 Metropolitan) Bob Steele. LOC: California: Unidentified ranch in Placerita Canyon.

Riders of the Santa Fe (1944 Universal) Rod Cameron. LOC: California: Agoura.

Riders of the Timberline (1941 Paramount) William Boyd. LOC: California: Big Bear; Cedar Lake; California Studio backlot.

Riders of the West (1942 Monogram) Rough Riders. LOC: California: Walker Ranch; Rancho Placeritos.

Riders of the Whistling Pines (1949 Columbia) Gene Autry. LOC: California: Big Bear; Cedar Lake; I. S. Ranch; Hitchcock Ranch; Janss Janss Conejo Ranch; Conejo Valley Airport; Columbia Ranch.

Riders of the Whistling Skull (1937 Republic) Three Mesquiteers. LOC: California: Iverson Ranch; Mecca: Painted Canyon; Republic Studio backlot.

Ridin' Down the Canyon (1942 Republic) Roy Rogers. LOC: California: Kernville.

Ridin' Down the Trail (1947 Monogram) Jimmy Wakely. LOC: California: Iverson Ranch.

Ridin' Fool, The (1931 Tiffany) Bob Steele. LOC: California: Walker Ranch; Ralph M. Like Studio backlot.

Ridin' for Justice (1932 Columbia) Buck Jones. LOC: California: Jauregui Ranch; Paramount Ranch.

Ridin' Gents (1934 Reliable) Jack Perrin. LOC: California: Trem Carr Ranch.

Ridin' Law (1930 Big 4) Jack Perrin. LOC:

Ridin' On (1936 Commodore) Tom Tyler. LOC: California: Walker Ranch; Trem Carr Ranch; Frank LaSalle Ranch.

Ridin' On a Rainbow (1941 Republic) Gene Autry. LOC: California: Agoura; Big Bear.

Ridin' the Cherokee Trail (1941 Monogram) Tex Ritter. LOC: California: Walker Ranch; Jauregui Ranch.

Ridin' the Lone Trail (1937 Republic) Bob Steele. LOC: California: Iverson Ranch; Walker Ranch.

Ridin' the Outlaw Trail (1951 Columbia) Charles Starrett. LOC: California: Iverson Ranch; Columbia Ranch.

Ridin' the Trail (1940 Ziehm Inc) Fred Scott. LOC: California: Walker Ranch; Jauregui Ranch.

Ridin' Thru (1935 Reliable) Tom Tyler. LOC: California: French Ranch.

Riding Avenger, The (1936 Grand National) Hoot Gibson. LOC: California: Kernville.

Riding High (1943 Paramount) Dick Powell. LOC: California: Arcadia; Santa Anita Race Track.

Riding Shotgun (1954 Warner Bros) Randolph Scott. LOC: California: Iverson Ranch; Corriganville; Berry Ranch.

Riding Speed (1934 Superior) Buffalo Bill, Jr. LOC: California: North Verde Ranch/Kemper Campbell Ranch, Upper Narrows, Victorville; Quartzite Mountain Area, Upper Desert Knolls Area, Apple Valley.

Riding the California Trail (1947 Monogram) Gilbert Roland. LOC: California: Rancho Placeritos.

Riding the Sunset Trail (1941 Monogram) Tom Keene. LOC: California: Rancho Placeritos; Walker Ranch; Jauregui Ranch.

Riding the Wind (1942 RKO) Tim Holt. LOC: California: Burro Flats; Lake Sherwood.

Riding Through Nevada (1942 Columbia) Charles Starrett. LOC: California: Iverson Ranch.

Riding Tornado, The (1932 Columbia) Tim McCoy. LOC: California: Brandeis Ranch.

Riding West (1944 Columbia) Charles Starrett. LOC: California: Columbia Ranch.

Riding Wild (1935 Columbia) Tim McCoy. LOC: California: Iverson Ranch; Jauregui Ranch.

Riding With Buffalo Bill (1954 Columbia) Marshall Reed. LOC: California: Iverson Ranch; Columbia Ranch; Ingram Ranch.

Righteous and the Wicked, The (2010 505 Films) Craig Myers. LOC: New Mexico: Bonanza Creek Ranch; Makarios Ranch Cerrillos.

Rim of the Canyon (1949 Columbia) Gene Autry. LOC: California: Iverson Ranch; Corriganville; Vasquez Rocks; Columbia Ranch.

Rimfire (1949 Lippert/Screen Guild) James Millican. LOC: California: Iverson Ranch.

Rio Bravo (1959 Warner Bros) John Wayne. LOC: Arizona: Old Tucson; Starr Pass.

Rio Conchos (1964 20th Century Fox) Richard Boone. LOC: California: Century Ranch; Utah: Arches National Park; Castle Valley; Moab; Professor Valley; White's Ranch.

Rio Diablo (1993 Kenny Rogers Productions) Kenny Rogers. LOC: Texas: Alamo Village; Big Bend Ranch State Park; Lajitas/Mexican set.

Rio Grande (1938 Columbia) Charles Starrett. LOC: California: Agoura Ranch; Columbia Ranch.

Rio Grande (1950 Astor) Sunset Carson. LOC: Texas: Juanita.

Rio Grande (1950 Republic) John Wayne. LOC: Utah: Castle Valley; Ida Gulch; Professor Valley; Onion Creek Narrows; White's Ranch.

Rio Grande Patrol (1950 RKO) Tim Holt. LOC: California: Iverson Ranch; Corriganville; Antelope Valley; RKO Encino Ranch.

Rio Grande Raiders (1946 Republic) Sunset Carson. LOC: California: Iverson Ranch; Republic Studio backlot.

Rio Lobo (1970 National General) John Wayne. LOC: Arizona: Old Tucson; Sonoita Creek; MEXICO: Morelos: Cuernevaca area and railway depot.

Rio Rattler (1935 Commodore) Tom Tyler. LOC: California: Jauregui Ranch; Towsley Canyon; Frank LaSalle Ranch.

Rio Rita (1929 RKO) Bebe Daniels. LOC: California: Tarzana Ranch.

Rio Rita (1942 MGM) Abbott & Costello. LOC: California: Hemet; Palm Springs.

Rip Roarin' Buckaroo (1936 Victory) Tom Tyler. LOC: California: Brandeis Ranch; Sable Ranch; Lone Pine.

River Lady (1948 Universal) Rod Cameron. LOC: California: Big Bear.

River of No Return (1954 20th Century Fox) Marilyn Monroe. LOC: Idaho: Clearwater River; CANADA: Banff National Park; Jasper National Park.

River of Skulls, A (2010 Sheep Ranch Prod) Trent Anderson. LOC: California: Calaveras County.

River's Edge, The (1957 20th Century Fox) Ray Milland. LOC: MEXICO: Mexico: Amecacameca; Itzaccihuati.

River's End (1940 Warner Bros) Dennis Morgan. LOC: California: Big Bear.

Road Agent (1941 Universal) Leo Carrillo. LOC: California: Iverson Ranch; Corriganville.

Road Agent (1952 RKO) Tim Holt. LOC: California: Iverson Ranch; Walker Ranch; Jauregui Ranch.

Road to Denver, The (1955 Republic) John Payne. LOC: Utah: St. George; Snow Canyon; Santa Clara River; Biglow Ranch on the Magotsu Wash north of Gunlock; Ervine and Nelson Ranches, Motoqua.

Road to Utopia (1945 Paramount) Crosby, Hope, & Lamour. LOC: California:

June Lake.

Roamin' Wild (1936 Reliable) Tom Tyler. LOC: California: Brandeis Ranch; Frank LaSalle Ranch.

Roaming Cowboy, The (1937 Spectrum) Fred Scott. LOC: California: Brandeis Ranch; Walker Ranch.

Roar of the Iron Horse (1951 Columbia) Jock Mahoney. LOC: Nevada: Carson City; Carson Valley.

Roarin' Guns (1936 Puritan) Tim McCoy. LOC: California: Brandeis Ranch; Towsley Canyon; Trem Carr Ranch; Chatsworth Train Depot.

Roarin' Lead (1936 Republic) Three Mesquiteers. LOC: California: Iverson Ranch; Walker Ranch; Republic Studio backlot.

Roaring Frontiers (1941 Columbia) Bill Elliott. LOC: California: Iverson Ranch.

Roaring Ranch (1930 Universal) Hoot Gibson. LOC: California: Universal Studio backlot.

Roaring Rangers (1946 Columbia) Charles Starrett. LOC: California: Iverson Ranch; Providencia Ranch; Columbia Ranch.

Roaring Six Guns (1937 Ambassador) Kermit Maynard. LOC: California: Brandeis Ranch.

Roaring Timber (1937 Columbia) Jack Holt. LOC: Oregon: Astoria.

Roaring West, The (1935 Universal) Buck Jones. LOC: California: Bronson Canyon; Kernville; Lone Pine; Frank Straubinger Ranch.

Roaring Westward (1949 Monogram) Jimmy Wakely. LOC: California: Walker Ranch; Oliver Drake Ranch.

Robbers of the Range (1941 RKO) Tim Holt. LOC: California: Burro Flats; Morrison Ranch; RKO Encino Ranch.

Robbers' Roost (1933 Fox) George O'Brien. LOC: California: Tuolumne County; Sonora; Arizona: Sedona; Oak Creek Canyon; Flagstaff.

Robbers' Roost (1955 United Artists) George Montgomery. LOC: MEXICO: Durango.

Robin Hood of El Dorado, The (1936 MGM) Warner Baxter. LOC: California: Tuolumne County; Dardanelle; Strawberry Flats; MGM backlot.

Robin Hood of Monterey (1947 Monogram) Gilbert Roland. LOC: California: Iverson Ranch; Rancho Placeritos.

Robin Hood of Texas (1947 Republic) Gene Autry. LOC: California: Iverson Ranch; Chatsworth Lake.

Robin Hood of the Pecos (1941 Republic) Roy Rogers. LOC: California: Burro Flats; Vasquez Rocks; Republic Studio backlot.

Robin Hood of the Range (1943 Columbia) Charles Starrett. LOC: California: Columbia Ranch.

Rock Island Trail (1950 Republic) Forrest Tucker. LOC: Oklahoma: McAlester.

Rock River Renegades (1942 Monogram) Range Busters. LOC: California: Walker Ranch; Jauregui Ranch.

Rockwell (1994 Inspired Corporation) Randy Gleave. LOC: Utah: Great Salt Lake; Pioneer Trail State Park Salt Lake City.

Rocky (1948 Monogram) Roddy McDowell. LOC: California: Bridgeport.

Rocky Mountain (1950 Warner Bros) Errol Flynn. LOC: New Mexico: Church Rock; Gallup; Navajo.

Rocky Mountain Mystery (1935 Paramount) Randolph Scott. LOC: California: Big Bear; Paramount Ranch.

Rocky Mountain Rangers (1940 Republic) Three Mesquiteers. LOC: California: Iverson Ranch; Republic Studio backlot.

Rocky Rhodes (1934 Universal) Buck Jones. LOC: California: Iverson Ranch.

Rodeo (1952 Monogram) John Archer. LOC:

Rodeo Day (1935 Skibo) Frank Luther. LOC: Rodeo scenes filmed at Hoot Gibson Rodeo Arena; rest of film has no exteriors.

Rodeo Girl (1980 CBS) Katharine Ross. LOC: California: Newhall; San Diego;

Rodeo King and the Senorita (1951 Republic) Rex Allen. LOC: California: Iverson Ranch.

Rodeo Rhythm (1942 PRC) Fred Scott. LOC: Missouri: Kansas City.

Rogue of the Range (1936 Supreme) Johnny Mack Brown. LOC: California: Walker Ranch; Jauregui Ranch; Ralph M. Like Studio.

Rogue River (1950 Eagle Lion) Rory Calhoun. LOC: Oregon: Grants Pass; Rogue River.

Roll Along, Cowboy (1937 20th Century Fox) Smith Ballew. LOC: California: Bishop.

Roll On, Texas Moon (1946 Republic) Roy Rogers. LOC: California: Iverson Ranch; Kernville; Doyle Ranch, Onyx.

Roll, Thunder, Roll (1949 Eagle Lion) Jim Bannon. LOC: California: Iverson Ranch; Rancho Placeritos.

Roll, Wagons, Roll (1940 Monogram) Tex Ritter. LOC: Utah: Cave Lake; Kanab Canyon; Johnson Canyon; Rockville; Virgin River; Duck Creek.

Rollin' Home to Texas (1940 Monogram) Tex Ritter. LOC: Arizona: Prescott; Granite Dells.

Rollin' Plains (1938 Grand National) Tex Ritter. LOC: California: Kernville; Ralph M. Like Studio backlot.

Rollin' Westward (1939 Monogram) Tex Ritter. LOC: California: Rancho Placeritos; Walker Ranch.

Rolling Caravans (1938 Columbia) Jack Luden. LOC: California: Iverson Ranch; Jauregui Ranch; Walker Ranch; Rancho Placeritos; Kernville; Paramount Ranch.

Rolling Down the Great Divide (1942 PRC) Frontier Marshal. LOC: California: Iverson Ranch; Kernville.

Rolling Home (1946 Screen Guild) Jean Parker. LOC: California: Corriganville; Pioneer Church.

Romance of Rosy Ridge, The (1947 MGM) Van Johnson. LOC: California: Mountain Ranch; Sheep Ranch; Calaveras County.
Romance of the Redwoods (1939 Columbia) Charles Bickford. LOC: California.
Romance of the Rio Grande (1929 Fox) Warner Baxter. LOC: California: Burro Flats; Vasquez Rocks.
Romance of the Rio Grande (1941 20th Century Fox) Cesar Romero. LOC: California: Iverson Ranch; Burro Flats; Vasquez Rocks.
Romance of the Rockies (1937 Monogram) Tom Keene. LOC: California: Iverson Ranch.
Romance of the West (1930 Capital Film Exchange) Jack Perrin. LOC:
Romance of the West (1946 PRC) Eddie Dean. LOC: California: Iverson Ranch; Corriganville.
Romance on the Range (1942 Republic) Roy Rogers. LOC: California: Iverson Ranch; Walker Ranch; Lake Sherwood; Vasquez Rocks.
Romance Revier (1934 Reliable) Fred Hume. LOC: California: Frank LaSalle Ranch.
Romance Rides the Range (1936 Spectrum) Fred Scott. LOC: California: Jauregui Ranch.
Rooster Cogburn (1975 Universal) John Wayne. LOC: Oregon: Bend; Deschutes National Park; Grants Pass; Rogue River.
Rootin' Tootin' Tenderfeet (1952 Columbia) Max Baer. LOC:
Rootin' Tootin' Rhythm (1937 Republic) Gene Autry. LOC: California: Dead Man Point; Lone Pine; Republic Studio backlot.
Rose and the Jackal, The (1990 TNT) Christopher Reeve) Georgia: MaconSavannah.
Rose Hill (1997 CBS) Jennifer Garner. LOC: CANADA: Alberta: CL Ranch; Longview; Quebec: Montréal.
Rose Marie (1936 MGM) Jeanette MacDonald. LOC: California: Lake Arrowhead; Lake Tahoe; Tuolumne County; Mammoth Lakes.
Rose Marie (1954 MGM) Howard Keel. LOC: California: Bishop; Mammoth Lakes; Nevada: Lake Tahoe CANADA: Jasper National Park, Alberta.
Rose of Cimarron (1952 20th Century Fox) Jack Buetel. LOC: California: Burro Flats; Republic Studio backlot.
Rose of the Rancho (1936 Paramount) John Boles. LOC: California: Paramount Ranch.
Rose of the Rio Grande (1938 Monogram) John Carroll. LOC: California: Walker Ranch.
Rose of the Yukon (1949 Republic) Steve Brodie. LOC:
Roseanna McCoy (1949 RKO) Farley Granger. LOC: California: Kennedy Meadow.
Rough Night in Jericho (1967 Universal) Dean Martin. LOC: Utah: Kanab; The Gap.
Rough Riders (1997 TNT) Tom Berenger. LOC: Texas: Bandera; CF Ranch Alpine;

Conroe; Texas State Railroad, Rusk; Palestine; San Antonio.

Rough Riders of Cheyenne (1945 Republic) Sunset Carson. LOC: California: Iverson Ranch; Republic Studio backlot.

Rough Riders of Durango (1951 Republic) Allan Lane. LOC: California: Iverson Ranch.

Rough Riders' Round-Up (1939 Republic) Roy Rogers. LOC: California: Iverson Ranch; Republic Studio backlot.

Rough Ridin' Justice (1945 Columbia) Charles Starrett. LOC: California: Iverson Ranch.

Rough Riding Ranger (1935 Superior) Rex Lease. LOC: California: Ralph M. Like Studio backlot.

Rough Riding Rhythm (1937 Ambassador) Kermit Maynard. LOC: California: Walker Ranch.

Rough Romance (1930 Fox) George O'Brien. LOC: Washington: Cascade Mountains; Rainier National Park; Oregon: upper lumber regions.

Rough, Tough West, The (1952 Columbia) Charles Starrett. LOC: California: Columbia Ranch; Corriganville.

Roughshod (1949 RKO) Robert Sterling. LOC: California: Janss Conejo Ranch; South of Sonora Pass.

Rounders, The (1965 MGM) Henry Fonda. LOC: Arizona: Sedona; Flagstaff.

Round-Up Time in Texas (1937 Republic) Gene Autry. LOC: California: Republic Studio backlot.

Round-Up, The (1941 Paramount) Richard Dix. LOC: California: Garner Ranch; Lone Pine.

Rovin' Tumbleweeds (1939 Republic) Gene Autry. LOC: California: Burro Flats; Chatsworth Train Depot; Republic Studio backlot.

Rowdy Girls, The (2000 Troma Entertainment) Shannon Tweed. LOC: California: Paramount Ranch.

Royal Mounted Patrol, The (1941 Columbia) Charles Starrett. LOC: California: Cedar Lake; Lake Arrowhead.

Royal Mounted Rides Again, The (1945 Universal) Bill Kennedy. LOC: California: Corriganville.

Ruby Jean and Jo (1996 Viacom Productions) Tom Selleck. LOC: Arizona: Bisbee; Douglas/Gadsden Hotel; Page.

Run for Cover (1955 Paramount) James Cagney. LOC: Colorado: Durango-Silverton Narrow Gauge Railroad; Silverton; Molas Lake; New Mexico: Aztec Ruins National Monument.

Run Home Slow (1965 Joshua Prod) Mercedes McCambridge. LOC: California.

Run of the Arrow (1957 RKO) Rod Steiger. LOC: Utah: Snow Canyon; St. George; Berry Spring; Virgin River; The Twist; Brown Hail's Ranch, airport; Chalk Mountain area; and Pine Valley.

Run to the High Country (1972 Sun International) Keith Larsen. LOC: Utah:

Zion National Park.

Run, Cougar, Run (1970 Buena Vista) Stuart Whitman. LOC: Arizona: Sedona; Utah: Arches National Park; Castle Valley; Dead Horse Point State Park; La Sal Mountains; Onion Creek; Professor Valley; Seven Mile Canyon.

Run, Simon, Run (1970 ABC-TV) Burt Reynolds. LOC: Arizona: San Xavier Del Bac Mission; Old Tucson; Santa Catalina Mountains.

Running Wild (1973 Golden Circle) Lloyd Bridges. LOC: Colorado: Cañon City; New Mexico: J. W. Eaves Ranch; Abiquiu Ghost Ranch.

Rustler's Roundup (1933 Universal) Tom Mix. LOC: California: Tuolumne County; Hoot Gibson Ranch.

Rustler's Roundup (1946 Universal) Kirby Grant. LOC: California: Iverson Ranch; Corriganville; Agoura.

Rustler's Valley (1937 Paramount) William Boyd. LOC: California: Tuolumne County; Columbia.

Rustlers (1949 RKO) Tim Holt. LOC: California: Garner Ranch.

Rustlers of Devil's Canyon (1947 Republic) Allan Lane. LOC: California: Iverson Ranch; Corriganville.

Rustlers of Red Dog, The (1935 Universal) Johnny Mack Brown. LOC: California: Bronson Canyon; Vasquez Rocks; Lasky Mesa.

Rustlers of the Badlands (1945 Columbia) Charles Starrett. LOC: California: Iverson Ranch.

Rustlers on Horseback (1950 Republic) Allan Lane. LOC: California: Iverson Ranch.

Rustlers' Ransom (1950 Universal) Tex Williams) LOST/MISSING/UNAVAILABLE

Rustlers' Hideout (1944 PRC) Buster Crabbe. LOC: California: Corriganville.

Rustlers' Paradise (1935 Ajay Films) Harry Carey. LOC: California: Iverson Ranch; Brandeis Ranch.

Rustlers' Rhapsody (1985 Paramount/Phoenix Co./Impala Films/Tesauro Sa) Tom Berenger. LOC: SPAIN: Rancho Leone Tabernas; Texas-Hollywood/Western town; La Calahorra Railroad east of Guadix, Granada province; La Pedriza Manzanares El Real, Madrid.

Rusty Rides Alone (1933 Columbia) Tim McCoy. LOC: California: Trem Carr Ranch; Jauregui Ranch.

Ruthless Four, The (1969 Goldstone Film Enterprises) Van Heflin. LOC: SPAIN: Almería.

Sabata (1970 United Artists) Lee Van Cleef. LOC: SPAIN: Almería.

Sacketts, The (1979 NBC-TV) Tom Selleck. LOC: Arizona: Old Tucson; Mescal; Patagonia; Sonoita; Colorado: Buckskin Joe; Fremont County.

Sacred Ground (1983 Pacific International) Tim McIntire. LOC: Oregon: Chiloquin; Jerry Withlatch Ranch; Klamath Falls; Medford; Mickey Wampler Ranch; Rocky Point Resort; Ray Driscoll Ranch; Sprague River; Winema National Forest.

Saddle Aces (1935 Resolute) Rex Bell. LOC: California: Lake Sherwood; Saugus

Train Depot; Brandeis Ranch.

Saddle Buster, The (1932 RKO) Tom Keene. LOC: California: Frank LaSalle Ranch; Hoot Gibson Rodea Arena; Agoura Ranch.

Saddle Leather Law (1944 Columbia) Charles Starrett. LOC: California: Corriganville.

Saddle Legion (1951 RKO) Tim Holt. LOC: California: Garner Ranch.

Saddle Mountain Roundup (1941 Monogram) Range Busters. LOC: California: Corriganville; Jauregui Ranch.

Saddle Pals (1947 Republic) Gene Autry. LOC: California: Malibou Lake; Valsteve Ranch; Republic Studio backlot.

Saddle Serenade (1945 Monogram) Jimmy Wakely. LOC: California: Walker Ranch; Circle J Ranch.

Saddle the Wind (1958 MGM) Robert Taylo. LOC: Colorado: Royal Gorge; Canon City.

Saddle Tramp (1950 Universal) Joel McCrea. LOC: California: Iverson Ranch; Jauregui Ranch; Universal Studios backlot.

Saddlemates (1941 Republic) Three Mesquiteers. LOC: California: Iverson Ranch.

Saddles and Sagebrush (1943 Columbia) Russell Hayden. LOC: California: Jauregui Ranch.

Saga of Death Valley (1939 Republic) Roy Rogers. LOC: California: Iverson Ranch; Lone Pine; Owenyo Train Depot.

Saga of Hemp Brown, The (1958 Universal) Rory Calhoun. LOC: California: Janss Conejo Ranch; Universal Studio backlot.

Sagebrush Heroes (1945 Columbia) Charles Starrett. LOC: California: Columbia Ranch.

Sagebrush Law (1943 RKO) Tim Holt. LOC: California: Agoura.

Sagebrush Trail (1933 Monogram) John Wayne. LOC: California: Bronson Canyon; Trem Carr Ranch.

Sagebrush Troubadour, The (1935 Republic) Gene Autry. LOC: California: Kernville; Kernville Movie Street.

Saginaw Trail (1953 Columbia) Gene Autry. LOC: California: Walker Ranch; Rancho Placeritos.

Salome, Where She Danced (1945 Universal) Rod Cameron. LOC: California: Corriganville; Lone Pine; Monterey.

Salt Lake Raiders (1950 Republic) Allan Lane. LOC: California: Iverson Ranch.

Sam Whiskey (1969 United Artists) Burt Reynolds. LOC: California: Lake Camanche, Ione; Orvis Ranch, Stockton; stock footage of Jamestown Railroad; Universal Studio backlot; Warner Bros backlot; Florida: Silver Springs.

San Antone (1953 Republic) Rod Cameron. LOC: California: Vasquez Rocks; Red Rock Canyon; Republic Studio backlot.

San Antone Ambush (1949 Republic) Monte Hale. LOC: California: Iverson Ranch.

San Antonio (1945 Warner Bros) Errol Flynn. LOC: California: Warner Ranch; Janss Conejo Ranch; Tuolumne County; Warnerville.

San Antonio Kid, The (1944 Republic) Bill Elliott. LOC: California: Iverson Ranch; Republic Studios backlot.

San Fernando Valley (1944 Republic) Roy Rogers. LOC: California: Iverson Ranch; Kentucky Park Farms; Republic Studio backlot.

San Francisco (1936 MGM) Clark Gable. LOC: California: San Francisco.

San Francisco Story, The (1952 Warner Bros) Joel McCrea. LOC: California: San Francisco.

Sand (1949 20th Century Fox) Rory Calhoun. LOC: California: Lake Arrowhead; Lone Pine; Colorado: La Plata Canyon; Durango; Pagosa Springs; Molas Lake.

Sandflow (1937 Universal) Buck Jones. LOC: California: Lone Pine.

Santa Fe (1951 Columbia) Randolph Scott. LOC: California: Iverson Ranch.

Santa Fe Bound (1936 Reliable) Tom Tyler. LOC: California: Brandeis Ranch; Frank LaSalle Ranch.

Santa Fe Marshal (1940 Paramount) William Boyd. LOC: California: Rancho Placeritos; Garner Ranch; Keen Camp; Bronson Canyon.

Santa Fe Passage (1955 Republic) John Payne. LOC: Utah: St. George; Snow Canyon; Dammeron Valley; Berry Springs; Virgin River.

Santa Fe Rides (1937 Reliable) Bob Custer. LOC: California: Brandeis Ranch; Jauregui Ranch.

Santa Fe Saddlemates (1945 Republic) Sunset Carson. LOC: California: Iverson Ranch; Republic Studio backlot.

Santa Fe Scouts (1943 Republic) Three Mesquiteers. LOC: California: Iverson Ranch.

Santa Fe Stampede (1938 Republic) Three Mesquiteers. LOC: California: Brandeis Ranch; Corriganville; Republic Studio backlot.

Santa Fe Trail (1930 Paramount) Richard Arlen. LOC: California: Paramount Ranch.

Santa Fe Trail (1940 Warner Bros) Errol Flynn. LOC: California: Warner Ranch; Lasky Mesa.

Santa Fe Uprising (1946 Republic) Allan Lane. LOC: California: Iverson Ranch.

Santee (1973 Crown Prod) Glenn Ford. LOC: California: Bell Ranch; New Mexico: J. W. Eaves Ranch; Galisteo.

Sarah Padden in Across the Border (1928 Vitaphone) Sarah Padden. LOC:

Sarah, Plain and Tall: Winter's End (1999 CBS) Glenn Close. LOC: Kansas: Emporia; The Old Cowtown/Wichita.

Saskatchewan (1954 Universal) Alan Ladd. LOC: CANADA: Banff National Park; Bow Lake Crowfoot Glacier; Stoney Reserve.

Satan's Cradle (1949 United Artists) Duncan Renaldo. LOC: California: Pioneertown.

Savage Frontier (1953 Republic) Allan Lane. LOC: California: Iverson Ranch; Corriganville; Burro Flats.

Savage Guns, The (1962 MGM) Richard Basehart. LOC: SPAIN: Sierra Alhamilla; Turrillas, Almería.

Savage Horde, The (1950 Republic) Bill Elliott. LOC: California: Iverson Ranch; Lasky Mesa; Agoura; Red Rock Canyon; Republic Studio backlot.

Savage Land (1994 Motion Picture Village/Savage Land Productions) Graham Greene. LOC: CANADA: Alberta: Millarville.

Savage Pampas (1967 Comet) Robert Taylor) Spain.

Savage Sam (1963 Buena Vista) Brian Keith. LOC: California: Albertson Ranch; Golden Oak Ranch; Escondido Canyon.

Savage, The (1952 Paramount) Charlton Heston. LOC: South Dakota: Black Hills.

Savages (1974 Spelling/Goldberg TV) Andy Griffith. LOC: California: Red Rock Canyon.

Savate (1995 PM Entertainment Group) Olivier Gruner. LOC: California: Veluzat Motion Picture Ranch Saugus.

Scalawag (1973 Paramount) Kirk Douglas. LOC: YUGOSLAVIA.

Scalphunters, The (1968 United Artists) Burt Lancaster. LOC: MEXICO: Coahuila: Torreon; Durango; Sonora: Guaymas; Zacatecas: Sierra de Organos.

Scalplock (1966 Columbia-TV) Dale Robertson. LOC: California: Tuolumne County; Railtown, Jamestown; Columbia Ranch.

Scalps (1987 Beatrice Films/Multivideo) Vassili Karis. LOC: SPAIN: Fort El Cóndor Tabernas, Almería; La Pedriza Manzanares El Real, Madrid.

Scandalous John (1971 Buena Vista) Brian Keith. LOC: Arizona: Old Tucson; New Mexico: Oliver Lee State Park, Alamogordo; White Sands National Monument; South Dakota: Black Hills.

Scape (2010 Mythmaker Ent.) Ben Furmaniak. LOC: California: Santa Cruz.

Scarlet Angel (1952 Universal) Rock Hudson. LOC: California: Universal backlot; Tuolumne County.

Scarlet Brand, The (1932 Big 4) Bob Custer. LOC: California: Ralph M. Like Studio backlot.

Scarlet Horseman, The (1946 Universal) Peter Cookson. LOC: California: Iverson Ranch; Universal Studio backlot.

Scarlet Letter, The (1995 Cinergi Pictures Entertainment) Demi Moore. LOC: CANADA: British Columbia: Oyster River; Strathcona Provincial Park; Vancouver Island; Nova Scotia: Shelburne; Yarmouth.

Scarlet River (1933 RKO) Tom Keene. LOC: California: Vasquez Rocks.

Scarlet Worm, The (2011 Wild Dogs Prod) Aaron Stielstra. LOC: California: Agua Dulce; Angeles National Forest; Big Tujunga Canyon; Sunland; Malibu; Menifee; Nuevo; Paramount Ranch; Pioneertown; Santa Clarita; Alaska.

Scouts to the Rescue (1939 Universal) Jackie Cooper. LOC: California: Dardanelle, below Sonora Pass.

Scream (1985 Calendary International/Cougar Films, Limited) Pepper Martin.

LOC: California: Paramount Ranch Agoura.

Screen Snapshots: Hollywood Bronc Busters (1956 Columbia) LOC:

Screen Snapshots: Hollywood Cowboys (1947 Columbia) Buck Jones. LOC:

Screen Snapshots: My Pal Ringeye (1947 Columbia) Smiley Burnette. LOC:

Sea of Grass, The (1947 MGM) Spencer Tracy. LOC: California: Iverson Ranch; Vasquez Rocks; New Mexico: Gallup; Plains of St. Augustin near Magdalena; Nebraska.

Search, The (1956 Wrather) Clayton Moore. LOC: California: Iverson Ranch; Corriganville; Ingram Ranch; Tuolumne County; Columbia.

Searchers, The (1956 Warner Bros) John Wayne. LOC: California: Bronson Canyon; Arizona: Monument Valley; Colorado: Gunnison; Utah: San Juan River; Mexican Hat; CANADA: Edmonton, Alberta.

Second Chance (1972 ABC-TV) Brian Keith. LOC: Arizona: Apacheland.

Second Greatest Sex, The (1955 Universal) Jeanne Crain. LOC: California: Universal Studio backlot.

Second Time Around, The (1961 20th Century Fox) Debbie Reynolds. LOC: California: Century Ranch; 20th Century Fox backlot.

Secret of Convict Lake, The (1951 20th Century Fox) Glenn Ford. LOC: Colorado: Durango.

Secret of Giving (1999 CBS) Reba McEntire. LOC: CANADA: British Columbia: Wild Horse Town/Western town Kamloops.

Secret of Navajo Cave, The (1976 Key Intl) Holger Kasper. LOC:

Secret of Outlaw Flats (1953 Allied Artists) Guy Madison. LOC: California: Iverson Ranch; Walker Ranch.

Secret of the Wasteland (1941 Paramount) William Boyd. LOC: California: Lone Pine; Rancho Placeritos; Anchor Ranch.

Secret of Treasure Mountain (1956 Columbia) Raymond Burr. LOC: California: Iverson Ranch.

Secret Patrol (1936 Columbia) Charles Starrett. LOC: CANADA: Victoria, British Columbia.

Secret Valley (1937 20th Century Fox) Richard Arlen. LOC: California: Lone Pine.

Seein' Injuns (1931 Pathe) Daphne Pollard. LOC:

Seguin (1982 PBS) A Martinez. LOC: Texas: Alamo Village.

Seminole (1953 Universal) Rock Hudson. LOC: California: Universal backlot; Los Angeles County Arboretum.

Seminole Uprising (1955 Columbia) George Montgomery. LOC: California: Iverson Ranch; Corriganville.

Senor Americano (1929 Universal) Ken Maynard. LOC: California: Universal backlot.

Senorita from the West (1945 Universal) Allan Jones. LOC: California: Universal backlot.

September Dawn (2007 Voice Pictures) Jon Voight. LOC: CANADA: Alberta: Albertina/Augustina Farms Calgary; CL Ranch Calgary.

September Gun (1983 CBS) Robert Preston. LOC: Arizona: MescalOld Tucson.

Sequoia (1934 MGM) Jean Parker. LOC: California: Iverson Ranch; Sequoia National Park; Springville.

Seraphim Falls (2006 Icon Productions) Liam Neeson. LOC: New Mexico: El Rancho de las Golondrinas; La Bajada; Lordsburg/The Playas; San Cristobal Ranch; Santa Fe/Hyde State Park; Taos Ski Valley; The Valles Caldera National Preserve Los Alamos; Zia Pueblo; Oregon: Koosah Falls/McKenzie River; Sahalie Falls/McKenzie River, Willamette National Forest.

Sergeant Rutledge (1960 Warner Bros) Jeffrey Hunter. LOC: Arizona: Monument Valley; Utah: San Juan River; Mexican Hat.

Sergeants 3 (1962 United Artists) Frank Sinatra. LOC: Utah: Paria; Kanab Canyon; Kanab Movie Fort; Kimball Valley; Bryce Canyon National Park.

Seven Alone (1974 Doty-Dayton) Dewey Martin. LOC: Wyoming: Cokeville; Snake River; Lyman; Fort Bridger.

Seven Angry Men (1955 Allied Artists) Raymond Massey. LOC: California: Warner Ranch.

Seven Brides for Seven Brothers (1954 MGM) Howard Keel. LOC: California: MGM backlot; Tioga Pass.

Seven Brides for Seven Brothers (1982 television series) Richard Dean Anderson. LOC: California: Murphys Calaveras County.

Seven Cities of Gold (1955 20th Century Fox) Anthony Quinn. LOC: MEXICO: Colima: Manzanillo beaches; Jalisco: Guadalajara deserts.

Seven Guns to Mesa (1958 Allied Artists) James Griffith. LOC: California: Iverson Ranch.

Seven Men from Now (1956 Warner Bros) Randolph Scott. LOC: California: Lone Pine; Olancha Sand Dunes; Warner Ranch.

Seven Ways from Sundown (1960 Universal) Audie Murphy. LOC: California: Universal Studio backlot; Nevada: Valley of Fire State Park; Red Rock Canyon; Mt. Charleston; Utah: St. George.

Seventh Cavalry (1956 Columbia) Randolph Scott. LOC: MEXICO: Mexico: Amecameca.

Shadow of Chikara, The (1977 AVCO Embassy) Joe Don Baker. LOC: Arkansas.

Shadow of the Wolf (1992 Canal+/Films A2) Lou Diamond Phillips. LOC: CANADA: Quebec: Montréal; NorthWest Territories

Shadow Ranch (1930 Columbia) Buck Jones. LOC: California: Kernville; Paramount Ranch.

Shadow Riders, The (1982 CBS) Tom Selleck. LOC: California: Columbia Tuolumne County.

Shadow Valley (1947 Eagle Lion) Eddie Dean. LOC: California: Iverson Ranch; Corriganville.

Shadowheart (2009 Desert Moon Pictures/JBA Productions) Angus MacFadyen.

LOC: California: Paramount Ranch; Golden Oak Ranch.

Shadows of Death (1945 PRC) Buster Crabbe. LOC: California: Corriganville.

Shadows of the Hawk (1976 Columbia) Jan-Michael Vincent. LOC: CANADA: Vancouver, British Columbia.

Shadows of the West (1949 Monogram) Whip Wilson. LOC: California: Walker Ranch; Rancho Placeritos.

Shadows of Tombstone (1953 Republic) Rex Allen. LOC: California: Burro Flats.

Shadows on the Range (1946 Monogram) Johnny Mack Brown. LOC: California: Walker Ranch.

Shadows on the Sage (1942 Republic) Three Mesquiteers. LOC: California: Iverson Ranch; Walker Ranch; Lone Pine.

Shadows Tombstone (1953 Republic) Rex Allen. LOC: California: Burro Flats.

Shakiest Gun in the West, The (1968 Universal) Don Knotts. LOC: California: Universal Studios Backlot; North Ranch; El Mirage Dry Lake.

Shalako (1968 Cinerama Releasing Corp) Seam Connery. LOC: SPAIN: Almeria.

Shame, Shame on the Bixby Boys (1978 Terry Fraze Prod/Calendar Corp) Monte Markham. LOC: California: Paramount Ranch.

Shane (1953 Paramount) Alan Ladd. LOC: California: Iverson Ranch; Wyoming: Antelope Flats; Elk Refuge, Jackson Hole; Kelly; Teton Valley Ranch; Wilson.

Shanghai (2000 Touchstone Pictures) Jackie Chan. LOC: CANADA: Alberta: CL Ranch Calgary; Drumheller/badlands; Morley.

Shaughnessy (1996 Aces & Eights Productions) Matthew Settle. LOC: California: Railtown; Red Hills Ranch; Sacramento/California State Railroad Museum.

She Came to the Valley (1989 A Band Company Production) Dean Stockwell. LOC: Texas: Mission; Rio Grande Valley.

She Wore a Yellow Ribbon (1949 RKO) John Wayne. LOC: Arizona: Monument Valley; House Rock Valley; Utah: Kanab; San Juan River; Mexican Hat.

Sheepman, The (1958 MGM) Glenn Ford. LOC: California: MGM Studio backlot; Colorado: Montrose.

Shenandoah (1965 Universal) James Stewart. LOC: California: Golden Oak Ranch; Janss Conejo Ranch; Universal Studio backlot; Oregon: Eugene.

Shepherd of the Hills, The (1941 Paramount) John Wayne. LOC: California: Big Bear; Cedar Lake.

Shepherd of the Hills, The (1964 Howco International) Richard Arlen) Missouri: Branson.

Sheriff of Cimarron (1945 Republic) Sunset Carson. LOC: California: Iverson Ranch; Republic Studio backlot.

Sheriff of Contention (2010 Rock Wayne Pictures) Angelo Ortega. LOC: California: Hutchings Ranch, Julian; KQ Ranch, Julian; White Horse Movie Ranch, Landers; Woodward Museum, Ramona.

Sheriff of Las Vegas (1944 Republic) Bill Elliott. LOC: California: Iverson Ranch; Corriganville.

Sheriff of Medicine Bow, The (1948 Monogram) Johnny Mack Brown. LOC: California: Rancho Placeritos.

Sheriff of Redwood Valley (1946 Republic) Bill Elliott. LOC: California: Iverson Ranch.

Sheriff of Sage Valley (1942 PRC) Buster Crabbe. LOC: California: Rancho Placeritos; Walker Ranch.

Sheriff of Sundown (1944 Republic) Allan Lane. LOC: California: Iverson Ranch; Corriganville.

Sheriff of Tombstone (1941 Republic) Roy Rogers. LOC: California: Iverson Ranch; Vasquez Rocks; Republic Studio backlot.

Sheriff of Wichita (1949 Republic) Alan Lane. LOC: California: Iverson Ranch; Corriganville.

Sheriff With the Gold, The (1966 Wonder Film) Louis McJulian. LOC: ITALY: Sardinia.

Sheriff's Secret, The (1931 Cosmos) Jack Perrin) LOST/MISSING

Shiloh Falls (2008 Radio London Films) Brad Greenquist. LOC: California: Sable Ranch.

Shine On Harvest Moon (1938 Republic) Roy Rogers. LOC: California: Jauregui Ranch; Towsley Canyon.

Shoot First and Pray You Live Because Luck Has Nothing to Do with It (2008 Wounded Knee) Richard Tyson. LOC: New Mexico: Bonanza Creek Ranch Santa Fe.

Shoot Out (1971 Universal) Gregory Peck. LOC: California: Mammoth Lakes; Hot Springs; New Mexico: Cumbres and Toltec Scenic Railroad; Los Alamos; Cerrillos.

Shoot Out at Beaver Falls (1970 August-Knight Prod) Tanya O'Rourke. LOC:

Shoot the Sun Down (1981 Jads Films International) Christopher Walken. LOC: New Mexico: Chaco Culture National Historic Park; J.W. Eaves Movie Ranch; Las Cruces; White Sands National Monument.

Shooter, The (1997 Royal Oaks Entertainment, Inc.) Michael Dudikoff. LOC: California: Melody Ranch; Sable Ranch; Vasquez Rocks.

Shooting High (1940 20th Century Fox) Gene Autry. LOC: California: Iverson Ranch; Corriganville; Santa Susanna Pass Road; 20th Century Fox backlot.

Shooting, The (1967 Jack H Harris Ent) Jack Nicholson. LOC: Utah: Glen Canyon National Recreation Area; Paria.

Shootist, The (1976 Paramount) John Wayne. LOC: California: Warner Bros. backlot; Nevada: Carson City.

Shoot-Out at Medicine Bend (1957 Warner Bros) Randolph Scott. LOC: California: Bell/Berry Ranch; Warner Ranch; Warner Bros. Studio backlot.

Shootout in a One-Dog Town (1974 Hanna Barbera Prod-TV) Richard Crenna. LOC: Arizona; MEXICO: Durango: Sonora: Bavispe; Zacatecas: Sierra de Organos; Sombrerete; Pilares de Nacozari.

Shootout of Luck (2008 Dark Universe Productions) Willie Nelson. LOC: Texas: Luck Ranch/Willieville/Nelson Ranch Spicewood, Austin.

Short Grass (1950 Allied Artists) Rod Cameron. LOC: California: Garner Ranch; New Mexico: Albuquerque.

Shotgun (1955 Allied Artists) Sterling Hayden. LOC: California: Rancho Placeritos; Vasquez Rocks; Arizona: Sedona.

Shotgun Pass (1931 Columbia) Tim McCoy. LOC: California: Towsley Canyon.

Showboat (1936 Universal) Irene Dunne. LOC: California: Universal Studio backlot.

Showdown (1940 Paramount) William Boyd. LOC: California: Kernville; Kernville Movie Street; Kern River Falls; Tuolumne County; Chatsworth Train Depot.

Showdown (1963 Universal) Audie Murphy. LOC: California: Lone Pine; Universal Studio backlot.

Showdown (1973 Universal) Dean Martin. LOC: California: Universal Studio backlot; Kernville; Sequoia National Forest; Greenhorn Mountains; Colorado: Costilla County; New Mexico: Abiquiu Ghost Ranch; Tierra Amarilla; Chama; Cumbres and Toltec Scenic Railroad.

Showdown at Abilene (1956 Universal) Jock Mahoney. LOC: California: Agoura Ranch; Universal Studio backlot.

Showdown at Boot Hill (1958 20th Century Fox) Charles Bronson. LOC: California: 20th Century Fox backlot.

Showdown at Devil's Butte (2005 Skeleton Creek Productions) Geoff Baron. LOC: Kansas: New Mexico: Oklahoma.

Showdown at Eagle Gap (1982) Madison Mason. LOC: MEXICO: Durango: Chupaderos.

Showdown, The (1950 Republic) Bill Elliott. LOC: California: Iverson Ranch.

Showdown, The (2009 Sand Prairie Productions) Dan Barth) Illinois: Hopedale.

Shut My Big Mouth (1942 Columbia) Joe E. Brown. LOC: California: Iverson Ranch; Columbia Ranch.

Sidekicks (1974 Warner Bros-TV) Larry Hagman. LOC: California: Big Sky Ranch; Valencia Oaks; Warner Bros backlot.

Siege at Red River, The (1954 20th Century Fox) Van Johnson. LOC: California: 20th Century Fox Studio backlot; Utah: Professor Valley; Castle Valley; Ida Gulch; Onion Creek; Dead Horse Point State Park; Colorado: La Plata County.

Sierra (1950 Universal) Audie Murphy. LOC: California: Universal Studio backlot; Utah: Aspen Mirror Lake; Kanab Canyon; Duck Creek; Cedar Breaks National Monument.

Sierra Baron (1958 20th Century Fox) Brian Keith. LOC: MEXICO: Mexico: Near Mexico City; Cortez Pass in La Marquesa Mountains.

Sierra Passage (1951 Monogram) Wayne Morris. LOC: California: Corriganville; Tuolumne County; Red Hills, Columbia, Jamestown.

Sierra Stranger (1957 Columbia) Howard Duff. LOC: California: Iverson Ranch;

Corriganville; Bell Ranch; Ralph M. Like Studio backlot.

Sierra Sue (1941 Republic) Gene Autry. LOC: California: Bishop; Mammoth Lakes; Republic Studio backlot.

Sign of the Wolf, The (1931 Metropolitan) Rex Lease. LOC: California: Fat Jones Ranch.

Sign of Zorro, The (1960 Buena Vista) Guy Williams. LOC: California: Bell Ranch.

Silence of the North (1980 Universal Pictures Canada) Ellen Burstyn. LOC: CANADA: Alberta: Fort McMurray; NorthWest Territories: Forth Smith, Great Slave Lake; Ontario: Kenora.

Silent Barriers (1937 Gaumont-British) Richard Arlen. LOC: CANADA: Lake Louise; Revelstoke, British Columbia.

Silent Code, The (1935 International Pictures) Kane Richmond. LOC: California: Big Bear.

Silent Conflict (1948 United Artists) William Boyd. LOC: California: Lone Pine; Anchor Ranch.

Silent Gun, The (1969 Paramount-TV) Lloyd Bridges. LOC: California: Paramount Studio backlot.

Silent Men (1933 Columbia) Tim McCoy. LOC: California: Walker Ranch; Jauregui Ranch.

Silent Tongue (1993 Trimark Pictures) Alan Bates. LOC: New Mexico: Diamond A Ranch; Flying A Ranch; Mescalero Sands Recreation Area Roswell.

Silent Valley (1935 Reliable) Tom Tyler. LOC: California: Frank LaSalle Ranch.

Silks and Saddles (1936 Victory) Bruce Bennett. LOC: California: Brandeis Ranch.

Sillie Billies (1936 RKO) Wheeler & Woolsey. LOC:

Silver Bullet (1949 Universal) Tex Williams. LOC:

Silver Bullet, The (1935 Commodore) Tom Tyler. LOC: California: Frank LaSalle Ranch.

Silver Bullet, The (1942 Universal) Johnny Mack Brown. LOC: California: Corriganville.

Silver Canyon (1951 Columbia) Gene Autry. LOC: California: Iverson Ranch; Pioneertown.

Silver City (1951 Paramount) Edmond O'Brien. LOC: California: Bronson Canyon; Tuolumne County; Columbia.

Silver City Bonanza (1951 Republic) Rex Allen. LOC: California: Iverson Ranch; Corriganville; Walker Ranch; Cedar Lake.

Silver City Kid (1944 Republic) Allan Lane. LOC: California: Iverson Ranch; Corriganville.

Silver City Raiders (1943 Columbia) Russell Hayden. LOC: California: Corriganville.

Silver Dollar (1932 First National) Edward G. Robinson. LOC: California: Warner Bros. backlot; Nevada: Carson City.

Silver Lode (1954 RKO) John Payne. LOC: California: Republic Studio backlot.

Silver on the Sage (1939 Paramount) William Boyd. LOC: California: Kernville; Kernville Movie Street.

Silver Queen (1942 United Artists) George Brent. LOC: no exteriors.

Silver Raiders (1950 Monogram) Whip Wilson. LOC: California: Iverson Ranch.

Silver Range (1946 Monogram) Johnny Mack Brown. LOC: California: Walker Ranch.

Silver River (1948 Warner Bros) Errol Flynn. LOC: California: Warner Ranch; Bronson Canyon; The Buttermilks, Bishop.

Silver Spurs (1936 Universal) Buck Jones. LOC: California: Iverson Ranch; Vasquez Rocks; Lasky Mesa.

Silver Spurs (1943 Republic) Roy Rogers. LOC: California: Iverson Ranch; Kernville; Kernville Movie Street.

Silver Stallion (1941 Monogram) David Sharpe. LOC: Arizona.

Silver Star, The (1955 Lippert) Edgar Buchanan. LOC: California: Paramount Ranch.

Silver Trail, The (1937 Reliable) Rex Lease. LOC: California: Frank LaSalle Ranch; Ralph M Like Studio.

Silver Trails (1948 Monogram) Jimmie Wakely. LOC: California: Iverson Ranch; Walker Ranch; Rancho Placeritos.

Silver Whip, The (1953 20th Century Fox) Dale Robertson. LOC: California: Donnell Lake and vicinity, Tuolumne County; 20th Century Backlot; Century Ranch.

Silverado (1985 Columbia Pictures) Kevin Kline. LOC: New Mexico: Abiquiú Ghost Ranch; Bonanza Creek Ranch; Cook Ranch/Cerro Pelon Ranch; J.W. Eaves Movie Ranch/Western town and Mexican set Santa Fe; Río Chama; Santa Ana Pueblo sand dunes; Tent Rocks Cochiti Pueblo; The White Place/Plaza Blanca Abiquiú; White Rock Overlook.

Sin Town (1942 Universal) Broderick Crawford. LOC: California: Universal backlot.

Sing Me a Song of Texas (1945 Columbia) Tom Tyler. LOC: California: Columbia Ranch.

Sing, Cowboy, Sing (1937 Grand National) Tex Ritter. LOC: California: Rancho Placeritos.

Sing, Cowboy, Sing (1981 DEFA) Dean Reed. LOC: EAST GERMANY.

Singer Not the Song, The (1961 Rank) John Mills. LOC: SPAIN: Torremolinos, Malaga, Andalucia.

Singin' in the Corn (1946 Columbia) Judy Canova. LOC: California: Columbia Ranch.

Singing Buckaroo, The (1937 Spectrum) Fred Scott. LOC: California: Brandeis Ranch.

Singing Cowboy, The (1936 Republic) Gene Autry. LOC: California: Iverson

Ranch; Brandeis Ranch; Agoura.

Singing Cowgirl, The (1939 Grand National) Dorothy Page. LOC: Arizona: Mesa.

Singing Guns (1950 Republic) Vaughn Monroe. LOC: Arizona: Sedona.

Singing Hill, The (1941 Republic) Gene Autry. LOC: California: Jauregui Ranch; Red Rock Canyon.

Singing on the Trail (1946 Columbia) Ken Curtis. LOC: California: Columbia Ranch.

Singing Outlaw, The (1938 Universal) Bob Baker. LOC: California: Kernville.

Singing Sheriff, The (1944 Universal) Bob Crosby. LOC: California: Corriganville.

Singing Spurs (1948 Columbia) Kirby Grant. LOST/MISSING/UNAVAILABLE

Singing Vagabond, The (1936 Republic) Gene Autry. LOC: California: Kernville; Republic Studio backlot.

Single-Handed Saunders (1932 Monogram) Tom Tyler. LOC: California: Trem Carr Ranch.

Sinister Journey (1948 United Artists) William Boyd. LOC: California: Lone Pine; Keeler Train Depot; Anchorville.

Sioux City Sue (1946 Republic) Gene Autry. LOC: California: Corriganville; Morrison Ranch; Chatsworth Lake; Towsley Canyon; Sherwood Forest; Republic Studio backlot.

Siringo (1994 Rysher Entertainment) Brad Johnson. LOC: California: Lake Los Angeles.

Sitting Bull (1954 United Artists) Dale Robertson. LOC: California: Iverson Ranch; MEXICO: Mexico: Salazar area of La Marquesa National Park.

Six Black Horses (1962 Universal) Audie Murphy. LOC: Utah: St. George; Snow Canyon; Ivins Reservoir; Sand Mountain area; Harrisburg.

Six Gun Gospel (1943 Monogram) Johnny Mack Brown. LOC: California: Iverson Ranch; Rancho Placeritos.

Six Gun Justice (1935 Spectrum) Bill Cody. LOC: California: Brandeis Ranch; Ralph M. Like Studio backlot.

Six Gun Mesa (1950 Monogram) Johnny Mack Brown. LOC: California: Walker Ranch; Soledad Canyon; Mint Canyon.

Six Reasons Why (2008 Campagna Brothers Independent Productions) Jeff Campagna. LOC: CANADA: Alberta; Ontario: Toronto.

Six-Gun Decision (1953 Allied Artists) Guy Madison. LOC: California: Iverson Ranch; Rancho Placeritos.

Six-Gun Gold (1941 RKO) Tim Holt. LOC: California: Iverson Ranch; Corriganville; Burro Flats.

Six-Gun Law (1948 Columbia) Charles Starrett. LOC: California: Iverson Ranch; Columbia Ranch.

Six-Gun Man (1946 PRC) Bob Steele. LOC: California: Iverson Ranch; Corriganville.

Six-Gun Rhythm (1939 Grand National) Tex Fletcher. LOC: California: Brandeis

Ranch; Antelope Valley.

Six-Gun Serenade (1947 Monogram) Jimmie Wakely. LOC: California: Iverson Ranch; Corriganville.

Six-Gun Trail (1938 Victory) Tim McCoy. LOC: California: Brandeis Ranch.

Six-Shootin' Sheriff (1938 Grand National) Ken Maynard. LOC: California: Walker Ranch; Rancho Placeritos.

Skin Game (1971 Warner Bros) James Garner. LOC: California: Valencia Oaks; Warner Bros Studio backlot; Disney's Golden Oak Ranch; Vasquez Rocks.

Skipalong Rosenbloom (1951 United Artists) Maxie Rosenbloom. LOC: California: Corriganville.

Skull and Crown (1935 Reliable Pictures) Rin-Tin-Tin, Jr. LOC: California: Big Bear.

Sky Bandits (1940 Monogram) James Newill. LOC: California: Rancho Placeritos; Big Bear; Big Bear Airport.

Sky Full of Moon (1952 MGM) Carleton Carpenter. LOC: Nevada: Las Vegas.

Slaughter Trail (1951 RKO) Brian Donlevy. LOC: California: Corriganville.

Slave Girl (1947 Universal) Yvonne De Carlo. LOC: California: Iverson Ranch.

Sledopyt (1987 Gorki Film Studios) Yuri Avsharov. LOC: SOVIET UNION.

Slim Carter (1957 Universal) Jock Mahoney. LOC: California: Hidden Valley.

Slowest Gun in the West, The (1960 Tra-Nan Productions) Phil Silvers. LOC: California: Universal Studio backlot.

Smith (1969 Buena Vista) Glenn Ford. LOC: California: Jauregui Ranch; Oregon: Washington.

Smoke Lightning (1933 Fox) George O'Brien. LOC: Arizona: Northern Arizona.

Smoke Signal (1955 Universal) Dana Andrews. LOC: Utah: Professor Valley; Ida Gulch; San Juan River.

Smoke Tree Range (1937 Universal) Buck Jones. LOC: California: Vasquez Rocks; Mojave Desert.

Smokey and the Bandit (1977 Universal) Burt Reynolds. LOC: Georgia: Atlanta.

Smokey Smith (1935 Commodore) Bob Steele. LOC: California: Iverson Ranch; Red Rock Canyon; Lone Pine.

Smoking Guns (1934 Universal) Ken Maynard. LOC: California: Bronson Canyon; Walker Ranch; South America.

Smoky (1933 Fox) Victor Jory. LOC: Arizona: Flagstaff; Oak Creek Canyon.

Smoky (1946 20th Century Fox) Fred MacMurray. LOC: Arizona: Fredonia; Utah: Aspen Mirror Lake; Duck Creek; Kanab Canyon; Kanab Rodeo Grounds; Kolob Canyon; Mountains of the Moon; Ogden; Zion National Park; Wyoming: Cheyenne.

Smoky (1966 20th Century Fox) Fess Parker. LOC: MEXICO: Mexico: La Marquesa National Park.

Smoky Canyon (1951 Columbia) Charles Starrett. LOC: California: Iverson Ranch.

Smoky Mountain Melody (1948 Columbia) Roy Acuff. LOC:
Smoky Trails (1939 Metropolitan) Bob Steele. LOC: California: Walker Ranch.
Snake River Desperadoes (1951 Columbia) Charles Starrett. LOC: California: Iverson Ranch.
Snow Dog (1950 Monogram) Kirby Grant. LOC: California: Big Bear; Cedar Lake.
So This is Arizona (1931 Big 4) Wally Wales. LOC: California: Frank LaSalle Ranch.
Sodbusters (1994 Atlantis Films Limited) Kris Kristofferson. LOC: CANADA: Ontario: Kleinburg; Orangeville.
Soldier Blue (1970 Avco/Embassy) Peter Strauss. LOC: MEXICO: Durango; Morelos: Cuernavaca; Guanajuato: San Miguel de Allende.
Sombrero (1953 MGM) Ricardo Montalban. LOC: MEXICO: Morelos: Tepoztlan.
Sombrero Kid, The (1942 Republic) Don Barry. LOC: California: Iverson Ranch; Walker Ranch.
Something Big (1971 National General) Dean Martin. LOC: MEXICO: Durango: Casa Blanca.
Something for a Lonely Man (1968 NBC-TV/Universal) Dan Blocker. LOC: California: Jamestown, Columbia, Tuolumne County; Universal Studio backlot.
Sometimes a Great Notion (1971 Universal) Paul Newman) Oregon: Newport; Toledo; Central Coast.
Somewhere in Sonora (1933 Warner Bros) John Wayne. LOC: California: Deadman Hill, Deadman Point, North Verde Ranch/Kemper Campbell Ranch, Upper Desert Knolls Area; Warner Bros Studio backlot.
Sommersby (1993 Warner Bros) Richard Gere. LOC: Virginia: Appomattox; Charlotte Court House; Farmville; Hot Springs; Lexington; Warm Springs; West Virginia: Snowshoe Mountain Ski Resort.
Son of a Bad Man (1949 Screen Guild) Lash LaRue. LOC: California: Iverson Ranch; Ingram Ranch.
Son of a Gunfighter (1966 MGM) Russ Tamblyn. LOC: SPAIN: Colmenar Viejo.
Son of Belle Starr (1953 Allied Artists) Keith Larsen. LOC: California: Iverson Ranch.
Son of Billy the Kid (1949 Screen Guild) Lash La Rue. LOC: California: Iverson Ranch; Ingram Ranch.
Son of Davy Crockett, The (1941 Columbia) Bill Elliott. LOC: California: Iverson Ranch; Columbia Ranch.
Son of Geronimo: Apache Avenger (1952 Columbia) Clayton Moore. LOC: California: Iverson Ranch.
Son of God's Country (1948 Republic) Monte Hale. LOC: California: Walker Ranch; Republic Studio backlot
Son of Oklahoma (1932 World Wide) Bob Steele. LOC: California: Antelope Valley; Trem Carr Ranch.
Son of Paleface (1952 Paramount) Bob Hope. LOC: California: Iverson Ranch;

Paramount Studio backlot; Muroc Dry Lake; Pierre Domec's Adobe.

Son of Roaring Dan (1940 Universal) Johnny Mack Brown. LOC: California: Agoura Ranch.

Son of the Border (1933 RKO) Tom Keene. LOC: California: Sherwood Forest; Vasquez Rocks; RKO Encino Ranch.

Son of the Morning Star (1991 ABC) Gary Cole. LOC: Montana: Billings; South Dakota: Badlands National Park; Buffalo Gap.

Son of the Plains, A (1931 Syndicate) Bob Custer. LOC: California: Jauregui Ranch.

Son of the Renegade (1953 United Artists) John Carpenter. LOC: California: Ingram Ranch.

Son of Zorro (1947 Republic) George Turner. LOC: California: Iverson Ranch; Republic Studio backlot.

Song of Arizona (1946 Republic) Roy Rogers. LOC: California: Iverson Ranch; El Encino Ranch; Chatsworth Train Depot; Republic Studio backlot.

Song of Hiawata (1997 Hallmark Home Entertainment) Irene Bedard. LOC: CANADA: British Columbia.

Song of Idaho (1948 Columbia) Kirby Grant. LOC:

Song of Nevada (1944 Republic) Roy Rogers. LOC: California: Corriganville; French Ranch; Walker Ranch; Kernville; Republic Studio backlot.

Song of Old Wyoming (1945 PRC) Eddie Dean. LOC: California: Corriganville; Rancho Placeritos; Jauregui Ranch.

Song of Texas (1943 Republic) Roy Rogers. LOC: California: Corriganville; Lone Pine; Republic Studio backlot.

Song of the Buckaroo (1938 Monogram) Tex Ritter. LOC: California: Vasquez Rocks.

Song of the Caballero (1930 Universal) Ken Maynard. LOC: California: Walker Ranch; Providencia Ranch.

Song of the Drifter (1948 Monogram) Jimmy Wakely. LOC: California: Rancho Placeritos.

Song of the Gringo (1936 Grand National) Tex Ritter. LOC: California: El Monte; Ralph M. Like Studio backlot.

Song of the Prairie (1945 Columbia) Ken Curtis. LOC: California: Jauregui Ranch; Columbia Ranch.

Song of the Range (1944 Monogram) Jimmy Wakely. LOC: California: Walker Ranch; Rancho Maria.

Song of the Saddle (1936 Warner Bros) Dick Foran. LOC: California: Iverson Ranch; Jauregui Ranch.

Song of the Sierras (1946 Monogram) Jimmy Wakely. LOC: California: Kernville.

Song of the Trail (1936 Ambassador) Kermit Maynard. LOC: California: Iverson Ranch.

Song of the Wasteland (1947 Monogram) Jimmy Wakely. LOC: California: Walker

Ranch.

Song of the West (1930 Warner Bros) John Boles. LOC: California: Lone Pine.

Songs and Bullets (1938 Spectrum) Fred Scott. LOC: California: Walker Ranch.

Songs and Saddles (1938 Colony) Gene Austin. LOC: California: Columbia.

Songwriter (1984 TriStar Pictures) Kris Kristofferson. LOC: Texas: Austin.

Sonora Stagecoach (1944 Monogram) Trail Blazers. LOC: California: Corriganville; Rancho Placeritos.

Sons of Adventure (1948 Republic) Russell Hayden. LOC: California: Republic Studio backlot.

Sons of Katie Elder, The (1965 Paramount) John Wayne. LOC: MEXICO: Durango: Chupaderos; El Saltito waterfall; Gomez Palacio; Rancho Marley; Rio Chico.

Sons of New Mexico (1950 Columbia) Gene Autry. LOC: California: Iverson Ranch; French Ranch; Agoura Ranch; Deerwood Stock Farm; New Mexico: Roswell.

Sons of the Pioneers (1942 Republic) Roy Rogers. LOC: California: Iverson Ranch; Walker Ranch; Jauregui Ranch; Vasquez Rocks; Republic Studio backlot.

Sons of the Plains (1938 Warner Bros) Mauch Twins. LOC:

Sons of the Saddle (1930 Universal) Ken Maynard. LOC: California: Deadman Point.

Soul of Nigger Charley, The (1973 Paramount) Fred Williamson. LOC: Arizona: Sabino Canyon; Mescal.

South of Arizona (1938 Columbia) Charles Starrett. LOC: California: Agoura.

South of Caliente (1951 Republic) Roy Rogers. LOC: California: Lake Los Angeles; Willow Gates Stables; Republic Studio backlot.

South of Death Valley (1949 Columbia) Charles Starrett. LOC: California: Iverson Ranch; Columbia Ranch.

South of Heaven, West of Hell (2001 Cine Points Productions) Dwight Yoakam. LOC: Arizona: Mescal; San Rafael Valley Ranch San Rafael Valley.

South of Monterey (1946 Monogram) Gilbert Roland. LOC: California: Iverson Ranch.

South of Rio (1949 Republic) Monte Hale. LOC: California: Iverson Ranch.

South of Santa Fe (1932 World Wide) Bob Steele. LOC: California: Trem Carr Ranch.

South of Santa Fe (1942 Republic) Roy Rogers. LOC: California: Iverson Ranch; Walker Ranch; Republic Studio backlot;) .

South of Sonora (1930 Big 4) Jay Wilsey. LOST/MISSING.

South of St. Louis (1949 Warner Bros) Joel McCrea. LOC: California: Warner Ranch; Lasky Mesa; Kemper Campbell Ranch.

South of the Border (1939 Republic) Gene Autry. LOC: California: Corriganville; Baldwin Hills Oil Field; Antelope Valley; Republic Studio backlot.

South of the Chisholm Trail (1947 Columbia) Charles Starrett. LOC: California: Providencia Ranch.

South of the Rio Grande (1932 Columbia) Buck Jones. LOC: California: Iverson Ranch.

South of the Rio Grande (1945 Monogram) Duncan Renaldo. LOC: California: Rancho Placeritos.

South Pacific Trail (1952 Republic) Rex Allen. LOC: California: Iverson Ranch; Republic Studio backlot.

Southern Yankee, A (1948 MGM) Red Skelton. LOC: California: MGM backlot.

Southward, Ho! (1939 Republic) Roy Rogers. LOC: California: Jauregui Ranch; Burro Flats; Agoura Ranch; Frank LaSalle Ranch; Towsley Canyon; Republic Studio backlot.

Southwest Passage (1954 United Artists) John Ireland. LOC: Utah: Kanab Canyon; Johnson Canyon Movie Set; The Gap; Coral Pink Sand Dunes.

Spawn of the North (1938 Paramount) George Raft. LOC: California: Totem Pole Point, Lake Arrowhead; Lake Tahoe; Balboa Island; Nevada: Lake Tahoe; Alaska: Katchikan.

Spencer's Mountain (1963 Warner Bros) Henry Fonda. LOC: Wyoming: Jackson; Triangle X Dude Ranch; Moose.

Spikes Gang, The (1974 United Artists) Lee Marvin. LOC: SPAIN: Almería; Río Alberche.

Spirit of the Eagle (1991 Queens Cross Productions) Dan Haggerty. LOC: Oregon: Grants PassMerlin.

Spirit of the West, The (1932 Allied) Hoot Gibson. LOC: California: Jauregui Ranch.

Spirit of the Wind (1980 Raven Pictures) Chief Dan George. LOC: Alaska.

Spirit Rider (1993 Credo Entertainment Group) Graham Greene. LOC: CANADA: Manitoba: Winnipeg.

Spoilers of the Forest (1957 Republic) Rod Cameron. LOC: California: Big Bear; Republic Studio backlot.

Spoilers of the North (1947 Republic) Paul Kelly. LOC: California: Republic Studio backlot.

Spoilers of the Plains (1951 Republic) Roy Rogers. LOC: California: Iverson Ranch; Corriganville; Republic Studio backlot.

Spoilers of the Range (1939 Columbia) Charles Starrett. LOC: California: Columbia Ranch.

Spoilers, The (1930 Paramount) Gary Cooper. LOC: California: Point Hueneme.

Spoilers, The (1942 Universal) John Wayne. LOC: California: Sunland; Tujunga Canyon; Lake Arrowhead; Universal Studio backlot.

Spoilers, The (1956 Universal) Rory Calhoun. LOC: California: Universal Studio backlot.

Spook Town (1944 PRC) Texas Rangers. LOC: California: Corriganville; Rancho

Placeritos.

Springfield Rifle (1952 Warner Bros) Gary Cooper. LOC: California: Iverson Ranch; Warner Ranch; Lone Pine.

Springtime in Texas (1945 Monogram) Jimmy Wakely. LOC: California: Rancho Placeritos; Jauregui Ranch; Walker Ranch.

Springtime in the Rockies (1937 Republic) Gene Autry. LOC: California: Garner Ranch; Keen Camp; Tahquitz Lodge; Republic Studio backlot.

Springtime in the Sierras (1947 Republic) Roy Rogers. LOC: California: Walker Ranch; Republic Studio backlot.

Spurs (1930 Universal) Hoot Gibson. LOC: California: Lone Pine.

Squanto: A Warrior's Tale (1994 Buena Vista) Adam Beach. LOC: CANADA: Nova Scotia: Cape Breton Island, Louisbourg National Historic Site.

Square Dance Jubilee (1949 Lippert) Donald Barry. LOC: California: Iverson Ranch.

Square Dance Katy (1950 Monogram) Vera Vague. LOC:

Square Shooter (1935 Columbia) Tim McCoy. LOC: California: Jauregui Ranch; Trem Carr Ranch.

Squaw Man, The (1931 MGM) Warner Baxter. LOC: California: Iverson Ranch; Lake Sherwood; Arizona: Castle Hot Springs.

Stable Mates (1934 Columbia) George Sidney. LOC:

Stage Ghost (2002 Vintage Valor) Christopher Atkins. LOC: California: Bronson Canyon; Corriganville; Rancho Maria; Sable Ranch.

Stage to Blue River (1951 Monogram) Whip Wilson. LOC: California: Iverson Ranch.

Stage to Chino (1940 RKO) George O'Brien. LOC: California: Vasquez Rocks.

Stage to Mesa City (1947 Eagle Lion) Lash La Rue. LOC: California: Corriganville; Iverson Ranch; Rancho Placeritos.

Stage to Thunder Rock (1964 Paramount) Barry Sullivan. LOC: California: Janss Janss Conejo Ranch; Paramount Studio backlot; Big Bear.

Stage to Tucson (1951 Columbia) Rod Cameron. LOC: California: Corriganville; Lone Pine; Owens Lake; Columbia Ranch; Utah: stock footage of Kanab area.

Stagecoach (1939 United Artists) John Wayne. LOC: California: Iverson Ranch; Beale's Cut; Kernville; Lucerne Dry Lake; RKO Encino Ranch; Arizona: Kayenta; Mesa; Arizona/Utah: Monument Valley.

Stagecoach (1966 20th Century Fox) Alex Cord. LOC: Colorado: Arapaho Falls, Indian Peaks Wilderness; Arapaho Glacier, Indian Peaks Wilderness; Boulder County.

Stagecoach (1986 CBS) Kris Kristofferson. LOC: Arizona: MescalOld Tucson.

Stagecoach Buckaroo (1942 Universal) Johnny Mack Brown. LOC: California: Iverson Ranch; Universal Studio backlot.

Stagecoach Days (1938 Columbia) Jack Luden. LOC: California: Iverson Ranch; Walker Ranch; Towsley Canyon.

Stagecoach Driver (1951 Monogram) Whip Wilson. LOC: California: Iverson Ranch.

Stagecoach Express (1942 Republic) Don Barry. LOC: California: Iverson Ranch.

Stagecoach Kid (1949 RKO) Tim Holt. LOC: California: Lone Pine; RKO Encino Ranch.

Stagecoach Outlaws (1945 PRC) Buster Crabbe. LOC: California: Corriganville.

Stagecoach to Dancer's Rock (1962 Universal) Warren Stevens. LOC: California: Palmdale.

Stagecoach to Denver (1946 Republic) Allan Lane. LOC: California: Iverson Ranch; Republic Studio backlot.

Stagecoach to Fury (1956 Regal) Forrest Tucker. LOC: Utah: Paria.

Stagecoach to Monterey (1944 Republic) Allan Lane. LOC: California: Iverson Ranch.

Stagecoach War (1940 Paramount) William Boyd. LOC: California: Kernville; Rancho Placeritos.

Staircase, The (1998 Craig Anderson Productions) Barbara Hershey. LOC: New Mexico: Abiquiú Ghost Ranch; Bonanza Creek Ranch; Diablo Canyon; El Rancho de las Golondrinas; J.W. Eaves Movie Ranch; Río Chama; San Juan Pueblo.

Stalking Moon, The (1969 National General) Gregory Peck. LOC: Nevada: Tule Springs; Pine Creek; Valley of Fire State Park; Red Rock Canyon.

Stallion Canyon (1949 Kayson/Screencraft) Ken Curtis. LOC: California: Lone Pine; Utah: around the Jacob Hamblin home in Santa Clara; Ivins; on the Red Hill north of St. George; in the Escalante area; Kanab.

Stallion Road (1947 Warner Bros) Ronald Reagan. LOC: California: Sierra Madre Range north of Los Angeles.

Stampede (1936 Columbia) Charles Starrett. LOC: California: Holcomb Valley; Big Bear; Rancho Placeritos.

Stampede (1949 Allied Artists) Rod Cameron. LOC: California: Iverson Ranch; Rancho Placeritos; Tuolumne County.

Stand at Apache River, The (1953 Universal) Stephen McNally. LOC: California: Deadman Point; Fairview Valley/Reeves Dry Lake, Apple Valley; Universal Studio backlot.

Stand Up and Fight (1939 MGM) Robert Taylor. LOC: California: Chico; Sterling City; MGM backlot; Maryland.

Star in the Dust (1956 Universal) John Agar. LOC: California: Universal Studio backlot.

Star of Texas (1953 Allied Artists) Wayne Morris. LOC: California: Iverson Ranch; Corriganville.

Star Packer, The (1934 Monogram) John Wayne. LOC: California: Trem Carr Ranch; Kernville.

Starbird and Sweet William (1973 Howco Intl) A Martinez. LOC: California: San

Bernardino National Forest; Tennessee.

Stardust on the Sage (1942 Republic) Gene Autry. LOC: California: Agoura; Chatsworth Train Depot; Republic Studio backlot.

Starlight over Texas (1938 Monogram) Tex Ritter. LOC: California: Corriganville; Rancho Placeritos.

Stars in My Crown (1950 MGM) Joel McCrea. LOC: California: MGM backlot.

Stars over Arizona (1937 Monogram) Jack Randall. LOC: California: Rancho Placeritos; Jack Garner Ranch; Lake Hemet.

Stars over Texas (1946 PRC) Eddie Dean. LOC: California: Corriganville; Rancho Placeritos.

Station West (1948 RKO) Dick Powell. LOC: Arizona: Sedona.

Stay Away, Joe (1968 MGM) Elvis Presley. LOC: Arizona: Sedona.

Steamboat Round the Bend (1935 Fox) Will Rogers. LOC: California: Sacramento River.

Stick to Your Guns (1941 Paramount) William Boyd. LOC: California: Kernville; Lone Pine.

Still Holding On: The Legend of Cadillac Jack (1998 CBS) Clint Black. LOC: Texas: Cleburne; Farmersville; McKinney.

Sting of the West, The (1975 Film Ventures) Jack Palance. LOC: SPAIN: Almería; La Calahorra.

Stoker, The (1932 Allied) Monte Blue. LOC: California: Tec-Art Studio backlot.

Stolen Woman, Captured Hearts (1997 CBS) Janine Turner. LOC: Kansas: The Old Cowtown/Wichita.

Stone Fox (1987 Hanna Barbera Prod./Taft Entertainment) Buddy Ebsen. LOC: CANADA: Alberta: Fort Edmonton Park/Edmonton.

Stone of Silver Creek (1935 Universal) Buck Jones. LOC: California: Vasquez Rocks.

Storm over Wyoming (1950 RKO) Tim Holt. LOC: California: Agoura; Bridgeport.

Storm Rider, The (1957 Regal) Scott Brady. LOC: California: Iverson Ranch; Bronson Canyon; Republic Studio backlot.

Stormy (1935 Universal) Noah Beery Jr. LOC: California: Vasquez Rocks; Arizona: Painted Desert; Tuba City.

Stormy Trails (1936 Colony) Rex Bell. LOC: California: Brandeis Ranch.

Story of Will Rogers, The (1952 Warner Bros) Will Rogers Jr. LOC: California: Will Rogers State Historic Park, Pacific Palisades; Harry Warner Ranch; Warner Ranch; Warner Bros Studio backlot.

Straight Shooter (1939 Victory) Tim McCoy. LOC: California: Brandeis Ranch.

Straight to Hell (1987 Island Pictures/Initial Pictures/Commies From Mars Pictures) Sy Richardson. LOC: SPAIN: Nueva Frontera/Western town Almería.

Strange Gamble (1948 United Artists) William Boyd. LOC: California: Lone Pine; Anchorville.

Strange Lady in Town (1955 Warner Bros) Greer Garson. LOC: Arizona: Old Tucson; Sabino Canyon.

Stranger and the Gunfighter, The (1976 Columbia) Lee Van Cleef. LOC: SPAIN: Almería; La Calahorra; Daganzo.

Stranger at My Door (1956 Republic) Macdonald Carey. LOC: California: Morrison Ranch; Republic Studios backlot.

Stranger from Arizona, The (1938 Columbia) Buck Jones. LOC: California: Corriganville; Chatsworth Train Depot; SP train tracks next to Corriganville including tunnel opening; Columbia Ranch.

Stranger from Pecos, The (1943 Monogram) Johnny Mack Brown. LOC: California: Iverson Ranch; Rancho Placeritos.

Stranger from Ponca City, The (1947 Columbia) Charles Starrett. LOC: California: Iverson Ranch; Providencia Ranch; Columbia Ranch.

Stranger from Santa Fe (1945 Monogram) Johnny Mack Brown. LOC: California: Walker Ranch; Rancho Placeritos.

Stranger from Texas, The (1939 Columbia) Charles Starrett. LOC: California: Agoura.

Stranger on Horseback (1955 United Artists) Joel McCrea. LOC: California: Rancho Placeritos; Arizona: Sedona.

Stranger on the Run (1967 Universal) Henry Fonda. LOC: California: Janss Janss Conejo Ranch.

Stranger Wore a Gun, The (1953 Columbia) Randolph Scott. LOC: California: Iverson Ranch; Corriganville; Lone Pine; Columbia Ranch.

Strangers at Sunrise (1969 Commonwealth Unlimited) George Montgomery. LOC: SOUTH AFRICA.

Strawberry Roan (1933 Universal) Ken Maynard. LOC: California: Kernville; Red Rock Canyon.

Strawberry Roan, The (1948 Columbia) Gene Autry. LOC: California: Jauregui Ranch; Arizona: Sedona.

Streets of Ghost Town (1950 Columbia) Charles Starrett. LOC: California: Iverson Ranch; Corriganville; Columbia Ranch.

Streets of Laredo (1949 Paramount) William Holden. LOC: California: Corriganville; Rancho Placeritos; New Mexico: Gallup.

Streets of Laredo (1995 CBS) James Garner. LOC: Texas: Alamo Village; Big Bend National Park; CF Ranch Alpine; Lajitas/Mexican set; Rancho Rio Grande/Moody's Ranch; Villa de la Mina Terlingua.

Strictly in the Groove (1943 Universal) Richard Davies. LOC: California: Universal backlot.

Strike It Rich (1949 Allied Artists) Rod Cameron. LOC: Texas: Kilgore; Tyler; Turnertown; Lindale.

Stronghold (1952 Lippert) Veronica Lake. LOC: MEXICO: Guerrero: Acapulco; Taxco.

Sudden Bill Dorn (1937 Universal) Buck Jones. LOC: California: Kernville.

Suddenly (1954 United Artists) Frank Sinatra. LOC: California: Saugus; Saugus Railroad Depot; Newhall.

Sugarfoot (1951 Warner Bros) Randolph Scott. LOC: California: Vasquez Rocks; Warner Ranch.

Sugarland Express, The (1974 Universal) Ben Johnson. LOC: Texas: Del Rio; San Antonio.

Sukiyaki Western Django (2007 Dentsu Productions/Geneon Entertainment/Sedic International/Sony Pictures/TV Ashai/Toei Company) Hideaki Ito. LOC: JAPAN.

Sun Shines Bright, The (1953 Republic) Charles Winninger. LOC: California: Sacramento River; Republic Studio backlot.

Sun Valley Cyclone (1946 Republic) Bill Elliott. LOC: California: Iverson Ranch.

Sundown in Santa Fe (1948 Republic) Allan Lane. LOC: California: Iverson Ranch; Walker Ranch.

Sundown Jim (1942 20th Century Fox) John Kimbrough. LOC: California: Burro Flats; Lone Pine.

Sundown Kid, The (1942 Republic) Don Barry. LOC: California: Iverson Ranch.

Sundown on the Prairie (1939 Monogram) Tex Ritter. LOC: California: Vasquez Rocks.

Sundown Rider, The (1933 Columbia) Buck Jones. LOC: California: Agoura.

Sundown Riders (1948 Film Enterprises) Russ Wade. LOC:

Sundown Saunders (1936 Superior) Bob Steele. LOC: California: Brandeis Ranch; Lone Pine; Ralph M. Like Studio backlot.

Sundown Trail (1931 RKO) Tom Keene. LOC: California: North Verde Ranch/Kemper Campbell Ranch; Upper Narrows, Victorville; RKO Encino Ranch.

Sundown Trail, The (1934 Imperial) Wally Wales. LOC: California.

Sundown Valley (1944 Columbia) Charles Starrett. LOC: California: Iverson Ranch.

Sundowners, The (1950 Eagle Lion) Robert Preston. LOC: Texas: Palo Duro Canyon; Amarillo; Davis Mountains.

Sundowners, The (1960 Warner Bros) Robert Mitchum. LOC: AUSTRALIA: New South Wales: Cooma; South Australia: Iron Knob; Flinders Ranges.

Sunrise Trail (1931 Tiffany) Bob Steele. LOC: California.

Sunscorched (1966 Feature Film Corp) Mark Stevens. LOC: SPAIN: Esplugas City, Barcelona.

Sunset (1988 TriStar Pictures) James Garner. LOC: California: Bell Ranch; Hollywood/Roosevelt Hotel; Melody Ranch.

Sunset Carson Rides Again (1948 Astor) Sunset Carson. LOC: California: Oliver Drake Ranch.

Sunset in El Dorado (1945 Republic) Roy Rogers. LOC: California: Iverson Ranch; Walker Ranch; Antelope Valley; Hwy 126 near Del Valle/Piru; Republic Studio backlot.

Sunset in the West (1950 Republic) Roy Rogers. LOC: California: Walker Ranch; Train Scenes–Saugus to Fillmore; Leo Carrillo State Beach; Republic Studio backlot.

Sunset in Wyoming (1941 Republic) Gene Autry. LOC: California: Idyllwild; George Lewis Mansion; Walker Ranch; Republic Studio backlot.

Sunset of Power (1935 Universal) Buck Jones. LOC: California: Walker Ranch; French Ranch.

Sunset on the Desert (1942 Republic) Roy Rogers. LOC: California: Walker Ranch; Jauregui Ranch; Vasquez Rocks; Kernville; Republic Studio backlot.

Sunset Pass (1933 Paramount) Randolph Scott. LOC: California: Mojave Desert.

Sunset Pass (1946 RKO) James Warren. LOC: California: Lone Pine.

Sunset Range (1935 First Division) Hoot Gibson. LOC: California: Agoura Ranch; Chatsworth Train Depot.

Sunset Serenade (1942 Republic) Roy Rogers. LOC: California: Walker Ranch; Bronson Canyon; Mint Canyon; Republic Studio backlot.

Sunset Trail (1938 Paramount) William Boyd. LOC: California: Kernville; Kernville Movie Street; Kelso Valley.

Sunset Trail, The (1932 Tiffany) Ken Maynard. LOC: California: Iverson Ranch.

Support Your Local Gunfighter (1971 United Artists) James Garner. LOC: California: Disney Golden Oak Ranch; Republic Studio backlot; Colorado: Durango-Silverton Narrow Gauge Railroad.

Support Your Local Sheriff (1969 United Artists) James Garner. LOC: California: Iverson Ranch; Agoura Ranch; MGM backlot.

Surrender (1950 Republic) John Carroll. LOC: California: Indian Village, Death Valley; Republic Studios backlot.

Susanna Pass (1949 Republic) Roy Rogers. LOC: California: Iverson Ranch; Corriganville; Vasquez Rocks; Chatsworth Lake and Manor; Filmore's State Fish Hatchery; Republic Studio backlot.

Susannah of the Mounties (1939 20th Century Fox) Shirley Temple. LOC: California: Iverson Ranch; 20th Century Fox backlot.

Sutter's Gold (1936 Universal) Edward Arnold. LOC: California: Universal **backlot; San Bernardino Mountains; Barton Flats; Sandwich Islands.**

Sweet Creek County War, The (1979 Imagery Films/Key International) Richard Egan. LOC: Wyoming: Pinedale.

Swifty (1935 Diversion Pictures) Hoot Gibson. LOC: California: Kernville.

Swing in the Saddle (1944 Columbia) Guinn Williams. LOC: California: Columbia Ranch.

Swing, Cowboy, Swing (1946 Westernair) Carl Shrum. LOC: California: Corriganville.

Taggart (1964 Universal) Tony Young. LOC: California: Janss Conejo Ranch; Universal Studio backlot.

Tailor, The (2005 Lucent Films) Joe Estevez. LOC: California: Ocotillo; San Diego.

Take a Hard Ride (1975 20th Century Fox) Lee Van Cleef) Canary Islands.

Take It Big (1944 Paramount) Jack Haley. LOC:

Take Me Back to Oklahoma (1940 Monogram) Tex Ritter. LOC: California: Garner Ranch; Keen Camp.

Take Me to Town (1953 Universal) Sterling Hayden. LOC: California: Universal backlot.

Taku (1940 Monogram) Ben Webster. LOC: Alaska: Taku River.

Tale of Gold (1956 Wrather) Clayton Moore. LOC: California: Iverson Ranch; Ingram Ranch; Utah: Kanab; Johnson Canyon Movie Set.

Tales of Two Guns, A (2022 Koenig Pictures) Tom Berenger. LOC: California: Whitehorse Ranch; Landers.

Talion (1966 Circle Prod) Patrick Wayne. LOC: California: Lone Pine.

Talisman, The (1966 Gillman Film) Ned Romero. LOC: California: Bell Ranch; Angeles National Forest.

Tall in the Saddle (1944 RKO) John Wayne. LOC: California: Agoura Ranch; Lake Sherwood; RKO Encino Ranch; Arizona: Gates Pass; Sedona; Flagstaff.

Tall Man Riding (1955 Warner Bros) Randolph Scott. LOC: California: Iverson Ranch; Corriganville; French Ranch; Hidden Valley.

Tall Men, The (1955 20th Century Fox) Clark Gable. LOC: California: 20th Century Fox backlot; Idaho: Sun Valley; MEXICO: Durango: Vicente Guerrero; Zacatecas: Sierra de Organos.

Tall Stranger, The (1957 Allied Artists) Joel McCrea. LOC: California: Morrison Ranch; Russell Ranch.

Tall T, The (1957 Columbia) Randolph Scott. LOC: California: Lone Pine; Columbia Ranch.

Tall Tale (1995 Buena Vista) Patrick Swayze. LOC: Arizona: Antelope Canyon/Corkscrew Canyon Page; Lake Powell; Lee's Ferry balanced rocks; Marble Canyon; Monument Valley; California: Disney's Golden Oak Ranch; Colorado: Aspen; Grand Sand Dunes National Monument Alamosa.

Tall Target, The (1951 MGM) Dick Powell. LOC: California: MGM backlot.

Tall Texan, The (1953 Lippert) Lee J. Cobb. LOC: California: Iverson Ranch; Bronson Canyon; New Mexico: City of the Rocks State Park, near Deming.

Taming of the West (1939 Columbia) Bill Elliott. LOC: California: Iverson Ranch; Columbia Ranch.

Tap Roots (1948 Universal) Van Heflin. LOC: California: Universal Studio backlot; North Carolina: Smoky Mountains; Tennessee: Great Smoky Mountains National Park.

Target (1952 RKO) Tim Holt. LOC: California: Iverson Ranch; Agoura Ranch; RKO Encino Ranch.

Taste of Death (1968 Western World) John Ireland. LOC: ITALY: National Abruzzo Park.

Taza, Son of Cochise (1954 Universal) Rock Hudson. LOC: California: Vasquez Rocks; Utah: Courthouse Wash, Arches National Park; Devil's Garden, Arches National Park; Professor Valley; Castle Valley; Dead Horse Point State Park; White's Ranch.

Tecumseh: The Last Warrior (1995 TNT) Tantoo Cardinal. LOC: North Carolina: Winston Salem.

Telegraph Trail, The (1933 Warner Bros) John Wayne. LOC: California: Lasky Mesa; Providencia Ranch; Warner Bros Studio backlot.

Tell Them Willie Boy is Here (1970 Universal) Robert Redford. LOC: California: Lake Sherwood; Joshua Tree National Monument; Palm Springs; Riverside.

Ten Days to Tulara (1958 United Artists) Sterling Hayden. LOC: MEXICO: Mexico: Teotihuacan.

Ten Wanted Men (1955 Columbia) Randolph Scott. LOC: Arizona: Old Tucson; Sabino Canyon.

Ten Who Dared (1960 Buena Vista) Brian Keith. LOC: Arizona: Grand Canyon National Park; Utah: Park Avenue, Arches National Park; Big Bend; Dead Horse Point State Park; Ida Gulch; White's Ranch.

Tenderfoot, The (1932 First National) Joe E. Brown. LOC: California: Iverson Ranch; New York: New York City.

Tennessee's Partner (1955 RKO) John Payne. LOC: California: Iverson Ranch; Republic Studio backlot.

Tension at Table Rock (1956 RKO) Richard Egan. LOC: California: Rancho Placeritos; Red Rock Canyon.

Tenting Tonight on the Old Camp Ground (1943 Universal) Johnny Mack Brown. LOC: California: Iverson Ranch; Corriganville; Agoura.

Terror in a Texas Town (1958 United Artists) Sterling Hayden. LOC: California: Rancho Placeritos.

Terror of the Plains (1935 Reliable) Tom Tyler. LOC: California: Frank LaSalle Ranch; Towsley Canyon.

Terror of Tiny Town, The (1938 Principal) Billy Curtis. LOC: California: Rancho Placeritos; Brandeis Ranch.

Terror Trail (1933 Universal) Tom Mix. LOC: California: Mystery Adobe Ranch; Bronson Canyon; Lone Pine; Universal Studio backlot.

Terror Trail (1946 Columbia) Charles Starrett. LOC: California: Iverson Ranch; Corriganville; Russell Ranch; Columbia Ranch.

Terrors on Horseback (1946 PRC) Buster Crabbe. LOC: California: Corriganville.

Test, The (1935 Reliable) Grant Withers. LOC: California: Big Bear Lake; Big Bear Valley.

Tex (1982 Walt Disney Productions) Matt Dillon. LOC: Oklahoma: Bixby; Broken Arrow; Tulsa.

Tex and the Lord of the Deep (1985 RAI Radiotelevisione Italiana Rete 3) Giuliano Gemma. LOC: SPAIN: Cabo de Gata/sand dunes Almería; Cantocochino

Madrid; Nueva Frontera/Mexican set Tabernas, Almería; Rancho Leone/Western set Almería; Texas-Hollywood/Western town Almería; La Pedriza Manzanares El Real, Madrid.

Tex Granger (1948 Columbia) Smith Ballew. LOC: California: Columbia Ranch; Kernville.

Tex McLeod in a Rope and a Story (1928 Vitaphone) Tex McLeod. LOC:

Tex Rides with the Boy Scouts (1937 Grand National) Tex Ritter. LOC: California: Kernville; Kernville Movie Street; Frank LaSalle Ranch.

Tex Takes a Holiday (1932 First Division) Wallace Mc Donald. LOST /MISSING/UNAVAILABLE.

Texan Meets Calamity Jane, The (1950 Columbia) James Ellison. LOC: California: Iverson Ranch.

Texan, The (1930 Paramount) Gary Cooper. LOC: California: Paramount Ranch; Tuolumne County.

Texan, The (1932 Principal Attraction) Buffalo Bill Jr. LOC: California: Fat Jones Ranch; Jauregui Ranch.

Texans Never Cry (1951 Columbia) Gene Autry. LOC: California: Iverson Ranch; Columbia Ranch; Lone Pine.

Texans, The (1938 Paramount) Gary Cooper. LOC: California: Kernville; Texas: Cotulla; La Mota Ranch; Port Lavaca.

Texas (1941 Columbia) William Holden. LOC: California: Agoura Ranch; Lasky Mesa; Columbia Ranch.

Texas Across the River (1966 Universal) Dean Martin. LOC: California: Universal Studio; North Ranch; Lovejoy Buttes; Rutherford-Starr Ranch, Julian.

Texas Bad Man (1953 Allied Artists) Wayne Morris. LOC: California: Corriganville.

Texas Bad Man, The (1932 Universal) Tom Mix. LOC: California: Deadman Point; Universal Studio backlot.

Texas Buddies (1932 World Wide) Bob Steele. LOC: California: Chatsworth Train Depot; Trem Carr Ranch; Antelope Valley.

Texas Carnival (1951 MGM) Esther Williams. LOC: California: Beverly Wilshire Hotel; Agoura Ranch?; El Mirage Dry Lake; MGM backlot.

Texas City (1952 Monogram) Johnny Mack Brown. LOC: California: Iverson Ranch.

Texas Cowboy, A (1929 Syndicate) Bob Steele. LOC: California: Jauregui Ranch.

Texas Cyclone (1932 Columbia) Tim McCoy. LOC: California: Iverson Ranch; Jauregui Ranch; Trem Carr Ranch.

Texas Dynamo (1950 Columbia) Charles Starrett. LOC: California: Iverson Ranch.

Texas Gunfighter (1932 Tiffany) Ken Maynard. LOC: California: Warner Bros Studio backlot; Vasquez Rocks.

Texas Jack (1935 Reliable) Jack Perrin. LOC: California: Frank LaSalle Ranch; Newhall Train Depot.

Texas Justice (1942 PRC) George Houston. LOC: California: Iverson Ranch; Corriganville.

Texas Kid, The (1943 Monogram) Johnny Mack Brown. LOC: California: Iverson Ranch.

Texas Lady (1955 RKO) Barry Sullivan. LOC: California: Murphys, Tuolumne County; Salt Spring Valley, Calaveras County.

Texas Lawmen (1951 Monogram) Johnny Mack Brown. LOC: California: Iverson Ranch.

Texas Manhunt (1942 PRC) Frontier Marshal. LOC: California: Iverson Ranch; Walker Ranch; Rancho Placeritos.

Texas Marshal, The (1941 PRC) Tim McCoy. LOC: California: Walker Ranch; Jauregui Ranch; Rancho Placeritos.

Texas Masquerade (1944 United Artists) Bill Boyd. LOC: California: Kernville; Kelso Valley; California Studio backlot.

Texas Panhandle (1945 Columbia) Charles Starrett. LOC: California: Iverson Ranch; Columbia Ranch.

Texas Pioneers (1932 Monogram) Bill Cody. LOC: California: Trem Carr Ranch.

Texas Rambler, The (1935 Spectrum) Bill Cody. LOC: California: Brandeis Ranch; Agoura Ranch?.

Texas Ranger, The (1931 Columbia) Buck Jones. LOC: California: Walker Ranch; Vasquez Rocks.

Texas Rangers (2001 Miramax/Dimension Films) Dylan McDermott. LOC: CANADA: Alberta: Brooks; Claresholm; Drumheller/badlands; High River; Longview Calgary; MEXICO: Durango: Chupaderos.

Texas Rangers Ride Again, The (1940 Paramount) John Howard. LOC: Arizona: Mesa.

Texas Rangers, The (1936 Paramount) Fred MacMurray. LOC: Arizona: Lupton; Colorado: Durango; New Mexico: Gallup; San Ildefonso Pueblo.

Texas Rangers, The (1951 Columbia) George Montgomery. LOC: California: Iverson Ranch; Corriganville; Tuolumne County.

Texas Renegades (1940 PDC) Tim McCoy. LOC: Arizona: Prescott.

Texas Stagecoach (1940 Columbia) Charles Starrett. LOC: California: Corriganville; Columbia Ranch.

Texas Stampede (1939 Columbia) Charles Starrett. LOC:

Texas Terror (1935 Monogram) John Wayne. LOC: California: Trem Carr Ranch; Jack Garner Ranch.

Texas Terrors (1940 Republic) Don Barry. LOC: California: Iverson Ranch; Burro Flats.

Texas to Bataan (1942 Monogram) Range Busters. LOC: California: Corriganville.

Texas Tornado (1932 Kent) Lane Chandler. LOC: California: Chatsworth Reservoir.

Texas Trail (1937 Paramount) William Boyd. LOC: California: Walker Ranch; Jauregui Ranch; Red Rock Canyon; Arizona: Tuba City; Sedona; Painted Desert.

Texas Trouble Shooters (1942 Monogram) Range Busters. LOC: California: Corriganville.

Texas Wildcats (1939 Victory) Tim McCoy. LOC: California: Iverson Ranch; Walker Ranch; Kernville.

Texican, The (1966 Columbia) Audie Murphy. LOC: SPAIN: Fraga, Aragón.

That Texas Jamboree (1946 Columbia) Ken Curtis. LOC: California: Walker Ranch; Columbia Ranch

The Assassination of Jesse James by the Coward Robert Ford (2007 Warner Bros) Brad Pitt. LOC: CANADA: Alberta: Calgary/Heritage Park; Fort Edmonton Park/Railway; McKinnon Flats; Manitoba: Winnipeg.

Then Came Jones (2003 ABC) Melissa Gilbert. LOC:

There Was a Crooked Man (1970 Warner Bros) Kirk Douglas. LOC: California: Warner Bros backlot; Joshua Tree National Monument; New Mexico: La Joya area.

These Thousand Hills (1959 20th Century Fox) Don Murray. LOC: Colorado: Durango; La Plata County; Towaoc.

They Came to Cordura (1959 Columbia) Gary Cooper. LOC: Nevada: Moapa Valley; Utah: Snow Canyon; Harrisburg.

They Died with Their Boots On (1942 Warner Bros) Errol Flynn. LOC: California: Iverson Ranch; Lasky Mesa; Warner Ranch; Busch Gardens.

They Ran for Their Lives (1969 Color Vision) John Payne. LOC: Nevada: Valley of Fire State Park; Red Rock Canyon; Bonnie Springs Ranch.

They Rode West (1954 Columbia) Robert Francis. LOC: California: Corriganville; Burro Flats; Columbia Ranch.

They Went That-A-Way and That-A-Way (1978 International Picture Show) Tim Conway. LOC: Georgia: Powder Springs; Atlanta.

This Man Can't Die (1970 Capitol Prod) Guy Madison. LOC: ITALY.

This Rugged Land (1970 Universal) Richard Egan. LOC:

This Savage Land (1969 Universal) George C. Scott. LOC: California: Janss Conejo Ranch; Agoura.

Thomasine and Bushrod (1974 Columbia) Max Julien. LOC: New Mexico: J. W. Eaves Ranch, Santa Fe; Santa Clara Pueblo.

Thousand Pieces of Gold, A (1991 Greycat Films) Rosalind Chao. LOC: Montana: Butte; Ennis; Nevada City.

Three Amigos (1986 Columbia) Chevy Chase. LOC: Arizona: MescalOld Tucson, Sabino Canyon.

Three Bad Men (2005 Iron Horse Productions) George Kennedy. LOC: California: American River Indio; Columbia Tuolumne County; Forest Hill/American Bar Quartz Mining Company; Helendale/church; Jamestown Tuolumne County; Placer County; San Bernardino County; Spears Ranch Lincoln; Luzerne Dry Lake.

Three Burials of Melquiades Estrada, The (2005 Europa Corp.) Tommy Lee Jones. LOC: Texas: Big Bend National Park/Santa Elena Canyon Rio Grande; Big Bend Ranch State Park; Chisos Mountains; Cibola Creek; Crow Town/Mexican set; Lajitas/Mexican set; Monahans; Shafter; Van Horn.

Three Desperate Men (1951 Lippert) Preston Foster. LOC: California: Corriganville.

Three Faces West (1940 Republic) John Wayne. LOC: California: Lone Pine.

Three Godfathers (1936 MGM) Chester Morris. LOC: California: Red Rock Canyon; RKO Encino Ranch.

Three Guns for Texas (1968 Universal) Neville Brand. LOC: California: Janss Conejo Ranch.

Three Hours to Kill (1954 Columbia) Dana Andrews. LOC: California: Columbia Ranch; Lake Sherwood.

Three in the Saddle (1945 PRC) Texas Rangers. LOC: California: Corriganville.

Three Men from Texas (1940 Paramount) William Boyd. LOC: California: Rancho Placeritos; Lone Pine; Anchor Ranch.

Three Mesquiteers, The (1936 Republic) Three Mesquiteers. LOC: California: Kernville; Republic Studio backlot.

Three on the Trail (1936 Paramount) William Boyd. LOC: California: Kernville; Kernville Movie Street; Lone Pine.

Three Outlaws, The (1956 Associated Film Releasing Corp) Neville Brand. LOC: California: Corriganville; Chatsworth Train Depot; SP train tracks next to Corriganville; Piute Butte.

Three Texas Steers (1939 Republic) Three Mesquiteers. LOC: California: Brandeis Ranch; Corriganville; Devonshire Downs; Republic Studio backlot.

Three Violent People (1957 Paramount) Charlton Heston. LOC: Arizona: Tucson.

Three Warriors (1977 United Artists-Fantasy Films) Randy Quaid. LOC: Oregon: Mount Hood National Forest; Oneonta Gorge, Columbia River Gorge; Simnasho, Warm Springs Indian Reservation.

Three Young Texans (1954 20th Century Fox) Jeffrey Hunter. LOC: Colorado: Durango-Silverton Narrow Gauge Railroad.

Three-Ten to Yuma (1957 Columbia) Glenn Ford. LOC: Arizona: Sedona; Old Tucson; Elgin; Willcox Dry Lake; Texas Canyon.

Thrill Hunter, The (1933 Columbia) Buck Jones. LOC: California: Walker Ranch.

Throw a Saddle on a Star (1946 Columbia) Ken Curtis. LOC: California: Columbia Ranch; Provi-dencia Ranch.

Throwback, The (1935 Universal) Buck Jones. LOC: California: Agoura Ranch?; Lasky Mesa; Vasquez Rocks.

Thunder at the Border (1969 Columbia) Rod Cameron) Croatia: Solin, Split; Strobec; Yugoslavia; Vrlika.

Thunder in God's Country (1951 Republic) Rex Allen. LOC: California: Iverson Ranch; Burro Flats.

Thunder in the Desert (1938 Republic) Bob Steele. LOC: California: Iverson Ranch; Walker Ranch.

Thunder in the Sun (1959 Paramount) Susan Hayward. LOC: California: Lone Pine; Olancha Sand Dunes.

Thunder in the Valley (1947 20th Century Fox) Lon McCallister. LOC: Utah: Kanab Canyon; Duck Creek; Strawberry Valley.

Thunder Mountain (1935 20th Century Fox) George O'Brien. LOC: California: Lake Sherwood; Tuolumne County: Columbia; Kennedy Meadow; Stanislaus River.

Thunder Mountain (1947 RKO) Tim Holt. LOC: California: Lone Pine; Anchor Ranch; RKO Encino Ranch.

Thunder of Drums, A (1961 MGM) Richard Boone. LOC: Arizona: Sabino Canyon; Saguaro National Monument; California: Vasquez Rocks; MGM backlot.

Thunder over Arizona (1956 Republic) Skip Homeier. LOC: California: Iverson Ranch; Republic Studio backlot.

Thunder over Texas (1934 Beacon) Big Boy Williams. LOC: California: Acton; Ranch01.

Thunder over the Plains (1953 Warner Bros) Randolph Scott. LOC: California: Agoura.

Thunder over the Prairie (1941 Columbia) Charles Starrett. LOC: California: Iverson Ranch; Columbia Ranch.

Thunder Pass (1954 Lippert) Dane Clark. LOC: California: Corriganville; Bronson Canyon; Fairview Mountain, Apple Valley; North Verde Ranch/Kemper Campbell Ranch, Victorville.

Thunder River Feud (1942 Monogram) Range Busters. LOC: California: Iverson Ranch; Brandeis Ranch.

Thunder Town (1946 PRC) Bob Steele. LOC: California: Iverson Ranch; Corriganville.

Thunder Trail (1937 Paramount) Gilbert Roland. LOC: California: Big Bear; Kernville.

Thunder Warrior (1983 Thunder Fulvia Film International) Mark Gregory. LOC: Arizona: Bitter Springs; Glen Canyon; Monument Valley; Navajo Bridge; Page; Sedona.

Thunder Warrior II (1986 Thunder II Fulvia Film International) Mark Gregory. LOC: Arizona: Kaibito; Monument Valley; Page.

Thunderbolt and Lightfoot (1974 United Artists) Clint Eastwood. LOC: Montana: Great Falls; Fort Benton.

Thunderhead—Son of Flicka (1945 20th Century Fox) Preston Foster. LOC: California: Century Ranch; Hidden Valley; Utah: Bryce Canyon National Park; Kanab Canyon; Duck Creek; Strawberry Valley; Zion National Park; Cedar Mountain.

Thunderheart (1992 TriStar Pictures) Val Kilmer. LOC: South Dakota: Badlands

National ParkPine Ridge Indian ReservationWounded Knee Cemetery - Washington D.C.

Thunderhoof (1948 Columbia) Preston Foster. LOC: California: Corriganville; Lake Los Angeles; Vasquez Rocks.

Thundering Caravans (1952 Republic) Allan Lane. LOC: California: Iverson Ranch; Corriganville.

Thundering Frontier (1940 Columbia) Charles Starrett. LOC: California: Iverson Ranch; Columbia Ranch.

Thundering Gun Slingers (1944 PRC) Buster Crabbe. LOC: California: Corriganville.

Thundering Herd, The (1933 Paramount) Randolph Scott. LOC: California: Paramount Ranch; Lone Pine.

Thundering Hoofs (1941 RKO) Tim Holt. LOC: California: Iverson Ranch; Corriganville; Jauregui Ranch.

Thundering Rails (1950 Universal) Tex Williams. LOC:

Thundering Trail, The (1951 Western Adventure) Lash LaRue. LOC: California: Iverson Ranch.

Thundering Trails (1943 Republic) Three Mesquiteers. LOC: California: Iverson Ranch; Republic Studio backlot.

Thundering West, The (1939 Columbia) Charles Starrett. LOC: California: Iverson Ranch; Alonzo Morrison Ranch.

Ticket to Tomahawk, A (1950 20th Century Fox) Dan Dailey. LOC: Colorado: Durango-Silverton Narrow Gauge Railroad; Silverton.

Tide of Empire (1929 MGM) George Duryea. LOC: California: Agoura; Beale's Cut; San Fernando Mission; MGM backlot.

Timber (1942 Universal) Dan Dailey. LOC: California: Universal backlot.

Timber Country Trouble (1955 Allied Artists) Guy Madison. LOC: California: Rancho Placeritos; Cedar Lake.

Timber Fury (1950 Eagle Lion) David Bruce. LOC:

Timber Queen (1944 Paramount) Mary Beth Hughes. LOC: California: Big Bear.

Timber Stampede (1939 RKO) George O'Brien. LOC: California: Tuolumne County; Columbia; Sonora.

Timber Terrors (1935 Stage & Screen) John Preston. LOC: California: Big Bear; Stillwell's #2.

Timber Trail, The (1948 Republic) Monte Hale. LOC: California: Iverson Ranch.

Timber Tramps (1975 Howco International) Joseph Cotton) Alaska.

Timber War (1935 Ambassador) Kermit Maynard. LOC: California: Scotia.

Timberjack (1955 Republic) Sterling Hayden. LOC: Montana: Glacier National Park; Polson; Wester; CANADA: British Columbia.

Timberwolf (2009 Collective Development) Dan Haggerty. LOC: Arizona: Mescal; Michigan: North Carolina: Maggie Valley.

Time for Dying, A (1969 Fipco Prod) Audie Murphy. LOC: Arizona: Apacheland.

Time for Killing, A (1967 Columbia) Glenn Ford. LOC: Arizona: Old Tucson; Utah: Kanab Movie Fort; Zion National Park; Glen Canyon National Recreation Area.

Timerider (1983 Jensen Farley) Fred Ward. LOC: New Mexico: J.W.Eaves Movie Ranch/Mexican set Santa FeThe White Place/Plaza Blanca Abiquiú.

Timestalkers (1987 Fries Entertainment) Forrest Tucker. LOC: California: Newhall.

Tin Star Void (1988 Six-Shooter Films/Double Helix Films) Daniel Chapman.) Connecticut: New Haven.

Tin Star, The (1957 Paramount) Henry Fonda. LOC: California: Janss Conejo Ranch; Janss Ranch; Prado Dam area south of Chino; Morrison Ranch; Paramount Studio backlot.

Tioga Kid, The (1948 Eagle Lion) Eddie Dean. LOC: California: Corriganville; Rancho Placeritos.

Titled Tenderfoot, The (1955 Allied Artists) Guy Madison. LOC: California: Cedar Lake.

To The Last Man (1933 Paramount) Randolph Scott. LOC: California: Big Bear; Cedar Lake; Pine Knot; Bear Valley.

Toll of the Desert (1935 Commodore) Fred Kohler, Jr. LOC: California: Brandeis Ranch; Vasquez Rocks; Frank LaSalle Ranch; Ralph M. Like Studio backlot.

Tom Horn (1980 Warner Bros) Steve McQueen. LOC: Arizona: MescalRio RicoSan Rafael Ranch San Rafael ValleySonoita.

Tomahawk (1951 Universal) Van Heflin. LOC: South Dakota: Badlands National Park.

Tomahawk Trail (1957 United Artists) Chuck Conners. LOC: Utah: Kanab; Kanab Movie Fort; The Gap.

Tomboy and the Champ (1961 Universal) Ben Johnson. LOC: Alabama: Illinois: Chicago; Texas: Houston.

Tombstone (1994 Buena Vista) Kurt Russell. LOC: Arizona: Babocomari Ranch/Babocomari River and set Elgin; Mescal; Old Tucson; Sabino Canyon Tucson; Willcox Playa dry lake.

Tombstone Canyon (1932 World Wide) Ken Maynard. LOC: California: Red Rock Canyon; Trem Carr Ranch.

Tombstone Terror (1935 Commodore) Bob Steele. LOC: California: Garner Ranch.

Tombstone, the Town too Tough to Die (1942 Paramount) Richard Dix. LOC: California: Iverson Ranch; Lone Valley; Lone Pine.

Tonka (1958 Buena Vista) Sal Mineo. LOC: Oregon: Bend; Warm Springs Indian Reservation.

Tonto Basin Outlaws (1941 Monogram) Range Busters. LOC: California: Corriganville.

Tonto Kid, The (1935 Resolute) Rex Bell. LOC: California: Vasquez Rocks; Mystery Adobe Ranch; RKO Encino Ranch.

Too Much Beef (1936 Colony) Rex Bell. LOC: California: Iverson Ranch.

Top Gun (1955 United Artists) Sterling Hayden. LOC: California: Ingram Ranch; Iverson Ranch.

Topeka (1953 Allied Artists) Bill Elliott. LOC: California: Iverson Ranch; Corriganville.

Topeka Terror, The (1945 Republic) Allan Lane. LOC: California: Iverson Ranch; Republic Studio backlot.

Torch, The (1950 Eagle Lion) Paulette Goddard. LOC: MEXICO: Pueblo: Cholula, El Portal Guerrero, Plaza de la Concordia, Casa del Caballero Aguilla, San Bernardino Tlaxcalancingo.

Tornado in the Saddle, A (1942 Columbia) Russell Hayden. LOC: California: Iverson Ranch.

Tornado Range (1948 Eagle Lion) Eddie Dean. LOC: California: Iverson Ranch.

Touch of Evil (1958 Universal) Charlton Heston. LOC: California: Venice.

Tough Assignment (1949 Lippert) Don Barry. LOC: California: Iverson Ranch.

Tougher They Come, The (1950 Columbia) Wayne Morris. LOC: California: Iverson Ranch.

Toughest Gun in Tombstone (1958 United Artists) George Montgomery. LOC: California: Iverson Ranch; Rancho Placeritos.

Toughest Man in Arizona (1952 Republic) Vaughn Monroe. LOC: California: Red Rock Canyon; Black Rock Area; Republic Studio backlot; Utah: Snow Canyon; Ivins Bence.

Town Tamer (1965 Paramount) Dana Andrews. LOC: California: Paramount Studio backlot.

Town That Dreaded Sundown, The (1977 American Int'l) Ben Johnson) Arkansas/Texas: Texarkana.

Track of the Cat (1954 Warner Bros) Robert Mitchum. LOC: Washington: Mt. Rainier National Park.

Tracker, The (1988 ITC Entertainment Group) Kris Kristofferson. LOC: Colorado: Durango-Silveron Narrow Gauge Railroad; Mesa Verde; Towaoc La Plata County; New Mexico: Bonanza Creek Ranch; Diablo Canyon; Galisteo area; J.W. Eaves Movie Ranch; Río Chama; San Ildefonso Pueblo.

Tracker, The (2002 Vertigo Productions Pty. Ltd.) David Gulpilil) Australia: South Australia: Arkaroola Wilderness SanctuaryFlinders RangesGammon Ranges.

Trackers (1956 Wrather) Clayton Moore. LOC: California: Corriganville; Ingram Ranch; Tuolumne County; Jamestown; Utah: Kanab; Paria.

Trackers, The (1971 Aaron Spelling Prod-TV) Ernest Borgnine. LOC: California: Paramount backlot.

Tracy Rides (1935 Commodore) Tom Tyler. LOC: California: Agoura.

Trail Beyond, The (1934 Monogram) John Wayne. LOC: California: Trem Carr Ranch; General Grant National Park/Kings Canyon National Park.

Trail Blazers, The (1940 Republic) Three Mesquiteers. LOC: California: Iverson Ranch; Corriganville; Republic Studio backlot.

Trail Drive, The (1933 Universal) Ken Maynard. LOC: California: Kernville; Miller and Lux Ranch.

Trail Dust (1936 Paramount) William Boyd. LOC: California: Tuolumne County.

Trail Guide (1952 RKO) Tim Holt. LOC: California: Iverson Ranch; Jauregui Ranch.

Trail of '98, The (1929 MGM) Dolores Del Rio) Alaska; Colorado.

Trail of Kit Carson (1945 Republic) Allan Lane. LOC: California: Iverson Ranch; Corriganville.

Trail of Robin Hood (1950 Republic) Roy Rogers. LOC: California: Iverson Ranch; Cedar Lake; Chatsworth Lake; Republic Studio backlot.

Trail of Terror (1935 Superior) Bob Steele. LOC: California: Agoura.

Trail of Terror (1943 PRC) Texas Rangers. LOC: California: Corriganville.

Trail of the Arrow (1952 Monogram) Guy Madison. LOC: California: Rancho Placeritos; Walker Ranch.

Trail of the Lonesome Pine, The (1936 Paramount) Henry Fonda. LOC: California: Iverson Ranch; Paramount Ranch; Big Bear; Cedar Lake; I. S. Ranch.

Trail of the Mounties (1947 Screen Guild) Russell Hayden. LOC: California: Corriganville.

Trail of the Rustlers (1950 Columbia) Charles Starrett. LOC: California: Iverson Ranch; Columbia Ranch.

Trail of the Silver Spurs (1941 Monogram) Range Busters. LOC: California: Corriganville; Brandeis Ranch.

Trail of the Vigilantes (1940 Universal) Franchot Tone. LOC: California: Iverson Ranch; Corriganville; Walker Ranch; Lake Sherwood; Kernville; Lone Pine; Tuolumne County; Kennedy Meadow; Universal Studio backlot.

Trail of the Yukon (1949 Monogram) Kirby Grant. LOC: California: Big Bear; Cedar Lake.

Trail of Vengeance (1937 Republic) Johnny Mack Brown. LOC: California: Iverson Ranch.

Trail Riders (1942 Monogram) Range Busters. LOC: California: Walker Ranch; Jauregui Ranch.

Trail Street (1947 RKO) Randolph Scott. LOC: California: RKO Encino Ranch; Jauregui Ranch.

Trail to Gunsight (1944 Universal) Eddie Dew. LOC: California: Agoura.

Trail to Hope Rose, The (2004 Hallmark Entertainment) Lou Diamond Phillips. LOC: California: Paramount Ranch; Sable Ranch; Veluzat Motion Picture Ranch.

Trail to Laredo (1948 Columbia) Charles Starrett. LOC: California: Iverson Ranch; Providencia Ranch.

Trail to Mexico (1946 Monogram) Jimmy Wakely. LOC: California: Walker Ranch.

Trail to San Antone (1947 Republic) Gene Autry. LOC: California: Lone Pine; Anchor Ranch; Columbia Ranch; Deerwood Stock Farm.

Trail to Vengeance (1945 Universal) Kirby Grant. LOC: California: Corriganville; Agoura.

Trailin' Trouble (1930 Universal) Hoot Gibson. LOC: California: Iverson Ranch; Lone Pine.

Trailin' West (1936 Warner Bros) Dick Foran. LOC: California: Iverson Ranch; Burro Flats; Beale's Cut; Kernville.

Trailing Danger (1947 Monogram) Johnny Mack Brown. LOC: California: Iverson Ranch; Corriganville; Walker Ranch; Rancho Placeritos.

Trailing Double Trouble (1940 Monogram) Range Busters. LOC: California: Iverson Ranch; Brandeis Ranch; Rancho Placeritos.

Trailing North (1933 Monogram) Bob Steele. LOC: California: Kernville.

Trailing Trouble (1937 Grand National) Ken Maynard. LOC: California: Iverson Ranch; Brandeis Ranch.

Trails End (1949 Monogram) Johnny Mack Brown. LOC: California: Walker Ranch.

Trails of Adventure (1935 American) Buffalo Bill, Jr. LOST/MISSING.

Trails of Peril (1930 Big 4) Wally Wales. LOST/MISSING.

Trails of the Golden West (1931 Cosmos) Buffalo Bill, Jr. LOST/MISSING.

Trails of the Wild (1935 Ambassador) Kermit Maynard. LOC: California: Big Bear.

Train Robbers, The (1973 Warner Bros) John Wayne. LOC: MEXICO: Coahuila: Bilbao sand dunes; Durango: El Saltito waterfall; La Joya Ranch; Zacatecas: Sierra de Organos.

Train to Tombstone (1950 Lippert) Don Barry. LOC: California: Iverson Ranch; Nevada: Carson City; Carson Valley.

Traitor, The (1936 Puritan) Tim McCoy. LOC: California: Walker Ranch; Trem Carr Ranch.

Tramplers, The (1966 Embassy) Joseph Cotton. LOC: ITALY.

Trap on Cougar Mountain (1972 Sun International) Keith Larsen. LOC:

Trap, The (1966 Continental) Oliver Reed. LOC: CANADA: Bowen Island, British Columbia.

Trapped (1937 Columbia) Charles Starrett. LOC:

Traveling Saleslady, The (1950 Columbia) Joan Davis. LOC: California: Iverson Ranch.

Treachery Rides the Range (1936 Warner Bros) Dick Foran. LOC: California: Warner Bros Studio backlot.

Treason (1933 Columbia) Buck Jones. LOC: California: Paramount Ranch.

Treasure of Lost Canyon (1952 Universal) William Powell. LOC: California: McArthur Burney State Park; Universal Studio backlot.

Treasure of Pancho Villa, The (1955 RKO) Rory Calhoun. LOC: MEXICO: Guerrero: Taxco; Morelos: Cuernavaca.

Treasure of Ruby Hills (1955 Allied Artists) Zachary Scott. LOC: California: Iverson Ranch; Corriganville; Rancho Placeritos; Vasquez Rocks.
Treasure of Silver Lake, The (1965 Columbia) Lex Barker. LOC: CROATIA: Paklenica National Park; YUGOSLAVIA; Grobnik Polje; Plitvice.
Treasure of Tayopah (1974 Reina Prod) Rena Winters. LOC: Arizona: Rio Rico.
Treasure of the Aztecs (1965 Ccc/Filmkunst) Lex Barker. LOC: SPAIN: Barcelona; Monserrat; YUGOSLAVIA: Kravica Fortress; Orjen Passage.
Treasure of the Sierra Madre, The (1948 Warner Bros) Humphrey Bogart. LOC: California: Iverson Ranch; Kernville; Kelly's Rainbow Mine, Salmon Creek Falls area; Warner Bros Studio backlot; MEXICO: Durango: Santiago Papasquiaro; Guerrero: Acapulco; Michoacan: Ocurio; San Jose Purua; San Miguel Chichimequillas; San Pancho; Tamaulipas: Tampico, Plaza de la Libertad.
Trespasses (1986 XIT Prods./Saphiro Entertainment) Robert Kuhn. LOC: Texas: Bastrop.
Trial of Billy Jack, The (1974 Warner Bros) Tom Laughlin. LOC: Arizona: Canyon de Chelly; Old Tucson; Arizona/Utah: Monument Valley; New Mexico: Bandelier National Monument; J. W. Eaves Movie Ranch, Santa Fe; Santa Clara Pueblo.
Tribute to a Badman (1956 MGM) James Cagney. LOC: California: MGM backlot; Colorado: Ouray County.
Trigger Fingers (1939 Victory) Tim McCoy. LOC: California: Brandeis Ranch; Walker Ranch; Jauregui Ranch.
Trigger Fingers (1946 Monogram) Johnny Mack Brown. LOC: California: Walker Ranch.
Trigger Law (1944 Monogram) Hoot Gibson. LOC: California: Iverson Ranch.
Trigger Pals (1939 Grand National) Art Jarrett. LOC: California: Ranch01.
Trigger Smith (1939 Monogram) Jack Randall. LOC: California: Rancho Placeritos; Walker Ranch; Vasquez Rocks; Lake Los Angeles.
Trigger Tom (1936 Reliable) Tom Tyler. LOC: California: Frank LaSalle Ranch; Towsley Canyon; Big Bear.
Trigger Trail (1944 Universal) Rod Cameron. LOC: California: Iverson Ranch; Corriganville.
Trigger Tricks (1930 Universal) Hoot Gibson. LOC: California: Agoura.
Trigger Trio, The (1937 Republic) Three Mesquiteers. LOC: California: Kernville; Republic Studio backlot.
Trigger, Jr. (1950 Republic) Roy Rogers. LOC: California: Lake Los Angeles; Republic Studio backlot.
Triggerman (1948 Monogram) Johnny Mack Brown. LOC: California: Iverson Ranch; Walker Ranch; Rancho Placeritos; Bronson Canyon.
Triggerman (2009 DAP Italy) Terence Hill. LOC: New Mexico: Bonanza Creek Ranch, Santa Fe.
Trinity & Bambino: The Legend Lives On (1995 Rialto Film Trinidad

Film/Motion Picture) Heath Kizzier. LOC: SPAIN: Texas-Hollywood/Western town and Mexican set Almería.

Trinity Goes East (1998 Jef Films) Steve Tartalia. LOC:

Trinity is Still My Name (1972 Avco Embassy) Terence Hill. LOC: YUGOSLAVIA.

Triple Justice (1940 RKO) George O'Brien. LOC: California: Iverson Ranch; Deadman Point; Rabbit Dry Lake; RKO Encino Ranch.

Triumphs of a Man Called Horse (1984 Shunka Wakan Jensen Farley Pictures) Richard Harris. LOC: Montana: Cooke City Red Lodge.

Trooper Hook (1957 United Artists) Joel McCrea. LOC: California: Rancho Placeritos; Utah: Kanab; Kanab Movie Fort; Johnson Canyon; The Gap; Three Lakes.

Troopers Three (1930 Tiffany) Rex Lease. LOC: California: Monterey Presidio.

Trouble at Midnight (1937 Universal) Noah Beery, Jr. LOC: California: Universal backlot.

Trouble Busters (1933 Majestic) Jack Hoxie. LOC: California: Trem Carr Ranch; Agoura Ranch; Frank LaSalle Ranch.

Trouble in High Timber County (1980 ABC) Eddie Albert. LOC:

Trouble in Sundown (1939 RKO) George O'Brien. LOC: California: Walker Ranch; Jauregui Ranch.

Trouble in Texas (1937 Grand National) Tex Ritter. LOC: California: Rancho Placeritos.

Trouble on the Trail (1954 Allied Artists) Guy Madison. LOC: California: Walker Ranch; Rancho Placeritos.

Truce (2005 Top Knot Productions) Buck Taylor. LOC:

True Grit (1969 Paramount) John Wayne. LOC: California: Mammoth Lakes; Hot Springs; Colorado: Gunnison area; Ridgway; Montrose County; San Juan National Forest.

True Grit (1978 ABC–TV) Warren Oates. LOC: Colorado: Buckskin Joe; Ridgway; Pagosa Springs.

True Grit (2010 Paramount Pictures) Matt Damon. LOC: New Mexico: Buena Vista Ranch, Mora; Charles R Ranch; Española; Monastery Ranch, Pecos; Rowe Mesa; San Cristobal Ranch; Santa Clara Pueblo; Texas: Granger.

True Story of Jesse James, The (1957 20th Century Fox) Robert Wagner. LOC: California: Century Ranch; 20th Century Fox Studio backlot.

True Women (1997 Craig Anderson Productions) Dana Delany. LOC: Texas: Austin; Bastrop; McDade; Mission San José State and National Historic Site, San Antonio;

Trumpet Blows, The (1934 Paramount) George Raft. LOC: California: Paramount Ranch.

Trusted Outlaw, The (1937 Republic) Bob Steele. LOC: California: Iverson Ranch; Ralph M. Like Studio backlot.

Truth, The (1956 Wrather) Clayton Moore. LOC: California: Iverson Ranch; Corriganville.

Tucson (1949 20th Century Fox) Jimmy Lydon. LOC: California: Santa Monica.

Tucson Raiders (1944 Republic) Bill Elliott. LOC: California: Iverson Ranch.

Tulsa (1949 Eagle Lion) Robert Preston. LOC: Oklahoma: Davis; Tulsa; Sulphur Springs.

Tulsa Kid, The (1940 Republic) Donald Barry. LOC: California: Iverson Ranch; Corriganville.

Tumbledown Ranch in Arizona (1941 Monogram) Range Busters. LOC: California: Corriganville; Arizona: University of Arizona's annual rodeo.

Tumbleweed (1953 Universal) Audie Murphy. LOC: California: Vasquez Rocks; Red Rock Canyon; Death Valley; Universal Studio backlot.

Tumbleweed Tempo (1946 Universal) Spade Cooley. LOC:

Tumbleweed Trail (1942 PRC) Frontier Marshal. LOC: California: Corriganville; Jauregui Ranch; Rancho Placeritos.

Tumbleweed Trail (1946 PRC) Eddie Dean. LOC: California: Corriganville; Jauregui Ranch; Rancho Placeritos.

Tumbleweeds (1925 William S. Hart Prod) William S. Hart. LOC: California: Agoura Ranch; Lucerne Valley.

Tumbling Tumbleweeds (1935 Republic) Gene Autry. LOC: California: Trem Carr Ranch; Agoura Ranch; Deadman Point, Luzerne Valley; Republic Studio backlot.

Twenty Mule Team (1940 MGM) Wallace Beery. LOC: California: Death Valley.

Twilight in the Sierras (1950 Republic) Roy Rogers. LOC: California: Iverson Ranch; Corriganville.

Twilight on the Prairie (1944 Universal) Johnny Downs. LOC: California: Universal backlot.

Twilight on the Rio Grande (1947 Republic) Gene Autry. LOC: California: Antelope Valley; Republic Studio backlot.

Twilight on the Trail (1941 Paramount) William Boyd. LOC: California: Kernville.

Twinkle in God's Eye, The (1955 Republic) Mickey Rooney. LOC: California: Lake Los Angeles; Republic Studio backlot.

Twisted Rails (1934 Imperial) Jack Donovan. LOC: California: Santa Fe Train Station, Los Angeles.

Two Fisted Justice (1931 Monogram) Tom Tyler. LOC: California: Jauregui Ranch; Trem Carr Ranch.

Two Fisted Stranger (1946 Columbia) Charles Starrett. LOC: California: Corriganville.

Two Flags West (1950 20th Century Fox) Joseph Cotton. LOC: New Mexico: San Ildefonso Pueblo.

Two for Texas (1998 TNT) Kris Kristofferson. LOC: Texas: AustinCaddo LakeMarshallSan Antonio

Two from Rio Bravo, The (1963 Constantine-Jolly-Trio Films) Rod Cameron.

LOC: SPAIN: Almería.

Two Gun Caballero (1931 Imperial) Robert Frazer. LOST/MISSING.

Two Gun Ginsberg (1929 Radio) Nat Carr. LOC:

Two Gun Law (1937 Columbia) Charles Starrett. LOC: California: Iverson Ranch; Walker Ranch; Jauregui Ranch.

Two Gun Man from Harlem (1938 Merit Pictures, Inc.) Herb Jeffries. LOC: California.

Two Gun Man, The (1931 Tiffany) Ken Maynard. LOC: California: Ralph M. Like Studio backlot; Walker Ranch; Jauregui Ranch.

Two Gun Sheriff (1941 Republic) Don Barry. LOC: California: Iverson Ranch.

Two Gun Teacher, The (1954 Allied Artists) Guy Madison. LOC: California: Iverson Ranch; Rancho Placeritos; Walker Ranch.

Two Gun Troubadour (1939 Spectrum) Fred Scott. LOC: California: Jauregui Ranch.

Two Guns and a Badge (1954 Allied Artists) Wayne Morris. LOC: California: Iverson Ranch; Corriganville.

Two Guys from Texas (1948 Warner Bros) Dennis Morgan. LOC: California: Warner Bros. backlot.

Two in Revolt (1936 RKO) John Arledge. LOC: Arizona: Sedona.

Two Mules For Sister Sara (1970 Universal) Clint Eastwood. LOC: MEXICO: Morelos: Cuautla area; ex Hacienda de Coahuixtla; San Pedro Apatlaco; ex Hacienda Pantitlan San Nicolas, Oaxtepec; Jantetelco; Tlayacapan.

Two Rode Together (1961 Columbia) James Stewart. LOC: Texas: Alamo Village; Fort Clark; Del Rio.

Two-Fisted Justice (1943 Monogram) Range Busters. LOC: California: Corriganville.

Two-Fisted Law (1932 Columbia) Tim McCoy. LOC: California: Walker Ranch; Jauregui Ranch; Trem Carr Ranch.

Two-Fisted Rangers (1940 Columbia) Charles Starrett. LOC: California.

Two-Fisted Sheriff (1937 Columbia) Charles Starrett. LOC: California: Jauregui Ranch; Agoura; Columbia Ranch.

Two-Gun Justice (1938 Monogram) Tim McCoy. LOC: California: Brandeis Ranch.

Two-Gun Lady (1956 Associated Film Releasing Corp) Peggie Castle. LOC: California: Ingram Ranch.

Two-Gun Marshal (1953 Allied Artists) Guy Madison. LOC: California: Walker Ranch; Rancho Placeritos.

Ulzana's Raid (1972 Universal) Burt Lancaster. LOC: Arizona: Nogales; Sonoita Creek; Nevada: Valley of Fire State Park; Lake Mead.

Uncivil Warriors (1935 Columbia) Three Stooges. LOC: California: Columbia Ranch.

Unconquered (1948 Paramount) Gary Cooper. LOC: Idaho: Ashton; McCall; Pennsylvania: Cook National Forest.

Unconquered Bandit (1935 Reliable) Tom Tyler. LOC: California: Frank LaSalle Ranch.

Undefeated, The (1969 20th Century Fox) John Wayne. LOC: Louisiana: Baton Rogue; MEXICO: Durango: ex Hacienda La Ferreria de Flores; Zacatecas: Sierra de Organos.

Under a Texas Moon (1930 Warner Bros) Frank Fay. LOC: California: Red Rock Canyon; Palm Springs Canyon.

Under Arizona Skies (1946 Monogram) Johnny Mack Brown. LOC: California: Iverson Ranch; Rancho Placeritos.

Under California Stars (1948 Republic) Roy Rogers. LOC: California: Walker Ranch; Republic Studios; Republic Studio backlot.

Under Colorado Skies (1947 Republic) Monte Hale. LOC: California: Iverson Ranch; Walker Ranch; Republic Studio backlot.

Under Fiesta Stars (1941 Republic) Gene Autry. LOC: California: Iverson Ranch; Corriganville; Bronson Canyon; Republic Studio backlot.

Under Mexicali Stars (1950 Republic) Rex Allen. LOC: California: Lone Pine.

Under Montana Skies (1930 Amity) Kenneth Harlan. LOC: California: Universal Studio backlot; Ralph M. Like Studio backlot.

Under Nevada Skies (1946 Republic) Roy Rogers. LOC: California: Corriganville; French Ranch; Republic Studio backlot.

Under Strange Flags (1937 Crescent) Tom Keene. LOC: Arizona: Nogales.

Under Texas Skies (1930 Syndicate) Bob Custer. LOC: California: Frank LaSalle Ranch; Towsley Canyon.

Under Texas Skies (1940 Republic) Three Mesquiteers. LOC: California: Iverson Ranch; Corriganville; Republic Studio backlot.

Under the Cock-Eyed Moon (1930 Pathe) Bob Carney. LOC: Arizona.

Under the Pampas Moon (1935 Fox) Warner Baxter. LOC: California: Santa Anita Race Track; 25 miles west of Bakersfield.

Under the Tonto Rim (1933 Paramount) Kent Taylor. LOC: California: Paramount Ranch.

Under the Tonto Rim (1947 RKO) Tim Holt. LOC: California: Fairview Mountain, Apple Valley; Highway 18/Joshua Road Area, Apple Valley; RKO Encino Ranch.

Under Western Skies (1945 Universal) Noah Beery, Jr. LOC: California: Iverson Ranch; Burro Flats.

Under Western Stars (1938 Republic) Roy Rogers. LOC: California: Lake Sherwood; Tinemaha Dam; Lone Pine; Winnedumah Hotel, Independence; Republic Studio backlot.

Undercover Man (1936 Republic) Johnny Mack Brown. LOC: California: Iverson Ranch; Walker Ranch; Kernville; Kernville Movie Street.

Undercover Man (1942 United Artists) William Boyd. LOC: California: Iverson Ranch.

Undercover Men (1935 Dominion Motion Pictures) Charles Starrett. LOC:

Underground Rustlers (1941 Monogram) Range Busters. LOC: California: Iverson Ranch; Corriganville.

Undersea Kingdom, The (1936 Republic) Ray Corrigan. LOC: California: Iverson Ranch; Republic Studio backlot.

Undressed West, The (1964 J M Nercesian Prods) Tawny Angel. LOC:

Unexpected Guest (1947 United Artists) William Boyd. LOC: California: Lone Pine; Anchor Ranch.

Unforgiven (1992 Warner Bros) Clint Eastwood. LOC: California: Hetch Hetchy Junction Tuolumne County - CANADA: Alberta: BrooksDrumheller/badlandsHigh RiverLongview.

Unforgiven, The (1960 United Artists) Burt Lancaster. LOC: MEXICO: Durango: El Arenal; Guadiana Desert.

Union Pacific (1939 Paramount) Barbara Stanwyck. LOC: California: Bronson Canyon; Canoga Park; Iowa: Council Bluffs; Utah: Cedar City; Iron Springs.

Unknown Ranger, The (1936 Columbia) Bob Allen. LOC: California: Kernville.

Unknown Valley (1933 Columbia) Buck Jones. LOC: California: Iverson Ranch; Rabbit Dry Lake; Universal Studio backlot.

Unsinkable Molly Brown, The (1964 MGM) Debbie Reynolds. LOC: California: MGM backlot; Colorado: Cortez; Black Canyon of the Gunnison National Monument.

Untamed (1940 Paramount) Ray Milland. LOC: California: Big Bear; Cedar Lake; Lake Arrowhead.

Untamed Breed, The (1948 Columbia) Sonny Tufts. LOC: California: Iverson Ranch; Lone Pine.

Untamed Frontier (1952 Universal) Joseph Cotton. LOC: California: Agoura; Arizona: Douglas.

Untamed Heiress (1954 Republic) Donald Barry. LOC: California: Iverson Ranch.

Uphill All the Way (1985 New World Pictures) Burt Reynolds. LOC: Texas: Alamo Village Brackettville; Big Bend Ranch State Park; Lajitas/Mexican set; Texas State Railroad, Rusk-Palestine.

Utah (1945 Republic) Roy Rogers. LOC: California: Iverson Ranch; Agoura; Lone Pine; Chatsworth Train Station; Los Angeles Stock Yard.

Utah Blaine (1957 Columbia) Rory Calhoun. LOC: California: Angels Camp; Murphys; San Andreas; Columbia Ranch.

Utah Kid, The (1930 Tiffany) Rex Lease. LOC: California: Iverson Ranch.

Utah Kid, The (1944 Monogram) Hoot Gibson. LOC: California: Walker Ranch; Rancho Placeritos.

Utah Trail, The (1938 Grand National) Tex Ritter. LOC: California: Corriganville; Chatsworth Train Depot; Grand National Studio backlot.

Utah Wagon Train (1951 Republic) Rex Allen. LOC: California: Iverson Ranch; Burro Flats.

Vacation Days (1947 Monogram) Freddie Stewart. LOC: California: Rancho

Placeritos.

Valdez the Half Breed (1973 Dino de Laurentiis) Charles Bronson. LOC: SPAIN: Almeria.

Valerie (1957 United Artists) Sterling Hayden. LOC: California: Iverson Ranch.

Valiant Hombre, The (1949 United Artists) Duncan Renaldo. LOC: California: Iverson Ranch; Pioneertown.

Valley of Fear (1947 Monogram) Johnny Mack Brown. LOC: California: Walker Ranch.

Valley of Fire (1951 Columbia) Gene Autry. LOC: California: Lone Pine; Columbia Ranch.

Valley of Hunted Men (1942 Republic) Three Mesquiteers. LOC: California: Iverson Ranch; Corriganville; Lake Sherwood.

Valley of Terror (1937 Ambassador) Kermit Maynard. LOC: California: Brandeis Ranch.

Valley of the Giants (1938 Warner Bros) Wayne Morris. LOC: California: Eureka; Orick.

Valley of the Lawless (1936 Superior) Johnny Mack Brown. LOC: California: Warner Ranch.

Valley of the Sun (1942 RKO) Lucille Ball. LOC: California: RKO Encino Ranch; New Mexico: Taos.

Valley of Vanishing Men, The (1942 Columbia) Bill Elliott. LOC: California: Iverson Ranch; Rancho Placeritos.

Valley of Vengeance (1944 PRC) Buster Crabbe. LOC: California: Corriganville.

Valley of Wanted Men (1935 Ambassador) Frankie Darro. LOC: California: Big Bear.

Vampire Black: Trail of the Dead (2008 Light Source Films) Scott Shaw. LOC: California: Hollywood Los Angeles.

Vanishing American, The (1955 Republic) Scott Brady. LOC: California: Republic Studio backlot; Utah: Snow Canyon; Bloomington area; Berry Springs area.

Vanishing Frontier, The (1932 Paramount) Johnny Mack Brown. LOC: California: Paramount Ranch; Trem Carr Ranch.

Vanishing Legion, The (1931 Mascot) Harry Carey. LOC: California: Iverson Ranch; Bronson Canyon; Kernville; Old Kernville; Tec-Art Studio backlot.

Vanishing Men (1932 Monogram) Tom Tyler. LOST/MISSING.

Vanishing Outpost, The (1951 Western Adventure) Lash LaRue. LOC: California: Iverson Ranch.

Vanishing Riders, The (1935 Spectrum) Bill Cody. LOC: California: Brandeis Ranch; Walker Ranch; Ralph M. Like Studio backlot.

Vanishing Westerner, The (1950 Republic) Monte Hale. LOC: California: Iverson Ranch; Red Rock Canyon.

Vanquished, The (1953 Paramount) John Payne. LOC: California: Paramount backlot.

Variety News #171: Gaucho Fiesta (1948 Universal) Narrated by Ben Grauer. LOC:

Variety News #173: Call of the Canyon (1948 Universal) Narrated by Kenneth Banghart. LOC:

Variety Views #112: Canadian Patrol (1942 Universal) Narrated by Larry Elliott. LOC:

Variety Views #113: Western Whoopee (1942 Universal) Narrated by Howard Petrie. LOC:

Vengeance (1965 Crown) William Thourlby. LOC: California: Ingram Ranch; Berry/Bell Ranch.

Vengeance of Pancho Villa, The (1966 Lacy) John Ericson. LOC: SPAIN.

Vengeance of Rannah (1936 Reliable) Bob Custer. LOC: California: Kernville; Kernville Movie Street.

Vengeance of the West (1942 Columbia) Bill Elliott. LOC: California: Iverson Ranch.

Vengeance Trail (2006 Triple Dare Films) Jeff Dolan. LOC: California: Disney Golden Oak Ranch.

Vengeance Valley (1951 MGM) Burt Lancaster. LOC: California: MGM backlot; Colorado: Royal Gorge; Cañon City.

Vengeance Vow (1956 Wrather) Clayton Moore. LOC: California: Iverson Ranch; Corriganville.

Vera Cruz (1954 United Artists) Burt Lancaster. LOC: MEXICO: Mexico: ex Hacienda Molino de Flores; San Juan Teotihuacan; Mexico City, Chapultepec Castle; Morelos: ex Hacienda Cocoyoc; Tlayacapan.

Via Pony Express (1933 Majestic) Jack Hoxie. LOC: California: Beale's Cut; Palmdale.

Vigilante Force (1976 United Artists) Kris Kristofferson. LOC: California: Corriganville; Santa Susana Pass; RKO 40 Acres.

Vigilante Hideout (1950 Republic) Allan Lane. LOC: California: Iverson Ranch; Burro Flats.

Vigilante Terror (1953 Allied Artists) Bill Elliott. LOC: California: Iverson Ranch; Corriganville.

Vigilante, The (1947 Columbia) Ralph Byrd. LOC: California: Iverson Ranch; Corriganville; Walker Ranch; Jauregui Ranch; French Ranch; Lake Sherwood; Hoot Gibson Rodeo Arena, Saugus.

Vigilantes Are Coming, The (1936 Republic) Robert Livingston. LOC: California: Mission San Luis Rey; San Fernando Mission; Kernville; Republic Studio backlot.

Vigilantes of Boomtown (1947 Republic) Allan Lane. LOC: California: Iverson Ranch; Antelope Valley; Republic Studio backlot.

Vigilantes of Dodge City (1944 Republic) Bill Elliott. LOC: California: Iverson Ranch.

Vigilantes Return, The (1947 Universal) Jon Hall. LOC: California: Iverson Ranch; Universal Studio backlot.

Vigilantes Ride, The (1944 Columbia) Russell Hayden. LOC: California: Corriganville.

Villa Rides (1968 Paramount) Yul Brynner. LOC: SPAIN: Madrid area; Aranjuez; Avila; Colmenar Viejo; Navalcarnero; Titulcia; Rio Jarama; Villamanta; Escalona; El Casar de Talamanca.

Villa!! (1958 20th Century Fox) Brian Keith. LOC: MEXICO.

Villain, The (1979 Columbia) Kirk Douglas. LOC: California: Bronson Canyon; Arizona: Old Tucson; San Manuel; Rio Rico; Arizona/Utah: Monument Valley.

Violent Men, The (1955 Columbia) Glenn Ford. LOC: California: Lone Pine; Columbia Ranch.

Violent Saturday (1955 20th Century Fox) Victor Mature. LOC: Arizona: Bisbee.

Virgin Cowboy (1975 Cal Vista) John Armond. LOC: California: Bell/Berry Ranch; Corriganville

Virginia City (1940 Warner Bros) Errol Flynn. LOC: California: Lake Sherwood; Red Rock Canyon; Warner Ranch; Arizona: Sedona; Painted Desert.

Virginian, The (1929 Paramount) Gary Cooper. LOC: California: Paramount Ranch; Tuolumne County.

Virginian, The (1946 Paramount) Joel McCrea. LOC: California: Jauregui Ranch; Rancho Placeritos; Paramount Ranch; Kernville.

Virginian, The (1999 TNT) Bill Pullman. LOC: CANADA: Alberta: DrumhellerJohn Scott Ranch CalgaryLongview.

Viva Cisco Kid (1940 20th Century Fox) Cesar Romero. LOC: California: 20th Century Fox backlot; Arizona: Sedona.

Viva Villa! (1934 MGM) Wallace Beery. LOC: Texas: El Paso; MEXICO: Chihuahua: Jaurez; Hidalgo: Hacienda de Santiago Tetlapayac; Jalisco: Guadalajara: Mexico City.

Viva Zapata! (1952 20th Century Fox) Marlon Brando. LOC: California: Century Ranch; Warner Ranch; Colorado: Denver and Rio Grande Railroad; Porter; Texas: Roma; Dolores; San Ygnacio.

Voice of Hollywood #9 (1929 Tiffany) Ken Maynard. LOC: no exteriors.

Wackiest Wagon Train in the West, The (1976 Metromedia) Bob Denver. LOC: California: Iverson Ranch; 20th Century Fox backlot.

Waco (1952 Monogram) Bill Elliott. LOC: California: Iverson Ranch; Corriganville.

Waco (1966 Paramount) Howard Keel. LOC: California: Paramount Studio backlot.

Wagon Master, The (1929 Universal) Ken Maynard. LOC: California: Lone Pine.

Wagon Team (1952 Columbia) Gene Autry. LOC: California: Iverson Ranch; Corriganville; Pioneertown; Columbia Ranch.

Wagon Tracks West (1943 Republic) Bill Elliott. LOC: California: Iverson Ranch; Bronson Canyon; Lake Sherwood.

Wagon Trail (1935 Ajay Films) Harry Carey. LOC: California: Walker Ranch;

Jauregui Ranch; Ralph M. Like Studio backlot.

Wagon Train (1940 RKO) Tim Holt. LOC: Utah: Kanab Canyon; Paria.

Wagon Wheels (1934 Paramount) Randolph Scott. LOC: California: Tuolumne County; Sonora.

Wagon Wheels West (1943 Warner Bros) Robert Shayne. LOC: California.

Wagon Wheels Westward (1945 Republic) Bill Elliott. LOC: California: Iverson Ranch; Bronson Canyon.

Wagonmaster (1950 RKO) Ben Johnson. LOC: Utah: Moab; Fisher Canyon; Professor Valley; Colorado River; Spanish Valley.

Wagons East (1994 TriStar Pictures) John Kandy. LOC: MEXICO: Durango: Chupaderos; Zacatecas: Sierra de Organos.

Wagons West (1952 Monogram) Rod Cameron. LOC: California: Corriganville; Burro Flats.

Wagons Westward (1940 Republic) Chester Morris. LOC: California: Iverson Ranch; Lone Pine.

Walk LIke a Dragon (1960 Paramount) Jack Lord. LOC: California: Paramount Studio backlot.

Walk Tall (1960 20th Century Fox) Williard Parker. LOC: California: Cedar Lake; San Bernardino National Forest; Tennessee.

Walk the Proud Land (1956 Universal) Audie Murphy. LOC: Arizona: Bear Canyon; Old Tucson; Cortaro.

Walker (2009 Universal) Ed Harris. LOC: Arizona: Old Tucson; NICARAGUA: Granada; San Juan del Sur.

Walking Hills, The (1949 Columbia) Randolph Scott. LOC: California: Lone Pine; Death Valley; California/MEXICO: Calexico/Mexicali.

Walking Thunder (1997 Majestic Entertainment Group/Rated Geel) James Read. LOC: Utah: Mount Timpanogos; Alpine.

Wall Street Cowboy (1939 Republic) Roy Rogers. LOC: California: Iverson Ranch; Red Rock Canyon; Towsley Canyon; Republic Studio backlot.

Wanda Nevada (1979 Pando/United Artists) Brooke Shields. LOC: Arizona: Glen Canyon National Recreation Area; Grand Canyon; Prescott; Flagstaff; Lee's Ferry.

Wanderer of the Wasteland (1935 Paramount) Dean Jagger. LOST/MISSING.

Wanderer of the Wasteland (1945 RKO) James Warren. LOC: California: Lone Pine.

Wanderers of the West (1941 Monogram) Tom Keene. LOC: California: Iverson Ranch; Burro Flats; Arizona: Prescott; Watson Lake.

Wanted: Dead or Alive (1951 Monogram) Whip Wilson. LOC: California: Iverson Ranch.

Wanted: That Sundance Woman (1976 20th Century Fox) Katharine Ross. LOC: Arizona: Old Tucson; San Manuel.

Wanted: Undead or Alive (2007 Dark Lot Entertainment/Media 8 Entertainment)

James Denton. LOC: New Mexico: Bonanza Creek Ranch Santa Fe; Millennium Turquoise Mine Santa Fe; Waldo Canyon; White Rock Overlook Los Alamos.

War Arrow (1954 Universal) Jeff Chandler. LOC: California: Universal Studio backlot; Arizona: Sonoita; San Rafael Valley.

War Drums (1957 United Artists) Lex Barker. LOC: Utah: Kanab Canyon; Johnson Canyon; John Canyon Movie Sets; Turkey Crossing, Kanab Creek.

War of the Wildcats (1943 Republic) John Wayne. LOC: California: Taft; Arizona: Kaibab National Forest; Utah: Kanab; Paria.

War on the Range (1933 Freuler/Monarch) Tom Tyler. LOC: California: Agoura.

War Paint (1953 United Artists) Robert Stack. LOC: California: Death Valley.

War Party (1965 20th Century Fox) Davey Davison. LOC: California: Iverson Ranch; Lone Pine.

War Party (1989 TriStar Pictures) Billy Wirth. LOC: Montana: Choreau; Glacier National Park.

War Wagon, The (1967 Universal) John Wayne. LOC: California: Universal Studios backlot; MEXICO: Durango: Chupaderos; Zacatecas: Sierra de Organos.

Warden of Red Rock (2001 Viacom) James Caan. LOC: MEXICO: Durango: Chupaderos; Hacienda La Providencia; Ojuela, Puente de Ojuela.

Warlock (1959 20th Century Fox) Henry Fonda. LOC: California: 20th Century Fox Studio backlot; Utah: Arches National Park; Moab; Professor Valley; Dead Horse Point State Park; Kings Bottom.

Warpath (1951 Paramount) Edmond O'Brien. LOC: Montana: Billings; Broadview; Laurel; Pryor.

Warrior Spirit (1994 Trimark Pictures) Lukas Haas. LOC: CANADA: Yukon Territory.

Water Rustlers (1939 Grand National) Dave O'Brien. LOC: California: Lone Pine; Arizona: Mesa.

Waterhole #3 (1967 Paramount) James Coburn. LOC: California: Janss Janss Conejo Ranch; Red Rock Canyon; Dolomite; Cerro Gordo; Owens Dry Lake; Paramount Studio backlot.

Way Down South (1939 RKO) Bobby Breen. LOC: California: Uplifters Club; Providencia Ranch; RKO Encino Ranch.

Way of a Gaucho (1952 20th Century Fox) Rory Calhoun) Argentina; Argentine Pampas.

Way of the West, The (1934 Superior) Wally Wales. LOC: California: Agoura Ranch; Ralph M. Like Studio backlot.

Way Out West (1930 MGM) William Haines. LOC: New Mexico: Ácoma Pueblo; Laguna Pueblo.

Way Out West (1937 MGM) Laurel & Hardy. LOC: California: Trem Carr Ranch; Lake Sherwood; Hal Roach Ranch.

Way to the Gold, The (1957 20th Century Fox) Jeffrey Hunter. LOC: Arizona: Florence; Phoenix; Glendale; Nevada: Lake Mead; Hoover Dam.

Way Up Thar (1935 Educational) Joan Davis. LOC: no exteriors
Way West, The (1967 United Artists) Kirk Douglas. LOC: Oregon: Crooked River Gorge; Eugene; Bend; Burn; Chimney Rock; Ft. Rock.
Webb Pierce and His Wanderin' Boys (1955 Universal) Webb Pierce. LOC:
Welcome to Blood City (1977 Famous Players) Jack Palance. LOC: CANADA: Kleinberg, Ontario.
Welcome to Hard Times (1967 MGM) Henry Fonda. LOC: California: Janss Janss Conejo Ranch.
Wells Fargo (1937 Paramount) Joel McCrea. LOC: California: Paramount Ranch; Kernville; Napa Valley; Angels Camp; Columbia; Chico; Sonora; Parrott's Ferry.
Wells Fargo Days (1944 Warner Bros) Dennis Moore. LOC: California: Brandeis Ranch.
Wells Fargo Gunmaster (1951 Republic) Allan Lane. LOC: California: Iverson Ranch; Walker Ranch.
West Is Still Wild/Mulefeathers, The (1977 Monarch) Rory Calhoun. LOC: California: Paramount Ranch.
West of Abilene (1940 Columbia) Charles Starrett. LOC: California: Columbia Ranch
West of Broadway (1931 MGM) John Gilbert. LOC: California: Tejon Ranch
West of Carson City (1940 Universal) Johnny Mack Brown. LOC: California: Iverson Ranch; Agoura.
West of Cheyenne (1931 Syndicate) Tom Tyler. LOC: California: Walker Ranch; Jauregui Ranch; Ralph M. Like Studio backlot.
West of Cheyenne (1938 Columbia) Charles Starrett. LOC: California: Agoura Ranch; Jauregui Ranch.
West of Cimarron (1941 Republic) Three Mesquiteers. LOC: California: Iverson Ranch; Agoura.
West of Dodge City (1947 Columbia) Charles Starrett. LOC: California: Iverson Ranch; Columbia Ranch.
West of Eldorado (1949 Monogram) Johnny Mack Brown. LOC: California: Rancho Placeritos; Walker Ranch.
West of Laramie (1949 Universal) Tex Williams. LOC:
West of Nevada (1936 Colony) Rex Bell. LOC: California: Lone Pine.
West of Pinto Basin (1940 Monogram) Range Busters. LOC: California: Corriganville; Rancho Placeritos.
West of Rainbow's End (1938 Monogram) Tim McCoy. LOC: California: Walker Ranch; Towsley Canyon.
West of Sonora (1948 Columbia) Charles Starrett. LOC: California: Iverson Ranch; Columbia Ranch.
West of Texas (1943 PRC) Texas Rangers. LOC: California: Iverson Ranch; Corriganville.
West of the Alamo (1946 Monogram) Jimmy Wakely. LOC: California: Walker

Ranch.

West of the Brazos (1950 Lippert) Jimmy Ellison. LOC: California: Iverson Ranch.

West of the Divide (1934 Monogram) John Wayne. LOC: California: Trem Carr Ranch; Jauregui Ranch.

West of the Law (1934 Imperial) Wally Wales. LOC: California: Antelope Valley.

West of the Law (1942 Monogram) Rough Riders. LOC: California: Walker Ranch; Rancho Placeritos.

West of the Pecos (1935 RKO) Richard Dix) LOST/MISSING/UNAVAILABLE.

West of the Pecos (1945 RKO) Robert Mitchum. LOC: California: Lone Pine.

West of the Rio Grande (1944 Monogram) Johnny Mack Brown. LOC: California: Walker Ranch.

West of the Rockies (1929 J Charles Davis Prod) Art Mix. LOST/MISSING.

West of the Rockies (1941 Warner Bros) Richard Travis. UNAVAILABLE.

West of the Santa Fe (1938 Columbia) Charles Starrett. LOC: California: Columbia Ranch.

West of Thunder (2012 Button and Reel Ent) Dan Davies. LOC: California: Caravan West Ranch; Colorado: Denver; Wisconsin: Hortonville; Stonefield Village, Cassville.

West of Tombstone (1942 Columbia) Charles Starrett. LOC: California: Iverson Ranch; Brandeis Ranch.

West of Wyoming (1950 Monogram) Johnny Mack Brown. LOC: California: Iverson Ranch; Walker Ranch.

West on Parade (1934 Reliable) Dennis Moore. LOC: California: Mentryville; Pico Canyon; Frank LaSalle Ranch.

West to Glory (1947 PRC) Eddie Dean. LOC: California: Iverson Ranch.

Westbound (1959 Warner Bros) Randolph Scott. LOC: California: Warner Ranch; Warner Bros Studio backlot.

Westbound Mail (1937 Columbia) Charles Starrett. LOC: California: Columbia Ranch.

Westbound Stage (1939 Monogram) Tex Ritter. LOC: Utah: Cave Lake; Kanab.

Western Caravans (1939 Columbia) Charles Starrett. LOC: California: Iverson Ranch; Agoura.

Western Code, The (1932 Columbia) Tim McCoy. LOC: California: El Escorpion Ranch; Trem Carr Ranch.

Western Courage (1935 Columbia) Ken Maynard. LOC: California: Iverson Ranch; Trem Carr Ranch.

Western Courage (1950 Universal) Tex Williams. LOC:

Western Cyclone (1943 PRC) Buster Crabbe. LOC: California: Iverson Ranch.

Western Frontier (1935 Columbia) Ken Maynard. LOC: California: Trem Carr Ranch; Lone Pine.

Western Gold (1937 20th Century Fox) Smith Ballew. LOC: California: Kernville; Kernville Movie Street; Lone Pine.

Western Heritage (1948 RKO) Tim Holt. LOC: California: Lone Pine; RKO Encino Ranch.

Western Jamboree (1938 Republic) Gene Autry. LOC: California: Iverson Ranch; Bronson Canyon.

Western Justice (1935 Commodore) Bob Steele. LOC: California: Kernville.

Western Knights (1930 Educational) Eddie Lambert. LOC: California: Paramount Ranch.

Western Mail (1942 Monogram) Tom Keene. LOC: California: Walker Ranch; Rancho Placeritos.

Western Pacific Agent (1950 Lippert) Robert Lowery. LOC: California: Feather River.

Western Racketeers (1935 Aywon) Bill Cody. LOC: California: Towsley Canyon; Idylwild.

Western Renegades (1949 Monogram) Johnny Mack Brown. LOC: California: Walker Ranch.

Western Romance (1930 Syndicate) Jack Hoxie. LOST/MISSING.

Western Trails (1938 Universal) Bob Baker. LOC: California: Iverson Ranch; Brandeis Ranch; Idyllwild; Universal Studio backlot.

Western Union (1941 20th Century Fox) Robert Young. LOC: California: 20th Century Fox Studio backlot; Arizona: House Rock Valley; Utah: The Gap; Paria; Johnson Canyon; Cedar City; Zion National Park.

Western Welcome, A (1938 RKO) Ray Whitley). LOC:

Westerner, The (1934 Columbia) Tim McCoy. LOC: California: Walker Ranch; Jauregui Ranch; Trem Carr Ranch.

Westerner, The (1940 United Artists) Gary Cooper. LOC: Arizona: Tucson, Canoa Ranch.

Westward Bound (1931 Syndicate) Buffalo Bill Jr. LOC: California: Jauregui Ranch; Walker Ranch.

Westward Bound (1944 Monogram) Trail Blazers. LOC: California: Corriganville; Rancho Placeritos.

Westward Ho (1935 Republic) John Wayne. LOC: California: Lone Pine; Owens Dry Lake.

Westward Ho the Wagons! (1957 Buena Vista) Fess Parker. LOC: California: Janss Conejo Ranch.

Westward Ho! (1942 Republic) Three Mesquiteers. LOC: California: Iverson Ranch.

Westward Ho-Hum (1941 RKO) Edgar Kennedy. LOC: California: RKO Encino Ranch.

Westward the Women (1952 MGM) Robert Taylor. LOC: California: Mojave Desert; Death Valley; Utah: Kanab Canyon; The Gap; William Mackelprang Ranch Movie Sets; Paria; Surprise Valley.

Westward Trail, The (1948 Eagle Lion) Eddie Dean. LOC: California: Iverson

Ranch.

Westworld (1973 MGM) Yul Brynner. LOC: California: Warner Bros. backlot; Red Rock Canyon; Harold Lloyd Estate.

Wheels of Destiny (1934 Universal) Ken Maynard. LOC: California: Lone Pine; Miller and Lux Ranch.

When a Man Rides Alone (1933 Freuler/Monarch) Tom Tyler. LOC: California: Frank LaSalle Ranch; Towsley Canyon; Newhall.

When a Man Sees Red (1934 Universal) Buck Jones. LOC: California: Red Rock Canyon; Kernville.

When a Man's a Man (1935 Fox) George O'Brien. LOC: California: Vasquez Rocks; Utah: Snow Canyon; St. George; Ivins Bench; Ivins Reservoir.

When Lightning Strikes (1934 Regal) Frances X. Bushman Jr. LOC:

When the Daltons Rode (1940 Universal) Randolph Scott. LOC: California: Iverson Ranch; Tuolumne County; Universal Studio backlot.

When the Legends Die (1972 20th Century Fox) Richard Widmark. LOC: Colorado: Durango; Ignacio; New Mexico: Farmington.

When the Redskins Rode (1951 Columbia) Jon Hall. LOC: California: Corriganville; Columbia Ranch.

Where the Buffalo Roam (1938 Monogram) Tex Ritter. LOC: California: Lone Pine; Rancho Placeritos.

Where the Hell's That Gold?! (1988 Willie Nelson Productions) Willie Nelson. LOC: Colorado: Cumbres and Toltec Scenic RailroadGrand Sand Dunes National Monument Alamosa - New Mexico: J.W. Eaves Movie Ranch/Mexican set Santa Fe.

Where the North Begins (1947 Screen Guild) Russell Hayden. LOC: California: Corriganville.

Where the West Begins (1938 Monogram) Jack Randall. LOC: California: Brandeis Ranch.

Where Trails Divide (1937 Monogram) Tom Keene. LOC: California: Walker Ranch; Rancho Placeritos; Red Rock Canyon; Death Valley.

Where Trails End (1942 Monogram) Tom Keene. LOC: California: Walker Ranch; Jauregui Ranch.

Whirlwind (1951 Columbia) Gene Autry. LOC: California: Pioneertown; Columbia Ranch.

Whirlwind Horseman (1938 Grand National) Ken Maynard. LOC: California: Brandeis Ranch.

Whirlwind Raiders (1948 Columbia) Charles Starrett. LOC: California: Corriganville; Columbia Ranch.

Whirlwind Rider, The (1935 American) Buffalo Bill Jr. LOC: California: Walker Ranch.

Whirlwind, The (1933 Columbia) Tim McCoy. LOC: California: Trem Carr Ranch.

Whispering Skull, The (1944 PRC) Texas Rangers. LOC: California: Corriganville.

Whispering Smith (1949 Paramount) Alan Ladd. LOC: California: Vasquez Rocks; Tuolumne County; Paramount Studio backlot.

Whispering Smith Speaks (1935 20th Century Fox) George O'Brien. LOC: California: Fillmore to Saugus Railroad.

Whistlin' Dan (1932 Tiffany) Ken Maynard. LOC: California: Iverson Ranch; Vasquez Rocks; Trem Carr Ranch.

Whistling Bullets (1937 Ambassador) Kermit Maynard. LOC: California: Walker Ranch; Jauregui Ranch.

Whistling Hills (1951 Monogram) Johnny Mack Brown. LOC: California: Iverson Ranch.

White Apache (1987 Beatrice Films/Multivideo) Sebastian Harrison. LOC: SPAIN: Rancho Leone/Western set Almería; Texas-Hollywood/Western town Almería; La Pedriza Manzanares El Real, Madrid.

White Buffalo, The (1977 United Artists) Charles Bronson) Colorado: Buckskin Joe; Custer and Fremont Counties; New Mexico: Chama; Cumbres and Toltec Scenic Railroad.

White Comanche (1968 International Producers Corp) Joseph Cotton. LOC: SPAIN: Colmenar Viejo.

White Eagle (1932 Columbia) Buck Jones. LOC: California: Paramount Ranch.

White Eagle (1941 Columbia) Buck Jones. LOC: California: Sequoia National Park.

White Fang (1991 Buena Vista) Klaus Maria Brandauer. LOC: Alaska: Haines; Skagway.

White Fang II: Myth of the White Wolf (1994 Buena Vista) Scott Bairstow. LOC: Colorado: Aspen. CANADA: British Columbia: Bordertown/Western town Maple Ridge, Vancouver; Squamish River North of Vancouver; Whistler Hope.

White Feather (1955 20th Century Fox) Robert Wagner. LOC: MEXICO: Durango: ex Hacienda La Ferreria de Flores.

White Hell (2006 Stefano Jacurti Productions) Stefano Jacurti. LOC: ITALY: Assergi; Campo Felice Lucoli; Campo Imperatore, Parco Nazionale del Gran Sasso Abruzzo.

White Outlaw, The (1929 J. Charles Davis Prod) Art Acord. LOC: California: Lone Pine.

White Renegade (1931 Artclass) Tom Santschi. LOC: New Mexico: Artesia; Carlsbad Caverns National Park; Hagerman; Roswell, Ruidoso.

White Squaw, The (1956 Columbia) David Brian. LOC: California: Iverson Ranch; Vasquez Rocks.

White Water Sam (1979 Monterey Home Video) Keith Larsen. LOC: Colorado: Wyoming.

White Wolves II: Legend of the Wild (1995 Concorde-New Horizons) Jeremy London. LOC: Montana; Wyoming: Yellowstone National Park.

Who Killed Johnny R? (1966 Ccc/Filmkunst) Lex Barker. LOC: SPAIN: Aragón,

Cataluña.

Whoopee (1930 United Artists) Eddie Cantor. LOC: California: Palm Springs.

Whoops, I'm an Indian (1936 Columbia) Three Stooges. LOC: California: Franklin Canyon Reservoir.

Wichita (1955 Allied Artists) Joel McCrea. LOC: California: Rancho Placeritos; Janss Janss Conejo Ranch; Tuolumne County.

Wicked Die Slow, The (1968 Canon Releasing) Gary Allen) New Jersey.

Wicked Wicked West, The (1998 BBC Films) Kelly McGillis. LOC: CANADA: Saskatchewan.

Wide Open Spaces, The (1931 RKO) Ned Sparks. LOC: Warner Bros backlot.

Wide Open Town (1941 Paramount) William Boyd. LOC: California: 20th Century Fox backlot; Lone Pine; Laws Train Depot

Wild and the Innocent, The (1959 Universal) Audie Murphy. LOC: California: Big Bear; Universal Studio backlot.

Wild and Wooly (1978 ABC-TV) Doug McClure. LOC: Arizona: Old Tucson.

Wild Beauty (1946 Universal) Don Porter. LOC: California: Iverson Movie Ranch; Red Rock Canyon.

Wild Bill (1995 United Artists/MGM) Jeff Bridges. LOC: California: Angeles National ForestBig Sky Ranch Simi ValleyMelody Ranch Newhall.

Wild Bill Hickok Rides (1942 Warner Bros) Bruce Cabot. LOC: California: Iverson Ranch.

Wild Brian Kent (1936 Principal/RKO Radio) Ralph Bellamy. LOC: California: Paso Robles; Clarence Hillman Ranch; Templeton; Cottage Hotel in Paso Robles.

Wild Bunch, The (1969 Warner Bros) William Holden. LOC: MEXICO: Coahuila: Parras; El Durazno; Rio Nazas; Bilbao sand dunes; Durango: La Goma; Comarca Lagunera.

Wild Country (1947 PRC) Eddie Dean. LOC: California: Corriganville.

Wild Country, The (1971 Buena Vista) Steve Forrest. LOC: Wyoming: Hunter Hereford Ranch; Curtis Canyon, Jackson Hole; Kelly; DuBois; Brooks Lake.

Wild Dakotas (1956 Associated) Bill Williams. LOC: California: Iverson Ranch.

Wild Frontier, The (1947 Republic) Allan Lane. LOC: California: Iverson Ranch.

Wild Gals of the Naked West (1962 Films Pacifica) Sammy Gilbert. LOC: California: Ingram Ranch.

Wild Geese Calling (1941 20th Century Fox) Henry Fonda. LOC: California: Big Bear; Lake Arrowhead.

Wild Girl (1932 Fox) Charles Farrell. LOC: California: Sequoia National Park.

Wild Gold (1934 Fox) John Boles. LOC: California: Iverson Ranch; Kernville.

Wild Harvest (1947 Paramount) Alan Ladd. LOC: Florida: Homestead.

Wild Hearts (2006 Hallmark Channel) Richard Thomas. LOC: California: Bronson Canyon HollywoodHidden Valley.

Wild Heritage (1959 Universal) Will Rogers, Jr. LOC: California: Lasky Mesa; Universal Studio backlot.

Wild Horse (1931 Allied) Hoot Gibson. LOC: California: Hoot Gibson Rodeo Arena; Frank LaSalle Ranch; Towsley Canyon.

Wild Horse Ambush (1952 Republic) Michael Chapin. LOC: California: Iverson Ranch.

Wild Horse Canyon (1938 Monogram) Jack Randall. LOC: California: Walker Ranch; Jauregui Ranch.

Wild Horse Hank (1979 Film Consortium of Canada) Linda Blair. LOC: CANADA: Alberta; Dinosaur Provincial Park; Waterton Lakes National Park.

Wild Horse Mesa (1932 Paramount) Randolph Scott. LOC: California: Paramount Ranch; Vasquez Rocks; Arizona: Flagstaff.

Wild Horse Mesa (1947 RKO) Tim Holt. LOC: California: Lone Pine; RKO Encino Ranch.

Wild Horse Phantom (1944 PRC) Buster Crabbe. LOC: California: Iverson Ranch; Corriganville.

Wild Horse Range (1940 Monogram) Jack Randall. LOC: California: Walker Ranch.

Wild Horse Rodeo (1937 Republic) Three Mesquiteers. LOC: California: Lone Pine; Republic Studio backlot.

Wild Horse Round-up (1936 Ambassador) Kermit Maynard. LOC: California: Iverson Ranch.

Wild Horse Rustlers (1943 PRC) Bob Livingston. LOC: California: Iverson Ranch.

Wild Horse Stampede (1943 Monogram) Trail Blazers. LOC: California: Corriganville; Rancho Placeritos.

Wild Horse Valley (1940 Metropolitan) Bob Steele. LOC: California: Walker Ranch.

Wild Horses (1984 CBS) Kenny Rogers. LOC: Wyoming: Sheridan.

Wild Horses (1984 Satori Entertainment) Keith Aberdein.) New Zealand: Tongariro National Park.

Wild Mustang (1935 Ajay Films) Harry Carey. LOC: California: Walker Ranch; Jauregui Ranch; Ralph M. Like Studio backlot.

Wild North, The (1952 MGM) Stewart Granger. LOC: Idaho: Sun Valley; Lewiston; Pierce; Reubens; Selway River; Wyoming: Jackson Hole; Jenny Lake; String Lake.

Wild Pony, The (1983 Huntington Films) Art Hindle. LOC: CANADA.

Wild Rovers (1971 MGM) William Holden. LOC: Arizona: Old Tucson; Sedona; Hale Ranch, Patagonia; San Rafael Valley; San Rafael Ranch; Flagstaff; Arizona/Utah: Monument Valley; Utah: Arches National Park; Professor Valley.

Wild Seven (2006 Beat Pirate Films) Robert Loggia. LOC: Arizona: Apacheland Apache JunctionPhoenixScottsdale.

Wild Stallion (1952 Monogram) Ben Johnson. LOC: California: Iverson Ranch; Corriganville.

Wild Times (1980 Golden Circle) Sam Elliott. LOC: New Mexico: Bonanza Creek Ranch Santa FeEl Rancho de las Golondrinas Santa Fe - J.W. Eaves Movie Ranch/Mexican set Santa Fe.

Wild Waters (1935 Imperial) David Sharpe. LOC: California: Pacoima Dam.

Wild West (1946 PRC) Eddie Dean. LOC: California: Iverson Ranch; Corriganville; Rancho Placeritos.

Wild West Days (1937 Universal) Johnny Mack Brown. LOC: California: Vasquez Rocks; Kernville.

Wild West Whoopee (1931 Allied) Jack Perrin. LOST/MISSING.

Wild Westerners, The (1962 Columbia) James Philbrook. LOC: California: Iverson Ranch; Lake Sherwood.

Wild Wild West (1999 Warner Bros) Kevin Kline. LOC: California: Disney's Golden Oak Ranch; Sacramento/Yolo Shortline; Vasquez Rocks; Warner Bros backlot; Arizona: Monument Valley; Idaho: Camas Prairie Railroad, Lewiston; New Mexico: Cook Ranch/Cerro Pelon Ranch; Galisteo; Río Chama.

Wild Wild West Revisited, The (1979 CBS-TV) Robert Conrad. LOC: California: Republic Studio backlot; Arizona: Old Tucson.

Wild Women of Chastity Gulch, The (1982 ABC) Priscilla Barnes. LOC: California: Century Ranch; Warner Bros Studio backlot.

Wildcat of Tucson (1940 Columbia) Bill Elliott. LOC: California: Iverson Ranch.

Wildcat Saunders (1936 Atlantic) Jack Perrin. LOC: California: Jauregui Ranch.

Wildcat Trooper (1936 Ambassador) Kermit Maynard. LOC: California: Big Bear.

Wilderness Mail (1935 Ambassador) Kermit Maynard. LOC: California: Big Bear.

Wildfire, the Story of a Horse (1945 Screen Guild) Bob Steele. LOC: California: Corriganville; Rancho Placeritos.

Wildside (1985 ABC) William Smith. LOC: California: Disney Studio backlot/Western street Burbank; Disney's Golden Oak Ranch Placerita Canyon, Newhall.

Will Penny (1968 Paramount) Charlton Heston. LOC: California: Bishop; Inyo National Forest; James L. C. Sherwin Ranch.

Winchester '73 (1950 Universal) James Stewart. LOC: California: Universal Studio backlot; Arizona: Old Tucson; Cortaro; Empire Ranch, Sonoita; Rain Valley.

Winchester '73 (1967 Universal-TV) Tom Tryon. LOC: Arizona: Old Tucson.

Wind River (1998 Family Movie Partners/High Voltage Entertainment) Blake Heron. LOC: Utah: Park City.

Wind Walker (1981 Pacific International Enterprises) Trevor Howard. LOC: Utah: Mirror Lake; Wasatch Mountains east of Provo.

Winds of Autumn, The (1976 Howco-International) Jack Elam. LOC: Montana: Kalispell.

Winds of the Wasteland (1936 Republic) John Wayne. LOC: California: Brandeis Ranch; Agoura Ranch; Republic Studio backlot.

Wings of Chance (1961 Universal) James Brown. LOC: CANADA: Edmonton, Alberta; Jasper National Park.

Wings of the Hawk (1953 Universal) Van Heflin. LOC: California: Burro Flats; Universal Studio backlot.

Winners of the West (1940 Universal) Dick Foran. LOC: California: Agoura; Universal Studio backlot.

Winnetou and Shatterhand in the Valley of Death (1968 CCC/Filmkunst) Lex Barker. LOC: Arizona: Grand Canyon; Yugoslavia: Roski Falls; Zrmanja Canyon.

Winnetous Rückkehr (1998 Regina Ziegler Filmproduktion)) Pierre Brice. LOC: SPAIN: Texas-Hollywood/Western town AlmeríaLa Calahorra Railroad east of Guadix, Granada province.

Winning of the West (1953 Columbia) Gene Autry. LOC: California: Iverson Ranch; Pioneertown; Lone Pine; Columbia Ranch.

Winterhawk (1976 Howco International) Leif Erikson. LOC: Colorado: Durango; Montana: Kalispell.

Wistful Widow of Wagon Gap, The (1947 Universal) Abbott & Costello. LOC: California: Iverson Ranch; Universal Studio backlot.

Without Honor (1932 Weiss) Harry Carey. LOC: California: Kernville; Kernville Movie Street.

Wolf Call (1939 Monogram) John Carroll. LOC: California: Big Bear.

Wolf Dog (1958 Regal Films) Jim Davis. LOC: CANADA: Markdale, Ontario.

Wolf Hunters, The (1949 Monogram) Kirby Grant. LOC: California: Big Bear; Cedar Lake.

Wolf Riders (1935 Reliable) Jack Perrin. LOC: California: Frank LaSalle Ranch.

Wolf Song (1929 Paramount) Gary Cooper. LOC: California: Paramount Ranch; Sierra Nevada; Mammoth Lakes.

Wolves of the Range (1943 PRC) Bob Livingston. LOC: California: Corriganville; Rancho Placeritos.

Woman of the North Country (1952 Republic) Ruth Hussey. LOC: California: MGM backlot; Minnesota: Frazier National Park.

Woman of the Town, The (1943 United Artists) Claire Trevor. LOC: California: Corriganville; California Studio backlot.

Woman They Almost Lynched, The (1953 Republic) Joan Leslie. LOC: California: Lone Pine.

Wonderful Country, The (1959 United Artists) Robert Mitchum. LOC: MEXICO: Durango; Mexico: San Miguel de Allende; La Punta. Guanajuato.

Wooden Gun, The (2002 Providence Productions) Jon Jacobs. LOC: Wyoming.

Wooly Boys (2001 PFG Entertainment) Peter Fonda. LOC: Minnesota: Minneapolis; Woodbury; North Dakota: Medora.

Wrangler's Roost (1941 Monogram) Range Busters. LOC: California: Corriganville.

Wrath of God, The (1972 MGM) Robert Mitchum. LOC: MEXICO: Mexico City;

Guanajuato.

Wyatt Earp (1994 Warner Bros) Kevin Costner. LOC: Colorado: Cumbres & Toltec Scenic Railroad; Antonito; New Mexico: Abiquiú Ghost Ranch; Chama/railroad depot; Cook Ranch/Cerro Pelon Ranch; El Rancho de las Golondrinas; Governor Bruce King's Ranch cornfield; J.W. Eaves Ranch; Río Chama Black Mesa; Santa Clara Pueblo; Tesuque Pueblo; The White Place/Plaza Blanca Abiquiu; Zia Pueblo; South Dakota: 777 Bison Ranch; Washington: Port Angeles.

Wyatt Earp: Return to Tombstone (1994 Orion Home Video) Hugh O'Brien. LOC: Arizona: Tombstone.

Wyatt Earp's Revenge (2012 Lancom Ent) Val Kilmer. LOC: Paramount Ranch; Santa Clarita.

Wyoming (1940 MGM) Wallace Beery. LOC: Wyoming: Jackson Hole; Signal Mountain, Jackson Hole; Grand Tetons; Jackson Lake.

Wyoming (1947 Republic) William Elliott. LOC: California: Iverson Ranch; Bronson Canyon; Kernville; Republic Studio backlot.

Wyoming Bandit, The (1949 Republic) Allan Lane. LOC: California: Iverson Ranch; Rancho Placeritos.

Wyoming Hurricane (1944 Columbia) Russell Hayden. LOC: California: Corriganville; Walker Ranch.

Wyoming Mail (1950 Universal) Stephen McNally. LOC: California: Toulumne County; Jamestown; Red Hills; Universal Studio backlot.

Wyoming Outlaw (1939 Republic) Three Mesquiteers. LOC: California: Iverson Ranch; Corriganville; Lancaster; Republic Studio backlot.

Wyoming Renegades (1955 Columbia) Phil Carey. LOC: California: Iverson Ranch; Bronson Canyon; Columbia Ranch.

Wyoming Roundup (1952 Monogram) Whip Wilson. LOC: California: Iverson Ranch.

Wyoming Whirlwind (1932 Kent) Lane Chandler. LOC: California: Ralph M. Like Studio backlot; Paramount Ranch.

Wyoming Wildcat (1941 Republic) Don Barry. LOC: California: Iverson Ranch; Burro Flats; Agoura; Republic Studio backlot.

Yahsi Bati (2009 Fida Film) Cem Yilmaz. LOC: TURKEY: Usak.

Yankee Don (1931 Capitol) Richard Talmadge. LOC: California: Universal Studios; MEXICO: Sonora: Nogales.

Yaqui Drums (1956 Allied Artists) Rod Cameron. LOC: California: Iverson Ranch; Corriganville.

Yearling, The (1946 MGM) Gregory Peck. LOC: California: Lake Arrowhead; L.A. County Arboretum; Florida: Silver Springs; Ocala National Forest; Hawthorne.

Yearling, The (1994 CBS) Peter Strauss. LOC: Florida: Ocala; Juniper Prairie Wilderness; Silver Springs.

Yellow Dust (1936 RKO) Richard Dix. LOC: California: Kernville; Tuolumne County; Sonora; RKO Encino Ranch.

Yellow Hair and the Pecos Kid (1984 Continental Movie Productions/Cinestar Films) Laurene Landon. LOC: SPAIN: Fort El Cóndor Almería; Playa de Mónsul Almería; Texas-Hollywood/Western town Almería.

Yellow Haired Kid, The (1952 Monogram) Guy Madison. LOC: California: Rancho Placeritos.

Yellow Mountain, The (1954 Universal) Lex Barker. LOC: California: Mojave area; Muroc Dry Lake; Universal Studio backlot.

Yellow Rock (2011 Black Elk Mountan Prod) Michael Biehn. LOC: California: Veluzat Motion Picture Ranch.

Yellow Rose of Texas, The (1944 Republic) Roy Rogers. LOC: California: Iverson Ranch; Republic Studio backlot.

Yellow Sky (1948 20th Century Fox) Gregory Peck. LOC: California: Death Valley; Lone Pine; Owens Dry Lake; 20th Century Fox backlot; RKO Encino Ranch.

Yellow Tomahawk, The (1954 United Artists) Rory Calhoun. LOC: Utah: Kanab Canyon; Kanab Movie Fort; Three Lakes; Turkey Crossing; Strawberry Valley.

Yellowneck (1955 Republic) Lin McCarthy. LOC: Florida: Everglades.

Yellowstone (1936 Universal) Henry Hunter. LOC: Wyoming: Yellowstone National Park; Jenny Lake, Grand Teton National Park.

Yellowstone Kelly (1959 Warner Bros) Clint Walker. LOC: California: Warner Bros backlot; Arizona: Flagstaff; Lake Mary and Mormon Lake, Coconino National Forest; Sedona.

Yes, We Have No Bonanza (1939 Columbia) Three Stooges. LOC: California: Columbia Ranch.

Yodelin' Kid from Pine Ridge (1937 Republic) Gene Autry. LOC: California: Idyllwild; Republic Studio backlot.

You Know My Name (1999 TNT) Sam Elliott. LOC: CANADA: Alberta: CL Ranch Calgary.

Young Bill Hickok (1940 Republic) Roy Rogers. LOC: California: Walker Ranch; Jauregui Ranch; Vasquez Rocks; Republic Studio backlot.

Young Billy Young (1969 United Artists) Robert Mitchum. LOC: Arizona: Old Tucson; The Magma Arizona Railroad, Superior; Lazy K Bar Ranch, Tucson.

Young Blood (1932 Monogram) Bob Steele. LOC: California: Walker Ranch; Jauregui Ranch; Frank LaSalle Ranch.

Young Buffalo Bill (1940 Republic) Roy Rogers. LOC: California: Iverson Ranch; Vasquez Rocks; Red Rock Canyon; Republic Studio backlot.

Young Daniel Boone (1950 Monogram) David Bruce. LOC: California: Iverson Ranch; Corriganville.

Young Fury (1964 Paramount) Rory Calhoun. LOC: California: Paramount Studios backlot; Vasquez Rocks.

Young Guns (1988 Morgan Creek/20th Century-Fox) Emilio Estevez. LOC: New Mexico: Abiquiú Ghost Ranch; Bonanza Creek Ranch Santa Fe; Cerrillos; El Rancho de las Golondrinas Santa Fe; Galisteo Dam area; Ojo Caliente; Río

Chama; Tent Rocks Cochiti Pueblo; Tesuque Pueblo; The White Place/Plaza Blanca Abiquiú.

Young Guns II (1990 Morgan Creek/20th Century-Fox) Emilio Estevez. LOC: Arizona: Helvetia ghost town; Old Tucson; San Rafael Ranch San Rafael Valley; Tumacacori Mission; New Mexico: Abiquiú Ghost Ranch; Cook Ranch/Cerro Pelon Ranch Galisteo; Galisteo; Tent Rocks Cochiti Pueblo; The White Place/Plaza Blanca Abiquiú; White Sands National Monument Alamogordo.

Young Guns of Texas (1963 20th Century Fox) James Mitchum. LOC: Arizona: Old Tucson; Cortaro.

Young Guns, The (1956 Allied Artists) Russ Tamblyn. LOC: California: Corriganville; Arizona: Sonoita.

Young Jesse James (1960 20th Century Fox) Willard Parker. LOC: California: 20th Century Fox backlot; Century Ranch.

Young Land, The (1959 Columbia) Patrick Wayne. LOC: California: Janss Conejo Ranch; MEXICO: Durango.

Young Mr. Lincoln (1939 20th Century Fox) Henry Fonda. LOC: California: Sacramento.

Young Pioneers, The (1978 ABC-TV) Roger Kern. LOC: Arizona: Sonoita.

Younger Brothers, The (1949 Warner Bros) Wayne Morris. LOC: California: Iverson Ranch; Warner Ranch.

Yukon Flight (1939 Monogram) James Newill. LOC: California: Big Bear.

Yukon Gold (1952 Monogram) Kirby Grant. LOC: California: Big Bear; Cedar Lake.

Yukon Manhunt (1951 Monogram) Kirby Grant. LOC: California: Big Bear; Cedar Lake.

Yukon Patrol (1942 Republic) Allan Lane. LOC: California: Cedar Lake.

Yukon Vengeance (1954 Allied Artists) Kirby Grant. LOC: California: Big Bear; Cedar Lake.

Yuma (1971 ABC-TV) Clint Walker. LOC: Arizona: Old Tucson; Horsehead Canyon.

Zachariah (1971 ABC) John Rubinstein. LOC: MEXICO: Baja California Norte: Laguna Salada, Mexicali.

Zandy's Bride (1974 Warner Bros) Gene Hackman. LOC: California: Carmel; Big Sur.

Zapata. El sueño del héroe (2004 Latin Arts LLC/Comala Films/Rita Rusic Co.) Alejandro Fernández. LOC: MEXICO: Morelos: El Hacienda de Coahuixtla;San Pedro Apatlaco; Ayala.

Zorro Rides Again (1937 Republic) John Carroll. LOC: California: Iverson Ranch; Bronson Canyon; Chatsworth Trains; Red Rock Canyon; Pacoima Dam; Southern Pacific Railroad/San Fernando Pass; Fillmore to Valencia Railroad; Republic Studio backlot.

Zorro the Avenger (1959 Disney) Guy Williams. LOC: California: Walt Disney Studio backlot; Bell/Berry Ranch.

Zorro, the Gay Blade (1981 20th Century-Fox) George Hamilton. LOC: MEXICO: Mexico City; Morelos.

Zorro's Black Whip (1944 Republic) George J. Lewis. LOC: California: Iverson Ranch; Republic Studio backlot.

Zorro's Fighting Legion (1939 Republic) Reed Hadley. LOC: California: Iverson Ranch; Burro Flats; San Fernando Mission; Republic Studio backlot.

www.ingramcontent.com/pod-product-compliance
Lightning Source LLC
Chambersburg PA
CBHW080548230426
43663CB00015B/2754